OVID

METAMORPHOSES

BOOK XIV

EDITED BY

K. SARA MYERS

Associate Professor of Classics

University of Virginia

CAMBRIDGE
UNIVERSITY PRESS

CAMBRIDGE UNIVERSITY PRESS
Cambridge, New York, Melbourne, Madrid, Cape Town, Singapore,
São Paulo, Delhi, Dubai, Tokyo

Cambridge University Press
The Edinburgh Building, Cambridge CB2 8RU, UK

Published in the United States of America by Cambridge University Press, New York

www.cambridge.org
Information on this title: www.cambridge.org/9780521007931

First published 2009

Printed in the United Kingdom at the University Press, Cambridge

A catalogue record for this publication is available from the British Library

Library of Congress Cataloguing in Publication data
Ovid, 43 B.C.-17 or 18 A.D.
[Metamorphoses. Liber 14]
Metamorphoses. Book XIV / Ovid ; edited by K. Sara Myers.
p. cm. – (Cambridge Greek and Latin classics)
Text in Latin; introduction and commentary in English.
Includes bibliographical references and indexes.
1. Mythology, Classical – Poetry. 2. Metamorphosis – Mythology – Poetry. 3. Fables, Latin.
I. Myers, K. Sara, 1961– II. Title.
PA6519.M6A14 2009
873′.01 – dc22 2009037747

ISBN 978 0 521 81025 8 Hardback
ISBN 978 0 521 00793 1 Paperback

For John, Peter, and Nikolas

CONTENTS

PREFACE

Metamorphoses 14 has generated a great deal of recent critical interest, much of which focuses on Ovid's allusive reworking of Virgil's *Aeneid* (13.623–14.573). Less discussed, but not less interesting or significant, is the book's introduction of Roman material into the epic. This commentary hopes to complement Neil Hopkinson's on *Metamorphoses* 13 by elucidating and making more accessible this important book.

Over the (too) many years of the writing of this commentary I have been encouraged and assisted by family, friends, colleagues, and students. I owe my greatest debt to my editor Professor E. J. Kenney for his firm guidance and for his countless improvements to this commentary. The unparalleled breadth and learning of his scholarship on Ovid has been an inspiration and model for the current generation of Ovidians and myself. I will always cherish the memories of his warm hospitality at Peterhouse. I also wish to thank especially Professor E. Courtney, teacher and colleague, who meticulously read through early drafts of the commentary and made many suggestions and corrections. He continues to teach me about Latin poetry by sharing his endless store of learning. Professor Philip Hardie generously allowed me to read his own important forthcoming commentary on book 14, from which I benefited greatly, and hosted me at Trinity College. At an early stage Professor Richard Tarrant kindly made available a draft of his *Metamorphoses* OCT and his immensely useful textual notes on book 14. Professor Tony Woodman heroically read through the final draft and made many helpful comments and corrections. It is a pleasure to acknowledge the encouragement and assistance received from friends and colleagues, Professor Carole Newlands (fellow commentator and unfailing supporter and listener), Professors Jim McKeown, Cynthia Damon, Alison Keith, Alex Hardie, Neil Hopkinson, and John Miller. F. Bömer's commentary on the *Metamorphoses*, as well as the first two volumes of the series on the *Metamorphoses* for Fondazione Lorenzo Valla (by A. Barchiesi and G. Rosati) were of great use in the writing of this commentary. I also benefited from the close scrutiny of the Commentary Seminar organized by Professors Alex Sens and Douglas Olsen at Georgetown in 2005.

My work has been supported by the University of Virginia with two sesqui leaves. I owe a great debt to Harvard's Loeb Classical Library Foundation for a grant for a sabbatical leave to finish this book at Cambridge University in 2008, where I was privileged to be a visiting fellow of Trinity College. The Cambridge University Faculty of Classics generously offered me the use of its library and stimulation of its Latin seminars (thanks especially to Professor Stephen Oakley). The Classics Department at UVA, my colleagues, and students, have all offered much help and encouragement. Michael Sharp and Muriel Hall (copy-editor extraordinaire) helped guide this book through publication. I dedicate this book to my family: my husband John Dillery, and my sons Peter and Nikolas, with the deepest gratitude for their love and support.

November 2008

INTRODUCTION

1. *BOOK 14 AND THE* METAMORPHOSES

At *Metamorphoses* 1.1–4 Ovid announces that his poem will begin from the origins of the world (*primaque ab origine mundi*) and continue to his own times (*ad mea . . . tempora*). In book 14 the poem enters for the first time the legendary period of proto-Roman Italian myth and history. The book occupies an important position in the *Metamorphoses*, continuing and concluding Ovid's reworking of Virgil's *Aeneid* begun in book 13 (13.623–14.573) and introducing Italian and Roman themes. The final erotic tale of the poem appears in this book (Pomona and Vertumnus), as do the first of the many Roman apotheoses (Aeneas, Romulus, and Hersilie), which will close the poem. The tales of book 14 recapitulate many of the central themes of the poem (erotic passion, sex and violence, speech and punishment, the relationship of the human and divine) and chart a pattern of cultural transition from Greece to Rome.[1]

Chronology and cosmogony

The chronological and cosmological framework of the *Metamorphoses* is initiated by the opening account of the creation of the world from chaos (1.1–75) and concludes with the imperial apotheoses of books 14 and 15, which bring us up to (and indeed past) Ovid's own times in the prediction of Augustus' and Ovid's future apotheoses (15.807–49, 871–9). These temporal references are supported by prolepses in books one and two looking forward to Rome and Augustus,[2] which are not activated again until book 14. Ring composition is further created by the cosmogonic opening of the poem and the cosmogony of Pythagoras' speech in book 15. Developing the Hellenistic catalogue tradition of metamorphosis,[3] and following the mythological trajectory of the pattern of Hesiod's *Theogony* and its 'sequel' the Hesiodic *Catalogue of Women*, Ovid claims to present a unified and universalizing version of the metamorphosis theme in Greek and Roman mythology in an aetiological *perpetuum carmen* (*Met.* 1.4). The complex proem aligns Ovid's unorthodox epic with two poetic traditions often seen as opposed: *perpetuum* (1.4) suggests the tradition of grand heroic (Homeric) epic, while *noua* (1.1) and *deducite* (1.4) evoke Alexandrian poetics of refinement, brevity, and discontinuity.[4] The *Metamorphoses*' cosmological themes embrace both

[1] Barchiesi 1997b: 185.

[2] 1.175–6, 199–205, 560–3, 2.254–9, 538–9, 642–54. See Feeney 1999: 27.

[3] On the earlier literary traditions of metamorphosis poetry, see Myers 1994a: 22–5, Hutchinson 2006.

[4] See Kenney 1976, Hinds 1987a: 18–20, 121, Heyworth 1994: 72–6, Myers 1994a, Wheeler 1999: 8–33, Feeney 1999, Rosati 1999: 247, van Tress 2004: 24–71, Barchiesi 2005: 133–45.

traditions, while with a light touch the epic incorporates most ancient genres.[5] The poem frequently changes style and tone. Unity and continuity are achieved mainly through Ovid's narrative control and his technique of self-consciously drawing attention to the mechanisms of his narrative.[6] Through his ingenious transitions between episodes and books,[7] Ovid defers closure, generating a multiplicity of beginnings and endings, and creating continuity, while destabilizing any scheme of structured sequentiality.[8]

There are strikingly few temporal markers in the *Metamorphoses*. By book 14 the poem has reached the 'historical period', signalled traditionally by the Trojan war (11.194 Troy built, cf. 13.623 Troy falls), a date (traditionally 1184/3 BCE), which tended to mark the dividing line between myth and history.[9] After the mention of Troy the narrative becomes to some extent more linear, following loosely the plot lines of Homer's and Virgil's epics, and the fates of the survivors of the Trojan war, Aeneas, Odysseus, and Diomedes. The canonical temporal demarcation of the Olympiads[10] (Eratosthenes dated the first Olympiad to 776 BCE) is mentioned in the anachronistic context of the Homeric narrator Macareus' story-telling at 14.324–5, i.e. about four hundred years too early.[11] At 14.609 the Alban king list initiates a genealogy of Roman rulers, which will continue until Numa in book 15 and segue eventually into Rome's new leaders Caesar and Augustus. Near the end of book 14 at lines 774–5 we arrive at the foundation of Rome (traditionally dated to 754/3 BCE). The establishment of the cult of Aesculapius on the Tiber island (15.622–744) is a piece of Roman history traditionally dated to the year 291 BCE. This and the tale of Cipus (also in Book 15) are the only events from the early Republic. Three centuries pass between that event and the imperial apotheoses, which close the poem (Julius Caesar 44/43 BCE (15.745–870) and that projected for Augustus at 15.807–39).

Ovid's complex handling of chronology in the *Metamorphoses* has been explored in a number of recent studies,[12] and becomes particularly interesting as the poem enters for the first time the legendary period of proto-Roman Italian myth and history in the final two books. Some scholars have pointed out Ovid's indebtedness in the structure of his poem to the dominant systems of mythological chronology found in earlier works, especially Varro's *De gente populi romani*.[13] Varro's triadic periodization

[5] See Hardie 1986: 66–9 on the cosmic tradition of Hesiod and Homer; also Feeney 1991, Hardie 1993, Myers 1994a. See Lafaye 1904, Kenney 1986: xviii on the poem as an 'anthology of genres', Barchiesi 2005: cxliv.

[6] Wheeler 1999, Barchiesi 2001: 49, Kenney 2002: 58, Rosati 2002: 304.

[7] See Solodow 1988: 41–6 on Ovid's transitional techniques. [8] Hardie 2004: 165.

[9] Coleman 1971: 472n.1, Kenney 1986: 439; Feeney 1999: 15, 19, 2007: 81–3. On the whole, however, no authoritative temporal demarcations between *fabula* and *historia* were established in the Roman tradition; see Feeney 1991: 257, 2007: 68–137.

[10] See Feeney 2007: 81–5. [11] See Feeney 1999: 21.

[12] See Feeney 1999, Hinds 1999, Zissos and Gildenhard 1999, Rosati 2002.

[13] Feeney 1999, Cole 2004, who stresses Varro's dependence on Castor of Rhodes; cf. Cameron 2004: 261–303, who finds parallels in the mythographers. On the *Metamorphoses* and universal history, see Ludwig 1965: 74–86, Wheeler 2000, Graf 2002: 119.

of history[14] corresponds to a widely accepted structural pattern in the *Metamorphoses* of three divisions: gods (1.452–6.420), heroes (6.421–11.193, introduced by the city of Athens), and historical figures (11.194–15.870, introduced by the city of Troy).[15] Thomas Cole has argued that Ovid follows Varro in presenting 'a continuous record of the series of post-diluvian generations that begins with Deucalion and Inachus . . . and ends [in Varro's case] with Romulus' (in Ovid's case with Augustus).[16] Ovid can be seen as loosely structuring his narrative according to the royal dynasties of Greek and Roman myth and the generations of great mythological houses (*Met.* 1–5 Argive, 6–9 Athenian, 12–15 Latino-Trojan), using them as coherent frameworks for metamorphosis stories, many of which are thematically and dramatically related, but which cannot be linked to any 'datable' figure or event.[17]

Yet, despite these elaborate chronological underpinnings, throughout most of the poem 'linearity takes second place to patterns of thematic association and contrast'.[18] The vast chronological horizon created by the cosmic framework encompasses stories linked by connected themes, characters, places, which tend to nullify an awareness of temporal sequence.[19] Individual episodes and thematic cycles (e.g. the contests in books 5 (Muses and Pierides) and 6 (Athena and Arachne), the song of Orpheus in book 10), most of indeterminate chronology, are more prominent than overarching diachronic structures. The seemingly totalizing frame of the poem (from chaos to Rome) is belied by the majority of tales in which there is no mention of Rome,[20] and the repeated regressions, digressions, and anachronisms challenge any attempts to impose a teleological interpretation on the poem.[21] Even in the opening books, the cosmogonies have a tendency to collapse again into chaos. To a great extent the chronological and narratological structural order of the *Metamorphoses* allows for the constant disordering and transformation of Ovid's narrative.[22] 'The secret was to keep the narrative moving and the reader guessing'.[23] The temporal world the *Metamorphoses* creates is ultimately one internal to the poem, a history of

[14] First 'unclear' from the beginning of humankind to the flood, second 'mythical' from the flood to first Olympiad, third 'historical' from the first Olympiad to the present, see Censorinus *DN* 20.12–21.2.

[15] Crump 1931: 204–14, 274–8. Cf. Ludwig 1965 on the tripartite division of the *Met.* into three 'epochs': early (1.5–451), mythological (1.452–11.193) and historical (11.194–15.870). Others emphasize the division of the poem into pentads; see Galinsky 1975: 85, Rieks 1980: 95, Holzberg 1998. Otis 1970: 77–8, 83–6 saw instead four thematic sections (Divine Comedy 1–2, Avenging Gods (3–6.400), Pathos of Love (6.401–11), Rome and the Deified Ruler (12–15).

[16] Cole 2004: 562, 2008: 63–79. [17] See Cameron 2004: 279. [18] Hinds 2003: 1085.

[19] See Rosati 2002: 277, on Ovid's double structural principle, combining chronological order with analogic order.

[20] Rome is first mentioned during the reign of Romulus at 14.800, also 809, 837, 849.

[21] See Due 1974: 120, Galinsky 1975: 3, 251–61, Solodow 1988: 162–8, Feeney 1999, Hinds 1999, Zissos and Gildenhard 1999, Wheeler 2000: 109, Rosati 2002: 280–1, Andrae 2003. See Granobs 1997: 26–31, and Tissol 2002 on the chronology of the final books.

[22] Barchiesi 2005: cxxxiii 'l'annalisi della struttura delle *Metamorfosi* diventa allora l'analisi di un disfare, di un trasformare l'ordine in dissonanza.'

[23] Kenney (forthcoming).

the world in a '*narrative* order', unfolding within the time of the narration.[24] The stories take place in relation to the other myths of the poem[25] and references to recent and future time usually refer to the internal time sequence of the narrative.[26] Ovid's play with different temporal realms (time of narration, mythological /cosmological time, temporal frame of earlier literary tradition) becomes especially complex in his treatment of his epic models in *Metamorphoses* 11–15 (see below on his '*Aeneid*').

Narrative structures in Metamorphoses *14*

Metamorphoses 14 opens within the '*Aeneid*' frame of the poem, begun in the previous book (13.623) and continued until 14.573 (see further below). The apotheosis of Aeneas follows (581–608), which performs a pivotal function in creating continuity with the '*Aeneid*' section of the book and initiating the second 'Italo-Roman' portion. The catalogue of Alban kings at 609–22 brings the poem swiftly forward chronologically to the time of Romulus (772–851). The Italian focus and landscape of book 14 unite the two sections, as do a number of themes, most obviously metamorphosis and eros. Venus figures prominently in the book, first appearing in her vengeful guise at its opening (27), and then in the stories of Diomedes (476–9) and Vertumnus and Pomona (622–771). Venus' other role as protectress of Rome and the Caesars is first displayed in her association with Aeneas' victory over Turnus (572–3) and then in her active participation in the deification of Aeneas at 581–608, and the defence of Janus' Gate at 775–804, which prefigures her later role in the deification of Julius Caesar at 15.760–851.[27] Venus' prominence at the end of the poem forms a frame with Cupid's introduction of eros in book 1 (452–73) and suggests a fulfilment of her imperialist ambitions expressed to Cupid in book 5.371–2 *cur non matrisque tuumque | imperium profers?*[28]

As the final section or pentad of the *Metamorphoses* enters 'historical' time with Troy, it also deals directly with the material of Ovid's epic predecessors Homer, Virgil, and Ennius. Ovid's narration of the Trojan war is prefaced by his description of the house of *Fama* at 12.39–55, which, with its emphasis on poetic authority and the transmission of stories (12.58 *auditis aliquid nouus adicit auctor*), serves as an introduction to his direct confrontation with his epic predecessors.[29] The frequent use of internal narrators and audiences in this section of the poem allows Ovid to refashion his models through

[24] See Rosati 2002: 279–80, Hinds 2003: 1085; also Feeney 1999: 24, Wheeler 1999: 117.

[25] Barchiesi 2001: 15.

[26] Rosati 2002: 279; cf. 157n. on *nondum*. At 7.232–3 the tale of Glaucus (13.900–14.74) is anticipated: *gramen | nondum mutato uulgatum corpore Glauci.*

[27] See Döpp 1968: 121, von Albrecht 1982, Barchiesi 1999.

[28] On Venus' imperialism in *Met.* 5.363–79, see Johnson 1996. On Ovid's association of the amatory and Augustan Venus, cf. *AA* 1.60 *mater in Aeneae constitit urbe sui, Am.* 1.8.42 *at Venus Aeneae regnat in urbe sui.*

[29] Feeney 1991: 247–9, Tissol 2002: 307–9, Barchiesi 2002b: 195–6.

new perspectives and reflect on the very processes of storytelling, which has been rightly seen as one of the most important concerns of the poem.[30]

The literary models of Virgil's *Aeneid* and Homer's *Odyssey*, which dominate the material of the first part of book 14, give way in the remainder to such diverse models as Propertius, Livy, and, finally, Ennius. Ovid's indebtedness to Ennius is famously signalled by the verbatim quotation by Mars at 14.814 of a line spoken to him by Jupiter in the earlier poem (*Ann.* 54 Sk., cf. *F.* 2.487). Ennius' original fifteen-book *Annales*, which began from Aeneas and continued to 187 BCE, offered an important structural model for the *Metamorphoses*.[31] *Met.* 14, like *Annales* 1, ends with Romulus' apotheosis, and *Met.* 15, like *Annales* 2, begins with Numa. The last book of the *Met.* also opens with the Speech of Pythagoras, which reworks the speech of Homer with which Ennius began the first book of his epic. The Ennian allusions are important signals preparing for the epic elevation of the cosmogony, apotheosis, and panegyric of the final book. At the same time, the preponderance of amatory tales in *Met.* 14 (five, occupying just under half of the lines of the book (around 375)) signals a continuity with the rest of the poem, and can also be seen to challenge Ovid's epic models in this section of the poem by activating again the generic tensions between elegiac and erotic themes on the one hand and the traditional national, historical, and philosophical themes of epic on the other, which are reintroduced emphatically at the poem's end. In *Met.* 14, as at the beginning of the poem in the episodes of Daphne and Syrinx (1.452–567), neoteric and elegiac themes are juxtaposed with those of lofty epic.[32]

The linearity of Ovid's narrative has been seen to take a more coherent form in his last five books, yet Ovid's treatment of Homer's and Virgil's epics and Roman 'history' in this section is marked by the same chronological complexity and irreverence as the rest of his poem. 'Ovidian imperialism'[33] integrates the Trojan and Roman material into the metamorphic world of the poem. *Met.* 14 begins in the middle of a 300-line amatory digression in the '*Aeneid*' framework of the poem, and the plot of the *Aeneid* and the Roman history of the last 250 or so lines function essentially as frameworks for the expanded tales of metamorphosis.[34] This is typical of Ovid's procedure and is found also at the beginning of book 11, where the foundation of Troy serves essentially as a narrative introduction to the long amatory tale of Ceyx and Alcyone,[35] while in book 15 the reign of Numa becomes the frame for the foundation of Croton and Pythagoras' long philosophical discourse.

After the end of the '*Aeneid*' section of the book (573) Aeneas' death/deification and Ascanius' subsequent accession initiate the chronological sequence of Alban kings (609–22), which leads to Romulus and Rome. Virgil had offered only an abbreviated

[30] Hinds 2003: 1085; Wheeler 2000, Rosati 2002: 274, Barchiesi 2002b: 181. Edmunds 2001: 76–7 charts the levels of narrative in Ovid's '*Aeneid*' (685 of 964 lines (72%) are embedded narratives).

[31] Knox 1986a: 69–71, Hardie 1993: 13, 2002d: 106.

[32] See most recently on genre in *Met.* 1, Keith 2002.

[33] Barchiesi 2005: cxi.

[34] Tissol 2002: 306–10.

[35] Feeney 1999: 19.

version of this regal catalogue (*Aen.* 6.760–70), which was a creation and traditional feature in early Roman historians and appears in Livy 1.3.1–11.[36] However, even as Ovid's catalogue begins to fast-forward the poem to Rome's foundation, it is interrupted by the amatory tale of Pomona and Vertumnus, the first episode presented in 'Italian' time, which takes place during the reign of the legendary Italian king Proca. The leisurely erotic story (with its Cypriot inset tale of Iphis and Anaxarete) interrupts and delays (by 150 lines) the Roman chronology and the poem's historical and teleological move towards Rome,[37] reducing the king list to a mere narrative framework.[38] The episode of Pomona and Vertumnus (622–771) draws heavily on erotic models of elegiac poetry, creating a sort of 'super-episode' representing the genre so central to the themes and poetics of the *Met.*[39] Vertumnus himself is the narrator of the erotic and aetiological inset tale of Iphis and Anaxarete, about a statue on Cyprus, which reflects his literary pedigree as a speaking statue in Propertius' elegy 4.2.[40] The episode of Pomona and Vertumnus is the final erotic tale of the poem and functions programmatically in providing a closural frame with the first erotic tale of the poem, Apollo and Daphne (1.452 *primus amor*). This ring-composition is thematized in Vertumnus' speech to Pomona at 682–3 *tu primus et ultimus illi | ardor eris*.[41]

Closural signals are evident throughout book 14, as the poem 'begins to gloss its own closure.'[42] Apotheosis dominates the Italian section of the *Met.* and serves as a final version of metamorphosis (see further below).[43] The apotheoses of Aeneas and Romulus in book 14 anticipate the imperial deifications of Caesar and Augustus in the following book and represent a return at the end of the poem to the Augustan themes of its opening. Elsewhere, in the only episode from Romulus' reign, the flooding of Janus' gate by Venus and Ausonian naiads to block Tatius and the Sabines (14.778–99),[44] Juno opens (what will be) Janus' gates of war (as she did in Virg. *Aen.* 7.621–2), but Venus' swift blocking of these gates constitutes another closural gesture, as war (and epic martial narrative) is prevented from commencing.

Italian and Roman myth in Metamorphoses *14*

The *Metamorphoses* arrives in Italy at the beginning of book 14 with Glaucus' arrival at Circei, a location with Homeric as well as Italian associations. It is Circe who dominates as the poem first moves into Italian realms, signalling the metamorphic focus of Ovid's narrative and, perhaps, the transformative proclivities of Italy, as Virgil had also suggested by his placement of Circe at the beginning of *Aeneid* 7.[45] Circe

[36] Cf. the almost identical version at *Fasti* 4.39–56.
[37] See Johnson 1997: 373–4, Kyriakidis 2002.
[38] Hardie 2002d: 192, where he cites Callimachus' Acontius and Cydippe as a parallel.
[39] See Rosati 2002: 287, on internal narratives as genre paradigms.
[40] Myers 1994b. [41] See Myers 1994b, Davis 1983: 67.
[42] Barchiesi 1997b: 187, Wheeler 2000: 110–14. [43] See Theodorakopoulos 1999: 148.
[44] An obscure story also in *Fasti* 1.259–74, where Janus' closing of the gates of war has similarly been seen as a programmatic exclusion of martial themes from his elegiac work.
[45] See Segal 1968, Hardie 1992, Tissol 1997: 210.

is a liminal figure, a remnant of the Greek (Homeric) literary past, but also firmly rooted to the Italian landscape (cf. 348 *nomine dicta suo Circaea reliquerat arua*); as such she represents the movement of the poem from Greece to Rome, but also blurs the boundaries between the two.[46] The first tale involving native Italian characters in the poem is the erotic tale of Circe, Picus, and Canens, which occurs within the '*Aeneid*' (and '*Odyssey*') frame of the epic (14.308–434). A number of commencement strategies are employed in this episode to signal the poem's movement into this new geographic and poetic territory. Reminders of the story's new Italian locale are frequent, (e.g. 14.320 *in Ausoniis . . . terris*, 326 *Latiis in montibus*, 390 *Latiis . . . siluis*, 422 *Latios . . . per agros*). A catalogue of Italian rivers introduces Picus' Naiad admirers and performs an initiatory function (326–32). Numerous native nymphs in these Italian tales,[47] especially Canens, who seems to be a muse-like figure (see 433–4n.), signal the new movement of the poem towards Italian landscape and myth. Continuity with the rest of the poem is confirmed in the tale's erotic focus, which shares its structure especially with the two preceding love-triangles (Galatea, Acis, Polyphemus 13.750–897, Scylla, Glaucus, Circe 13.898–14.74). The tale, which explains a statue of Picus and an Italian (invented) toponym, programmatically introduces Ovid's aetiological and Callimachean treatment of much of his Italian material. Picus' venerated statue also prefigures the upcoming statue tales of the Vertumnus and Pomona episode and the apotheoses of Aeneas and Romulus, both of whom will be represented by statues in Augustus' forum.

It is well known that when Ovid approaches Italian themes in the final two books of the *Met.* his treatment of Roman myth differs in some respects from his earlier treatment of Greek myths.[48] Most notably, the Italian myths for the most part share with the *Fasti* the theme of religious aetiology.[49] The characters in Ovid's Italian stories of the *Met.* include relatively obscure, but ancient, native Italian agricultural and rustic deities, such as Picus, Vertumnus, Pomona, (in book 15 Virbius and Tages), some of whom have a rather more sophisticated literary background (Picus, Vertumnus, Virbius). They are mixed with a number of Ovidian inventions (Canens, Hersilie/Hora), Greek gods (Aesculapius, Hippolytus/Virbius), as well as the deified heroes and emperors of Roman cult (Aeneas and Romulus, in book 15 Caesar and Augustus). Other religious aetia include the Cumaean Sibyl (14.101–53), the Cypriot cult statue of Anaxarete/ *Venus Prospiciens* (14.753–61), Janus' gate (14.778–99), Egeria's spring (15.547–51), Etruscan rites of haruspicy (15.558–9), and Cipus (15.565–621). Italian tales in book 14 also include the brief geographical and aetiological episodes of

[46] Segal 2003: 21 instead attempts to distinguish two registers of myth in Ovid's Italian section, the Greek/Odyssean register of fantastic creatures and the Roman/Virgilian register of origins and history.

[47] Fantham 1990. Cf. Italian nymphs (14.512–26), the nymphs transformed from the Trojan ships who now patriotically never assist Greek ships (14.561), and the nymphs who assist in defending Rome from the Sabines at 14.785, and Egeria (15.482–551).

[48] See Feeney 1998: 71, on Ovid's 'regular amputation of the religious aetiological elements from his Greek myths in the *Metamorphoses*'; also Graf 2002: 118–19.

[49] See Knox 1986a: 65–83; Graf 1988, Myers 1994a: 95–132, 2004, Tissol 1997: 177–91.

the Cercopians turned into apes on the island of Pithecusae (90–100, really a Greek tale), the Apulian shepherd turned into a wild olive tree (512–26), and the creation of the heron from the ashes of Ardea (573–80). The Italian tales of books 14 and 15 are interspersed with Greek tales and narratives (see the Homeric narratives at 14.158–307, Iphis and Anaxarete 14.698–761), which threaten at times to overshadow the Roman element (see especially Pythagoras' long philosophical narrative at 15.75–478). The only tales in book 14 that feature rustic Italian figures are those of Picus and Canens, the Apulian shepherd, and Pomona and Vertumnus. All three tales also include 'foreign' characters such as Circe, Pan, and Iphis and Anaxarete. The Apulian shepherd's tale, in appearance a genuinely 'rustic' Italian tale, is probably from the Alexandrian poet Nicander (fr. 47 Gow-Scholfield). In book 15 the major themes of book 14 are continued in the (repeated) movement from Greece to Rome (Hercules, Myscelos, and Croton, Pythagoras, Hippolytus/Virbius, Aesculapius) and in the apotheoses of Hippolytus/Virbius, Aesculapius, Caesar, Augustus, and Ovid.

Apotheosis

Aeneas' apotheosis into a *Deus Indiges* (14.581–608) introduces the theme that dominates the Roman/Italian remainder of the poem in books 14 and 15.[50] This new transformative tendency was prefigured in the tales of Acis and Glaucus, both turned into water deities (13.885–97, 920–65). The divinizations of Aeneas, Romulus, and Hersilie in book 14 anticipate those of Caesar and Augustus in the final book and have been seen as reflecting on contemporary imperial dynastic politics concerning ruler cult.[51] Aeneas and Romulus, with whom Julius Caesar and Augustus of course also claimed family ties,[52] provided important models for the early development of the imperial ruler cult in Roman state religion[53] and recall Augustus' juxtaposition of the two heroes in his new Forum.[54] The idea that mortal benefactors of mankind might be divinized is found in Hellenistic philosophy and had been a commonplace of praise poetry since the courts of Alexandria.[55] Aeneas' deification, however, like those of Hippolytus and Aesculapius in book 15, is not that of a native Roman, as Ovid stresses in Caesar's case (15.746 *Caesar in urbe sua deus est*). Romulus provided the primary precedent for a Roman ruler attaining divinity and his apotheosis is a much treated theme in Latin literature (see 805–28n.).[56] After the assassination of

[50] Earlier deifications in the poem include Callisto and Arcas (2.505–7), Ino and her son (4.539–42), Hercules (9.242–72), Acis (13.885–87), Glaucus (13.920–63); see Lieberg 1970, Petersmann 1976, Schmidt 1991: 133–8, Salzman 1998, Tissol 2002: 322–7.

[51] Feeney 1991: 207–24, Tissol 2002: 321, Hardie 2002d: 208.

[52] Gee 2000: 164–73 emphasizes the dynastic aspect of Caesar's catasterism.

[53] On the development of Roman ruler cult, see Scott 1925, Weinstock 1971, Price 1987, Galinsky 1996: 288–331, Gradel 2002, Scheid 2003.

[54] Zanker 1988: 201–3, Barchiesi 2002a, Tissol 2002: 311–12.

[55] Knox 1986a: 75–83, Cameron 2004: 278.

[56] See Herbert-Brown 1994: 49–52, Barchiesi 1997a: 112–23, 154–64, 166–77. On the episode in the *Metamorphoses* see Feeney 1991: 122–3, 208, Granobs 1997: 58–61, Tissol 2002: 328–32.

Julius Caesar Romulus' death and deification were inevitably linked with his fate (cf. Appian, *BC* 2.114) and Augustus' identification with Romulus was closely related to the question of his own apotheosis (see 772–851n.).

Ovid's depiction of Roman deifications in the *Met.* shares an epic emphasis on divine action rather than on panegyrical enumeration of exploits, which seemed to have formed the basis of the earlier Roman tradition, initiated probably by Ennius' euhemeristic account of Romulus' apotheosis, and important also to Varro's mythological chronography.[57] Venus' canvassing of the gods for Aeneas (14.585 *ambieratque Venus superos*) on the other hand reflects Roman political realities,[58] and strikes an overly explicit and comic note in the world of mythological epic. Her diffident request for the bestowal of at least a *paruum numen* (589) further deflates the tone of the episode. Earlier in the poem the deification of Hercules, who provided an important paradigm for human apotheosis in the Greek and Roman world,[59] is achieved through similar divine dynastic politicking (9.251–5).[60] Ovid's narrative crowds out an enumeration of the hero's great deeds and 'we hear more about the labours of Hercules' mother than we do about those of Hercules himself' (9.134–5, cf. 182–98).[61] Romulus' deification in *Met.* 14 is motivated solely by divine intervention, while in the *Fasti* version there is brief mention of his achievements (2.481–2 *postquam noua moenia uidit | multaque Romulea bella peracta manu)*. His father Mars declares that it is time (808 *tempus adest*) for Romulus to receive his rewards and calls upon Jupiter to fulfill his earlier (in Ennius' *Annales*) promise. Ovid's use of the technological comparison of a slingshot simile to describe the physical process of Romulus' apotheosis (824–6) conflicts with and undermines the supernatural gravity of the event.[62] His wife Hersilie's apotheosis also springs solely from Juno's divine initiative – or rather, Ovid's own imagination (it is only attested here), a bold move amidst this escalation of political divinizations. Her apotheosis looks forward both to the similar catasterism of Caesar and the future apotheosis of Ovid, which will close book 15.

Ovid's apotheoses are indebted to Alexandrian models, such as Callimachus and Theocritus, who exhibit a similar strategy of treating panegyric in a frequently offbeat and witty manner.[63] The confrontation of Ovidian myth with contemporary Roman political discourses in *Met.* 14 and 15 blurs the traditional distinctions between history (*historia*) and myth, which was considered fiction (*fabula*). This juxtaposition of myth and history, combined in book 15 with Pythagoras' philosophical discourse, reveals Ovid's consistent interest in the *Met.* in exploring the creation of authority, both poetic and political, through different narrative modes.[64] His mythologizing of the apotheoses of Roman leaders may be understood as celebrating a new age of

[57] Skutsch 1985: 260–1; on Varro, see Cole 2004: 365.

[58] Feeney 1991: 207; cf. 15.760–1.

[59] For his presence in the traditional canon of deified human benefactors, see 581–608n.

[60] Due 1974: 82–3. [61] Feeney 1991: 206. [62] Due 1974: 86.

[63] Knox 1986a: 77–8, Barchiesi 1997a: 82 'political *laudes* and playfulness are [not] mutually incompatible', Gee 2000: 188.

[64] See Feeney 1991: 188–249, Myers 1994a, Hardie 1997b, Graf 2002: 119, Schiesaro 2002.

imperial demi-gods, in line with Augustus' own political mythologizing,[65] but it may simultaneously invite the reader to explore the implications this may have against the background of the violent world of the *Met.*[66]

The prominence of these Italian apotheoses has led some to argue that Ovid's Italo-Roman stories represent an amelioration of myth and thus that Italy is presented as a place of restoration.[67] However, not all metamorphoses in the final two books are 'upward'. Violence and grief, important themes in the poem as a whole, are not entirely absent from Italy, and are indeed present at the beginning of book 14 in the menacing figure of Circe. Denis Feeney has argued that we should resist one line of interpretation of the *Fasti* which constructs a progress in the poem from Greek frivolity to Roman seriousness, and the same might be said for the *Met.*[68] Surrounding the apotheoses of Italo-Roman leaders are some less edifying mythological transformations into divine or quasi-divine forms, which explore some of the possible ambiguities of the translation from human to god. Transformed into a sea deity, Glaucus assures Scylla that he is not a sea monster (13.917 *nec sum fera belua*), which is precisely what his attentions will cause Scylla herself to become. The Sibyl is given by Apollo a debased form of immortality (1000 years) of a particularly unpleasant variety,[69] while Picus' transformation into a woodpecker is hardly a positive one from his perspective. The commemoration of mourning is mapped onto the Italian landscape in the mournful evanescence of Canens (cf. the similar liquefaction of Egeria at 15.482–55),[70] the death of Caieta, and the destruction of the city of Ardea.[71] The abuses and punishments of the Cercopians, Acmon, and the Apulian shepherd seem to challenge further the notion of a dramatic change in the tone and content of the poem upon arrival in Italy.

Italian myth and the Fasti

The Italian themes of the *Metamorphoses* and their aetiological treatment overlap with the poetic territory of the *Fasti*, Ovid's poem on the Roman calendar, which shares similar tensions between myth and politics. As Philip Hardie has argued, the two poems 'represent Ovid's typically indirect answer to the challenge of Virgil's epic, on the one hand a Callimachean elegy on the central subjects of the *Aeneid* and on the other a hexameter epic on themes for the most part not Roman'.[72] A number of the myths and characters in the final two books of the *Met.* also appear in

[65] Feeney 2007: 83, cf. Galinsky 1999.

[66] See Hinds 1988: 25–6, Feeney 1991: 224.

[67] Porte 1985, Theodorakopoulos 1999, Hardie 2002d: 198, Cole 2008: 146–52, 167–9; cf. Parker 1997.

[68] Feeney 1998: 132, see Myers 2004–5.

[69] Cf. her dismissal of divine honors at 130–1 '*nec sacri turis honore | humanum dignare caput*'.

[70] Of the three mourning Italian widows, only Hersilie is deified and reunited with her husband.

[71] Cf. the suicide of the Cypriot Iphis for love.

[72] Hardie 1991: 47.

the *Fasti* (Romulus, Picus, Tatius and Tarpeia, Vertumnus, Hersilie, Numa, Egeria, Virbius). Versions of the apotheosis of Romulus (*F.* 2.475–512), the Alban king list (*F.* 4.39–56) and the flooding of Janus' gate (*F.* 1.260–76) appear in the *Fasti* and *Met.* 14. Such episodes shared by the two poems have been used to illustrate Ovid's dual explorations of the generic limits of epic and elegy.[73] It has been observed that at a very basic level the *Met.* and *Fasti* share a common structure, beginning with cosmogony (in the *Fasti* represented by the figure of Janus) and ending with apotheosis (sharing the figure of Aesculapius).[74] The establishment of the cult of Aesculapius on 1 Jan. 291 BCE, described in *Met.* 15, looks to the beginning of the calendar and the *Fasti.* Alessandro Barchiesi has suggested that through this cross-reference Ovid encourages a continuous reading from the *tempora* of his epic to the *tempora* of the *Fasti* (*F.* 1.1 *tempora cum causis Latium digesta per annum*).[75]

2. *OVID'S* 'AENEID' (METAMORPHOSES *13.623–14.573*)

Book 14 begins within the '*Aeneid*' frame of the poem, Ovid's tendentious treatment of the events of Virgil's epic in *Met.* 13 and 14.[76] The *Aeneid* frame begins at *Met.* 13.623 with Aeneas' escape from Troy and ends in the middle of line 573 of book 14 with the death of Turnus (cf. 572 *tandem*).[77] Virgil's influence is evident throughout the *Metamorphoses,* in Ovid's language, and in the many stories and characters that evoke Virgilian themes and types.[78] This section, however, constitutes a unique case of literary 'annexation',[79] in which the issues of literary continuation, appropriation, and repetition are central. The comprehensiveness of Ovid's treatment of the *Aeneid* contrasts with his incorporation of Homer's *Iliad* and *Odyssey* and Apollonius' *Argonautica,* which are recalled by only selected episodes, avoiding direct repetition.[80]

[73] See especially Heinze 1919, Hinds 1987b.

[74] Barchiesi 1991: 6–7, Hardie 1991.

[75] Barchiesi 1991: 6–7, Hardie 1991: 52–3.

[76] On Ovid's 'Aeneid', see Stitz 1962, Due 1974: 36–42, 83–5, Galinsky 1975: 217–51, Ellsworth 1986; Fabre-Serris 1986, Solodow 1988: 110–56, Döpp 1991: 6; Esposito 1994: 11–36; Myers 1994: 95–132; Baldo 1995: 29–141; Casali 1995; Smith 1997: 104–15; Tissol 1997: 177–91, 2002, Hinds 1998: 104–22; Andrae 2003: 164–207, Papaioannou 2005.

[77] Many scholars include the apotheosis of Aeneas (581–608) within this section as well. His apotheosis in a sense continues the *Aeneid*'s narrative by fulfilling a prophecy given by Jupiter twice in the *Aeneid* (1.259–60 to Venus and at 12.794–5 to Juno), but it occurs after the end of Virgil's poem.

[78] The conflict of Turnus and Aeneas, for example, has been seen to be more fully represented in the conflicts between Phineus and Perseus in book 5.1ff. (Keith 2002: 242–5) or Achelous and Hercules in book 9.1ff. Hardie 1990 has suggested that the Theban cycle represents a Virgilian foundation story. The storm-scene of *Aen.* 1.84–156 is the model for the storm of *Met.* 11.474–571. See further Baldo 1995, Tarrant 2002: 26, Andrae 2003.

[79] Hinds 1998: 104.

[80] *Argonautica*: 6.719–7.158, where the voyage of the Argo to Colchis is elided at the book division and the return journey accomplished in one verse (7.154–8). *Iliad*: 12.1–13.428, including the episodes of Achilles and Cycnus (12.72–188), Lapiths and Centaurs (12.189–535), Ajax and Ulysses' contest over the arms of Achilles (13.1–398). Odysseus' adventures in *Odyssey*: 9–10 are represented in 14.158–440. See Ellsworth 1988, Dippel 1990, Baldo 1995: 111–41.

Ovid's reworking of Virgil marks the first of many poetic responses and challenges to the *Aeneid* and its closures in imperial Roman epic.[81] Ovid's engagement with Virgil of course extends throughout his whole poetic career, beginning with the first poem of his *Amores*, where he announces his new elegies as a non-Virgilian work by the renunciation of *arma* (*Am.* 1.1.1).[82] Concentrated reworkings of the *Aeneid* are found also in *Heroides* 7, where Ovid rewrites *Aeneid* 1–4 through the focalization of Dido, and in *Fasti* 3.545–656 in the story of Anna. A virtuoso compressed version of the epic is given in three and a half lines by Venus at *Metamorphoses* 15.771–4.

In *Metamorphoses* 13 and 14 Ovid follows the narrative and geographical line of the *Aeneid* closely, but only briefly mentions Virgil's major characters and events, while foregrounding and expanding Virgil's metamorphoses and inserting his own. His allusive treatment relies throughout on his readers' knowledge of his model. In a manoeuvre typical of Alexandrian confrontations with the earlier tradition, which sees a 'refocusing of poetic subject matter onto what in earlier traditions had been the margins of interest',[83] Virgil's imperial plot is made subordinate to Ovid's privileged tales of love and metamorphosis, while Aeneas' journey serves mainly as a narrative itinerary or framework.[84] Characteristically, major episodes of the *Aeneid* serve merely as swift transitions to Ovid's own tales (14.75–89 = *Aen.* 4–5, 14.116–19 = *Aen.* 6, 14.445–53 = *Aen.* 7). In general, 'wherever Virgil is elaborate, Ovid is brief, and wherever Virgil is brief, Ovid elaborates'.[85] As the Trojans proceed, their different stopovers provide occasions for stories, only some of which are Virgilian, but all of which must be read as engaging with the Virgilian frame. Throughout the *Metamorphoses* Ovid refines traditional epic plots, which provide the appearance of unity to sections of the poem through a notional framework, into briefer, often oblique or merely tangential episodes. (Cf. the early history of Thebes 3.1–4.603, 'Perseid' 4.610–5.251, Argonauts 6.719–7.158, Hercules 9.1–272, Theseus 7.402–8.84.) Ovid's indirect and marginalizing treatment of Aeneas himself is paralleled earlier in the poem by the similar narrative displacement of the heroes Hercules, Theseus, Perseus, Jason, and Achilles, who play subsidiary roles and whose famous feats are routinely glossed over.[86] Ovid avoids martial narrative throughout his '*Aeneid*', as in the poem as a whole, with the exception of two epic battle narratives, which, as Carole Newlands has observed, occur incongruously at weddings (5.1–249 Perseus and Phineus, 12.210–531 Battle of the Lapiths and Centaurs).[87]

[81] See Hardie 1993: 11–18, 1997a, Casali 1995, Thomas 2001: 55 'intertextuality is a form of hermeneutics'.

[82] Kenney 2002: 59 'all Ovid's work is shot through and through with Virgilian reminiscences'; see Zingerle 1869: *passim*, Bömer 1959, Myers 1999: 195–6, Tarrant 2002: 23–7. On *Amores* 1.1, see McKeown ad loc., Barchiesi 1997a: 16–17.

[83] Goldhill 1991: 285.

[84] Cf. the geographical routes of Phaethon 2.78ff., Medea 7.350ff.

[85] Hinds 1998: 106. [86] See Nagle 1988b.

[87] Newlands 2005: 481–2. A third, briefer battle between the Greeks and Trojans at 12.64–145 introduces Cycnus' metamorphosis into a swan. Cf. the epic Calydonian boar hunt at 8.267–444.

Famously, prophetic elements central to the Virgilian plot and to its teleological thrust towards Augustus and Rome are omitted throughout Ovid's '*Aeneid*', while personal histories and backgrounds dominate.[88] Rome is nowhere mentioned by name and Ovid's episodes have notoriously little to do with Aeneas or public Augustan themes.[89] The whole of Ovid's 'Aeneid' tends to look backwards, rather than forwards to Rome, giving us in flashbacks pre-*Aeneid* and even pre-Homeric events, such as the Cyclops in love (13.750–897), Circe's transformation of Scylla (14.51–67), the Sibyl and Apollo (104–53), Picus and Canens (308–434). In the Underworld Aeneas sees only his ancestors, not his descendants, and learns only of the impending war, not its aftermath. An issue long debated is whether in his treatment of the *Aeneid* Ovid is undermining Virgil's Augustan vision or rather drawing out and bringing attention to unsettling or subversive readings already present in the *Aeneid* itself (and thus freeing the earlier epic from its Augustan canonization).[90] Casali suggests that Ovid's anti-Augustan reading of the *Aeneid* aims at implicating Virgil himself in the charge.[91] By stripping the plot of the *Aeneid* of its Augustan teleology, Ovid enforces a critical rereading of Virgil's epic which brings out instead some of its oppositional themes (or 'other voices') and internal tensions, such as the destructive power of passion, personal loss, the devaluation of Homeric heroism, and the issue of the justification of violence.[92]

Ovid's incorporation of the *Aeneid* into the *Metamorphoses* may be seen as a kind of 'bid for teleological and authorial control'.[93] As Stephen Hinds has suggested, Ovid constructs his poem as preceding Virgil's by highlighting metamorphoses already in his model, suggesting that there was a '*Metamorphoses* latent in the *Aeneid*.'[94] Episodes from the *Aeneid* directly reworked include Achaemenides' retelling of the Homeric Cyclops episode at 14.158–220 (augmented by Ovid's addition of a second Homeric narrator who continues an Odyssean narrative through the episode of Circe's transformation of Odysseus' men 221–440), the metamorphosis of Diomedes' men (457–511), and the metamorphosis of the Trojan ships into nymphs (527–65).[95] Where Virgil had avoided having the Trojans encounter either the Homeric Scylla or Circe, Ovid reincorporates Scylla through his prequel and Circe appears in no fewer than

88 Solodow 1988: 156, Baldo 1995: 108, Tissol 1997: 177–91, Feeney 1999: 27. The prophecy of Rome's rise is supplied by Pythagoras in 15.431–52 (in the context of the rise and fall of cities).

89 Kenney 1982: 44, Feeney 1999: 27, Tarrant 2002: 26.

90 See Thomas 2001: 79 on collaborative imitation and see also his cautions against a reductive approach to Virgil's text and teleology.

91 Casali 1995, cf. Barchiesi 1997a: 30–3 on Ovid's hints at possible 'deviant readings' of the *Aeneid*, Fabre-Serris 1986: 184 'opposer Virgile à Virgile', and Hardie 1990 on the 'darker reading' of the *Aeneid* in *Met.* 3–4 (Thebes). Cf. Knox *Heroides* 1995: 202 and Desmond 1993 on similar strategies in *Heroides* 7.

92 See 380, 451, 574–5nn. for possible criticisms of Aeneas' mission.

93 Hinds 1998: 106. 94 Hinds 1998: 106. Cf. Hardie 1992.

95 Other metamorphoses from the *Aeneid* are treated elsewhere in the poem: Virbius *Aen.* 7.761–89 = *Met.* 15.492–546, Cycnus *Aen.* 10.187–93 = *Met.* 2.367–80. At 13.628–30 Ovid briefly alludes to the omitted episode of Polydorus (*Aen.* 3.19–68), see Hopkinson ad loc., Smith 1997: 104–15, Casali 2007: 182–8.

three episodes in *Metamorphoses* 14, as erotic pursuer of Glaucus (1–74), Odysseus (254–307 the Homeric version), and Picus (308–434).

An important way in which Ovid appropriates the *Aeneid* is to play with the relative narrative and mythological time-frames of the two epics, and those between Virgil and his model Homer. It is well known that 'Ovid has a rare appetite for reflexively highlighting these moments of intersection between different temporal realities.'[96] Many of the events of Ovid's '*Aeneid*' are set at a time either prior to or just after the dramatic time of Virgil's narrative. The Virgilian characters of Anius, Polyphemus, Circe, Scylla, Picus, and the Cumaean Sibyl all feature in Ovid's '*Aeneid*' in non-Virgilian prequels to Aeneas' journey. Major stages in Aeneas' journey are also anticipated and usurped by Ovidian characters. It is not Aeneas' journey towards Rome that brings the poem to Italy at the opening of *Met.* 14, but Glaucus' swim to Italy to enlist the aid of Circe.[97] The Italian nymph Canens arrives at the Tiber (426) just before the Trojans do so at 447–8, and her birthplace on the Palatine (333) constitutes the first mention of the city since the proleptic reference to the Palatine at 1.175–6. Elsewhere Ovid acknowledges the belatedness of his '*Aeneid*' by placing his narrative slightly after the events of the *Aeneid*. In Ovid's remake of Virgil's Achaemenides episode from *Aen.* 3 Achaemenides repeats his Virgilian narrative of the Cyclops (which is placed temporally shortly after Odysseus' departure in Homer), but at a later time, after having been rescued already by the Trojans in the *Aeneid* (see 165–6n.). So also Scylla's transformation into a rock at 73–4 marks Aeneas' journey in Ovid's text as occurring just after that in Virgil's, when she had still posed a threat. Scylla's petrifaction also effectively ends the possibility of any further literary repetition. Visions of the future in Ovid's *Aeneid* tend to refer to the literary pasts of Homer or Virgil, as when the Trojans ships are metamorphosed into nymphs and look forward to the metamorphosis of the Phaeacians' ship (563–5n.) or when at 192–7 the Cyclops looks forward to a future revenge on Odysseus in lines that recall his behaviour in Homer (*Odyssey* 9.289–91, 311) and Virgil (*Aen.* 3.626–7),[98] as at 13.863–6, 882–4 where a Theocritean Cyclops in love anticipates his future acts of violence as told in the *Odyssey* (9.289–93, 480–3).[99]

The story of Aeneas begins at 13.623–31 with the fall of Troy and Aeneas' escape from the city with his father and son and their arrival in Delos, where Ovid has Aeneas meet Anius, king of Delos and priest of Delian Apollo, as in *Aeneid* 3.80–120. At this point he replaces Apollo's prophecy to the Trojans (later mentioned at 13.677–9) with Anius' story about the sad transformation of his daughters into doves (640–74) and an ecphrasis with a similar tale about the daughters of Orion (the Coroni 679–99). Both episodes have been seen to have thematic associations with the *Aeneid* frame,

96 Baldo 1986: 121, Hinds 1998: 115. Virgil also frequently adopts this strategy in his treatment of his model Homer.

97 The Trojans reach Italy in *Aeneid* 7; Ovid acknowledges Virgil's bipartite structure by his division between the two parts of his treatment of the 'Aeneid' at the moment of arrival in Italy.

98 See Hinds 1998: 115.

99 See Hopkinson ad locc. On 'future reflexive allusion' see Barchiesi 1993.

in their stories of sacrifice for a city at a time of war (Trojan and Theban).[100] The following lines (705–29) swiftly allude to Aeneas' travels from Delos to Sicily in *Aeneid* 3 (128–560). The Trojans arrive at Zancle (13.729), where the mention of Scylla and Charybdis serves as a narrative cue for the introduction of the two love-triangles of Galatea, Acis, Polyphemus, and Scylla, Glaucus, and Circe. For over 300 lines Virgil's plot is left behind until the Trojans' journey is resumed at 14.75. Omitted is Virgil's episode of Achaemenides' retelling of the Homeric Cyclops (*Aen.* 3.558–691), which will appear later in book 14, having been replaced in book 13.740–897 by the pre-Homeric Polyphemus in love. Polyphemus and Circe are figures whose multiple appearances in the *Metamorphoses* serve as reminders of the temporal and literary layering of Ovid's '*Aeneid*'. Both figures appear first in scenes that represent pre-Homeric events and then reappear in Italy in their Homeric incarnations.

The opening of Book 14 continues the geographical route begun by Glaucus at the end of the previous book. Glaucus' journey takes him – and the poem – for the first time to Italy, as he leaves Sicily to swim to Circe's promontory on the western coast of Latium, bridging the division between Books 13 and 14 and signalling the movement of the poem from Greek to Italian themes. With the first word *iamque* in line 1 the reader of *Metamorphoses* 14 is perhaps bound to be somewhat at a loss initially as to where she has arrived in the narrative. In lines 1–7 the catalogue of the locations Glaucus has already left behind him in his journey lists some of the most formidable dangers faced by the Trojans in *Aeneid* 3: Aetna, the Cyclopes, and the straits of Messina. At the beginning of book 14 these episodes all lie in the (narrative) future. The narrowness of the strait between Sicily and Italy (14.6–7 *nauifragumque fretum, gemino quod litore pressum | Ausoniae Siculaeque tenet confinia terrae*) glosses the blurred boundaries between the two books, which are linked by Glaucus' continuing journey.[101] The dangerous nature of the strait perhaps signals metaphorically Ovid's confrontation with Virgil's epic in this section of the poem (although Virgil's Aeneas avoids precisely this route, see 1–74n.), while its narrowness and proximity to the shore stress Ovid's own Alexandrian approach to epic.[102]

After the metamorphoses of Scylla (monster/rock) we return to the Trojans' journey at 14.75 and follow it to Libya, where in four notorious lines Ovid dispatches with epigrammatic brevity Aeneas' affair with Dido in *Aen.* 4 (78–81). The treatment of the episode from Dido's perspective (as in *Heroides* 7) brings out an oppositional voice of the *Aeneid*, which seems to call into question Aeneas' actions and mission.[103] The theme

[100] The mention of Thebes in association with the Coroni once again associates Roman and Thebes, see Galinsky 1975: 221, Hardie 1990.

[101] See Wills 1997: 199 'Coastlines are obvious signals of liminality; they provide a sort of narrative punctuation which encloses separate books but also articulates the connections between them.'

[102] On the image of the open sea as grandiose epic poetry, see Wimmel 1960: 227–33, Kambylis 1965: 137–55, Call. *Hymn to Apollo* 106, Hor. *C.* 1.3, 4.15.3–4, Virg. *G.* 2.41–5. In elegiac imagery the poetic ship stays close to the shore, e.g. Ovid, *Tr.* 2.239–30, Prop. 3.23–4, 3.9.3–4. Contrast Pythagoras in *Met.* 15.176–7 *et quoniam magno feror aequore plenaque uentis | uela dedi.*

[103] Casali 1995, Thomas 2001: 82.

of deception and its punishment will be taken up in the following metamorphosis tale.[104] After some perfunctory highlights of episodes in *Aen.* 5 (82–8), the mention of the island of Pithecusae prompts the narration of the non-Virgilian tale of the metamorphosis of its inhabitants, the Cercopians, who are transformed into apes for their perjury (90–100). The narrative then moves on to Cumae and the Sibyl of *Aeneid* 6. Here again, instead of the pageant of the Roman future seen by Aeneas in Virgil's poem, Aeneas hears from the Sibyl her retrospective tale of Apollo's unsuccessful attempt to seduce her (10–153). Ovid's Aeneas reaches Caieta/Gaeta after the Sibyl episode at 14.157, where Ovid 'corrects' with *nondum* Virgil's chronological 'mistake' of prematurely naming the port before explaining how it came to be so called. Hinds has suggested that Ovid here 'salutes' Virgil's unusually non-closural division between *Aeneid* 6 and 7 by creating a gap between his two halves of Aeneas' story.[105] In Ovid's text it is not until lines 441–4 that he will fulfill the narrative expectation set up here, by giving us Caieta's burial and her epitaph, an epigram which both acknowledges Virgil's opening of *Aeneid* 7 and serves as a closural signal – immediately afterwards the Trojans arrive at the Tiber. This long narrative deferral creates a frame enclosing a series of Homeric (Cyclops and Circe) and Ovidian (Picus and Canens) tales narrated by two (non-Homeric) internal narrators in a scene which takes its cue from Virgil's Achaemenides episode in *Aeneid* 3. 558–691 (where Achaemenides also narrates the Cyclops episode).

The first Italian tale of the poem, that of Circe, Picus (Latinus' grandfather at *Aen.* 7.187–91) and Canens, appears in this section, filling in again the retrospective history of Italy before the arrival of the Trojans and taking advantage of a narrative gap in Homer as to what Odysseus' men did during the year he lingered with Circe. The story accounts for a religious statue of Picus (also the woodpecker) and a (non-existent) toponym for a *locus Canens* and functions programmatically in introducing the new Italian material of the poem and its largely aetiological treatment. The tale moves Circe's sexual malevolence deeper into the Italian landscape and a number of passages suggest that the erotic triangle also resonates with that of Aeneas, Lavinia, and Turnus in the *Aeneid*. The tale ends with Canens' evanescence from grief at the banks of the Tiber. The Trojans' subsequent arrival in Italy is signalled by the burial of Caieta (441–4) and the sighting of the Tiber (447–8). In another condensed summary the main plot of *Aeneid* 7–12 is introduced (449–53). The episode of Diomedes follows, closely reworked from *Aeneid* 11, but with the metamorphosis of his men expanded (457–511). The episode has a closural function as a miniature recapitulation of the plot of the *Aeneid*.[106] Appended to this story, and geographically and thematically related, is the non-Virgilian tale of the Apulian *pastor*, transformed, like Diomedes' men, for his verbal crime (512–26). Another Virgilian scene of metamorphosis follows at 530–65, where the Trojan ships are transformed into nymphs.

After this tale the plot of the *'Aeneid'* is swiftly resolved and ends, like Virgil's poem, with Turnus' death in the middle of line 573. At 14.566–72 the climax of the battle

104 Lamacchia 1969: 157.   105 Hinds 1998: 109.   106 See Hinds 1998: 116–19.

between Aeneas and the Latins is reached, only to be treated in a compressed and stark manner in five and a half very difficult lines. Here Ovid, in keeping with his anti-teleological reading, strips away any distinction between the two combatants' motivations and goals, beyond victory itself (569–72). However, Venus' appearance in 472–3, in language replete with imperial implications (*Venus uictricia nati* | *arma uidet*), recalls the Virgilian mission and prepares the way for Aeneas' imminent apotheosis. Aeneas' agency in Turnus' death is conspicuously omitted (*Turnusque cadit: cadit Ardea*), although in the following line his *barbarus ignis* is damagingly implicated in Ardea's destruction (574–5).[107] The emphasis is deflected from Turnus by Ovid's swift transition to the story of the creation of the heron (*ardea*) from the ashes of Turnus' destroyed town of Ardea, while the motifs of destruction and mourning provide thematic continuity. While signalling the continuation of his own poem, as well as his freedom to continue the Virgilian plot, Ovid's story of Ardea seems to supply retrospectively the closural ritual of lament which many have seen as so conspicuously omitted at the end of Virgil's *Aeneid*.[108] The continuation of the '*Aeneid*' narrative with Aeneas' destruction of an Italian city may, however, call into question his Virgilian civilizing mission (*Aen.* 1.5).[109]

A number of significant patterns emerge in the relationship of Ovid's 'inserted' narratives to the Virgilian frame, which confirm their participation in Ovid's overall project of a critical and tendentious reading of the *Aeneid*. Many of the tales are told by internal character narrators (Anius, Galatea, Glaucus, Sibyl, Achaemenides, Macareus, Diomedes) – a strategy that allows Ovid, as we have seen, to highlight the personal experience of Homeric and Virgilian characters, giving familiar events a fresh perspective. Achaemenides and Macareus offer first-person flashbacks of the same adventures Odysseus had narrated in the *Odyssey*, with the notable difference that Macareus actually experienced metamorphosis at the hands of Circe. The Virgilian characters Anius, the Sibyl, and Diomedes offer personal narratives of their own earlier losses, which contrast with their appearances in the *Aeneid*, where Anius and the Sibyl are associated with prophecies concerning Rome's rise (Anius *Aen.* 3.73–120, Sibyl *Aen.* 6.77–97) and Diomedes encourages Aeneas' mission (*Aen.* 11.225–95). Many of the tales involve loss and sacrifice (especially of children; see Anius' daughters 13.643–74, the Coroni 685–99, Molossus 716–18). A number share an emphasis on the loss of speech as punishment for the misuse or abuse of speech (Cragaleus, Cercopians, the Sibyl, Diomedes' men, Apulian shepherd), a story-pattern found throughout the poem, but perhaps especially relevant in this Virgilian and Augustan framework.[110] The tales of the poetic Canens and the ineptly imitative and crudely rustic Apulian shepherd seem to comment on Italian literary origins, fame, and imitation.[111] The preponderance of amatory tales (four; three are erotic triangles) can be seen to

[107] See 574n. for the textual difficulties of this line.

[108] See Hardie 1997b: 143–44, 151. [109] Casali 2006: 159–65.

[110] See Keith 1992 on book 2, also Feeney 1992 on Augustus and 'free speech', cf. *Fama* 12.39–55 above.

[111] See on Canens A. Hardie (forthcoming).

contrast generically with Ovid's epic model in this section of the poem, while also bringing out the erotic element in Virgil's text.[112] The motif of death and mourning is prominent in the tale of Picus and Canens and continued in the burial of Caieta and the destruction of Ardea (cf. Egeria in 15). Of the eleven non-Virgilian tales in Ovid's *Aeneid*, many are Greek (Anius' daughters, Coroni, Cercopians) and betray Alexandrian sensibilities (four may be derived from Nicander (Crageleus (Ant.Lib. 4), Molossus' sons (A.L. 14), Apulian shepherd (A.L. 31), Coroni (A.L. 25)). A number of geographical locations provide opportunities for aetiological stories, much in the tradition of Virgil himself (*Aen.* 6.232–5 Misenum, 7.1–4 Caieta), such as Ambracia (13.714–15), Chaonia (717–18), Pithecusae, and the Apulian shepherd.

3. *VIRGIL'S* AENEID *IN* METAMORPHOSES *13.623–14.573*

Metamorphoses	*Aeneid*
13.623–7 Escape from Troy	Book 2 Troy's fall, 2.721–804 escape from Troy, Creusa
628–31 Thrace	3.1–68 Thrace, Polydorus
[Polydorus 13.429ff.]	
632–704 Delos, Anius	3.69–130 Delos, Anius
prophecy 675–9	prophecy of Apollo 3.84–120
Anius' daughters, Orion's daughters	
705–8 Crete (bad weather)	3.131–91 Crete, Pergamum (plague) (dream of Aeneas 147ff.)
709–10 storm, Strophades (Aello)	3.192–208 storm (3 days)
	3.209–67 Strophades (Celaeno, prophecy)
711–13 Dulichium, Ithaca, Samos, Neritus	3.270–3 Zacynthus, Dulichium, Same, Neritus, Ithaca
713–15 Ambracia (*Cragaleus*= Actium)	3.274–90 Leucas, Actium (Trojan Games)
716–18 Dodona, Chaonia (*Molossus' sons*)	
719–20 Phaeacia, Epirus	3.291–2 Phaeacia, Epirus
720–3 Buthrotum, Helenus	3.293–505 Buthrotum, Helenus (Andromache) (prophecy, Scylla and Charybdis)
	3.506–52 Italy
724ff. Sicily, Scylla, Charybdis	3.553–67. Sicily (Scylaceum, Charybdis)
731–7 *Scylla I*	3.420–1

[112] Cf. Ovid's famous characterization of the *Aeneid* in *Tr.* 2.533–6. See Ellsworth 1986 and Nagle 1988c, on erotic triangles.

738–897 *Galatea, Acis, Cyclops*	(568–691 Achaemenides, Cyclops)
898–14.74 *Scylla, Glaucus, Circe*	
14.75–81 Carthage, Dido	Book 4 Dido
82–4 Eryx, Acestes, funeral rites for Anchises	Book 5 funeral rites for Anchises, games
85–6 ship-burning	5.604–99 ship-burning
86–8 Aeolian islands, Sirens	
88 Palinurus	5.833–71 Palinurus
	5.864–6 Sirens
89 Inarime, Prochyte	
89–100 Pithecusae, *Cercopians*	
101–3 Parthenope, Misenum	6.149–235 Misenus
103–56 Cumae, Sibyl and Underworld	Book 6 Sibyl and Underworld
Sibyl and Apollo	
157 Caieta (*nondum*) (cf. 14.441–4)	6.900–1, 7.1–6 Caieta
158–444 Aeneas in Caieta:	
158–222 Achaemenides, Cyclops	[3.570–691 Achaemenides, Cyclops]
223–307 *Macareus, 'Odyssey 9–10', Circe*	7.10–24 Circe
308–434 *Picus and Canens*	7.187–91 Picus
442–4 Caieta	7.1–6 Caieta
445–608 Aeneas in Latium	Books 7–12
(Lavinia, Latinus, Faunus, Turnus, *bellum*, Evander)	
457–511, 527–30 Venulus-Diomedes	8.9–17, 11.226–95 Venulus and Diomedes
512–26 *Apulian shepherd*	
530–65 Turnus, ship metamorphoses	9.69–122 Turnus, ship metamorphoses
566–73 war-death of Turnus	Book 12 *finis*
573–608 Ardea, Aeneas' deification	[7.411–13 Ardea, 1.259–60, 12.794–5 Aeneas]

4. ASPECTS OF OVID'S STYLE

Ovid's style and metre have been treated fully in a number of important studies; the following is meant to point out a number of characteristic features of Ovid's diction and narrative technique in *Metamorphoses* 14.[113] The poem is characterized by a blending of styles corresponding to its generic diversity, drawing from the entire range of Latin literary traditions, from lofty epic (didactic and heroic), philosophical and scientific discourse, to the humble themes of erotic and Alexandrian elegy.[114] Ovid includes

[113] Knox 1986a: 27–47, 1995: 25–34, Fantham 1998: 42–9, Kenney 2002. See also Wilkinson 1963, Horsfall 1995: 217–48.

[114] Knox 1986b: 100.

elements of colloquial speech for vividness of emotional effect, often in internal narratives (see the speech of Vertumnus at 657–764), scientific terminology (368–70, 791–3, 824–6), and draws throughout on the themes, vocabulary, and narrative devices of erotic elegy and neoteric poetry (the tale of Iphis and Anaxarete at 698–761 is especially indebted to love elegy). Venus attempts to cajole Jove with embraces into agreeing to Aeneas' deification in a scene of Alexandrian lightness and wit (585–91), while Mars, in order to secure Romulus' deification, quotes Ennius and speaks in weighty archaic language to Jupiter (806–15). Variations in tone and tempo are the norm. Increased enjambment speeds up transitional passages between episodes (e.g. 85–90, 445–53, 609–21)[115] and narrative swiftness is also achieved through mid-line transitions to new tales (e.g. 514, 573).

The narrative of the *Met.* combines a seemingly effortless lucidity and fluency with a continual alertness to the effects of word choice and placement. Ovid's choice of diction has been characterized by Kenney as directed towards 'establishing what might be called a standard literary dialect of Latin'.[116] Many features of Ovid's style are dictated by the desire to keep the narrative and rhythm fast-moving. In the case of the rhythm, this means lightening it by cutting down on elision and introducing a high proportion of dactyls.[117] For the latter purpose Ovid draws heavily on the usage of the poetic plural (use of the plural when sing. expected), especially in neuter nouns which provide nom./acc. plurals in *-a*, often of dactylic shape; use of this resource goes back to the earliest Latin poetry and has a basis in Greek usage (e.g. στήθεα in Homer).[118] In *Met.* 14 we have e.g. 499–500 *colla, pectora*, 616 *nomina*, 621 *uocabula*, 843 *ora*. Other forms providing dactylic endings include adjectives in *–ilis* (116 *formidabilis)*, abstract fourth declension substantive formations in *–us* (129 *suspiratibus*), neuter nouns in *–men* (808 *fundamine*), and the common poetic use of the shorter form of the third person plural perfect.[119]

In a poem whose subject matter is for the most part profoundly Greek, it is not surprising that among the linguistic features the most notable in the *Metamorphoses* is the profusion and variety of Greek proper names and adjectival derivatives of Greek names, which impart learned, emotive, and exotic colour to the narrative (cf. Cic. *Or.* 163 *locorum splendidis nominibus illuminatus*).[120] Ovid tends to prefer Greek inflections of Greek names, especially the acc. *-n*, even when not needed to avoid elision (see Quint. *Inst.* 12.10.31 for the appeal of this termination).[121] Greek declensions provide

[115] On Ovid's use of enjambment see Kenney 2002: 80–1. [116] Kenney 2002: 68.

[117] On Ovid's higher proportion of feet containing short syllables see Duckworth 1969: 71–80, Kenney 2002: 57–89.

[118] On the use of poetic plurals, primarily for metrically useful variants, but also for poetic color, see Löfstedt 1942: 27–65, esp. 29 (categories), 37 (metre), Norden on *Aen.* 6.408ff., Fordyce on *Aen.* 7.445, Maurach 1995: 84–6, Coleman 1999: 75.

[119] See Coleman 1999: 44. [120] Wilkinson 1955: 235–6, Kenney 2002: 68.

[121] See Coleman 1999: 46–7 on the increasing retention in poetry of Greek case forms in Greek nouns. For caution about the textual transmission of Greek proper names, see Tarrant's Appendix to his edition of the *Metamorphoses* (483–94), listing the textual variants of names in the MSS.

dactylic terminations, e.g. second-declension accusatives in *-on* (e.g. 223–4 *Aeolon*), third-declension acc. sing. in *-a* (e.g. 252 *Elpenora*, 472 *Capherea*, 497 *Acmona*), third-declension nom. and acc. plurals in *-es* and *-as* (e.g. 557, 786 *Naides*). Ovid's attachment to Greek forms of proper names goes so far that he gives Greek terminations to the Latin name *Hersilia* (830, 839, 848). Third-declension adjective endings in *-is, -idis* are also useful (e.g. 14 *Titani*, 376 *Titanida*).[122] So are the feminine and neuter endings *-a* of adjectives in *-eius* (e.g. 44 *Hecateia*, 47 *Zancleia*); for these Ovid takes a hint from Virgil, whose *Aeneia nutrix* he reproduces (441). Greek forms also provide convenient final long syllables (e.g. 669 *Helene*).[123]

Adjectival forms of Greek names often occur with variants, many of them unique to Ovid, and are employed with 'formulaic economy' for metrical convenience:[124] contrast *Hecateius* (44) with 6.139 *Hecateis* (both Ovidian coinages), *Zancleius* (47, only here) with *Zanclaeus* (13.729, *F.* 4.499, *Tr.* 5.2.73), *Acheloias* (87, only here) with *Achelois* (5.552) and *Acheloius* (9.413), *Aetolius* (461, only here) with *Aetolus* (528) and *Aetolis* (*Her.* 9.131), *Lapitheius* (670, 12.417, only here), *Lapitheus* (12.530), *Cytherea* (487) with *Cythereius* (584), *Cythereia* (4.190), *Cythereis* (4.288), and *Cytheriacus* (*Her.* 7.60, first here), *Cythereias* (15.386, only here), *Titanis* (14.376) with *Titanius* (382, 438), *Thaumanteus* (845, only here), *Thaumantias* (4.480), *Thaumantis* (11.647). Recherché mythological patronymics and periphrases standing for persons and places also add epic grandeur and demand learned readers: patronymics *Hippotades* (86, 224 Aeolus, which also functions as a literary allusion to Homer and Apollonius Rhodius), *Acheloias* (87 daughter of Achelous, a cross-reference to an earlier episode), *Aeolides* (103 Misenus), *Saturnia* (782 Juno, a literary allusion to Virgil), matronymics *Iliades* (781 Romulus, unique to Ovid), and papponymics *Oenides* (512 Diomedes, grandson of Oeneus of Calydon), *Titanis/Titania* (14, 376, 382, 438 Circe, descendant of Titan, underlining her formidable powers, see 36n.). Geographical periphrases include Glaucus as *Euboicus cultor aquarum* (4), Dido as *Sidonis* (80), Ulysses as *Dulichius . . . dux* (230), Diomedes as *Aetolius heros* (261), Aeneas as *Cytherius heros* (584), Venus as *Idalie* (694).

Ovid's well-known fondness for wordplay is rarely mere frivolity; rather it 'reflects an intellectual process that compels thought on the part of the reader by unexpected verbal effects'.[125] His verbal wit is displayed in etymological wordplay, explicit (e.g. 90, 338, 348, 396, 579–80, 614–16, 621, 626) or suggestive (e.g. 12, 29, 60, 82, 94).[126] A favourite means of piquing the reader and keeping her on her toes is polyptoton (e.g. 35 *spernentem sperne*, 81 *decepta . . . decipit*, 468 *a Virgine uirgine*). As with some of these instances, paradox is implicit; one may here note 93–4 *idem | dissimiles . . . similes*, 113 *inuia . . . uia*. In 536–7 *aera* (from *aer*) . . . *aeris* (from *aes*) we have an actual pun, and 649–50 *putator . . . putares* incorporates a correct etymology.

[122] Kenney 2002: 68. [123] Kenney 1973: 126–7. [124] Kenney 2002: 68–9.
[125] Knox 1995: 29; see Hinds 1987b: 6.
[126] On Ovid's love of etymological play, see McKeown 1987: 45–62, Tissol 1997: 167–77, Michalopoulos 2001.

One device of which Ovid makes much use is the figure of syllepsis, pervasive in all his work (78, 377, 417, 426, 449, 498). This trope, which confers point and wit, hinges on the merging of the literal and figurative meanings of an expression, usually for 'specific thematic purposes'.[127] An example in book 14 occurs in line 78 where Dido is said to have 'welcomed Aeneas there in her heart and home' (*excipit Aenean illic animoque domoque*). Here the verb *excipit* is applied literally to one word (*domo*) and metaphorically to another (*animo*) to express Dido's swift surrender to her passion for Aeneas. Tissol stresses the close connection of syllepsis with the similar 'shift from the conceptual to the physical in metamorphosis'.[128] In book 14, for example, the petrifaction of Anaxarete represents a realization of her literary characterization throughout the episode as a hard-hearted mistress (*dura puella*).[129]

Through complex word order Ovid enhances the meaning of his lines. Significant juxtaposition[130] of nouns can express such different notions as pointed opposition (e.g. 77 *Ausonium, Libycas*, 163 *barbara Graium*, 220 *Graiumque ratis Troiana*, 800 *Romana Sabinis*), oxymoron (711 *surgente cadentibus*, 623–4 *Latinas | inter Hamadryadas*), or (aspiring) closeness (699 *Iphis Anaxareten*). The epanalepsis (repetition) of *Aeolon* at 223–4 functions as an allusion to Homer,[131] while Circe's magical spell at 300–1 (*percutimurque caput conuersae uerbere uirgae, | uerbaque dicuntur dictis contraria uerbis*) is vividly illustrated by wordplay, polyptoton, and alliteration.

[127] Tissol 1997:19, see Kenney 1971: 160, 1972: 39–40, 2002: 45–7 and Tissol 1997: 219–20 (on the distinction between syllepsis and zeugma), also Galinsky 1975: 143, 156, 248, Tissol 1997: 18–20, 221–22.

[128] Tissol 1997: 20 'To blur the boundaries between literal and figurative meanings is the perfect linguistic representation of metamorphosis', cf. Solodow 1988: 184–5.

[129] Solodow 1988: 179. [130] Cf. Harrison 1991: 288–90. [131] Wills 1996: 162.

THE TEXT AND APPARATUS CRITICUS

Although over 400 manuscripts of the *Metamorphoses* survive, there are no extant complete codices from before the second half of the eleventh century (there are four fragments from the ninth and tenth centuries, and a number of codices from the end of the tenth to the end of the eleventh centuries), while many date from the twelfth century 'aetas Ovidiana'. No pure strain of the textual tradition can be identified or given preferential treatment. The present text relies primarily on readings reported in the Oxford Classical Text of R. Tarrant (2004), whose editorial approach is eclectic, allowing for horizontal contamination of the primary MSS and the preservation of authentic readings in the 'recentiores'.[1] Variants and conjectures are reported selectively. Particular textual problems are discussed in the commentary.

The following abbreviations are used:

M = reading of the whole MS tradition
m = reading of part of the MS tradition

[1] See Tarrant 1983: 276–82, 1982.

P. OVIDI NASONIS
METAMORPHOSEON
LIBER QVARTVS DECIMVS

P. OVIDI NASONIS
METAMORPHOSEON
LIBER QVARTVS DECIMVS

Iamque Giganteis iniectam faucibus Aetnen
aruaque Cyclopum quid rastra, quid usus aratri
nescia nec quidquam iunctis debentia bubus
liquerat Euboicus tumidarum cultor aquarum;
liquerat et Zanclen aduersaque moenia Regi
nauifragumque fretum, gemino quod litore pressum
Ausoniae Siculaeque tenet confinia terrae.
inde manu magna Tyrrhena per aequora uectus
herbiferos adiit colles atque atria Glaucus
Sole satae Circes, uariarum plena ferarum.
quam simul aspexit, dicta acceptaque salute,
'diua, dei miserere, precor. nam sola leuare
tu potes hunc' dixit, 'uidear modo dignus, amorem.
quanta sit herbarum, Titani, potentia nulli
quam mihi cognitius, qui sum mutatus ab illis.
neue mei non nota tibi sit causa furoris,
litore in Italico, Messenia moenia contra,
Scylla mihi uisa est. pudor est promissa precesque
blanditiasque meas contemptaque uerba referre;
at tu, siue aliquid regni est in carmine, carmen
ore moue sacro, siue expugnacior herba est,
utere temptatis operosae uiribus herbae
nec medeare mihi sanesque haec uulnera mando
(fine nihil opus est!); partem ferat illa caloris.'
At Circe (neque enim flammis habet aptius ulla
talibus ingenium, seu causa est huius in ipsa,
seu Venus indicio facit hoc offensa paterno)
talia uerba refert: 'melius sequerere uolentem
optantemque eadem parilique cupidine captam.
dignus eras ultro (poteras certeque) rogari,

10 uariarum *m*: uanarum *m* 13 dignus amorem *m:* dignus amore, dignior esse *m* 20 aliquid regni *m*: aliquod regnum *m* 24 fine nihil *m*: fineque nil *m* 30 certeque *m*: per teque *Burman*

et, si spem dederis, mihi crede, rogaberis ultro.
neu dubites adsitque tuae fiducia formae,
en ego, cum dea sim, nitidi cum filia Solis,
carmine cum tantum, tantum quoque gramine possim,
ut tua sim uoueo. spernentem sperne, sequenti
redde uices, unoque duas ulciscere facto.'
talia temptanti 'prius' inquit 'in aequore frondes'
Glaucus 'et in summis nascentur montibus algae,
sospite quam Scylla nostri mutentur amores.'
indignata dea est, et laedere quatenus ipsum
non poterat (nec uellet amans), irascitur illi
quae sibi praelata est; Venerisque offensa repulsa
protinus horrendis infamia pabula sucis
conterit et tritis Hecateia carmina miscet
caerulaque induitur uelamina perque ferarum
agmen adulantum media procedit ab aula,
oppositumque petens contra Zancleia saxa
Region ingreditur feruentes aestibus undas,
in quibus ut solida ponit uestigia terra
summaque decurrit pedibus super aequora siccis.
  Paruus erat gurges curuos sinuatus in arcus;
grata quies Scyllae, quo se referebat ab aestu
et maris et caeli, medio cum plurimus orbe
sol erat et minimas a uertice fecerat umbras.
hunc dea praeuitiat portentificisque uenenis
inquinat, hic pressos latices radice nocenti
spargit et obscurum uerborum ambage nouorum
ter nouiens carmen magico demurmurat ore.
Scylla uenit mediaque tenus descenderat aluo,
cum sua foedari latrantibus inguina monstris
aspicit; ac primo, credens non corporis illas
esse sui partes, refugitque abigitque timetque
ora proterua canum. sed quos fugit attrahit una,
et corpus quaerens femorum crurumque pedumque
Cerbereos rictus pro partibus inuenit illis;
statque canum rabie subiectaque terga ferarum
inguinibus truncis uteroque exstante coercet.

32 adsitque *m*: absitque *m* (*Heinsius*) 44 carmina *m*: gramina *m* 66 rabie *Heinsius*: rabies *M*

Fleuit amans Glaucus nimiumque hostiliter usae
uiribus herbarum fugit conubia Circes.
Scylla loco mansit, cumque est data copia primum,
in Circes odium sociis spoliauit Vlixem.
mox eadem Teucras fuerat mersura carinas,
ni prius in scopulum, qui nunc quoque saxeus exstat,
transformata foret; scopulum quoque nauita uitat.
Hunc ubi Troianae remis auidamque Charybdin
euicere rates, cum iam prope litus adessent
Ausonium, Libycas uento referuntur ad oras.
excipit Aenean illic animoque domoque
non bene discidium Phrygii latura mariti
Sidonis, inque pyra sacri sub imagine facta
incubuit ferro deceptaque decipit omnes.
Rursus harenosae fugiens noua moenia terrae
ad sedesque Erycis fidumque relatus Acesten
sacrificat tumulumque sui genitoris honorat.
quasque rates Iris Iunonia paene cremarat
soluit et Hippotadae regnum terrasque calenti
sulphure fumantes Acheloiadumque relinquit
Sirenum scopulos, orbataque praeside pinus
Inarimen Prochytenque legit sterilique locatas
colle Pithecusas, habitantum nomine dictas.
quippe deum genitor, fraudem et periuria quondam
Cercopum exosus gentisque admissa dolosae,
in deforme uiros animal mutauit. ut idem
dissimiles homini possent similesque uideri,
membraque contraxit naresque a fronte resimas
contudit et rugis perarauit anilibus ora
totaque uelatos flauenti corpora uillo
misit in has sedes. nec non prius abstulit usum
uerborum et natae dira in periuria linguae;
posse queri tantum rauco stridore reliquit.
Has ubi praeteriit et Parthenopeia dextra
moenia deseruit, laeua de parte canori
Aeolidae tumulum et, loca feta palustribus undis,
litora Cumarum uiuacisque antra Sibyllae

87 Acheloiadumque *Const. Fanensis, Naugerius*: Acheloidumque *m* 95 resimas *Salmasius*: remissas *M* 103 undis *m*: uluis *m*

intrat et ut manes adeat per Auerna paternos
orat. at illa diu uultum tellure moratum
erexit tandemque deo furibunda recepto
'magna petis' dixit, 'uir factis maxime, cuius
dextera per ferrum, pietas spectata per ignes.
pone tamen, Troiane, metum; potiere petitis
Elysiasque domos et regna nouissima mundi
me duce cognosces simulacraque cara parentis.
inuia uirtuti nulla est uia.' dixit et auro
fulgentem ramum in silua Iunonis Auernae
monstrauit iussitque suo diuellere trunco.
  Paruit Aeneas et formidabilis Orci
uidit opes atauosque suos umbramque senilem
magnanimi Anchisae. didicit quoque iura locorum,
quaeque nouis essent adeunda pericula bellis.
inde ferens lassos aduerso tramite passus
cum duce Cumaea mollit sermone laborem;
dumque iter horrendum per opaca crepuscula carpit,
'seu dea tu praesens, seu dis gratissima' dixit,
'numinis instar eris semper mihi, meque fatebor
muneris esse tui, quae me loca mortis adire,
quae loca me uisae uoluisti euadere mortis.
pro quibus aerias meritis euectus ad auras
templa tibi statuam, tribuam tibi turis honores.'
  Respicit hunc uates et suspiratibus haustis
'nec dea sum' dixit 'nec sacri turis honore
humanum dignare caput, neu nescius erres,
lux aeterna mihi carituraque fine dabatur,
si mea uirginitas Phoebo patuisset amanti.
dum tamen hanc sperat, dum praecorrumpere donis
me cupit, "elige" ait "uirgo Cumaea, quid optes;
optatis potiere tuis." ego pulueris hausti
ostendens cumulum, quot haberet corpora puluis,
tot mihi natales contingere uana rogaui;
excidit, ut peterem iuuenes quoque protinus annos.
hos tamen ille mihi dabat aeternamque iuuentam,
si Venerem paterer. contempto munere Phoebi
innuba permaneo; sed iam felicior aetas

114 in silua *m*: silua *m* 127 meritis *m*: uiuenti *m*

terga dedit, tremuloque gradu uenit aegra senectus,
quae patienda diu est. nam iam mihi saecula septem
acta uides; superest, numeros ut pulueris aequem,
ter centum messes, ter centum musta uidere.
tempus erit, cum de tanto me corpore paruam
longa dies faciet, consumptaque membra senecta
ad minimum redigentur onus, nec amata uidebor
nec placuisse deo, Phoebus quoque forsitan ipse
uel non cognoscet, uel dilexisse negabit.
usque adeo mutata ferar, nullique uidenda,
uoce tamen noscar; uocem mihi fata relinquent.'
Talia conuexum per iter memorante Sibylla
sedibus Euboicam Stygiis emergit in urbem
Troius Aeneas sacrisque ex more litatis
litora adit nondum nutricis habentia nomen.
hic quoque substiterat per taedia longa laborum
Neritius Macareus, comes experientis Vlixei.
desertum quondam mediis qui rupibus Aetnae
noscit Achaemeniden improuisoque repertum
uiuere miratus, 'quis te casusue deusue
seruat, Achaemenide? cur' inquit 'barbara Graium
prora uehit? petitur uestra quae terra carina?'
talia quaerenti, iam non hirsutus amictu,
iam suus et spinis conserto tegmine nullis,
fatur Achaemenides: 'iterum Polyphemon et illos
aspiciam fluidos humano sanguine rictus,
hac mihi si potior domus est Ithaceque carina,
si minus Aenean ueneror genitore; nec umquam
esse satis potero, praestem licet omnia, gratus.
quod loquor et spiro caelumque et sidera solis
respicio, possimne ingratus et immemor esse?
ille dedit, quod non anima haec Cyclopis in ora
uenit et, ut iam nunc lumen uitale relinquam,
aut tumulo aut certe non illa condar in aluo.
'Quid mihi tunc animi (nisi si timor abstulit omnem
sensum animumque) fuit, cum uos petere alta relictus

145 uides *m*: tamen *Clausen 1963* 152–3 *uu. secl. Tarrant* 158 per *m*: post *m* 159 Vlixei *m*: Vlixis *m* 160 qui *m*: e, in, sub, pr(a)e *m* 169 Ithaceque *m* (*Naugerius*): -cique *m* 173 immemor *m*: impius *m*

aequora conspexi? uolui inclamare, sed hosti
prodere me timui; uestrae quoque clamor Vlixis
paene rati nocuit. uidi, cum monte reuulsum
inmanem scopulum medias permisit in undas;
uidi iterum ueluti tormenti uiribus acta
uasta Giganteo iaculantem saxa lacerto,
et ne deprimeret fluctusue lapisue carinam
pertimui, iam me non esse oblitus in illa.
ut uero fuga uos a certa morte reduxit,
ille quidem totam gemebundus obambulat Aetnen
praetemptatque manu siluas et luminis orbus
rupibus incursat foedataque bracchia tabo
in mare protendens gentem exsecratur Achiuam
atque ait: "o si quis referat mihi casus Vlixem
aut aliquem e sociis, in quem mea saeuiat ira,
uiscera cuius edam, cuius uiuentia dextra
membra mea laniem, cuius mihi sanguis inundet
guttur et elisi trepident sub dentibus artus,
quam nullum aut leue sit damnum mihi lucis ademptae!"
haec et plura ferox; me luridus occupat horror
spectantem uultus etiamnum caede madentes
crudelesque manus et inanem luminis orbem
membraque et humano concretam sanguine barbam.
[mors erat ante oculos, minimum tamen ipsa doloris.]
et iam prensurum, iam nunc mea uiscera rebar
in sua mersurum; mentique haerebat imago
temporis illius, quo uidi bina meorum
ter quater affligi sociorum corpora terrae,
cum super ipse iacens hirsuti more leonis
uisceraque et carnes cumque albis ossa medullis
semianimesque artus auidam condebat in aluum.
me tremor inuasit; stabam sine sanguine maestus,
mandentemque uidens eiectantemque cruentas
ore dapes et frusta mero glomerata uomentem,
talia fingebam misero mihi fata parari.
perque dies multos latitans omnemque tremescens
ad strepitum mortemque timens cupidusque moriri,

185 –ue lapisue *m:* uentusue *m* 202 *u. om. m; secl. Tarrant* 205 bina *m*: uiua *m* 215 cupidusque *m*: cupiensque *m*

glande famem pellens et mixta frondibus herba
solus inops exspes, leto poenaeque relictus,
hanc procul aspexi longo post tempore nauem
orauique fugam gestu ad litusque cucurri,
et moui: Graiumque ratis Troiana recepit.
tu quoque pande tuos, comitum gratissime, casus
et ducis et turbae, quae tecum est credita ponto.'
Aeolon ille refert Tusco regnare profundo,
Aeolon Hippotaden, cohibentem carcere uentos;
quos bouis inclusos tergo, memorabile munus,
Dulichium sumpsisse ducem flatuque secundo
lucibus isse nouem et terram aspexisse petitam.
proxima post nonam cum sese aurora moueret,
inuidia socios praedaeque cupidine uictos,
esse ratos aurum, dempsisse ligamina uentis;
cum quibus isse retro, per quas modo uenerat undas,
Aeoliique ratem portus repetisse tyranni.
'Inde Lami ueterem Laestrygonis' inquit 'in urbem
uenimus; Antiphates terra regnabat in illa.
missus ad hunc ego sum numero comitante duorum,
uixque fuga quaesita salus comitique mihique,
tertius e nobis Laestrygonis impia tinxit
ora cruore suo. fugientibus instat et agmen
concitat Antiphates; coeunt et saxa trabesque
coniciunt merguntque uiros franguntque carinas.
una tamen, quae nos ipsumque uehebat Vlixem,
effugit. amissa sociorum parte dolentes
multaque conquesti terris adlabimur illis,
quas procul hinc cernis – procul hinc, mihi crede, uidenda
insula, crede mihi! tuque o iustissime Troum,
nate dea (neque enim finito Marte uocandus
hostis es, Aenea) moneo, fuge litora Circes!
nos quoque Circaeo religata in litore pinu
Antiphatae memores immansuetique Cyclopis,
ire negabamus et tecta ignota subire;
sorte sumus lecti, sors me fidumque Politen
Eurylochumque simul nimiique Elpenora uini

229 uictos *m*: captos *m* 240 frangunt *Kenney*: mergunt *M* 245 crede *Shackleton Bailey*: uisa *M*: pressa *Courtney 2005* 250 et *m*: sed, uel, nec *m*

bisque nouem socios Circaea ad moenia misit.
quae simul attigimus stetimusque in limine tecti,
mille lupi mixtique lupis ursique leaeque
occursu fecere metum. sed nulla timenda,
nullaque erat nostro factura in corpore uulnus;
quin etiam blandas mouere per aera caudas
nostraque adulantes comitant uestigia, donec
excipiunt famulae perque atria marmore tecta
ad dominam ducunt. pulchro sedet illa recessu,
sublimi solio pallamque induta nitentem
insuper aurato circumuelatur amictu.
Nereides nymphaeque simul, quae uellera motis
nulla trahunt digitis nec fila sequentia ducunt;
gramina disponunt sparsosque sine ordine flores
secernunt calathis uariasque coloribus herbas.
ipsa quod hae faciunt opus exigit ipsa quis usus
quoue sit in folio, quae sit concordia mixtis,
nouit et aduertens pensas examinat herbas.
haec ubi nos uidit, dicta acceptaque salute
diffudit uultus et reddidit omina uotis;
nec mora, misceri tosti iubet hordea grani
mellaque uimque meri cum lacte coagula passo,
quique sub hac lateant furtim dulcedine sucos
adicit. accipimus sacra data pocula dextra.
quae simul arenti sitientes hausimus ore
et tetigit summos uirga dea dira capillos
(et pudet et referam), saetis horrescere coepi
nec iam posse loqui, pro uerbis edere raucum
murmur et in terram toto procumbere uultu;
osque meum sensi pando occallescere rostro,
colla tumere toris, et qua modo pocula parte
sumpta mihi fuerant, illa uestigia feci.
cumque eadem passis (tantum medicamina possunt)
claudor hara; solumque suis caruisse figura
uidimus Eurylochum, solus data pocula fugit.
quae nisi uitasset, pecoris pars una manerem
nunc quoque saetigeri, nec tantae cladis ab illo

262 sublimi *m*: sollemni *m* 269 quoue *m*: quoque *m* 272 omina *m*: omnia *m* uotis *m*: uocis, uoce *m* 288 manerem *Gruter*: maneret *M*

certior ad Circen ultor uenisset Vlixes.
pacifer huic dederat florem Cyllenius album;
moly uocant superi, nigra radice tenetur.
tutus eo monitisque simul caelestibus intrat
ille domum Circes et ad insidiosa uocatus
pocula conantem uirga mulcere capillos
reppulit et stricto pauidam deterruit ense.
inde fides dextraeque datae thalamoque receptus
coniugii dotem sociorum corpora poscit.
spargimur ignotae sucis melioribus herbae
percutimurque caput conuersae uerbere uirgae,
uerbaque dicuntur dictis contraria uerbis.
quo magis illa canit, magis hoc tellure leuati
erigimur, saetaeque cadunt bifidosque relinquit
rima pedes, redeunt umeri et subiecta lacertis
bracchia sunt. flentem flentes amplectimur illis
haeremusque ducis collo, nec uerba locuti
ulla priora sumus quam nos testantia gratos.
'Annua nos illic tenuit mora, multaque praesens
tempore tam longo uidi, multa auribus hausi;
hoc quoque cum multis, quod clam mihi rettulit una
quattuor e famulis ad talia sacra paratis.
cum duce namque meo Circe dum sola moratur,
illa mihi niueo factum de marmore signum
ostendit iuuenale gerens in uertice picum,
aede sacra positum multisque insigne coronis.
quis foret et quare sacra coleretur in aede,
cur hanc ferret auem quaerenti et scire uolenti
"accipe" ait, "Macareu, dominaeque potentia quae sit
hinc quoque disce meae; tu dictis adice mentem.
' "Picus in Ausoniis, proles Saturnia, terris
rex fuit, utilium bello studiosus equorum.
forma uiro, quam cernis, erat; licet ipse decorem
aspicias fictaque probes ab imagine uerum.
par animus formae; nec adhuc spectasse per annos
quinquennem poterat Graia quater Elide pugnam.
ille suos Dryadas Latiis in montibus ortas
uerterat in uultus, illum fontana petebant

305 illis *m*: illum, ipsi *m* 324 per *m*: tot *m* 325 Elide pugnam *m*: edere pugna *m*

numina, Naiades, quas Albula, quasque Numici,
quas Anienis aquae cursuque breuissimus Almo
Narue tulit praeceps et opacae Farfarus umbrae,
quaeque colunt Scythicae stagnum nemorale Dianae
finitimosque lacus. spretis tamen omnibus unam
ille colit nymphen, quam quondam in colle Palati
dicitur Ionio peperisse Venilia Iano;
haec ubi nubilibus primum maturuit annis,
praeposito cunctis Laurenti tradita Pico est.
rara quidem facie, sed rarior arte canendi,
unde Canens dicta est; siluas et saxa mouere
et mulcere feras et flumina longa morari
ore suo uolucresque uagas retinere solebat.
'''Quae dum feminea modulatur carmina uoce,
exierat tecto Laurentes Picus in agros
indigenas fixurus apros, tergumque premebat
acris equi laeuaque hastilia bina ferebat,
poeniceam fuluo chlamydem constrictus ab auro.
uenerat in siluas et filia Solis easdem,
utque nouas legeret fecundis collibus herbas,
nomine dicta suo Circaea reliquerat arua.
quae simul ac iuuenem uirgultis abdita uidit,
obstipuit; cecidere manu quas legerat herbae,
flammaque per totas uisa est errare medullas.
ut primum ualido mentem collegit ab aestu,
quid cuperet fassura fuit; ne posset adire
cursus equi fecit circumfususque satelles.
'non' ait 'effugies, uento rapiare licebit,
si modo me noui, si non euanuit omnis
herbarum uirtus nec me mea carmina fallunt.'
dixit, et effigiem nullo cum corpore falsi
finxit apri praeterque oculos transcurrere regis
iussit et in densum trabibus nemus ire uideri,
plurima qua silua est et equo loca peruia non sunt.
haud mora, continuo praedae petit inscius umbram
Picus equique celer spumantia terga relinquit
spemque sequens uanam silua pedes errat in alta.
concipit illa preces et uerba precantia dicit

334 (h)ionio *m*: ancipiti *m* 345 constrictus *Salmasius, Liberman 2004*: contractus *m*
365 precantia *m*: uenefica *m*: potentia *Slater*

ignotosque deos ignoto carmine adorat,
quo solet et niueae uultum confundere lunae
et patrio capiti bibulas subtexere nubes.
tum quoque cantato densetur carmine caelum
et nebulas exhalat humus, caecisque uagantur
limitibus comites, et abest custodia regis.
nacta locum tempusque 'per o tua lumina' dixit,
'quae mea ceperunt, perque hanc, pulcherrime, formam,
quae facit ut supplex tibi sim dea, consule nostris
ignibus et socerum qui peruidet omnia Solem
accipe, nec durus Titanida despice Circen.'
dixerat; ille ferox ipsamque precesque relinquit
et 'quaecumque es' ait 'non sum tuus; altera captum
me tenet et teneat per longum, comprecor, aeuum,
nec Venere externa socialia foedera laedam,
dum mihi Ianigenam seruabunt fata Canentem.'
saepe retemptatis precibus Titania frustra
'non impune feres neque' ait 'reddere Canenti,
laesaque quid faciat, quid amans, quid femina disces
[rebus,' ait; 'sed amans et laesa et femina Circe.']
' "Tum bis ad occasus, bis se conuertit ad ortus,
ter iuuenem baculo tetigit, tria carmina dixit.
ille fugit, sed se solito uelocius ipse
currere miratur; pennas in corpore uidit,
seque nouam subito Latiis accedere siluis
indignatus auem, duro fera robora rostro
figit et iratus longis dat uulnera ramis.
purpureum chlamydis pennae traxere colorem;
fibula quod fuerat uestemque momorderat aurum
pluma fit, et fuluo ceruix praecingitur auro;
nec quidquam antiquum Pico nisi nomina restat.
' "Interea comites, clamato saepe per agros
nequiquam Pico nullaque in parte reperto,
inueniunt Circen (nam iam tenuauerat auras
passaque erat nebulas uentis ac sole recludi);
criminibusque premunt ueris regemque reposcunt
uimque ferunt saeuisque parant incessere telis.

385 *u. del. Korn* ait sed *m*: at est et *Postgate*: adest et *Watt 1995*

illa nocens spargit uirus sucosque ueneni
et Noctem Noctisque deos Ereboque Chaoque
conuocat et longis Hecaten ululatibus orat.
exsiluere loco (dictu mirabile) siluae,
ingemuitque solum, uicinaque palluit arbor,
sparsaque sanguineis maduerunt pabula guttis,
et lapides uisi mugitus edere raucos
et latrare canes et humus serpentibus atris
squalere et tenues animae uolitare silentum.
attonitum monstris uulgus pauet; illa pauentum
ora uenenata tetigit mirantia uirga.
cuius ab attactu uariarum monstra ferarum
in iuuenes ueniunt; nulli sua mansit imago.

‘ “Sparserat occiduus Tartessia litora Phoebus,
et frustra coniunx oculis animoque Canentis
exspectatus erat; famuli populusque per omnes
discurrunt siluas atque obuia lumina portant.
nec satis est nymphae flere et lacerare capillos
et dare plangorem (facit haec tamen omnia), seque
proripit ac Latios errat uesana per agros.
sex illam noctes, totidem redeuntia solis
lumina uiderunt inopem somnique cibique
per iuga, per ualles, qua fors ducebat, euntem;
ultimus aspexit Thybris luctuque uiaque
fessam et in gelida ponentem corpora ripa.
illic cum lacrimis ipsos modulata dolores
uerba sono tenui maerens fundebat, ut olim
carmina iam moriens canit exequialia cycnus;
luctibus extremum tenues liquefacta medullas
tabuit inque leues paulatim euanuit auras.
fama tamen signata loco est, quem rite Canentem
nomine de nymphae ueteres dixere Camenae.”

‘Talia multa mihi longum narrata per annum
uisaque sunt. resides et desuetudine tardi
rursus inire fretum, rursus dare uela iubemur.
ancipitesque uias et iter Titania uastum

427 in gelida *m*: iam longa *m* 428 ipsos . . . dolores *m*: ipso . . . dolore *m* 431 extremum *m*: extremis *m* 434 Camenae *m*: coloni *m*

dixerat et saeui restare pericula ponti;
pertimui, fateor, nactusque hoc litus adhaesi.'
  Finierat Macareus, urnaque Aeneia nutrix
condita marmoreo tumulo breue carmen habebat
HIC·ME·CAIETAM·NOTAE·PIETATIS·ALVMNVS
EREPTAM·ARGOLICO·QVO·DEBVIT·IGNE·CREMAVIT
  Soluitur herboso religatus ab aggere funis
et procul insidias infamataeque relinquunt
tecta deae lucosque petunt, ubi nubilus umbra
in mare cum flaua prorumpit Thybris harena.
Faunigenaeque domo potitur nataque Latini,
non sine Marte tamen; bellum cum gente feroci
suscipitur, pactaque furit pro coniuge Turnus.
concurrit Latio Tyrrhenia tota, diuque
ardua sollicitis uictoria quaeritur armis.
  Auget uterque suas externo robore uires,
et multi Rutulos, multi Troiana tuentur
castra. neque Aeneas Euandri ad moenia frustra,
at Venulus frustra profugi Diomedis ad urbem
uenerat; ille quidem sub Iapyge maxima Dauno
moenia condiderat dotaliaque arua tenebat.
sed Venulus Turni postquam mandata peregit
auxiliumque petit, uires Aetolius heros
excusat: nec se aut soceri committere pugnae
uelle sui populos, aut quos e gente suorum
armet habere ullos. 'neue haec commenta putetis,
admonitu quamquam luctus renouentur amaro,
perpetiar memorare tamen. postquam alta cremata est
Ilion, et Danaas pauerunt Pergama flammas,
Naryciusque heros, a Virgine uirgine rapta,
quam meruit poenam solus digessit in omnes,
spargimur et uentis inimica per aequora rapti
fulmina noctem imbres, iram caelique marisque
perpetimur Danai cumulumque Capherea cladis;
neue morer referens tristes ex ordine casus,
Graecia tum potuit Priamo quoque flenda uideri.
me tamen armiferae seruatum cura Mineruae

442 marmoreo *m*: marmorea *m* 461 auxiliumque petit *m*: auxilium petiit *m* 467 Ilion *m*: Ilios *m* flammas *m*: dextras *m*

fluctibus eripuit, patriis sed rursus ab agris
pellor, et antiquo memores de uulnere poenas
exigit alma Venus. tantosque per alta labores
aequora sustinui, tantos terrestribus armis,
ut mihi felices sint illi saepe uocati,
quos communis hiems importunusque Caphereus
mersit aquis, uellemque horum pars una fuissem.
ultima iam passi comites belloque fretoque
deficiunt finemque rogant erroris, at Acmon
feruidus ingenio, tum uero et cladibus asper,
"quid superest, quod iam patientia uestra recuset
ferre, uiri?" dixit "quid habet Cytherea quod ultra
(uelle puta) faciat? nam dum peiora timentur,
est locus in uotum; sors autem ubi pessima rerum est,
sub pedibus timor est securaque summa malorum.
audiat ipsa licet et, quod facit, oderit omnes
sub Diomede uiros; odium tamen illius omnes
spernimus, et †magno stat magna† potentia nobis."
talibus iratam Venerem Pleuronius Acmon
instimulat uerbis stimulisque resuscitat iram.
dicta placent paucis, numeri maioris amici
Acmona corripimus; cui respondere uolenti
uox pariter uocisque uia est tenuata, comaeque
in plumas abeunt, plumis noua colla teguntur
pectoraque et tergum, maiores bracchia pennas
accipiunt, cubitique leues sinuantur in alas;
magna pedis digitos pars occupat, oraque cornu
indurata rigent finemque in acumine ponunt.
hunc Lycus, hunc Idas et cum Rhexenore Nycteus,
hunc miratur Abas, et dum mirantur, eandem
accipiunt faciem; numerusque ex agmine maior
subuolat et remos plausis circumuolat alis.
si uolucrum quae sit subitarum forma requiris,
ut non cycnorum, sic albis proxima cycnis.
uix equidem has sedes et Iapygis arida Dauni
arua gener teneo minima cum parte meorum.'

476 agris *m*: argis *m* 489 uotum *Magnus*: uoto *m* 493 et magno *m*: et paruo *m* (*Heinsius*): haud magno *Ellis* magna *m*: tanta *m* (*Heinsius*): uicta (*e.g.*) *Shackleton Bailey 1981* 499 noua *m*: quoque *m* 508 subitarum *m*: dubiarum *m*

Hactenus Oenides. Venulus Calydonia regna
Peucetiosque sinus Messapiaque arua relinquit,
in quibus antra uidet, quae multa nubila silua
et leuibus guttis manantia semicaper Pan
nunc tenet, at quodam tenuerunt tempore nymphae.
Apulus has illa pastor regione fugatas
terruit et primo subita formidine mouit,
mox, ubi mens rediit et contempsere sequentem,
ad numerum motis pedibus duxere choreas.
improbat has pastor saltuque imitatus agresti
addidit obscenis conuicia rustica dictis,
nec prius os tacuit, quam guttura condidit arbor.
arbor enim est, sucoque licet cognoscere mores.
quippe notam linguae bacis oleaster amaris
exhibet; asperitas uerborum cessit in illas.
Hinc ubi legati rediere negata ferentes
arma Aetola sibi, Rutuli sine uiribus illis
bella instructa gerunt, multumque ab utraque cruoris
parte datur. fert ecce auidas in pinea Turnus
texta faces, ignesque timent quibus unda pepercit.
iamque picem et ceras alimentaque cetera flammae
Mulciber urebat perque altum ad carbasa malum
ibat, et incuruae fumabant transtra carinae,
cum memor has pinus Idaeo uertice caesas
sancta deum genetrix tinnitibus aera pulsi
aeris et inflati compleuit murmure buxi
perque leues domitis inuecta leonibus auras
'irrita sacrilega iactas incendia dextra,
Turne,' ait; 'eripiam, nec me patiente cremabit
ignis edax nemorum partes et membra meorum.'
intonuit dicente dea, tonitrumque secuti
cum saliente graues ceciderunt grandine nimbi,
aeraque et tumidum subitis concursibus aequor
Astraei turbant et eunt in proelia fratres.
e quibus alma parens unius uiribus usa
stuppea praerupit Phrygiae retinacula classis
fertque rates pronas medioque sub aequore mergit.

515 guttis *m*: cannis *m* 523 os tacuit *m*: obticuit *m* 534 transtra *m*: igne *m* 547 classis *m*: puppis *m*

robore mollito lignoque in corpora uerso
in capitum facies puppes mutantur aduncae,
in digitos abeunt et crura natantia remi,
quodque latus fuerat latus est, mediisque carina
subdita nauigiis spinae mutatur in usum;
lina comae molles, antemnae bracchia fiunt,
caerulus, ut fuerat, color est. quasque ante timebant,
illas uirgineis exercent lusibus undas
Naides aequoreae, durisque in montibus ortae
molle fretum celebrant, nec eas sua tangit origo.
non tamen oblitae quam multa pericula saeuo
pertulerint pelago, iactatis saepe carinis
supposuere manus – nisi si qua uehebat Achiuos.
cladis adhuc Phrygiae memores odere Pelasgos,
Neritiaeque ratis uiderunt fragmina laetis
uultibus et laetis uidere rigescere puppem
uultibus Alcinoi saxumque increscere ligno.
  Spes erat, in nymphas animata classe marinas,
posse metu monstri Rutulum desistere bello;
perstat, habetque deos pars utraque, quodque deorum est
instar, habent animos. nec iam dotalia regna
nec sceptrum soceri nec te, Lauinia uirgo,
sed uicisse petunt deponendique pudore
bella gerunt. tandemque Venus uictricia nati
arma uidet, Turnusque cadit; cadit Ardea, Turno
sospite dicta potens. quam postquam barbarus ignis
abstulit et tepida latuerunt tecta fauilla,
congerie e media tum primum cognita praepes
subuolat et cineres plausis euerberat alis.
et sonus et macies et pallor et omnia captam
quae deceant urbem, nomen quoque mansit in illa
urbis, et ipsa suis deplangitur Ardea pennis.
  Iamque deos omnes ipsamque Aeneia uirtus
Iunonem ueteres finire coegerat iras,
cum, bene fundatis opibus crescentis Iuli,
tempestiuus erat caelo Cythereius heros.
ambieratque Venus superos colloque parentis

552 latus[1] *m*: sinus *m*   574 quam *m*: quem *m*   barbarus *M*: Dardanus *Heinsius*   ignis *m*: ensis *m*   575 latuerunt *m*: patuerunt *m*

circumfusa sui 'numquam mihi' dixerat 'ullo
tempore dure pater, nunc sis mitissimus, opto,
Aeneaeque meo, qui te de sanguine nostro
fecit auum, quamuis paruum des, optime, numen,
dummodo des aliquod. satis est inamabile regnum
aspexisse semel, Stygios semel isse per amnes.'
adsensere dei, nec coniunx regia uultus
immotos tenuit placatoque adnuit ore.
tum pater 'estis' ait 'caelesti munere digni,
quaeque petis pro quoque petis: cape, nata, quod optas.'
fatus erat. gaudet gratesque agit illa parenti
perque leues auras iunctis inuecta columbis
litus adit Laurens, ubi tectus harundine serpit
in freta flumineis uicina Numicius undis.
hunc iubet Aeneae quaecumque obnoxia morti
abluere et tacito deferre sub aequora cursu.
corniger exsequitur Veneris mandata suisque
quidquid in Aenea fuerat mortale repurgat
et respergit aquis; pars optima restitit illi.
lustratum genetrix diuino corpus odore
unxit et ambrosia cum dulci nectare mixta
contigit os fecitque deum, quem turba Quirini
nuncupat Indigetem temploque arisque recepit.
  Inde sub Ascanii dicione binominis Alba
resque Latina fuit. succedit Siluius illi,
quo satus antiquo tenuit repetita Latinus
nomina cum sceptro. clarus subit Alba Latinum;
Epytus ex illo est. post hunc Capetusque Capysque,
sed Capys ante fuit. regnum Tiberinus ab illis
cepit et in Tusci demersus fluminis undis
nomina fecit aquae; de quo Remulusque feroxque
Acrota sunt geniti. Remulus maturior annis
fulmineo periit, imitator fulminis, ictu;
fratre suo sceptrum moderatior Acrota forti
tradit Auentino, qui quo regnarat eodem
monte iacet positus tribuitque uocabula monti.
  Iamque Palatinae summam Proca gentis habebat.

594 munere *m*: numine *m* 604 respergit *m* (*Heinsius*): –sit *M* 612 alba latinum *m*: ecce latino *m* 622 summam proca *anon. apud Naugerium*: summae loca *M*

rege sub hoc Pomona fuit, qua nulla Latinas
inter Hamadryadas coluit sollertius hortos,
nec fuit arborei studiosior altera fetus;
unde tenet nomen. non siluas illa nec amnes,
rus amat et ramos felicia poma ferentes.
nec iaculo grauis est, sed adunca dextera falce,
qua modo luxuriem premit et spatiantia passim
bracchia compescit, fisso modo cortice lignum
inserit et sucos alieno praestat alumno.
nec sentire sitim patitur bibulaeque recuruas
radicis fibras labentibus irrigat undis.
hic amor, hoc studium; Veneris quoque nulla cupido est.
uim tamen agrestum metuens pomaria claudit
intus et accessus prohibet refugitque uiriles.
quid non et Satyri, saltatibus apta iuuentus,
fecere et pinu praecincti cornua Panes
Siluanusque suis semper iuuenalior annis,
quique deus fures uel falce uel inguine terret,
ut poterentur ea? sed enim superabat amando
hos quoque Vertumnus, neque erat felicior illis.
o quotiens habitu duri messoris aristas
corbe tulit uerique fuit messoris imago!
tempora saepe gerens faeno religata recenti
desectum poterat gramen uersasse uideri;
saepe manu stimulos rigida portabat, ut illum
iurares fessos modo disiunxisse iuuencos;
falce data frondator erat uitisque putator;
induerat scalas, lecturum poma putares.
miles erat gladio, piscator harundine sumpta.
denique per multas aditum sibi saepe figuras
repperit, ut caperet spectatae gaudia formae.
Ille etiam picta redimitus tempora mitra,
innitens baculo, positis per tempora canis,
adsimulauit anum cultosque intrauit in hortos
pomaque mirata est 'tanto'que †'potentior!'† inquit,
paucaque laudatae dedit oscula, qualia numquam
uera dedisset anus, glaebaque incurua resedit

630 fisso *m*: fissa *m* 632 recuruas *m*: repugnans *m* 646 uersasse *m*: uersare *m* 648 iurares *m*: -asses *m* 651 *u. secl. Tarrant* 655 per *m*: ad *m* 657 potentior *m*: peritior *m*

suspiciens pandos autumni pondere ramos.
ulmus erat contra, speciosa nitentibus uuis;
quam socia postquam pariter cum uite probauit,
'at si staret' ait 'caelebs sine palmite truncus,
nil praeter frondes quare peteretur haberet.
haec quoque, quae iuncta uitis requiescit in ulmo,
si non nupta foret, terrae acclinata iaceret.
tu tamen exemplo non tangeris arboris huius,
concubitusque fugis nec te coniungere curas.
atque utinam uelles! Helene non pluribus esset
sollicitata procis nec quae Lapitheia mouit
proelia nec coniunx †timidi aut audacis† Vlixis.
nunc quoque, cum fugias auerserisque petentes,
mille uiri cupiunt et semideique deique
et quaecumque tenent Albanos numina montes.
sed tu si sapies, si te bene iungere anumque
hanc audire uoles, quae te plus omnibus illis,
plus quam credis, amo, uulgares reice taedas
Vertumnumque tori socium tibi selige, pro quo
me quoque pignus habes (neque enim sibi notior ille est
quam mihi). nec passim toto uagus errat in orbe:
haec loca sola colit; nec, uti pars magna procorum,
quam modo uidit amat: tu primus et ultimus illi
ardor eris, solique suos tibi deuouet annos.
adde quod est iuuenis, quod naturale decoris
munus habet formasque apte fingetur in omnes
et quod erit iussus, iubeas licet omnia, fiet.
quid quod amatis idem, quod quae tibi poma coluntur
primus habet laetaque tenet tua munera dextra?
sed neque iam fetus desiderat arbore demptos
nec quas hortus alit cum sucis mitibus herbas,
nec quidquam nisi te. miserere ardentis et ipsum
quod petit ore meo praesentem crede precari;
ultoresque deos et pectora dura perosam
Idalien memoremque time Rhamnusidis iram.
quoque magis timeas (etenim mihi multa uetustas

671 timidi aut audacis *M*: nimium tardantis *Riese*: prudens audacis *Possanza 2002* Vlixis *m*: Vlixei *m* 681 sola *m*: magna *m*

scire dedit), referam tota notissima Cypro
facta, quibus flecti facile et mitescere possis.
'Viderat a ueteris generosam sanguine Teucri
Iphis Anaxareten humili de stirpe creatus,
uiderat et totis perceperat ossibus aestum.
luctatusque diu, postquam ratione furorem
uincere non potuit, supplex ad limina uenit.
et modo, nutrici miserum confessus amorem,
ne sibi dura foret, per spes orauit alumnae;
et modo, de multis blanditus cuique ministris,
sollicita petiit propensum uoce fauorem.
saepe ferenda dedit blandis sua uerba tabellis,
interdum madidas lacrimarum rore coronas
postibus intendit posuitque in limine duro
molle latus tristisque serae conuicia fecit.
saeuior illa freto surgente cadentibus Haedis,
durior et ferro quod Noricus excoquit ignis
et saxo quod adhuc uiuum radice tenetur,
spernit et inridet factisque immitibus addit
uerba superba ferox et spe quoque fraudat amantem.
non tulit impatiens longi tormenta doloris
Iphis et ante fores haec uerba nouissima dixit:
"uincis, Anaxarete, neque erunt tibi taedia tandem
ulla ferenda mei. laetos molire triumphos
et Paeana uoca nitidaque incingere lauro.
uincis enim, moriorque libens. age, ferrea, gaude!
certe aliquid laudare mei cogeris, eritque
quo tibi sim gratus, meritumque fatebere nostrum.
non tamen ante tui curam excessisse memento
quam uitam, geminaque simul mihi luce carendum est.
nec tibi fama mei uentura est nuntia leti;
ipse ego, ne dubites, adero praesensque uidebor,
corpore ut exanimi crudelia lumina pascas.
si tamen, o superi, mortalia facta uidetis,
este mei memores (nihil ultra lingua precari

705–7 *uu. om. m; delendos esse censuit Merkel, Zwierlein* (705–6) 705 blanditus cuique ministris *m*: aliqui blanditus amicis *m* 711 haedis *m*: austris *m* 722 eritque *m*: amoris *m* 724 curam excessisse *m*: curamque egisse, curam fuisse *m*: fugisse *uel* cessisse *Heinsius* 725 carendum est *m*: carendum *m*

sustinet) et longo facite ut narremur in aeuo
et quae dempsistis uitae date tempora famae."
'Dixit et ad postes ornatos saepe coronis
umentes oculos et pallida bracchia tollens,
cum foribus laquei religaret uincula summis,
"haec tibi serta placent, crudelis et impia?" dixit
inseruitque caput, sed tum quoque uersus ad illam,
atque onus infelix elisa fauce pependit.
icta pedum motu trepidantum †et multa timentem†
uisa dedisse sonum est adapertaque ianua factum
prodidit. exclamant famuli frustraque leuatum
(nam pater occiderat) referunt ad limina matris.
accipit illa sinu complexaque frigida nati
membra sui postquam miserorum uerba parentum
edidit et matrum miserarum facta peregit,
funera ducebat mediam lacrimosa per urbem
luridaque arsuro portabat membra feretro.
forte uiae uicina domus, qua flebilis ibat
pompa, fuit, duraeque sonus plangoris ad aures
uenit Anaxaretes, quam iam deus ultor agebat.
mota tamen "uideamus" ait "miserabile funus"
et patulis iniit tectum sublime fenestris;
uixque bene impositum lecto prospexerat Iphin,
deriguere oculi, calidusque e corpore sanguis
inducto pallore fugit, conataque retro
ferre pedes haesit, conata auertere uultus
hoc quoque non potuit, paulatimque occupat artus,
quod fuit in duro iam pridem pectore, saxum.
neue ea ficta putes, dominae sub imagine signum
seruat adhuc Salamis, Veneris quoque nomine templum
Prospicientis habet. – quorum memor, o mea, lentos
pone, precor, fastus, et amanti iungere, nymphe;
sic tibi nec uernum nascentia frigus adurat
poma nec excutiant rapidi florentia uenti.'
Haec ubi nequiquam formas deus aptus in omnes
edidit, in iuuenem rediit et anilia demit

739 timentem *m*: gementem *m*: aperire iubentem *Shackleton Bailey 1981* 744 miserorum *m*: -arum *m* 758 pectore *m*: corpore *m* 765 formas deus aptus in omnes *m*: forma deus aptus anili *m*: formae deus apta senili *Housman*

instrumenta sibi talisque apparuit illi,
qualis ubi oppositas nitidissima solis imago
euicit nubes nullaque obstante reluxit;
uimque parat, sed ui non est opus, inque figura
capta dei nymphe est et mutua uulnera sensit.
Proximus Ausonias iniusti miles Amuli
rexit opes, Numitorque senex amissa nepotis
munere regna capit, festisque Palilibus urbis
moenia conduntur, Tatiusque patresque Sabini
bella gerunt, arcisque uia Tarpeia reclusa
dignam animam poena congestis exuit armis.
inde sati Curibus tacitorum more luporum
ore premunt uoces et corpora uicta sopore
inuadunt portasque petunt, quas obice firmo
clauserat Iliades. unam tamen ipsa reclusit
nec strepitum uerso Saturnia cardine fecit;
sola Venus portae cecidisse repagula sensit
et clausura fuit, nisi quod rescindere numquam
dis licet acta deum. Iano loca iuncta tenebant
Naides Ausoniae gelido rorantia fonte;
has rogat auxilium, nec nymphae iusta petentem
sustinuere deam uenasque et flumina fontis
elicuere sui. nondum tamen inuia Iani
ora patentis erant, neque iter praecluserat unda;
lurida supponunt fecundo sulphura fonti
incenduntque cauas fumante bitumine uenas.
uiribus his aliisque uapor penetrauit ad ima
fontis et, Alpino modo quae certare rigori
audebatis aquae, non ceditis ignibus ipsis.
flammifera gemini fumant aspergine postes,
portaque nequiquam rigidis promissa Sabinis
fonte fuit praestructa nouo, dum Martius arma
indueret miles; quae postquam Romulus ultra
obtulit, et strata est tellus Romana Sabinis
corporibus strata estque suis, generique cruorem
sanguine cum soceri permiscuit impius ensis,
pace tamen sisti bellum nec in ultima ferro
decertare placet Tatiumque accedere regno.

777 dignam *m*: digna *m* (*Heinsius*) exuit *m*: edidit *m*: expuit *Kenney* 804 accedere *m*: exc- *m*

Occiderat Tatius, populisque aequata duobus,
Romule, iura dabas, posita cum casside Mauors
talibus adfatur diuumque hominumque parentem:
'tempus adest, genitor, quoniam fundamine magno
res Romana ualet nec praeside pendet ab uno,
praemia iam promissa mihi dignoque nepoti
soluere et ablatum terris imponere caelo.
tu mihi concilio quondam praesente deorum
(nam memoro memorique animo pia uerba notaui)
"unus erit, quem tu tolles in caerula caeli"
dixisti: rata sit uerborum summa tuorum!'
adnuit omnipotens et nubibus aera caecis
occuluit tonitruque et fulgure terruit urbem.
quae sibi promissae sensit rata signa rapinae
innixusque hastae pressos temone cruento
impauidus conscendit equos Gradiuus et ictu
uerberis increpuit pronusque per aera lapsus
constitit in summo nemorosi colle Palati,
reddentemque suo non regia iura Quiriti
abstulit Iliaden. corpus mortale per auras
dilapsum tenues, ceu lata plumbea funda
missa solet medio glans intabescere caelo;
pulchra subit facies et puluinaribus altis
dignior, est qualis trabeati forma Quirini.
Flebat ut amissum coniunx, cum regia Iuno
Irin ad Hersilien descendere limite curuo
imperat et uacuae sua sic mandata referre:
'o et de Latia, o et de gente Sabina
praecipuum, matrona, decus, dignissima tanti
ante fuisse uiri, coniunx nunc esse Quirini,
siste tuos fletus et, si tibi cura uidendi
coniugis est, duce me lucum pete, colle Quirini
qui uiret et templum Romani regis obumbrat.'
paret et in terram pictos delapsa per arcus
Hersilien iussis compellat uocibus Iris.
illa uerecundo uix tollens lumina uultu
'o dea (namque mihi nec quae sis dicere promptum est,
et liquet esse deam) duc, o duc' inquit 'et offer

809 nec *m*: et *m* 817 urbem *m*: orbem *m* 825 ceu *m*: ut *m* lata *M* : torta *Hardie*

coniugis ora mihi, quae si modo posse uidere
fata semel dederint, caelum accepisse fatebor.'
nec mora, Romuleos cum uirgine Thaumantea
ingreditur colles; ibi sidus ab aethere lapsum
decidit in terras, a cuius lumine flagrans
Hersilie crines cum sidere cessit in auras.
hanc manibus notis Romanae conditor urbis
excipit et priscum pariter cum corpore nomen
mutat Horamque uocat, quae nunc dea iuncta Quirino est.

848 Hersilie crines *m*: -iliae crinis *m*: -ilia aetherias *Riese*

COMMENTARY

1–74 Glaucus, Scylla, and Circe

Book 14 begins within the '*Aeneid*' frame, with the continuation from book 13 of the tale of Scylla, Glaucus, and Circe (1–74). The plot of the *Aeneid* was left off at 13.729 and is not resumed until 14.75, where the Trojans quickly pass the traditional sea monsters Scylla and Charybdis and are driven to Libya. Ovid splits his *Aeneid* between books 13 and 14, suspending Aeneas' journey at the point between Virgil's books 3 and 4. At the same time, the arrival of the poem in Italy and the appearance here of Circe at the beginning of the book also gestures towards the opening of the second half of Virgil's *Aeneid*, where Aeneas sails past Circe's island on his way from Cumae to the Tiber mouth in book 7.10–24 (cf. 157n., 441–5n. on the book division between *Aen.* 6 and 7).

At 13.729 Aeneas and his men arrive in Zancle (Messina), near the Straits between Italy and Sicily, which corresponds to Aeneas' wanderings in *Aeneid* 3 (*Aen.* 3.707–8, although Virgil does not have Aeneas sail any further than Drepanum). In the *Aeneid* Aeneas and his men twice narrowly avoid Scylla and Charybdis (*Aen.* 3.555–67, 684–88), despite Helenus' earlier warning to avoid sailing near them (*Aen.* 3.410–32). At this point in his narrative (13.730–3 *Scylla latus dextrum, laeuum inrequieta Charybdis | infestat; uorat haec raptas reuomitque carinas, | illa feris atram canibus succingitur aluum, | uirginis ora gerens*) Ovid describes Scylla and Charybdis in lines that are closely indebted to the Virgilian account at *Aen.* 3.420–1 (see Hopkinson 2000: ad loc.). He follows this with the surprising claim that Scylla was once a girl: *si non omnia uates | ficta reliquerunt, aliquo quoque tempore uirgo* (733–4) and provides the first extant account of Scylla's metamorphosis from maiden to half-monster (and finally to stone).

In book 13 Scylla first listens to Galatea's story of her lover Acis, who was killed out of jealousy by Polyphemus and then turned by her into a river god (13.738–897). The narrative delay of Scylla's own story may acknowledge a similar structure in both Homer and Virgil, where Scylla and Charybdis are also twice presented, once in foretelling, and once in actual encounter (*Od.* 12.73–100, 234–59; *Aen.* 3.420–36, 555–69, cf. Ap. Rh. 4.789–832, 922–56). Galatea's tale of a love-triangle with a violent ending foreshadows Scylla's own transformation by the jealous Circe in book 14 (for parallels between the tales, see Nagle 1988c, Hopkinson 2000: 34, 41–2). After Galatea has finished her story (which should have warned her listener about the dangers of spurning affection), Scylla is seen near the shore by Glaucus, a fisherman transformed by magical grass into a half-fish marine deity (prefiguring Scylla's metamorphosis), and rejects his advances (13.900–68); whereupon Glaucus journeys to Italy to seek the help of Circe in winning her over (14.1f.).

Virgil had described Scylla as only half monster, her top half being that of a young woman: *prima hominis facies et pulchro pectore uirgo | pube tenus* (*Aen.* 3.426–7, cf. *Ecl.* 6.74–6, Xen. *Mem.* 2.6.31), a representation which already appears in archaic Greek art and coins (see Waser 1894, Roscher s.v. *Skylla I*). In Homer (*Od.* 12.73–100) Scylla is described as a monster with twelve feet and six heads with triple rows of teeth, hidden in a cave up to her middle and reaching out with her many necks to catch dolphins. She is said to have a voice like a new-born hound (*Od.* 12.86–7), which may be the origin of the later version we find in the *Aeneid* and elsewhere that she had dogs or wolves below the waist.

The story of Glaucus of Anthedon was popular in Alexandrian literature and Roman neoteric epyllia (see the list in Athenaeus' *Deipnosophistae* 7.296a–7b, Hopkinson 2000: 41–2). His prophetic powers (cf. Paus. 9.22.6, Eur. *Or.* 364) probably led to his mention in the *Aeneid* as the father of the Cumaean Sibyl (*Aen.* 6.36, cf. 5.823). The early third-century BCE poetess Hedyle is said to have treated the tale of Glaucus' love for Scylla in a poem entitled *Scylla* (*SH* 456; for her date see *HE* p. 289). Ovid may be indebted to this earlier version, but seems to be the first to add Circe to Scylla's story; otherwise the love-triangle is mentioned only by Serv. on *Ecl.* 6.74 and *Aen.* 3.420, Fulg. *Myth.* 2.9, and Hyg. *Fab.* 199 (probably the Ovidian version). Cornificius (mid first century BCE) wrote a *Glaucus* (fr. 2, *FLP* p. 226). The *Ciris* at 54–88 (an extremely corrupt passage) lists a number of variant versions of Scylla's transformation, among which is an erotic triangle involving Scylla, Neptune and his wife Amphitrite (70–6, with Lyne ad loc.); cf. Serv. *auct.* on Virg. *Ecl.* 6.74 (here Amphitrite is said to use *Circe's* poisons) and on *Aen.* 3.420.

1–74 Glaucus' itinerary takes him – and the poem – for the first time to Italy, as he leaves Sicily to swim to Circe's promontory on the western coast of Latium (9n.). A number of geographical routes at the end of the *Met.* repeat this trajectory: Aeneas' journey from Zancle (13.728–9) to Cumae (14.75–105), Myscelos' from Argos to Croton (15.49–54), Aesculapius' route from Epidaurus to Rome (15.697–744), and, in abbreviation, Canens' journey from Circeii to the Tiber (14.426–7); see Gassner 1972: 102–7, Granobs 1997: 148. Other book divisions in which a journey is continued are 1/2, 2/3, 6/7 (see Holzberg 1998: 89–95). Barchiesi 1997b: 183 observes that such geographical transitions delineate the three major divisions of the poem (gods, heroes, history) at 6.420/21, 11.193/4. Ovid utilizes a familiar literary trope of nautical imagery of a ship or sea-voyage (Glaucus is, in fact, swimming) as a metaphor for the movement of his poem (cf. 15.176–7). The '*Aeneid*' section of the poem was similarly launched by Aeneas' flight from Troy at 13.627–30 *profugaque per aequora classe | fertur ab Antandro scelerataque litora Thracum | et Polydoreo manantem sanguine terram | linquit.*

1 Iamque also opens books 3 and 7 (both journeys); cf. 8.1 *iam*, 5.1 *dumque*. Ovid typically bridges the divisions between his books with a continuing story, but there may be some surprise here in the reference to Glaucus' journey, rather than the more expected resumption of that of Aeneas and the Trojans (Guthmüller 1964: 103). The mention of Aetna and the Cyclopes reminds the reader that this famous episode from *Aen.* 3.569–681 was skipped by Ovid in book 13 in his treatment of Aeneas' wanderings (it will be related at 14.558–691). **Giganteis:** the use of a personal adjective (an adjectival form of a proper name) instead of possessive genitive is a feature of high epic style (Austin on *Aen.* 2.543, Harrison on *Aen.* 10.156–7, K–S I 209–12, Löfstedt 1942: 107–24). The volcanic nature of Mt Etna was attributed to Jupiter's crushing of the defeated giant Typhoeus (or Typhon) under Sicily. Ovid tells the story at *Met.* 5.346–55 *uasta Giganteis ingesta est insula membris* | *Trinacris et magnis subiectum molibus urguet* | *aetherias ausum sperare Typhoea sedes* (346–8); cf. 3.303–4 (punishment), 5.319–31 (battles of gods and giants), *F.* 4.491–2. The giant Typhoeus also appears in Pindar, *Pyth.* 1.15–24; Virgil at *Aen.* 3.578–82 names Enceladus instead, as in *Aetna* 71–3 (at *Aen.* 9.715–16 Typhoeus is said to be buried under Inarime). **faucibus:** *fauces* is used of the crater of a volcano (*OLD* 3e), but here, through a sort of syllepsis, the literal and figurative senses of *fauces* merge to form a picture of an anthropomorphic volcano and a 'volcanic' monster: 'Aetna heaped upon the Giant's throat'; cf. 5.352–3 *degrauat Aetna caput, sub qua resupinus harenas* | *eiectat flammamque ferox uomit ore Typhoeus, F.* 4.491 *alta iacet uasti super ora Typhoeos Aetne*, Lucr.1.724 *faucibus eruptos iterum uis ut uomat ignis, Aen.* 7.786 *Aetaeos efflantem faucibus ignes.* On such anthropomorphic representions of Etna in Lucretius and Virgil (with Gigantomachic overtones), see Hardie 1986: 211, 264–5, and 116 on the 'volcanic' monster Cacus. **Aetnen:** Ovid tends to prefer Greek inflections of Greek names, especially the acc. *-n*, even when not needed to avoid elision, as here (Fantham on *F.* 4.471); see Quint. *Inst.* 12.10.31.

2 aruaque Cyclopum: localized in Sicily in the area of Mt Etna by Virgil's time (*Aen.* 3.569, 588–654, 8.416–53, cf. Thuc. 6.2.1, Eur. *Cycl.* 95). This mention reminds us of the earlier episode of Polyphemus and Galatea at 13.740–897 and looks ahead to that of Odysseus and the Cyclops narrated at 14.158–222. The line is framed by the same etymology (*aratri*: *LALE* s.v. *aruum*). **quid . . . quid** introduce indirect questions (verbs omitted) dependent on *nescia* in the next line; suggesting perhaps parody of the repeated relatives of Virg. *G.* 1.1–4. The Cyclops' lack of cultivation corresponds to Homer's description at *Od.* 9.107–8 οἵ ῥα θεοῖσι πεποιθότες ἀθανάτοισιν | οὔτε φυτεύουσιν χερσὶν φυτὸν οὔτ' ἀρόωσιν ('trusting in the immortal gods they plant nothing with their hands nor plough', cf. 122–4). **rastra** 'a pronged mattock' (a tool like a pick-axe for loosening soil, from *rado*, 'scrape', see White 1967: 52–6); the noun is normally masc. in its pl. forms, cf. 11.36, Virg. *Ecl.* 4.40, etc.; neuter at Juv. 15.166, Stat. *Theb.* 3.589. At 13.765–6 Polyphemus humorously uses *rastra* to comb his hair instead (see Hopkinson ad loc.).

3 iunctis . . . bubus 'teams of oxen'.

4–5 liquerat . . . liquerat: the repetition underlines Glaucus' speed and perhaps also Ovid's *praeteritio* of these Sicilian dangers in book 13. **Euboicus tumidarum cultor aquarum:** epic periphrasis for Glaucus, who is actually from Anthedon, a town in Boeotia, opposite the island of Euboea, cf. 7.232 *Euboica . . . Anthedone*, 13.905. For the periphrasis, cf. 13.904 (Glaucus) *alti nouus incola ponti*; *Her.* 19.181 (Leander, another swimming lover) *iuuenis tumidarum uictor aquarum*, Virg. *G.* 1.14 (Aristaeus) *cultor nemorum* (with Serv. ad loc. '*cultor autem pro incola*'); Catull. 61.1–2 *collis o Heliconii* | *cultor, Vraniae genus.* The phrase *tumidarum . . . aquarum* may activate a programmatic reference here to the lofty style of epic poetry, which contrasts with Glaucus' upcoming passage through the narrow straits (6 *litore pressum*); on *tumidus* as a negative literary critical term for inflated or grand style, see *OLD tumidus* 6, Catull. 95.10, Hor. *AP* 94, Quint. 10.2.16, and cf. the poetic implications (epic/Callimachean) of the swollen Achelous (8.550 *tumens*, 853 *intumui*) in *Met.* 8, with Hinds 1987b: 19, Barchiesi 2001: 50–5. On the image of the open sea as grandiose epic poetry, see Wimmel 1960: 227–33, Kambylis 1965: 137–55, Call. *Hymn to Apollo* 106, Hor. *C.* 1.3, 4.15.3–4, Virg. *G.* 2.41–5. In elegiac imagery the poetic ship stays close to the shore (e.g. Ovid, *Tr.* 2.329–30, Prop. 3.3.23–4, 3.9.3–4). The dangers of the narrow strait (6 *nauifragum*) may hint at Ovid's audacity in rewriting Virgil's epic, see Introduction, p. 15.

5 Zanclen: the old name for Messana (modern Messina), a town located on the NE tip of Sicily, on the strait between Italy and Sicily, where the Trojans anchor at 13.729 (not mentioned in the *Aeneid*). The eighth-century Greek colony (Euboean) took its original name (found first in Ovid in Latin) from the indigenous word for 'sickle', said to have been derived either from the shape of its harbour (Thuc. 6.4.5) or from Kronos' discarded sickle (Call. *Ait.* 2 fr.50.68–72 Massimilla (= 43.68–72 Pf.), Nicander, *FGH* III A 271–2, F. 15). The Gk acc. sing. ending avoids elision (see 1n.). **Regi:** Rhegium, modern Reggio di Calabria, 7.5 m./12 km south-east of Messina, in south Italy. A Chalcidian colony also founded in the eighth century, it dominated the straits of Messina for much of its early history, see Vallet 1958. The name is connected etymologically with ῥηγνύναι 'to break off' (*LALE* s.v. Regium, *dictum est a rumpendo*). The Romans believed Sicily was once joined to Italy, as Pythagoras explains at 15.290–2, cf. Virg. *Aen.* 3.414–19 (with Serv. ad loc.); Plin. *Nat.* 2.204, 3.86, Val. Fl. 1.589, Lucan 2.435–8.

6 nauifragumque 'causing shipwrecks', a metrically convenient variant of the more common *naufragus* (cf. *F.* 4.500 *naufraga monstra* = Scylla), which seems to be Virgil's archaizing invention, appearing elsewhere only at *Aen.* 3.553 *nauifragum Scylaceum* (see Horsfall ad loc.). Paschalis 1997: 147 (also O'Hara 2001: 395) suggests Virgil's phrase points to the etymology of Scylla < σκύλλω 'trouble, molest' (cf. *uexasse* in *Ecl.* 6.76), Stat. *Theb.* 5.14. **gemino . . . litore pressum** 'narrowed, hemmed in' (*OLD premo* 9b) by the two coasts', cf. *F.* 1.292 *insula, diuidua quam premit amnis aqua.* On the narrowness of the channel, see also Virg. *Aen.* 3.418–19 *aruaque et urbes* | *litore diductas angusto interluit aestu,* Lucr. 1.720–1 *angustoque fretu rapidum mare diuidit undis* | *Italiae terrarum oras a finibus eius.* The Straits of Messina, which separate the Italian peninsula from Sicily and connect the Ionian and Tyrrhenian seas, are *c.* 20 m./32 km long and vary in width from 2 m./3 km (north) to 10 m./16 km (south). The currents, whirlpools, and winds of the strait still hamper navigation. On the liminal and programmatic function of coastlines in literature, see Wills 1997.

7 Ausoniae 'Italian', cf. 77, 320, 772, 786, etc. Ovid follows Virgil in using *Ausonius/Ausonia* for Italy and Italians in general (*G.* 2.385 is the first extant occurrence, 40x in the *Aeneid*). The name was originally applied to an ancient Italian tribe (*Ausones*) and was popularly derived from Auson, a son of Odysseus and Calypso (*LALE* s.v. *Ausonia*), and was adopted by the Hellenistic poets (Call. fr. 238.28 Pf., Ap. Rh. 4.660, 828, see Fordyce on *Aen.* 7.39, Harrison on *Aen.* 10.52). Cf. *Aen.* 3.418 *Hesperium Siculo latus abscidit.* **tenet confinia** 'occupies the borders of' (*TLL* IV 217.9 cites only Optatianus *leti et uitae confinia summa tenentem*).

8 manu magna 'with mighty strokes' (Melville). The expression is used in contexts of super-human power and size, originating in Homer (*Il.* 15.694–5) and imitated by Ennius (*Ann.* 581 Sk. *atque manu magna Romanos inpulit amnis*), and Virgil (*Aen.* 3.624 (Cyclops), 5.241–2 *pater ipse manu magna Portumnus euntem | impulit*). Here the phrase suggests Glaucus' divine strength and greater size (cf. 13.962 *ingentesque umeros*), while creating a humorous effect by the logical application of the epic cliché to swimming, where large hands are helpful (see Hill ad loc.). **Tyrrhena:** Greek for 'Etruscan' (cf. 452, for *Tuscus* see 223n.); the Tyrrhenian sea, an arm of the Mediterranean Sea, lies off the western coast of Italy, and is bounded by Corsica, Sardinia, and Sicily. **per aequora uectus** is Virgilian, cf. *Aen.* 1.376 *per aequora uectos*, 3.325, 6.335 , 692, 7.228, *G.* 1.206; in Ovid elsewhere only at 3.538, *Her.* 17.5, cf. *Met.* 14.470 *per aequora rapti*. The expression is usually considered to be derived from Catull. 101.1 (see Conte 1986: 32–9), but Horsfall on *Aen.* 3.325 suggests Ennius.

9 herbiferos . . . colles: *herbifer* is an Ovidian coinage found only here and at *F.* 4.468 *herbifer Aci*; cf. the more common alternatives *herbosus* (2.688, 10.128, 14.445, 15.574, Virg. *G.* 2.199, etc.), and *herbidus* (8.282, Varro *RR* 2.1.16); see Kenney 2002: 63. Circe grows herbs for her magic (cf. Hom. *Od.* 10.213 Circe's κακὰ φάρμακα); for *herbae* and magic, see 267–70 (Circe), 6.139–40, 7.224–33 (Medea), *Am.* 1.14.39, *Her.* 12.166–7, *AA* 2.100–1, Ap. Rh. 4.666–7 (Circe), Virg. *Aen.* 4.514, 7.19 (Circe), Hor. *Epod.* 5.67–8, Tib. 1.2.51; Tupet 1976: 59–64. Circe and Medea often represented archetypal witches (e.g. *AA* 2.103, Theocr. *Id.* 2.15–16, Tib. 1.2.51–2, 2.4.55–6, Prop. 2.1.53, Val. Fl. 6.440). Later authors attribute the toxicological skills of the Marsi to their descent from Circe (Plin. *Nat.* 7.15, 25.11, see Wiseman 1995: 47).

9–10 atria . . . Circes: echoes the final line of the previous book, 13.968 *petit Titanidos atria Circes. Circes* is Gk gen. fem. sg. While Homer had placed Circe's home, the island of Aeaea, in the extreme east (*Od.* 10.135–9, 12.3–4), post-Homeric legend, which situated Odysseus' ports of call in the western Mediterranean, had located it off the western shore of Italy (the tradition is as early as [Hes.] *Th.* 1011–16; Apollonius Rhodius relates her migration west at *Arg.* 3.309–13, cf. 4.659–63; see Hunter on 3.311–13). Virgil identifies Circe's western island (*Aen.* 3.386 *Aeaeae insula Circae*, cf. *Met.* 14.245), with the promontory of Circei on the coast of Latium half-way between Cumae and the mouth of the Tiber (cf. *Aen.* 7.799 *Circaeum iugum*, *Met.* 14.348 *nomine dicta suo Circaea reliquerat arua*, *F.* 4.70 *quod adhuc Circes nomina litus habet*).

Modern Monte Circeo, near Tarracina on the sw coast of Italy, rises steeply out of the sea and might have been taken for an island by early sailors (attempts were made to explain the discrepancy, see Serv. on *Aen.* 3.386 *Circeius mons . . . aliquando, ut Varro dicit, insula fuit, nondum siccatis paludibus, quae eam diuidebant a continenti*). Cicero (*ND* 3.48) and Strabo (5.3.6) mention the continuing worship of Circe at the site. See Fordyce on Virg. *Aen.* 7.10, Horsfall on *Aen.* 7.5–24, Tilly 1959: 200. **Sole satae:** *satus*, 'offspring', is the perfect participle of *sero*, 'sow' (*OLD sero*[1] 3); *Sole* is abl. of origin. *satus* is an archaic word which imparts a high epic style (Hopkinson on 13.123). At *Od.* 10.135–9 Circe is the daughter of Helios and the Oceanid Perse, cf. 4.205, [Hes.] *Th.* 956–62, 1011, Virg. *Aen.* 7.11 *Solis filia*, 282. **uariarum:** Circe's transformation of Odysseus' crew into flesh-and-blood animals is treated at 14.253–397 and that of Picus' men at 14.414–15 *uariarum monstra ferarum | in iuuenes ueniunt; nulli sua mansit imago* (contrast her creation of a phantom boar at 358–9 *effigiem nullo corpore falsi | fingit apri*).

11 dicta acceptaque salute 'when greetings had been exchanged', also at 14.271, *Tr.* 3.12.33 (the conventional greeting *OLD salus* 8).

12–24 Glaucus asks for Circe's help in winning over Scylla. The recourse to magic in erotic matters is both an attested practice in ancient Greek and Roman society and a topos in ancient literature, especially Roman elegy (e.g. Theocr. *Id.* 2; Tib. 1.2.41–64, 2.4.55–60; Prop. 1.1.19–24; Ovid, *Am.* 1.8.5–18, *AA* 2.327–30, *Her.* 6.83–94, *Med. Fac.* 35–8, cf. Virg. *Aen.* 4.487–8), where often, as here, magic is represented as ultimately unsuccesful in erotic conquest, cf. e.g. Ovid, *Rem.* 249–90 (263 *quid tibi profuerunt, Circe, Perseides herbae?*, 290 *deme ueneficiis carminibusque fidem*), *AA* 2.103–4 *Circe tenuisset Vlixem, | si modo seruari carmine posset amor*; see Tupet 1976, Fauth 1980, 1999, Sharrock 1994: 53–86, Graf 1997: 176–90, Faraone 1999: 13–14, 49–69, 112–19, Segal 2000. The danger of erotic magic was illustrated earlier in the story of Deianira and Nessus' poison at 9.134–210.

12–13 diua, dei: paronomasia (repetition of words (here synonyms) that are close in appearance or sound) underlines Glaucus' appeal to Circe, with a flattering (and self-important) vaunt of their divine affinities; cf. Hom. *Od.* 5.97 (Hermes to Calypso) Εἰρωτᾶις μ'ἐλθόντα θεὰ θεόν, Virg. *Aen.* 12 .138–9 (Juno to Juturna) *Turni sic est adfata sororem | diua deam.* **nam . . . tu potes:** formal, in the style of prayers, 'explaining why the functions of the divinity addressed are appropriate' (Austin on *Aen.* 1.65), cf. Hom. *Il.* 16.515, 21.379; Hes. *Th.* 420, Lucr. 1.31–2 *nam tu sola potes tranquilla pace iuuare | mortales;* Virg. *Aen.* 6.117 *alma, precor, miserere, potes namque omnia*, Hor. *Epod.* 17.45 *et tu – potes nam – solue me dementia* (see N-H on Hor. *C.* 1.28.28, Norden 1913: 152–4). **sola** is also part of the conventional language of entreaty (Norden 1913: 350 n.1), cf. 9.547, Lucr. 1.31–2 (above). The word may also be etymologically motivated here in its association with Sol, Circe's father, cf. Varro, *LL* 5.68 *sol uel quod ita Sabini, uel quod solus ita lucet, ut ex eo deo dies sit* (*LALE* s.v. *sol*, Michalopoulos 2001: 160–1). **uidear modo dignus** 'only provided that I seem worthy'; *modo* = *si modo*, with the concessive subjunctive (*OLD modo*[1] 4); cf. 4.702, 5.272, 8.38; *TLL* VIII 1301.67. The variants *dignus amore* and *dignior esse* for *dignus, amorem* require *hunc* = *me.*

14 herbarum . . . potentia: cf. 1.522 *herbarum . . . potentia*, 4.49 *potentibus herbis;* Virg. *Aen.* 7.19 *quos hominum ex facie dea saeua potentibus herbis | induerat Circe in uultus ac terga ferarum.* **Titani:** voc. fem. sing. (N–W I 444, nom. *Titanis*), cf. 376 *Titanida . . . Circen*, 13.968 *Titanidos . . . Circes*; she is *Titania* at 382, 438. Circe's father, Helios, the sun, is descended from Hyperion (Hom. *Od.* 12.176), one of the Titans, the children of Uranus and Ge (see Hes. *Th.* 371–2). For Titan as the sun, cf. 1.10, 2.118, *F.* 2.73–4, 4.180, Cic. *Arat.* 589 [343], Virgil, *Aen.* 4.119.

14–15 nulli | quam mihi cognitius: the comparative is found only here and *Tr.* 4.6.28 *cognitiora.* A wry reflection on Glaucus' earlier ignorance of the power of the transforming grass he ingests at 13.942 *'quae' tamen 'has' inquam 'uires habet herba?'* Ironically Glaucus does not guess that Circe's magical herbs may have the same transformative effect on Scylla as did those that turned him into a piscine sea god. **ab illis:** Ovid often adds *ab* to instrumental ablatives (primarily for metrical convenience), cf. 11.130, 13.105, 14.345, but here the preposition may personify the magic (see Guttmann 1890: 8–12, 15–20, Kenney 2001: 546).

16 neue = *et, ne* (*OLD neue* 2b), with the anticipatory use of *ne* (*OLD ne*[1] 13a) in a final purpose clause with an introductory verb omitted; a common Ovidian brachylogy, cf. 32, 131, 464, 473, 759. **furoris:** the 'madness' of passion (*OLD* 3, *TLL* VI 1631.32f., 74f.). Cf., e.g., 701, 9.541, Virg. *Aen.* 4.91, 101.

17 litore in Italico: cf. 15.9 *Italicis . . . in oris*, 15.59 *Italis in finibus*, 15.291 *Italiae*, 701 *Italiam.* Virgil does not use this form of the adj., but *Italus*, cf. *Aen.* 7.86 *Italae gentes*, etc.; see Kenney 2002: 41. The initial vowel of *Italico* is lengthened *metri gratia*, cf. e.g. 15.9, Virg. *Aen.* 1.2 *Italiam* (following Call. *H. Art.* 58, see Austin ad loc.), 3.185 *Itala regna*, Catull. 1.5 *Italorum.* **Messenia moenia contra:** i.e. near Rhegium, cf. 5 *aduersaque moenia Regi*, and 47–8 *contra Zancleia saxa | Region.* Ovid varies the geographical description; for the location, cf. 13.730–9, 898–911. Zancle, a Cumaean colony, was renamed Messana (Messene in Ionic) either from the Messenian origin of the tyrant of Rhegium (Thuc. 6.4.5–6) or from Messenian settlers there (Paus. 4.23.5–10), but this seems to be the only instance of the adj. referring to the Sicilian colony and not the Greek state in the south-west Peloponnese, as at 2.679 *Messeniaque arua* and 12.549 *Messenia moenia.*

18 Scylla mihi uisa est: the scene is described at 13.900–11. This Scylla is the daughter of Crateis (13.749 *Crataeide natam*, Hom. *Od.* 12.124–5) and Phorcys (Ap. Rh. 4.828), or Echidna and Typhon (Hyg. *Praef.* 39, *Fab.* 151, see Schmidt *RE* III A.1.647–55 for other variants). The story of the other Scylla, daughter of Nisus of Megara, is treated in *Met.* 8.6–151 (where Ovid hints at the monstrous Scylla at 8.100 *monstrum* and 144 *haeret comes inuidiosa carinae*). The conflation of these two Scyllas (e.g. *AA* 1.331–2, *Am.* 3.12.21–2, *Rem.* 737, *F.* 4.500, Virg. *Ecl.* 6.74–5, Prop. 4.4.39–40) was one of the 'most mannered and celebrated of all Alexandrian conflations' (Hinds 1993: 15 and n. 14); see *Ciris* 54–91 for complaints about the confusion.

18–19 pudor est . . . referre 'I am ashamed to repeat'. Perhaps a joke, since Glaucus' words of entreaty to Scylla are twice cut off by her and never appear in the narrative, see 13. 907–8 *quaecumque putat fugientem posse morari* | *uerba refert; fugit illa tamen* and 966–7 *talia dicentem, dicturum plura reliquit* | *Scylla deum.* **promissa precesque** | **blanditiasque:** erotic terminology, cf. 705n., *AA* 1.439–40 *blanditias ferat illa tuas imitataque amantum* | *uerba, nec exiguas, quisquis es, adde preces*; 631 *nec timide promitte, trahunt promissa puellas*, Pichon 1966: 94, 238–9, 241. **contemptaque uerba** 'all rejected words' (Hill); the third *-que* is epexegetic (adding a word that explains and enlarges on what precedes, *OLD* 6) and *contempta* thus qualifies all four substantives. Cf. 13.966–7 (quoted at 18n.).

20–1 siue aliquid regni est in carmine, carmen | **ore moue sacro** 'if there is any power in magical song, begin [*OLD mouere* 17] a spell with your divine voice'; *regni* is a partitive gen., cf. *Am.* 2.17.11 *tibi si facies nimium dat in omnia regni*, *OLD regnum* 4b. Ovid frequently uses *aliqui(s)* rather than *qui(s)* after *siue* (Bömer on 4.327). *si* clauses are regular in prayers, see N-H on Hor. *C.* 1.32.1. For *mouere* of song, cf.10.147 (Orpheus) *hoc uocem carmine mouit*, 11.40, *F.* 6.622 *sollemni satis est uoce mouere preces*, *Am.* 3.1.6; Virg. *Aen.* 1.262 *arcana mouebo*, 7.45 *cantusque mouete*, 641, 10.63; Enn. *Ann.* 403 Sk. The tone, with *ore* as well, is lofty and solemn, cf. 8.703 *Saturnius edidit ore*, *F.* 6.386 *Iuppiter . . . sacro quid uelit ore docet*, *AA* 2.509–10 *Phoebo parete monenti;* | *certa dei sacro est huius in ore fides*, *Tr.* 2.423 *utque suo Martem cecinit grauis Ennius ore.* For *carmen* = 'magic spell' or 'incantation', cf. e.g. 34, 44, 58, 357, 366, 369, 387, 7.137–8, 167, 10.397 (*carmine . . . et herbis*), 13.952, *Am.* 1.8.5,18, 2.1.23–8, 3.7.28–32 (*carmen et herba*), *Her.* 6.83, Virg. *Ecl.* 8.70 *carminibus Circe socios mutauit Vlixi*, and see Pease on *Aen.* 4.487 for further examples. **carmine, carmen:** polyptoton, for emphasis. On Ovid's fondness for such inflexional variation and repetition, see Kenney 1993: 460–1; Wills 1996: 213–16.

21 expugnacior 'more forceful', a hapax legomenon; on Ovid's sparing use of adjectives in *-ax* (and Heinsius' fondness for them), see Tarrant 1989b: 112–14. For *expugnare* in amatory contexts, see Pichon 1966: 139. Glaucus' diction is unusual in places (see Bömer on 13.920, 958, 14.23), and Tarrant (1989b: 113–14) has suggested that Ovid is drawing on the technical language of pharmacy.

22 'use the proven strength of an efficacious herb'. For *operosus* (in poetry first here) used in medical terminology, see *TLL* IX 2.699.75–8 (only Ovid and Caelius Aurelianus, a fifth-century CE doctor), Bömer ad loc. On Ovid's use of adjectives in *–osus*, see Knox 1986b (53 examples to Virgil's 28), McKeown on *Am.* 1.1.9–10 'the nuance of such formations ranges from the colloquial to the highly poetic', Kenney 2002: 37-8. *uiribus* also has a technical ring (*OLD* 23b), cf. 69, 793.

23 medeare: subj. in an ind. command with *mando.* Ovid evokes the elegiac metaphor of *medicina amoris*, cf. 1.521–4, 7.116 (of Medea's enchanted herbs) *tantum* *medicamina possunt*, 9.653; on the topos see Knox 1986a: 15–17. **uulnera:** for the wounds of love (*OLD uulnus* 1d), cf. 771, 4.207, 9.540, *Am.* 1.2.29, Lucr. 1.34, Virg. *Aen.* 4.1–2, Prop. 2.12.11–13 *ante ferit quoniam tuti quam cernimus hostem | nec quisquam ex illo uulnere sanus abit. | in me tela manent;* Pichon 1966: 302.

24 fine nihil is a reading attested only in a handful of late MSS. *fineque nil* of most MSS cannot here be right, as Ovid never attaches *-que* to a short *-e* (Platnauer 1951: 93); the iambic scansion of *nihil* is parallelled at 7.644, *Tr.* 5.14.41, *Pont.* 3.1.113 (see Housman 1972b: 925–6). For the *amor mutuus* topos, cf. 771n., 4.192, 9.718, Tib. 1.2.65–6 *non ego totus abesset amor sed mutuus esset | orabam*, Ter. *Eun.* 91; Catull. 76.23 expresses the opposite wish: *non iam illud quaero, contra me ut diligat illa.* Cf. also Prop. 1.1.21–2 (a request for help from witches) *en agedum dominae mentem conuertite nostrae, | et facite illa meo palleat ore magis!* On the *finis amoris* topos here rejected, cf. 10.397–8, *Rem.* 143. **opus est:** a relatively frequent idiom in Ovid, too colloquial for most other poets; see Bömer on 10.565.

25–36 Circe's reply to Glaucus, a *suasoria*, has much in common with love elegy, especially the erotodidactic voice of the *lena* (procuress) of *Am.* 1.8 and the *magister amoris* of the *Ars*; see Stitz 1962: 63. Circe delivers another unsuccessful entreaty to Picus at 372–6, and at *Rem.* 271–84 she attempts to persuade Ulysses to remain with her (*irrita . . . uerba* 286). Cf. Vertumnus' wooing of Pomona at 657–764 (765n.), Polyphemus at 13.789–869, Apollo's and Jove's attempts at seduction speeches (both failures) at 1.504–24 and 589–96, see Nagle 1988a, Gross 1985: 62–5, Tarrant 1995: 70–1. Circe's characterization as a sexually aggressive female (cf. 25n.) is indebted to Homer's scene between Circe and Odysseus in *Odyssey* 10.325ff., see Ellsworth 1988: 338, Segal 1968: 437.

25–7 (neque enim . . . paterno): on this type of explanatory parenthesis, cf. *AA* 2.565 *nec Venus oranti (neque enim dea mollior ulla est) | rustica Gradiuo difficilisque fuit;* von Albrecht 1964: 148, 161. The poet offers two explanations, cf. 4.519–20, 10.80–1.

25 flammis: conventionally of love, cf. 351 (of Circe) *flammaque per totas uisa est errare medullas*, 374–6 *consule nostris | ignibus*; 1.495 *sic deus in flammas abiit*; Virg. *Aen.* 4.23 *agnosco ueteris uestigia flammae*; see McKeown on *Am.* 1.1.26. While the ancients write frequently of the greater sex-drive of women as a whole (cf. e.g. *AA* 1.281–2 *parcior in nobis nec tam furiosa libido; | legitimum finem flamma uirilis habet*, 341–2 *omnia feminea sunt ista libidine mota; | acrior est nostra plusque furoris habet*, Prop. 3.19.1–2), Circe's genealogy as *filia Solis* may render her especially susceptible to the flames of passion, cf. 4.194–5 (of Sol) *nempe tuis omnes qui terras ignibus uris, | ureris igne nouo?* Ovid may acknowledge ancient allegorical interpretation of Homer's Circe as symbolic of greed and lust (Heraclit. *All.* 72.2–3, Xen. *Mem.* 1. 3.7). Circe was also characterized as a prostitute (Plaut. *Epid.* 604, Hor. *Ep.* 1.2.17–26, Serv. on *Aen.* 7.19 *clarissima meretrix*); see Buffière 1962: 237, 379, Yarnall 1994: 71–91, Kaiser 1964: 201–2, Gale 1997.

26 ingenium signifies the natural disposition of a person (*TLL* VII 1.1534.33–41 i. q. *cor, animus*); Circe is formed by her nature for love.

27 indicio . . . offensa paterno: Ovid tells the story of Sol's betrayal to Vulcan of Venus' and Mars's illicit liaison earlier in the poem at 4.169–89 (173–4 *marito | furta tori furtique locum monstrauit*), where Venus takes revenge on Sol by his unhappy love for Leucothoe 4.190–2 *exigit indicii memorem Cythereia poenam | inque uices illum, tectos qui laesit amores, | laedit amore pari* (the mention of Circe at 4.205, *nec tenet Aeaeae genetrix pulcherrima Circes,* constitutes a forward reference to this later scene). For the literary tradition of Venus' punishment of the sun, cf. *Her.* 4.53–62, Sen. *Phaed.* 124–7, Serv. *auct.* on Virg. *Ecl.* 6.47 *ob iram . . . Veneris, quae . . . subolem eius inhonestis amoribus subiecit ut Circen, Medeam, Pasiphaen.* The vengeful Venus assumes a thematic significance in this book (see 476–9n.).

28 talia uerba refert: a variant of an epic formula introducing a new speech, cf. 1.700 , *F.* 4.580, Virg. *Aen.* 1.94, 208 *talia uoce refert.* **melius sequerere uolentem** 'you would be doing better to pursue one who is willing', potential subj. (likelihood) (*NLS* §121, K–S I 195 (§49)). *melius* 'to better purpose' qualifies and expresses a judgement on the whole phrase, cf. 8.487, 13.321, *Her.* 7.151 (with Knox ad loc.), *Tr.* 5.6.13; see N–H on Hor. *C.* 1.2.22, H–S 827, K–S 1.795. For *sequor* in *sermo amatorius,* cf. e.g. *Am.* 1.9.10, 2.9.9–10, 2.19.36. Circe's suggestion conflicts with the typical behaviour of the lover, a commonplace in amatory contexts, cf. *Am.* 2.19.36 *quod sequitur, fugio; quod fugit, ipse sequor* (echoing Call. *Ep.* 31 Pf. (=*HE* 1039–40)), 2.9.9–10, Catull. 8.10, Hor. *Sat.* 1.2.105–8.

29 cupidine captam: cf. 13.762 (Polyphemus) *cupidine captus, F.* 6.119–20 (Janus), all echoes of Virg. *Aen.* 7.189 (Circe herself) *capta cupidine coniunx,* cf. *Aen.* 4.194 (Aeneas and Dido) *turpique cupidine captos.* On the etymological link between *cupido* and *capio,* see Isid. *Etym.* 10.42 *cupidus a capiendo multum, id est accipiendo, uocatus*; Michalopoulos 2001: 61–2.

30 'you deserved to be to be wooed spontaneously (and, what is more, without any doubt you might have been)'. The past tenses of *possum* are regularly used with a potential sense in the indicative, cf. 10.633, K–S I 172–3, *NLS* §125. For *rogo* in the erotic sense 'proposition' (*OLD* 7c), cf. e.g. *AA* 1.711, *Am.* 1.8.43, 2.2.5, Catull. 8.13, Tib. 1.4.55, Prop. 1.5.32, Pichon 1966: 254, Tränkle 1960: 163. On women in the active role of pursuer, see *Am.*1.8.44 *si rusticitas non uetat, ipsa rogat, AA* 1.277–8 *conueniat maribus ne quam nos ante rogemus, | femina iam partes uicta rogantis aget,* Sall. *C.* 25.3. **ultro** 'spontaneously', i.e. 'for your own sake' (*OLD* 5b), cf. 2.566, *Am.* 2.5.49. **certeque** 'and what is more (*OLD que* 11), without any doubt'; the *-que* belongs with *poteras*; postponements of *-que* are rare in the *Met.* The parenthesis seems anticlimactic, but perhaps betrays Circe's enthusiasm; alternatively Burman's suggestion *per teque* would bring out more forcefully the force of *ultro.*

31 mihi crede: a phrase reinforcing advice relatively common in Ovid (14x), but too colloquial for other poets (Hor. *Sat.* (3x), not in Virg., Tib., Prop.), cf. 244, *F.* 1.496, *Am.* 2.2.9 (with McKeown). Cf. *crede mihi,* e.g. 245, 1.361, *Am.* 1.8.62; Tränkle 1960:

9–10, Hofmann 1951: 126. **rogaberis ultro:** emphatic repetition (polyptoton), with chiasmus, of the previous line.

32 neu = *et, ne* 'and, so that you do not . . . '. Circe's syntax echoes that of Glaucus' entreaty at line 16(n.). **adsitque tuae fiducia formae** 'and instead have confidence in your beauty'; *ut* is to be understood from the preceding *ne*: K–S II 563–4. *formae* is an obj. gen. (*NLS* § 76). Heinsius' attractive suggestion of *absit* (attested in a few secondary MSS) would make parallel the two clauses 'but in case you doubt this and lack confidence in your beauty'. *tuae fiducia formae* is elegiac language, cf. *AA* 1.707–8 *a, nimia est iuueni propriae fiducia formae, | expectat si quis dum prior illa roget! Am.* 1.8.25 *nulli tua forma secunda est,* Prop. 3.24.1 *falsa est ista tuae, mulier, fiducia formae.* In the metamorphic world of the poem (1.1 *mutatas . . . formas*), confidence in one's own physical beauty invariably results in disaster for mortals (cf. 3.270 (Semele) *tanta est fiducia formae,* 4.687 (Andromeda's mother), 8.434–5 (Atalanta)), although not for gods (see Mercury in 2.731, Barchiesi 1999: 112); see Barkan 1986: 89–90.

33–4 cum . . . cum . . . cum: 'although' (*OLD cum*[2] 7a). Triple anaphora of *cum* in two clauses of 1/2 line and one full line creates a 'rising tricolon'. **filia Solis:** cf. *Aen.* 7.11 *Solis filia.* The appeal to genealogy is a typical divine amatory strategy, cf. 375–6 (Circe again), 1.517 (Apollo) *Iuppiter est genitor,* 595–6 (Jove) *nec de plebe deo, Rem.* 275–6 (Circe to Ulysses) *et tamen, ut coniunx essem tua, digna uidebar | quod dea, quod magni filia Solis eram.*

34 An intricately constructed line, with anaphora and chiastic juxtaposition of *tantum* at the main caesura (anadiplosis or gemination, cf. 2.284), the jingle of *carmine . . . gramine,* and *possim* taken with both halves of the line. Hill (ad loc.) suggests that it is 'intended, no doubt, to recall the kind of wordplay associated with magic spells'. Circe responds to Glaucus' request at 20–1 (*carmen/herba*), cf. 356–7. Similar word play with *gramen/carmen* at 7.137. **tantum . . . possim** 'although I have such power' (*OLD possum* 8a), cf. 285 *tantum medicamina possunt.*

35 ut tua sim uoueo 'I pray to be your love' (*OLD uoueo* 2). **spernentem sperne:** for Ovid's facility with this type of elegant verbal (participial) polyptoton see Wills 1996: 250, 316–25. For the sentiment cf. *Her.* 4.167–8 (Phaedra to Hippolytus) *per Venerem, parcas, oro, quae plurima mecum est; | sic numquam, quae te spernere possit ames.* For *spernere* of amatory rejection, cf. 332, 714.

36 redde uices 'return the favour' (*OLD uicis* 5). *uices* is poetic pl. only here, *metri gratia*; cf. *Am.* 1.6.23 (with McKeown ad loc.), *Pont.* 2.10.51, 3.5.35. **unoque duas:** Ovid is fond of such numerical juxtaposition (see Bömer on 3.544): cf. e.g. 332, 469, 496, 4.108 *una duos, inquit, nox perdet amantes,* 8.464 *trahunt unum duo nomina pectus*; Catull. 5.3; Virg. *G.* 4.184, *Aen.* 1.15, Hom. *Il.* 17.95, *Od.* 20.313. **ulciscere** 'give two women what they deserve'; a loose translation of the verb seems required: Circe suggests that Scylla be punished (*OLD* 1a 'take vengeance on') and herself requited (*OLD* 2a 'avenge'). The verb perhaps alludes to Circe's ancestry (14n.) and the derivation of Titan from τίσις (Hes. *Th.* 207–10, Serv. on *Aen.* 6.580, see McKeown 1987: 46); cf. 383–5.

37–9 Glaucus answers Circe with an *adynaton*, an impossible violation of the natural order, that the speaker claims will have to occur before he changes his mind, cf. Virg. *Ecl.* 1.59–60 (with Coleman); see Smith on Tib. 1.4.65–6, Otto 1890: 139. For similar lovers' oaths, cf. *Her.* 5.29–30, Prop.1.15.29–30, 2.15.31–5. Such a reversal of the natural order of things of course did occur after the flood in *Met.* 1.283–347, cf. Hor. *C.* 1.2.9–12. The confusion of land and water also resonates with Glaucus' and Scylla's own metamorphosed hybrid forms.

39 sospite . . . Scylla: sadly ironic; Glaucus seals Scylla's fate, as she won't be *sospes* after Circe has dealt with her, nor indeed loved by Glaucus. **mutentur:** potential subj. with *prius . . . quam*, referring to the future (*NLS* § 227). A hint at Scylla's metamorphosis; *nostri . . . amores* also can be understood as one's beloved (*OLD amor* 1b): cf., e.g., 1.617, 4.137, Tib. 1.6.35, Prop. 1.20.51, Catull. 6.16, 10.1.

40 indignata dea est = 6.204 (Latona against Niobe). **quatenus** 'inasmuch as' causal (*OLD* 8), cf. 6.204, 8.725.

41 non poterat: presumably because Glaucus was a god (and already transformed). **(nec uellet amans)** 'nor, since she was in love, would she have wanted to do so'; potential subjunctive (*NLS* §121). This claim is belied later in the book when Circe transforms Picus, the second object of her passions (382–96).

42 Venerisque offensa repulsa: an echo of Glaucus' own earlier reaction to Scylla's rejection of his overtures at 13.967: *furit ille inritatusque repulsa*, cf. 13.735, 15.503 (at line end) *offensane repulsae. Venus* is a common metonym for '*amor*' (love or sex, *OLD Venus* 4), cf. e.g. 141, 380, 634, *Am.* 2.4.40, 2.8.8. This begins a long sentence which does not end until line 50, with *protinus* in 43 signalling Circe's haste (Bömer ad loc.).

43 horrendis infamia pabula sucis 'plants ill-famed for their fearful juices'; *sucis* is causal abl. (cf. 13.400 *infames caede uirorum*). For *infamis* used in the context of poison see Bömer ad loc.; cf. 7.269 *strigis infames . . . alas, Am.* 1.12.10 *melle sub infami.* It is *pabula* that transform Glaucus earlier at 13.943, cf. *Her.* 6.84 *diraque pabula, Rem.* 249 *mala pabula.*

44 conterit et tritis: 'The resumption of a verb by a participle is a favorite of Ovid' (Wills 1996: 311); here the shift from a compound to a simple form with the force of the compound persisting (see Wills 1996: 319–20 for further examples) is an instance of a common Greek and Latin idiom: see Courtney on Juv. 1.55, Renehan 1977, and Wills 1996: 438–43. Cf. 4.504 (Tisiphone's potion) *omnia trita simul*, Prop. 2.17.14 *in nostras trita uenena manus*, [Tib.] 3.5.10 *trita uenena.* **tritis Hecateia carmina miscet** 'she mixes magical songs with her ground herbs'. For words as an ingredient, cf. 7.248 *uerba simul fudit*, Virg. *G.* 3.283 *miscueruntque herbas et non innoxia uerba. Hecateius* occurs first here (elsewhere only at Stat. *Ach.* 1.447), providing a favoured pentasyllabic form in ∪ ∪ – ∪ x. On Ovid's predilection for adjectival variations of Greek proper names, see Kenney 2002: 68–9. Hecate is the goddess traditionally invoked by magicians, see 405 (Circe), 7.194–5 (Medea) *tuque, triceps Hecate, quae coeptis conscia nostris | adiutrixque uenis cantusque artisque magorum*; cf. 6.139 *sucis Hecateidos herbae*, Virg. *Aen.* 4.511 (see Pease ad loc.), Hor. *Sat.* 1.8.33, Eur. *Med.* 395–400, Theocr. *Id.* 2.12–16. Hecate was the Underworld aspect of a triple deity (cf. 7.94–5 *triformis . . . deae*) comprising also Luna and Diana. In some versions Hecate (identified with Crataeis) is said to be the mother of Scylla (Hes. fr. 262 M–W, Ap. Rh. 4.827–9).

45 caerulaque: a bluish-green colour esp. associated with the sea (Serv. on *Aen.* 7.198 *caerulum est uiride cum nigro*); Circe chooses a matching garment. The Greek adjective is γλαυκός, cf. Ovid's pun on Glaucus' name at 13.962 *caerula bracchia* (see Hopkinson on 13.288, 913, Austin on *Aen.* 2.381); cf. 555n., Virg. *Aen.* 3.432 *Scyllam et caeruleis canibus resonantia saxa*, 5.122–3 (a boat) *Scyllaque . . . caerulea*. Ovid (like Virgil) uses both *caerulus* and *caeruleus* for metrical convenience (see Bömer on 3.342, McKeown on *Am.* 2.11.12). **induitur uelamina:** 'middle' voice with an accusative object (*OLD* 2b), see *NLS* §19 iii; Harrison 1991: 290–1 (iv), cf. 262, 345, 638, 11.589; the extension of this construction to finite forms of the verb begins with Virgil, *Aen.* 2.392–3, 7.640; see Courtney 2004: 426 (3), Coleman 1999: 81–3.

45–6 ferarum | agmen adulantum: cf. 259 *adulantes comitant uestigia*, where the beasts in Circe's halls are more fully described (255–61).

47–8 oppositumque . . . | Region 'seeking Rhegium facing opposite the cliffs of Zancle'; cf. 5 *aduersaque moenia Regi*. The Gk acc. termination of *Region* avoids elision. Circe's journey reverses that of Glaucus earlier at 14.5.

47 Zancleia: a hapax legomenon, created by Ovid for metrical convenience in place of the more common *Zanclaeus* (13.729, *F.* 4.499, *Tr.* 5.2.73).

48 ingreditur feruentes aestibus undas 'she steps on to the waves seething with swells'. The water reflects Circe's inner turmoil, cf. 2.602 *animus tumida feruebat ab ira*, 11.548–9 *tanta uertigine pontus | feruet. aestus* can be used of a rough sea (*OLD* 7) and of sexual passion (*OLD* 5a), cf. 52–3n.

49–50 'on which she plants her feet as if on solid land and skims along the surface of the water with dry feet'. The ability to walk on water is a traditional sign of divinity, cf. 10.654 (of Hippomenes and Atalanta) *posse putes illos sicco freta radere passu*, Virg. *Aen.* 5.819 (Neptune) *caeruleo per summa leuis uolat aequora curru*, 7.810–11 (Camilla) *uel mare per medium fluctu suspensa tumenti | ferret iter celeris nec tingeret aequore plantas*, Hom. *Il.* 20.226–9 (offspring of Boreas and the magic horses of Erichthonius), Ap. Rh. 1.182–4 (Euphemus, son of Poseidon).

49 ut solida . . . terra 'as if on solid land'.

51–54 The frenzied and threatening activity of the previous lines is interrupted by an ecphrasis describing Scylla's cove, creating a dramatic contrast between Scylla's previously peaceful, safe refuge and the harm she will soon receive there. For the pattern of such sheltered and idyllic landscapes as sites of violence, see Parry 1964, Segal 1969a: 28–9, 58–63 (on the tainting of pure water). Although her precise location is not specified by Homer (*Od.* 12.73–110), in later literature Scylla was situated traditionally in the Straits of Messina on the west coast of Calabria, 10 m./ 16 km north of Reggio, whereas Charybdis was opposite on the Sicilian side: cf. 13.730–3, Virg. *Aen.* 3.420–1 *dextrum Scylla latus, laeuum implacata Charybdis | obsidet*, Thuc. 4.24.5 (Charybdis), Ap. Rh. 4.825–31, Polyb. 34.3.9.

51 Paruus erat gurges: cf. 13.902–3 (on Scylla's refuge) *seductos nacta recessus, | gurgitis inclusa sua membra refrigerat unda.* Hardie (*per litteras*) points out that *paruus* may stand in pointed constrast to the *alto* of *Ecl.* 6.76 (of Scylla) *gurgite in alto.* On the verb 'to be' as a typical epic formula introducing a topographical ecphrasis, cf. e.g. 1.568 *est nemus,* 5.385 *lacus est,* 11.229, 13.429, 685 (see Hinds 1987a: 36–8). This *est locus* formula is almost invariably followed by some kind of relative (here *quo,* 52), and a demonstrative (here *hunc,* 55, *hic,* 56) to resume the main narrative. In the *Odyssey* Homer speaks of Scylla's 'hollow cave' (κοῖλον σπέος 12.84), while Virgil at *Aen.* 3.424 describes her lair as *caecis . . . spelunca latebris* (cf. *Aen.* 3.431 *uasto . . . sub antro*). **curuos sinuatus in arcus** 'curved like a bent bow' (Hill), cf. 11.229 (Thetis' retreat where she is captured by Peleus) *est sinus Haemoniae curuos falcatus in arcus,* 8.30 (of a real bow) *patulos sinuauerat arcus,* Virg. *Aen.* 3.533 (the Trojans first arrive in Italy at Castrum Mineruae) *portus ab euroo fluctu curuatus in arcum.* See Michalopoulos 2001: 35–6, on the etymological connection of *arcus* with *curuus.*

52 quies 'a resting-place', an unusual meaning (*OLD* 2b); cf. Lucr. 1.405 *intectas fronde quietes,* where it is used of animal lairs (the context of the hunt may be relevant here also for Scylla). See Parry 1964: 277 on the pattern of rape and violence at a place of refuge.

52–3 quo se referebat ab aestu | et maris et caeli: Ovid plays again with multiple meanings of *aestus* (syllepsis), of a rough sea as at 48 above, and of hot weather (*OLD* 2). The literal meanings of the word are fused also with its connotations of sexual passion (*OLD* 5a), which Scylla has also fled (Segal 1969a: 62); cf. 48, 352 (Circe), 700 (Iphis), 13.867 (Polyphemus) *exaestuat,* 9.465 (Byblis), *Am.* 3.2.39 *an magis hic meus est animi, non aeris, aestus?* (with McKeown ad loc.).

53–4 medio . . . umbras 'when the sun was at its most powerful in mid-course and created from its zenith the shortest shadows'; *plurimus* is predicative; cf. 3.50 *fecerat exiguas iam sol altissimus umbras* 11.353 *medio cum sol altissimus orbe.* Mid-day traditionally marks a time of danger, cf. 1.592 (Jupiter and Io) *medio sol est altissimus orbe,* 2.417 (Jupiter and Callisto) *ulterius medio spatium sol altus habebat,* 3.144–5 (Actaeon), Sen. *Phaed.* 777–80; see Gibson on *AA* 3.723–4.

55 hunc: sc. *gurgitem.* **praeuitiat portentificisque** are both new compounds invented by Ovid; like *demurmurat* below at 58 they are perhaps suggestive of the magical *uerba noua* (57) of Circe's spell. Ovid is fond of compounds with the prefix *prae* (here temporal), cf. 134 *praecorrumpere*, 189 *praetemptare*, 395 *praecingere*, 798 *praestruere*, etc. (see Bömer on 4.251, McKeown on *Am.* 1.4.33). For *portentificus* see Kenney 2002: 64, and cf. 5.553 *saxificos uultus Medusae*. The motif of the tainting of pure water appears also in the tale of Salmacis and Hermaphroditus, 4.388 *incesto fontem medicamine tinxit*; see Segal 1969a: 63. **portentificisque uenenis** 'poisons with supernatural force'.

57–8 obscurum uerborum ambage nouorum | . . . carmen 'a chant obscured by a confusion of strange words'; *ambage* is a causal abl. with *obscurum*. Of the enigmatic speech of oracles cf. 7.760–1 (Sphinx) *praecipitata iacebat | immemor ambagum uates obscura suarum*, Virg. *Aen.* 6.98–9 *Cumaea Sibylla | horrendas canit ambages*, Lucan 1.637–8, Sen. *Oed.* 214, and cf. Circe's later spell on Picus' men at 366 *ignotosque deos ignoto carmine adorat.* **ter nouiens:** three and its multiples had magical associations in Greek and Roman ritual and magic. Cf. e.g. 387, 7.153, 189, 261, 13.952, *F.* 2.573, 3.563–4, Varro, *RR* 1.2.27 *ter nouiens*, Virg. *Ecl.* 8.73–5 *terna . . . terque . . . numero deus impare gaudet*, *Aen.* 4.510, *Ciris* 371; see Gow on Theocr. *Id.* 2.43, *RAC* IV 286 s.v. Drei 'Lustrale Kulthandlungen', Tupet 1976: 396–7, Tavenner 1916. **demurmurat:** another Ovidian coinage (see Bömer on 4.340 on O's fondness for such *de-* compounds). *murmur* belongs to magical terminology, cf. (Medea) 7.251 *murmure longo*, Lucan 6.448, 567–8, 686, Stat. *Theb.* 4.418, 9.734, Theocr. *Id.* 2.11; see Baldini Moscadi 1976.

59–67 *Scylla's transformation into a sea monster.* Ovid focalizes the metamorphosis through Scylla, dwelling on her horrified realization of the grotesque corruption of her lower body caused by Circe's jealousy and poisons. Like Circe, Scylla was allegorized as a symbol of lust, with the dogs below her groin representing her shamelessness and rapacity (see *Ciris* 69 *inguinis est uitium et ueneris descripta libido* (with Lyne on 68f.), Heraclit. *All.* 70.11, Buffière 1962: 236, 379–80), but in Ovid's version she has shunned all male advances. Galatea ironically had earlier congratulated Scylla on her ability to escape suitors (13.737 *elusos . . . amores*) with impunity: 13.741 *potes his impune negare.* Circe's punishment of Scylla also echoes Glaucus' metamorphosis: plants cause both transformations (43–4, 51–67, 13.942–6) and both are made (marine) animals below the waist (64, 67, 13.963, cf. Acis 13. 893–4); see Hopkinson 2000: 42. Virgil describes Scylla's lower body as part-marine, part-wolf at *Aen.* 3.427–8 *postrema immani corpore pistrix | delphinum caudas utero commissa luporum*, and in most representations of Scylla in art she has a long fish-tail in addition to the dogs; see Andreae 1984: 49–54 for early illustrations of Scylla, and 156–76, 221–52 for the sculptural groups at Sperlonga and the Villa Hadriana.

59 mediaque tenus . . . aluo: Scylla will be transformed only where her body touches the poisoned waters, cf. 13.732 (Scylla) *feris atram canibus succingitur aluum*, Virg. *Aen.* 3.426–7 *prima hominis facies et pulchro pectore uirgo | pube tenus.* Glaucus (13.956–65, although his overall colour changes), the Sirens (5.552–63), and Midas (11.174–81) are the only other partial metamorphoses in the poem. Cf. 13.893 (Acis) *subito media tenus exsitit aluo*, 5.413 (Cyane).

60 foedari: a strong word, meaning to disfigure (*OLD* 2), often by wounding (*OLD* 3), but also connoting pollution (*OLD* 1), here, with *inguina,* suggestive of sexual violation; see Segal 1997–8: 31–2. Cf. Cornificius Glaucus (fr. 2 *FLP* p. 226) *centauros foedare bimembres* (with Deichgräber 1971: 60). **latrantibus inguina monstris** = Virg. *Ecl.*6.75, *Ciris* 59; cf. *Met.* 13.915 (Glaucus) *ultimaque excipiat quod tortilis inguina piscis, Am.* 2.16.23 (Scylla) *quae uirgineo portenta sub inguine latrant, Am.* 3.12.22 (Scylla) *pube premit rapidos inguinibusque canes, Pont.* 4.10.25, *Tr.* 4.7.13, Prop. 4.4.40 (Scylla) *candidaque in saeuos inguina uersa canes.* The barking of Scylla's dogs was etymologically connected with her name; in Homer her voice is said to be like that of a young hound σκύλαξ (*Od.* 12.85–7, for the association with σκύλλειν see 6n.); cf. *Met.* 7.65 *Scylla rapax canibus Siculo latrare profundo,* Catull. 60.2 *Scylla latrans infima inguinum parte.* Sallust offers a natural-historical explanation at *Hist.* fr. 4.27 *quia collisi ibi fluctus latratus uidentur exprimere.* **inguina:** poetic pl.

61–2 credens . . . partes 'not believing that those parts belonged to her own body'. On the incredulity of a character experiencing metamorphosis, cf. 11.[108] (Midas), 15.566–7 (Cipus) *falsamque in imagine credens | esse fidem. pars* or *partes,* with various adjectival complements, frequently serve as euphemisms for the sexual organs (Adams 1982: 45).

62–3 refugitque abigitque timetque: the triple verb repetition with multiple *-que,* found only here and at Stat. *Th.* 6.116–17 (Wills 1996: 377), underlines Scylla's shock and repulsion; cf. Io's reaction to her new form at 1.[638], 641 *cornua pertimuit seque exsternata refugit, Am.* 1.3.21 *exterrita cornibus Io, Her.* 14.92 (of Io) *territaque est forma, territa uoce sua, Ciris* 82 (Scylla) *quotiens heu pertimuit latratus.* **refugit . . . fugit:** Ovid varies here perhaps Virg. *Aen.* 12.753 *mille fugit refugitque uias,* which appears in a simile that represents Turnus fleeing from Aeneas as a quarry from an Umbrian hound (the passage is also recalled in Daphne's pursuit *Met.* 1.535 = *Aen.* 12.754). See Wills 1996: 448); cf. 2.409 *redit itque,* 8.163 *refluitque fluitque,* 537 *refouentque fouentque*; for the compound–simple verb variation see 44n. **sed quos fugit attrahit una** 'but in fleeing them, she drags them along with her'.

64 'and seeking the flesh of her thighs and shins and feet'; an unusual construction (*OLD corpus* 5), cf. 1.408, 7.291, *TLL* IV 1000.57f.

65 Cerbereos rictus 'jaws like those of Cerberus'. 'With the rare adjective *Cerbereus* (cf. 4.501) Ovid acknowledges Lucretius' deflation of the myth at *DRN* 4.732–3 *Scyllarum membra uidemus | Cerbereasque canum facies'* (Oliensis 1991: 113n.13); cf. the Lucretian echoes in Ovid's 'Centauromachy' at 12.393–428. Cerberus, guardian of the Underworld, was described as a black dog with heads ranging in number from three (cf. 4.450, 7.414) to 100 (Hor. *C.* 2.13.34 *belua centiceps*). In Homer, *Od.* 12.90 Scylla is a beast with six mouths, each with three rows of teeth (although number does not seem to be the point of the comparison here). In Virg. *Aen.* 6.286 *Scyllae biformes* appear as monsters at the entrance to the Underworld. For *rictus* in other human to animal metamorphoses, cf. 2.481 (Callisto), 3.674 (Medon), 6.378 (Lycian peasants), 13.568 (Hecuba). **inuenit:** at 2.346–63 the Heliades similarly discover their own metamorphosis (still in process) with surprise: 353 *dumque ea mirantur, complectitur inguina cortex*; cf. Scylla in *Ciris* 80–2 (80 *horribilis circum uidit se existere formas*).

66 statque canum rabie: 'she stands on raging dogs', (abstract noun + gen. for noun + adj.); cf. *Am.* 3.12.22 *pube premit rabidos inguinibusque canes*, Lucr. 5.892 *rabidis canibus succinctas semimarinis | corporibus Scyllas*, Virg. *Aen.* 1.200 *Scyllaeam rabiem*, Sen. *Med.* 351.

66–7 subiectaque . . . coercet 'and her mutilated groin and protruding belly are enclosed by the bodies of the beasts'; cf. *Am.* 3.12.22 (above). An example of the idiom by which a transitive verb (*coercet*) refers not to what the subject 'does' but to what the subject 'has happen to him or her'; see Kenney on Lucr. 3.490 and *Addenda*, p. 250. Cf. Glaucus 13.914 *caesariemque umeros subiectaque terga tegentem. terga ferarum* is from Virg. *Aen.* 7.20 (Circe's victims). *uteroque exstante* suggests both that the stomach (*utero* is womb for external belly, cf. *Aen.* 3.428 *delphinum caudas utero commissa luporum*) remains unchanged and 'stands out', cf. 73 *saxeus exstat*, 2.355 (Heliades) *exstabant tantum ora uocantia matrem* (*TLL* V 2.1929.52–71; 1932.6–71).

68 hostiliter: Ovid is more inclined than other poets to use adverbs in *-e*, *-o*, and *-(i)ter*, which seem to have been considered prosaic (Kenney on *Her.* 16.174, Axelson 62–3). On Ovid's use of prosaic diction, see Kenney 2002: 36 n.57.

69 uiribus herbarum: Glaucus now regrets his earlier (all too justified) confidence in *herbarum . . . potentia* (14n.). **conubia:** the scansion of this word is a problem. In this its most common form (in nom. and acc. pl.) the second syllable is, since Catullus, regularly long when it bears the ictus (e.g. Catull. 62.27, 57, Ovid, *F.* 3.195, Sen. *Tro.* 901, except Lucr. 3.776, Stat. *Silv.* 2.3.19, 3.3.10, etc.), probably by poetic licence, since originally the syllable seems to have been short; see Knox on *Her.* 2.81, Austin on *Aen.* 1.73, 4.126.

70 cumque . . . primum 'and as soon as an opportunity presented itself' (*OLD* *cum*[2] 1d).

71 in Circes odium 'to vent her hatred of Circe'; final *in* (*OLD* 21; see McKeown on *Am.* 1.1.22, *TLL* VII 1.767.31), cf. Tac. *Hist.* 1.12.3. The attribution of this motive for Scylla's attack on Odysseus seems original; cf. *Ciris* 74–6 *ast tamen exegit longo post tempore poenas* (74). At Hom. *Od.* 12.73–100 Circe warns Odysseus about Scylla, but she still seizes six of his men (*Od.* 12.234–59). Cf. the anti-Greek ship-nymphs at 562–5, also with reference to Odyssean events. **Vlixem:** the Latinized name of Ulysses (*Vlixes*) draws its forms from the fifth and also third declensions (Leumann 458, Housman 1972a: 834–5).

72–4 Although Scylla is mentioned as a monster at *Met.* 13.730–3, she evidently turns into stone between the earlier stage of Aeneas' journey and the present point in the narrative, just in time to save Aeneas and the Trojans. Ovid thereby suggests perhaps the passage of time taken up by this long narrative 'digression', and also distinguishes between the Homeric and Virgilian pasts (Odysseus reaches Italy first), while affirming their synchronism (see Barchiesi 2001: 166n.18). Ovid also thus marks a distance between his version of Aeneas' journey and Virgil's. Aeneas has been warned by Helenus in the *Aeneid* to avoid the Straits of Messina with its two monsters Scylla and Charybdis by sailing south around Sicily (3.416–32, 684–6 *contra iussa monent Heleni, Scyllamque Charybdinque | inter, utrimque uiam leti discrimine paruo | ni teneam cursus*), although the Trojans come close enough to hear them (3.555–67, cf. 1.200–1 *uos et Scyllaeam rabiem penitusque sonantis | accestis scopulos*). Ovid instead has Aeneas travel through the straits northwards towards Italy, perhaps because Scylla is now a harmless rock. Casali 1995a: 63–5 suggests subtle interplay between Ovid's presentation of two Scyllas, one mythological and one rationalizing, and Virgil's two references to Scylla. Helenus' account of the monster (*Aen.* 3.420–32) may be understood to conflict with the Trojans' later encounter with the straits (3.555–60), suggesting a recognition of the rationalizing tradition that Scylla was a mythological personification of cliffs dangerous to ships. Ovid unmasks Scylla's duality in poetic fiction (cf. the introduction to the Scylla story at 13.733–4 *si non omnia uates | ficta reliquerunt*, which recalls *Aen.* 3.434 *si qua fides, animum si ueris implet Apollo*), cf. Pinotti, *EV* IV 726a.

Scylla's transformation into a crag is mentioned first here, although she is often associated with a rock and is given the epithet 'rocky' (Ap. Rh. 4.789, 922, Hom. *Od.* 12.231 Σκύλλην πετραίην). We are not told how this second transformation is effected; the fifth-century CE Virgilian commentator Iunius Philargyrius on *Ecl.* 6.74 (pp. 122–3 Hagen) attributes Scylla's petrifaction to Neptune. Sallust (*Hist.* 4.27) relates a rationalizing interpretation of the myth of Scylla from certain resounding and distinctively shaped rock-formations in the straits (*Scyllam accolae saxum mari imminens appellant simile celebratae formae procul uisentibus unde et monstruosam speciem fabulae illi dederunt*), which Seneca later claims to have seen (*Epist.* 79.1 *Scyllam saxum esse . . . scio*, cf. Polyb. 34.2.12–13); the promontory is still known as Rocca di Scilla.

72 eadem 'she likewise' (*OLD* 7). **Teucras:** synonym for *Troianas;* cf. 698, 13.705 *Teucros a sanguine Teucri*, after the legendary Trojan king Teucrus or Teucer (Virg. *Aen.* 3.107–8 *maximus unde pater . . . Teucrus*). **fuerat mersura** 'would have sunk', a future participle with past tense indic. of *esse* in a contrary to fact ('unreal') condition (K–S II 401–2, *NLS* § 200); cf. *F.* 4.500 *naufraga monstra*, Virg. *Aen.* 3.425 *nauis in saxa trahentem*. Scylla usually pulls men off ships, while Charybdis sinks them (*Ciris* 61 *deprensos nautas canibus lacerasse marinis*, Hom. *Od.*12.98–100, 245–59). **carinas:** *carina* (keel or hull) is common in poetry for ship (synecdoche, part for whole); cf. 164, 169, 185, 240, 560.

73 nunc quoque 'even now to this day'; typical aetiological formula used by Ovid to signal the origin (aetion) and continuation of an event or landmark up to the present time, equivalent to the Greek expressions such as εἰσέτι καὶ νῦν, and frequent in the *Fasti* (15x), and *Met.* (17x), e.g. 1.235, 2.706, 4.561, 602, 750, 13.622.; cf. also *nunc* 516, 851, 13.715, *etiam nunc* 6.312, see Myers 1994a: 66–7, O'Hara 1996a: 90–1, Loehr 1996: 136. Scylla's transformation into an Italian landmark gives the narrative the feel of an aetiological itinerary; cf. Crageleus' transformation into a rock at 13.714–15, 90 (Pithecusae), 103–4 (Misenum). **saxeus** 'in rock form', proleptic adj. Bömer suggests the adj. is not mere poetic pleonasm, but a reference to the above-mentioned tradition of Scylla's rocky epithet. **exstat** 'is (still) to be seen' (*OLD* 3a), but also with the sense 'projects from', cf. 67 *uteroque exstante*; an aetiological formula: cf. 13.569–70 *locus exstat et ex re* | *nomen habet, Her.* 20.106 *nunc quoque Mygdonia flebilis exstat humo* (with Kenney ad loc.).

73–4 scopulum . . . scopulum: repetition, marking the end of the first half of 73 and the second half of 74. Ovid's fondness for assonance of repeated syllables (especially at line-end) is in evidence here: *saxeus exstat, transformata foret, nauita uitat.*

74 nauita: cf. 8.591 *Perimelen nauita dicit,* 9.228–9 *nautae calcare uerentur* | *appellantque Lichan.*

75–100 Aeneas in Carthage; the Cercopians

75–81 The Trojans' journey in *Aen.* 3 is now resumed from 13.729, where Aeneas and his followers had landed at Zancle near Scylla and Charybdis at nightfall. Relying on the reader's knowledge of the *Aeneid,* in this bridging passage Ovid swiftly and allusively summarizes Aeneas' arrival at Carthage (75–7), reached also at the end of *Aen.* 3 (line 715, cf. *Aen.* 1.157ff.) and his tragic love affair with Dido in *Aen.* 4 (79–81).

75 Hunc: sc. *scopulum Scyllae.* **auidamque Charybdin:** *auidam* gestures towards the Greek etymology of Charybdis' name from the verb 'to swallow': cf. Hom. *Od.* 12.104 Χάρυβδις ἀναρροιβδεῖ, *LALE* 124: *dicta quod . . . naues obsorbeat.* This recalls her mention at 13.730 *laeuum inrequieta Charybdis,* where she was still evidently a threat; cf. 7.63–5 *ratibusque inimica Charybdis . . . Scylla rapax,* Virg. *Aen.* 3.420 *implacata Charybdi,* Manil. 4.605 *auidam . . . Charybdin.*

76 euicere : *euinco* (*OLD* 2) is used of overcoming the same navigational dangers at 15.706 (Aesculapius' voyage) *euincitque fretum Siculique angusta Pelori*; cf. *Tr.* 1.10.33, *Her.* 19.155. Despite the real dangers of the strait, the verb seems a bit overblown here when we just been told that Scylla is now a rock. On the fondness of epic poets for this shortened form of the perfect, see Austin on Virg. *Aen.* 2.53, N–W III 190–9, Skutsch 1985: 62, Quint. *Inst.* 1.5.42, Bömer on *Met.* 15.615.

76–77 litus . . . Ausonium: cf. *Aen.* 7.198 *litus ad Ausonium.*

77 ~ *Aen.* 1.158 *Libyae uertuntur ad oras.* Aeneas is driven to the coast of north Africa to Dido's newly founded city of Carthage by the storm raised by Aeolus (*Aen.* 1.84–158, here reduced to *uento*!) at the instigation of Juno in Virg. *Aen.* 1.34–123, cf. *Aen.* 1.376–7 (Aeneas to Venus) *diuersa per aequora uectos* | *forte sua Libycis tempestas appulit oris.* See

Bömer ad loc. for other examples of the pointed opposition of *Ausonium, Libycas* (cf. *Aen.* 4.106 *quo regnum Italiae Libycas auerteret oras*).

78–81 In one loaded sentence in four much-discussed lines Ovid summarizes the tragic love affair of Dido and Aeneas told in *Aeneid* 1 and 4, probably the most famous episode of Virgil's epic (see *Tr.* 2.1.535–6 *nec legitur pars ulla magis de corpore toto,* | *quam non legitimo foedere iunctus amor*). The radical abbreviation of the episode focuses on and is focalized through the figure of Dido, representing a view hostile to Aeneas and his mission. In *Heroides* 7, an elegiac letter from Dido to Aeneas on his departure, Ovid explores in length the episode from the unique perspective of the suffering queen; see Knox ad loc. and Desmond 1993. Other passages in the poem allude to Dido's tragedy, cf. 7.68–74 (Medea), 7.852–92 (Procris), 1.618–21 (Sleep), see Smith 1997: 101–2, Tarrant 2002: 23–7.

78 'welcomed Aeneas there in her heart and home': a favourite Ovidian figure of speech, syllepsis, in which a word, here *excipit*, is applied literally to one word (*domo*) and metaphorically to another (*animo*); see Introduction, p. 22, Kenney 1972: 39–40 (on the distinction between syllepsis and zeugma), 2002: 45–7, Tissol 1997: 18–20, 219–22, Galinsky 1975: 143, 156, 248. Here the figure perhaps underlines the speed and completeness of Dido's surrender to her love for Aeneas, cf. 9.278–9 (Hyllus and Iole) *Herculis illam* | *imperiis thalamoque animoque receperat Hyllus, Her.* 6.55 (Hypsipyle and Jason) *urbe uirum uidua tectoque animoque recepi, AA* 2.407. Other examples of syllepsis include 377, 417, 426, 449, 498. Cf. Dido's complaints at *Her.* 7.89–90 *fluctibus eiectum tuta statione recepi* | *uixque bene audito nomine regna dedi,* and its model at Virg. *Aen.* 4.373–4 *nusquam tuta fides. eiectum litore, egentem,* | *excepi et regni demens in parte locaui.* The repetition of the correlative *-que*, typically occurring at the end of the line as here, is 'a feature of epic style, found already in Ennius, who took it over from the Homeric correlative τε . . . τε' (Austin on Virg. *Aen.* 1.18; Harrison on Virg. *Aen.* 10.91, G–L §476 n. 5d., Wills 1996: 372–85, Kenney on *Her.* 16.96). **Aenean:** Gk acc., as frequently with the name in Ovid and Virgil for metrical convenience, cf. 170.

79 non bene . . . latura 'destined to endure painfully'. *non bene* = *male*, but stronger (litotes). A dry précis of Dido's highly-wrought tragedy in Virgil. In the *Aeneid moritura* is a leitmotiv for Dido (Barchiesi 2001: 46); cf. *Aen.* 4.308 *nec moritura tenet crudeli funere Dido?*, 415, 519, 604. **discidium:** the noun (not in Virgil) strikes an elegiac note, recalling Tib. 1.5.1 *asper eram et bene discidium me ferre loquebar,* cf. Prop. 1.11.28, 2.24.32, *Eleg. in Maec.* 2.7. **Phrygii . . . mariti:** there is perhaps pointed irony behind Ovid's reuse of Juno's hostile appellation of Aeneas in her designing speech to Venus at *Aeneid* 4.103 *liceat Phrygio seruire marito* (cf. Austin ad loc. 'a venomous line, for *Phrygius* is often a term of contempt used by the enemies of Troy', cf. *Aen.* 4.216): see Bömer ad loc., Lamacchia 1969: 7, Casali 1995a: 68–9. *maritus* suggests also Dido's viewpoint in the *Aeneid,* where she characterizes her relationship with Aeneas as a marriage (4.172 *coniugium uocat, hoc praetexit nomine culpam*), while Aeneas denies the existence of such a marriage bond (*Aen.* 4.338–9 *nec coniugis umquam* | *praetendi taedas aut haec in foedera ueni*).

In *Her.* 7 Dido repeatedly insists on the existence of such a bond, 9 *certus es, Aenea, cum foedere soluere naues?*, 69 *coniugis ante oculos deceptae stabit imago.*

80 Sidonis 'Dido, woman of Sidon'; the story of Dido's flight from Sidon (or Tyre) to the coast of North Africa where she founded the city of Carthage is told by Venus to Aeneas at Virg. *Aen.* 1. 338–71 (cf. *Her.* 7.113–25). Virgil refers to Dido as *Sidonia Dido* (1.446, 613, 9.266, 11.74) and *Phoenissa* (1.670, 714, 4.529, 6.450). The prosody of the second syllable of the adj. *Sidonis* varies, being short in the nom. and voc. and long in the oblique cases; it is used of Dido only here, cf. 2.840 (Sidon), 10.267, *F.* 3.649 (Anna, Dido's sister, cf. Sil. 8.70), 5.610 (Europa), 617, *AA* 3.252. See Kenney 2002: 68 for Ovid's preference for the adjective ending *-is* for metrical convenience. **sacri sub imagine** 'under the pretext of a sacrifice'. At *Aen.* 4. 474–503 Dido decides on suicide and deceives her sister Anna by pretending that she has learned from a priestess how to end her sufferings by means of magical rites. She tells Anna to construct a pyre secretly on which to burn the relics of Aeneas (494–5 cf. 504), and Anna does so, not suspecting that Dido will use it instead to kill herself (500–1 *non tamen Anna nouis praetexere funera sacris | germanam credit*).

81 incubuit ferro 'she fell upon his sword'. At Virg. *Aen.* 4.641–64 Dido ascends the pyre and kills herself with Aeneas' sword; cf. *Aen.* 4.650 *incubuitque toro*, 663–4 *ferro | conlapsum* (with Austin ad loc. 'probably "upon the sword"'). In *Her.* 7 Dido explains that she writes holding the sword (184) *scribimus et gremio Troicus ensis adest* (cf. *Am.* 2.18.25 *quodque tenens strictum Dido miserabilis ensem*) and foretells her own death in a terse and incriminating epigram: 195–6 *praebuit Aeneas et causam mortis et ensem | ipsa sua Dido concidit usa manu* (repeated verbatim at *F.* 3.549–50, cf. *AA* 3.39–40). **deceptaque decipit omnes** 'herself deceived, deceived all'; the polyptoton (with Ovid's favourite passive/active contrast) creates wordplay; cf. *Her.* 7.61 *perdita ne perdam timeo, noceamque nocenti* (see Wills 1996: 249 for further examples). Dido's unexpected (*decipit*) suicide is a direct response to her feelings in the *Aeneid* of having been betrayed (*decepta*) by Aeneas, see *Aen.* 4.330 *non equidem omnino <u>capta</u> ac <u>de</u>serta viderer*, 541–2 *necdum | Laomedonteae sentis periuria gentis*; cf. also 4.296–7 *at regina dolos (quis fallere possit amantem?) | praesensit* and 4.17 (Dido on Sychaeus' death) *postquam primus amor <u>deceptam</u> morte fefellit. decepta* also confirms Dido's view of Aeneas' deceit in *Heroides* 7, e.g. *Her.* 7.67–8 *protinus occurrent falsae periuria linguae | et Phrygia Dido fraude coacta mori*, 69 *coniugis . . . <u>deceptae</u>*, 105 *<u>decepit</u> idoneus auctor*, see Thomas 2001: 80–1. Anna complains after Dido is dead at *Aen.* 4.675–6 '*hoc illud, germana, fuit? me fraude petebas? | hoc rogus iste mihi, hoc ignes araeque parabant?*'

82–88 The following lines touch very briefly on some of the main events of *Aeneid* 5, picking up Aeneas' route as he flees from Carthage at the end of *Aen.* 4 and reaches Sicily again at the opening of *Aen.* 5.

82 rursus . . . fugiens 'fleeing back', i.e. in the direction from which one has come (*OLD rursus* 1b.). It was after Anchises' death at Drepanum in Sicily that the Trojans were carried to Libya (*Aen.* 3. 707–15). **harenosae . . . terrae:** Libya;

cf. Virg. *Aen.* 4.257 *litus harenosum ad Libyae* (the unique appearance of the adj. in Virgil), Prop. 4.1.103 *harenosum Libyae Iouis antrum.* **noua moenia** reflects the Punic etymology of Carthage, see Servius on *Aen.* 1.366 *moenia surgentemque nouae Karthaginis arcem: 'Carthago' enim est lingua Poenorum 'noua ciuitas', ut docet Liuius* (= Livy fr. 6 W–M), cf. *Her.* 7.11–12 *noua Carthago* (with Knox ad loc. and see O'Hara 1996a: 123).

83 Cf. Virg. *Aen.* 5. 630 *hic Erycis fines fraterni atque hospes Acestes.* Eryx is Aeneas' half-brother, son of Venus and Butes (*Aen.* 5.23–4 *litora . . . fraterna Erycis*). An eponymous local hero, he gave his name to a famous mountain (Mt Eryx) and town on the N. coast of western Sicily (modern Erice). Acestes, the Sicilian king, *Troiano a sanguine clarus* (*Aen.* 1.550), received Aeneas in Sicily before his detour to Carthage (*Aen.* 1.195–6, 549–50) and later welcomes him there again in *Aen.* 5 after he has fled Dido (35ff.). Aeneas founds for him the city of Acesta (*Aen.* 5. 711–58, called Egesta by the Greeks, Segesta by the Romans), where he settles those of the Trojans who have no wish to sail further. On the Trojans in Sicily, see Thuc. 6.2.3, Dion. Hal. *Ant. Rom.* 1.53.1, Diod. 4.83.4, Cic. *Verr.* 4.33, Galinsky 1969a.

84 The funeral rites and games in honour of the first anniversary of the death of Aeneas' father Anchises are narrated in *Aeneid* 5 (cf. *Aen.* 5.94 *inceptos genitori instaurat honores*). **sacrificat:** usually prosaic (Axelson 1945: 69), but cf. *F.* 3.850, 4.414, Ennius *Ann.* 214 Sk. **genitoris** belongs to the elevated style, found first in Ennius (*Ann.* 108 Sk., see *TLL* VI 1816.56ff.).

85–90 A good example of O's 'fast-forwarding' mode: every verse is enjambed.

85 In Virg. *Aen.* 5.604–99 Juno bids Iris to persuade the Trojan women to set fire to the ships while the Trojan men are occupied with the funeral games. At the entreaty of Aeneas, Jupiter extinguishes the flames by a rain-storm and saves all but four ships. **quasque rates:** i.e. *ratesque quas;* the antecedent, as not infrequently, is incorporated into the relative clause; cf. *Am.* 2.2.4, *F.* 6.395, Kenney on *Her.* 21.100. **Iris Iunonia:** *Iunonius* occurs first at Virg. *Aen.* 1.671–2 (of Dido's hospitality) *uereor quo se Iunonia uertant | hospitia,* but appears as an epithet of Iris only here and at Statius, *Silv.* 5.1.103 *Iunonia uirgo*; cf. *Met.* 1.678 (Argus) *custos Iunonius,* 8.220–1 *Iunonia . . . Samos, Am.* 2.6.55 *ales Iunonia* (peacock). Iris (the rainbow) belongs to both pantheon and common meteorology. She is a messenger of the gods, especially of Juno (as Mercury is of Jupiter), cf. 14.829–48, 1.270 *nuntia Iunonis uarios induta colores,* 11.585 '*Iri, meae' dixit 'fidissima nuntia uocis'.* On Iris' role in fomenting strife in Homer and Virgil see Hardie on *Aen.* 9.2.

86 Hippotadae regnum: the Aeolian islands, identified with Lipara (Lipari), off the north-east coast of Sicily, are not mentioned in *Aeneid* 5 (but cf. *Aen.* 1.50–80 (Aeolus), 8.416–17 *Aeoliam Liparen*). *Hippotades* is a Greek patronymic (here in gen. sing.), 'son of Hippotes' (i.e. Aeolus, keeper of the winds), familiar from Hom. *Od.* 10.2, 36 and Ap. Rh. 4.819; only Ovid of the Augustan poets uses it (7x: see Kenney on *Her.* 18.46), cf. 223–4, 1.663, 11.431, 15.707 (Aesculapius' journey) *Hippotadae domos.* Patronymics of this form go into the first decl. (see G–L §182.11).

87 sulphure fumantes: on the volcanic nature of the Lipari islands see Plin. *Nat.* 35.174 *mira natura est sulphuris, quo pluruma domantur. nascitur in insulis Aeoliis inter Siciliam et Italiam, quas ardere diximus.* **Acheloiadumque** 'daughters of Achelous'. *Acheloias* is a patronymic; see 5.551–63 for the Sirens' genealogy (and the variant form *Achelois* at 5.552 *Acheloides*) and their metamorphoses, cf. Ap. Rh. 4.893 Ἀχελωίδες. On Ovid's predilection for such Greek feminine names in *–ias* (this form occurs only here (creating a four-word hexameter), cf. Sil. 12.34), see Kenney 1999a. Achelous, a river (god), appears in a long episode with Theseus at 8.547–9.97, to which this patronymic functions as a cross-reference.

88 Sirenum scopulos: cf. *Aen.* 5.864–5 *iamque adeo scopulos Sirenum aduecta subibat, | difficilis quondam.* The location of the Sirens was a matter of debate; Strabo 1.2.12–13 discusses the controversy and possibilities. They were associated with the area of Surrentum (Stat. *Silv.* 2.2.1, 116–17, 3.1.64, Plin. *Nat.* 3.62), and usually identified with three small islands in the Gulf of Salerno, near Capri, known as the Sirenusae (modern Isole Li Galli). The cult of the Sirens was firmly established in the area of Naples (see below 101n.), with a sanctuary near the promontory of Surrentum (see Van Dam on Stat. *Silv.* 2.2.1). According to legend (Lycophr. 712f., 1463f.), the Sirens killed themselves after Odysseus got past them (Hom. *Od.* 12.39–54, 165–200); so Virgil seems to confirm (above) at *Aen.* 5.865 *difficilis quondam* (see Williams on *Aen.* 5.864–7, Servius on *Aen.* 5.864, Hyg. *Fab.* 141). **orbataque praeside:** refers to the loss of Palinurus, steersman of the Trojan fleet, who was flung into the sea by Somnus and killed by native Italians upon beaching, see *Aen.* 5.833–71 (867–8 *pater amisso fluitantem errare magistro | sensit*) and 6.337–83. In Virgil he is lost before the ships pass the Sirens' rocks and provides the etymology of the headland on the Lucanian coast, south-east of Velia (*Aen.* 6.381 *aeternumque locus Palinuri nomen habebit*, modern Capo Palinuro), which is south of the region of the Sirens. **pinus:** poetic synecdoche ('material for object') for ship (*OLD* 2a), cf. e. g. 248, 535.

89–90 Ovid first names two islands off the coast of Italy near Cape Misenum and Cumae: Inarime (also called Aenaria, modern Ischia) and the small Prochyte (modern Procida), which are mentioned in Virgil, not in *Aen.* 5, but at 9.715–16 *Prochyta alta tremit durumque cubile | Inarime Iouis imperiis imposta Typhoeo.* Inarime seems to derive from a misreading, first attested in Virgil, of Homer *Il.* 2.783 εἰν Ἀρίμοις (his location for Typhoeus) as one word (cf. Serv. *auct.* on Virg. *Aen.* 9.712, Hardie on *Aen.* 9.715–16; O'Hara 1996a: 221–2 suggests deliberate 'reinterpretation' on Virgil's part). Pithecusae (not in the *Aeneid*), a settlement located on the NW coast of Ischia, was also another name for the island itself, but sometimes, as here, it seems to be confusingly presented as a separate island (cf. Liv. 8.22.6 with Oakley ad loc.); see Bömer ad loc. **legit** 'skirts' (*OLD lego*[2] 7b); for *legere* of navigation in a sea-voyage cf. 15.707, 709, *F.* 4.289, 566. **sterilique . . . colle:** the locatival abl. is used freely in poetry without a preposition (*NLS* 51 (iv)). Ischia is composed largely of porous volcanic tufa and areas of arable land are few. The remains of the acropolis of Pithecusae, the first western Greek settlement (founded by Euboeans *c.* 775–750 BCE), have been excavated at modern Monte di Vico; see Ridgway 1992: 35–7. Pithecusae was ordered to be destroyed by Sulla in 82 BCE because the community had sheltered Marius and his followers (Plut. *Marius* 40). **Pithecusas habitantum nomine dictas:** the etymology was disputed, see Plin. *Nat.* 3.82 *Pithecusa, non a simiarum multitudine* [πίθηκος] (*ut aliqui existimauere*) *sed a figlinis doliorum* [πίθος, πιθάκνη], and Serv. *auct.* on Virg. *Aen.* 9.712 *et quia in †eamdi contumeliam simiae missae sunt, quas Etruscorum lingua arimos dicunt: ob quam causam Pithecusam etiam uocitant.* On *nomen* as a common 'etymological marker', see O'Hara 1996a: 75–9, Cairns 1996: 29–31, Michalopoulos 2001: 4–5. Other toponyms in the book include 102–3 Misenum, 348 *arua Circaea*, 416–34 *locus Canens*, 157, 441–4 Caieta, 614–16 Tiber, 619–21 *Aventinus*; for a fuller list see Loehr 1996: 144.

91–100 Ovid inserts the non-Virgilian story of the metamorphosis of the Cercopes, motivated geographically and etymologically by the mention of Pithecusae, cf. 13.713–18, 14.512–26nn. Ovid imitates Virgil's technique of Alexandrian geographical aetiology, while only briefly alluding to Virgil's well-known examples of Palinurus (*Aen.* 5.380–1, see 88n.) and Misenus (*Aen.* 6.232–5, see 102–3n., but cf. Caieta 157, 443nn.). The Cercopes, known as proverbial cheats and liars, were the subject of a comic poem ascribed to Homer and are frequently mentioned in the comic poets (Adler *RE* XI 309.44–313.47). In some versions they were captured by Hercules, in others Zeus was involved. Pherecydes (*FGH* 3 F 77) is cited for a story that Zeus turned them into stone for lying. Ovid follows a version attested in Xenagoras, a third- or first-century BCE historian, in which they were transformed into apes and put on Pithecusae (*FGH* 240 F28, see Forbes Irving 1990: 292). The association of their name with κέρκος (tail) perhaps suggested the metamorphosis into apes (πίθηκος); both words, as well as Cercopes, were used as terms of abuse (e.g. Ar. *Ach.* 907, Plaut. *Mil.* 989, 284, Cic. *Fam.* 5.10a.1, 7.2.3, Hor. *Sat.* 1.10.18), see Otto 1890: 323, Keith 1992: 147–50, Connors 2004. The story is the first of a number of episodes in the book that share the theme of verbal misuse or abuse: see also the Sibyl 104–53, Diomedes' men 483–509, the Apulian shepherd 512–26; cf. Crageleus. 13.713–15. The tale has thematic links with the *Aeneid* frame through the theme of deception, recently stressed in the description of Dido at 81 *deceptaque decipit omnes*: cf. *Her.* 7.67–8 *protinus occurrent falsae periuria linguae | et Phrygia Dido fraude coacta mori,* which alludes to Dido's complaint at *Aen.* 4.541–2 *necdum | Laomedonteae sentis periuria gentis?* (Knox on *Her.* 7.67 observes that this is the only instance of *periurium* in the *Aen.*); cf. Casali 1995a: 69–70.

91 quippe 'for', explanatory (*OLD* 1). **deum genitor** is a grand epic periphrasis for Jupiter, modelled on the Homeric πατὴρ ἀνδρῶν τε θεῶν τε (*Il.* 1.544, *al.*; see McKeown on *Am.* 1.13.45), cf. 807n., *F.* 3.285, *Tr.* 2.37, Virg. *Aen.* 7.306. *deum* is an archaic form of the gen. pl., much used by epic poets. **periuria:** cf. 99; the word occurs in the poem elsewhere only at 11.206 (Laomedon's teachery) *perfidiae cumulum,* *falsis periuria uerbis* (cf. *Aen.* 4.541–2 above) and 2.705–6 (Battus) *periuriaque pectora uertit* | *in durum silicem.* **quondam** 'once (upon a time)' (*OLD* 1c).

92 exosus 'out of hatred of', causal use of the perfect participle (*NLS* §92), although *exodi* is not an extant form; cf. 7.367. **admissa** 'crimes'.

93 idem 'at the same time' (*OLD* 10).

94 dissimiles . . . similesque: the two adjs. form a polar pair in positive and negative forms, see Wills 1996: 451–8. The reader is left to pick up the latent wordplay in this line and the following (*resimas*) between *similis/simia*: see Enn. *Sat.* 23 *FLP* p. 19 *simia quam similis, turpissima bestia, nobis* (with Courtney ad loc.), Martial, *Ep.* 7.87.4, Isid. *Etym.* 12.2.30 *alii simias Latino sermone uocatos arbitrantur, eo quod multa in eis similitudo rationis humanae sentitur; sed falsum est,* and Connors 2004: 183–9. Differences in vowel quantity did not prevent such punning or etymologizing: see O'Hara 1996a: 61–2.

95–6 naresque a fronte resimas | contudit 'and crushed their noses in front (*OLD frons*[2] 5b) so that they were turned up'. *resimas,* a proleptic adjective, expressing the result of *contudit,* is a conjecture of Salmasius (17th century); the main MSS read *remissas.* The adj. not only describes the splayed noses of apes, but suggests their conspicuously omitted Latin name, *simia* (cf. Serv. on *Ecl.* 10.7 *'simiae' graecum est nomen, id est pressis naribus, unde et simias dicimus*).

96 perarauit 'furrowed': the compound verb appears first in Ovid (6x (2x in *Met.*), all other instances refer to writing); elsewhere only at Sen. *Med.* 650. Cf. 3.75–6 *simulauit anum posuitque ad tempora canos* | *sulcauitque cutem rugis, Med. Fac.* 46 *placitus rugis uultus aratus erit.*

97 totaque uelatos flauenti corpora uillo 'and after he had covered their bodies completely with tawny hair'; cf. 2.376 (Cycnus) *penna latus uelat,* 3.197 (Actaeon) *uelat maculoso uellere corpus. uelatos* is predicative (*NLS* §90–1) and a perfect passive participle with *corpora* as an accusative of 'respect' referring to a body-part, as in Greek; see Courtney 2004: 427 (5), *NLS* §19, ii, cf. 300, 432.

98–9 abstulit usum | uerborum . . . linguae: two nouns denoting speech enclose line 99; *usum* must be taken with both of these genitives. The loss of the faculty (*OLD usus* 3) of speech is a prominent feature of Ovidian metamorphosis, often, as here, as punishment for the misuse of speech; cf. 498 (Acmon), 523 (Apulian shepherd), 2.658 (Ocyroe) *plura loqui uocisque meae praecluditur usus,* 3.366–7 (Echo) *'huius' ait 'linguae, qua sum delusa, potestas*| *parua tibi dabitur uocisque breuissimus usus',* 4.412–13 (Minyades), 5.465–7 (Cyane), see Bömer on 3.193, Keith 1992: *passim,* Landolfi 2003. **natae dira in periuria linguae** 'tongues born for terrible perjuries', cf. 5.561 *ille canor mulcendas natus ad aures,* 13.111 *nataeque ad furta sinistrae,* Hor. *C.* 1.27.1 *natis in usum laetitiae scyphis.*

100 'he left to them only the ability to complain in a harsh shriek'; for the inf. used substantivally (as a neut. noun), cf. 2.483 (Callisto) *posse loqui eripitur* (with Bömer),

11.177 *dat posse moueri*, *AA* 2.626, *Pont.* 7.7.47 and *NLS* §25. For the construction of *relinquere* with the infin., cf. Hor. *Sat.* 1.1.52, Sil. 3.708. **rauco:** *raucus* is used in the *Met.* often for the animal voice of a transformed human, cf. e.g. 280 (pig/Macareus) *nec iam posse loqui, pro uerbis edere raucum | murmur*, 2.484 (bear/Callisto) *rauco de gutture*, 5.678, 6.377, 8.287, 13.567.

101–157 The Sibyl. Arrival at Caieta

101 Has ubi praeteriit: the lengthening of the final syllable of the third person singular of the perfect indicative of verbs forming their perfect in *-ii* (*-iīt*), is a revival of the original vowel quantity for metrical convenience that Ovid occasionally allows himself (Platnauer 1951: 60–1), cf. 519, 618, 766. The wording here and below (104–5) recalls somewhat Helenus' prophecy to Aeneas about this part of his voyage at *Aen.* 3.441–2 *huc ubi delatus Cumaeam accesseris urbem | diuinosque lacus et Auerna sonantia siluis.*

101–2 Parthenopeia . . . | moenia: Naples; cf. 15.711–12 (Aesculapius' journey) *in otia natam | Parthenopen et ab hac Cumaeae templa Sibyllae. Parthenopeia* (six syllables) is a hapax legomenon; Ovid is making free as usual with the prosody of proper names to suit his metre (cf. 44n., 47). Naples was said to have been called Parthenope after one of the Sirens who was washed ashore in the Bay of Naples; she had a tomb near the port and there was a famous cult of the Sirens, see Lycophr. 717–21, Plin. *Nat.* 3.62, Sil. It. 12.32 (see Frederikson 1984: 86, 105–6, Van Dam on Stat. *Silv.* 2.2.1–3). Although not mentioned by Virgil in the *Aen.*, Parthenope appears in his famous sphragis at *G.* 4.563–4 (*illo Vergilium me tempore dulcis alebat | Parthenope studiis florentem ignobilis oti*) and the city became associated with him after his burial there; see Stat. *Silv.* 1.2.260–2, 4.4.52–5 (with Coleman ad loc.). The reference activates again (cf. 88 *Sirenum scopulos*) the theme of speech, shared by the two juxtaposed episodes of the Cercopians and the Sibyl (see 152–3n.).

102–3 canori | Aeolidae tumulum: the tomb of Misenus, son of Aeolus (Virg. *Aen.* 6.164), the trumpeter of the Trojan fleet (for *canori*, cf. *Aen.* 6.172 *cantu uocat in certamina diuos*). *Aeolidae* (patronymic *Aeolides*) is Gk gen. sing., see 86n. Ovid once again plays with Virgilian chronology and geography by having the Trojans pass by Misenus' tomb before arriving in Cumae. At *Aen.* 6.149–235 Aeneas is told by the Sibyl that he must bury Misenus before he can enter the Underworld. The Trojans discover his drowned body on the beach and build him a tomb. Like that of Palinurus, his death is an aetiological legend, explaining the name of the Promunturium Misenum SSE of Cumae (Punta di Miseno) at *Aen.* 6.232–5 (see Austin on *Aen.* 6.162). Misenum lies on the coast of Italy, but juts out to form an arm, which could be seen to lie on the left (west) while one travelled north in the Bay of Pozzuoli. Bömer argues instead, perhaps rightly (cf. above 88n.), that Ovid is interested more in parallelism (*dextra . . . laeua*) than accurate geography (cf. 15.703–4); on the general lack of interest in topographical reality in the ancient authors, see Horsfall 1985 and Castagnoli 1983. **loca feta palustribus undis** is probably to be understood in apposition to *litora Cumarum* (with Bömer). Tarrant's punctuation (no comma after *et*) suggests that it refers backwards instead, and makes *litora* the start of the *intrat* clause. *uluis* for *undis* has some MS support, cf. 11.366 *uluisque palustribus*, 8.336. The hemistich recalls Virg. *Aen.* 1.50–1 *nimborum in patriam, loca feta furentibus Austris,* | *Aeoliam uenit,* where Juno goes to convince Aeolus to stir up a storm against Aeneas. Cf. Prop. 3.18.2 *fumida Baiarum stagna tepentis aquae,* Stat. *Silv.* 3.2.17 *Baianosque sinus et feta tepentibus undis.*

104–153 *Visit to the Sibyl.* In the *Aeneid* Aeneas arrives in Italy at Cumae at 6.2 (*tandem Euboicis Cumarum adlabitur oris*). Ovid's Sibyl episode focuses on her personal history (129–53) and omits the famous metaphysical explanation and historical prophecy of Virgil's sixth book (cf. his similar move away from Virgilian prophecy to another tale of metamorphosis in the episode of Anius at 13.632–704). His version also inverts the progression of the Virgilian episode by placing the main emphasis of the story on Aeneas' exit from the Underworld, rather than his entrance (see 120, 121nn.). Rather than learn about the future, as in Virgil, Aeneas here learns about the Sibyl's past. On Ovid's indebtedness to Virgil in this episode, see Bömer 1959, Stitz 1962: 72–9, Due 1974: 38–41, Lamacchia 1969: 7–9, Ellsworth 1988a, Baldo 1995: 80–8; see also Tissol 1997: 177–91, Papaioannou 2005: 43–74.

There were a number of Sibyls, women inspired by a god with prophecy, variously localized in the ancient world (Varro listed ten (Lactant. *DI* 1.6.7–12 = fr. 56a Cardauns)). The Cumaean Sibyl, usually inspired by Apollo (*Aen.* 6.12 *Delius inspirat uates*), was said in a number of sources to have come to Cumae from Erythrae in Asia Minor ([Arist.] *Mir.* 838, Serv. on *Aen.* 6.321, Parke 1988: 78–9). It is perhaps first Virgil who places her prophecy to Aeneas at Cumae. Called Deiphobe, daughter of Glaucus, in the *Aeneid* (6.36), the Cumaean Sibyl was also given other names (Varro, Cardauns fr. 56a.15–16, Serv. on *Aen.* 6.72), but Ovid mentions none. On Sibyls in antiquity, see Parke 1988, Potter 1994: 71–87.

104 uiuacisque 'long-lived': the proverbial longevity of the Sibyl is explained by the story she narrates at 129–53 (at 144–6 we learn her age is 700); cf. *F.* 4.875 *carmine uiuacis . . . Sibyllae,* Virg. *Aen.* 6.321, 628 *Phoebi longaeua sacerdos*, Prop. 2.2.15–16, Petron. *Sat.* 48, Stat. *Silv.* 4.3.149–52, Otto 1890: 321. The Sibyl appears as a young woman on coins issued by L. Manlius Torquatus in 65 BCE (*RRC* no. 441), see Potter 1994: 81–2. **antra:** poetic pl., cf. the Sibyl's cave at *Aen.* 6.11 *antrum immane.* The exact site of the Cumaean Sibyl's cave is disputed, although it is often identified with the underground complex at Cumae excavated by Maiuri in 1932. See Monti 1994 and Austin on *Aen.* 6.42–76 for discussion and illustrations.

105–6 ut manes adeat . . . paternos | **orat:** Ovid abbreviates the much longer Virgilian account of Aeneas' request at *Aen.* 6.103–24 (106–9 *unum oro: quando hic inferni ianua regis* | *dicitur et tenebrosa palus Acheronte refuso,* | *ire ad conspectum cari genitoris et ora* | *contingat*). **Auerna** 'the infernal regions', n. pl. subst. (as common in toponyms (*OLD Auernus*[2] 2), N–W 1.722, *TLL* II 1315.83–1316.15), cf. *Aen.* 3.442 *Auerna sonantia siluis*, 5.732 *Auerna per alta.* Ovid uses the sing. masc. noun at *Am.* 3.9.27 *nigro . . . Auerno.* Avernus, a lake formed in a volcanic crater, was long considered the entrance to the Underworld (Strab. 5.4.5, see McKay 1970: 201–17) and its name was often used of the Underworld itself, cf. 114n., *Aen.* 6.126–7 *facilis descensus Auerno: | noctes atque dies patet atri ianua Ditis*, 237–8, Serv. on *Aen.* 6.126 *inferorum significat et lacum pro inferis ponit.* **orat. at:** such assonance is common in Ovid: cf. e.g. 470 *aequora rapti*, 623 *nulla Latinas* (see Bömer on *Met.* 15.697).

106–7 diu uultum tellure moratum | erexit 'she raised her gaze after it had lingered long on the ground', cf. 13.125 (Ulysses) *oculos paulum tellure moratos | sustulit.* Ovid may here be taking over Virgil's description of Aeneas' reaction to the Sibyl's injunctions at *Aen.* 6.156 *Aeneas maesto defixus lumina uultu* (Bömer 1959: 281). From the beginning of the passage, Ovid emphasizes the humanity of the Sibyl.

107 deo furibunda recepto: *furibundus* here signifies the possession and inspiration of the Sibyl by Apollo (μαινομένη, cf. *Aen.* 3.443 *insanam uatem*); it is used of madness at 4.512 (Athamas) and Virg. *Aen.* 7.348 (Amata), but otherwise specifically of the madness of love at 8.107 (Scylla), 9.637 (Byblis), 10.410 (Myrrha), 13.871 (Cyclops), cf. Virg. *Aen.* 4.646 (Dido); see Due 1974: 39–40 and Bömer 1959: 281–2. Virgil's description of the Sibyl in the *Aen.* is the *locus classicus* of the divine *furor* of a *uates*: 6.46–51 (50–1 *adflata est numine quando | iam propiore dei*), 77–82, 98–102 (102 *ut primum cessit furor*), 262 *furens.* Virgil is imitated by Ovid more closely at 2.640–1 (Ocyroe) *ergo ubi uaticinos concepit mente furores | incaluitque deo, quem clausum pectore habebat.* The suggestion in *deo . . . recepto* is that although Apollo failed to seduce the Sibyl, he is still able to possess her in this way; cf. Apollo on the fate of Daphne at 1.557–8 '*at quoniam coniunx mea non potes esse, | arbor eris certe' dixit 'mea'.*

108 magna . . . maxime: escalation through polyptoton; see Wills 1996: 236–8. Cf. 8.328 *maius opus magni certaminis urget, F.* 1.603–6, *Her.* 9.107–8, 17.153–6, Virg. *G.* 2.169–70, Sen. *Tro.* 427, Sil. 6.416–17. Cf. the opening of the Virgilian Sibyl's speech at *Aen.* 6.83–4 *o tandem* <u>*magnis*</u> *pelagi defuncte periclis | (sed terrae* <u>*grauiora*</u> *manent).* **uir factis maxime:** Aeneas is called *maximus heros* at *Aen.* 6.192, while at *Met.* 13.644–5 *heros | maxime* refers instead to Anchises. *factis* is abl. of respect with *maxime*, cf. 12.623 *non bello maior et aeuo*, Virg. *Aen.* 1.544–5 *Aeneas . . . quo iustior alter | nec pietate fuit, nec bello maior et armis*, 2.339–40 *maximus armis | Epytus.* The tone is elevated, as is much of the Sibyl's direct speech (see Bömer on 14.130).

109 'whose right hand has been proved by sword, whose sense of duty by fire'; *spectata* 'proven' (*OLD spectare* 6) is taken ἀπὸ κοινοῦ ('in common') with *dextera* and *pietas*; see Kenney 2002: 73. Cf. *F.* 4.37–8 *hinc satus Aeneas: pietas spectata per ignes | sacra patremque umeris, altera sacra, tulit*, *Met.* 5.243 (of Perseus) *iuuenis uirtus per tot spectata labores*, 13.384–5 (Ajax) *qui ferrumque ignesque Iouemque | sustinuit totiens.* The line recalls a number of passages in the *Aen.*: 4.597–9 *en* <u>*dextra fidesque,*</u> *| quem secum patrios aiunt portare penates, | quem subiisse umeris confectum aetate parentum*, 6.403 *Troius Aeneas,* <u>*pietate insignis et armis,*</u> 6.687–8 *tuaque ex*<u>*spectata*</u> *parenti | uicit iter durum* <u>*pietas*</u> (this reference owed to Tony Woodman). While *pietas* is the essential characteristic of Aeneas in the *Aeneid* (cf. *Aen.* 1.10 *insignem pietate uirum*, see Austin on *Aen.* 2.708, 4.393), Ovid refers here to Aeneas' most famous display of *pietas* in his rescue of his father and the Trojan Penates from burning Troy in *Aen.* 2 (632–3 *ducente deo flammam inter et hostis | expedior: dant tela locum flammaeque recedunt*); cf. *Aen.* 6.110–11 *illum ego per flammas et mille sequentia tela | eripui his umeris medioque ex hoste recepi, Met.* 13.623–5, 15.441–2; see Austin on *Aen.* 2.708, *LIMC* I 1.386–90, 2.300–6. The statue of Aeneas in Augustus' portrait gallery of Roman heroes in the NW portico of the Temple of Mars Ultor in the Forum of Augustus included Anchises and Iulus: see *F.* 5.563 *hinc uidet Aenean oneratum pondere caro, LTUR* II.289–95; reconstructions in Fusco 2000, Zanker 1968; cf. 772–851n., 609–21n.

111–12 Elysias . . . cognosces: reminiscent of the Sibyl's words to Aeneas at *Aen.* 6.154 *sic demum lucos Stygis et regna inuia uiuis | aspicies* (see Baldo 1995: 84). **Elysiasque domos:** whereas Hom. *Od.* 4.561ff. and Hes. *Op.* 170ff. had located Elysium at the boundaries of Earth, Virgil conceived of this paradise for the virtuous as a special region of the Underworld (see Austin on *Aen.* 6.637–78). Cf. on Elysium *Met.* 11.62 *arua piorum, Aen.* 6.705 *domos placidas.* **regna nouissima mundi** 'the last realm of the world', i.e. the Underworld, last (*OLD nouissimus* 2 or perhaps 6) of the three divisions of the cosmos assigned to Jupiter (heaven), Neptune (sea), and Pluto (Underworld). *regna* is poetic pl. The division of the cosmos between the three sons of Kronos goes back to Hom. *Il.* 15.187–92. Cf. 5.368 [Pluto] *cui triplicis cessit fortuna nouissima regni,* 14.590 *inamabile regnum,* 15.859 *mundi regna triformis, F.* 4.584 *nupta Iouis fratri tertia regna tenet.* **simulacraque cara parentis** 'the ghost of your dear father'; *cara* is a 'transferred epithet' (enallage) in that it agrees grammatically with *simulacra* but in sense it refers to *parentis. simulacra* is poetic pl. Ovid transfers to his Sibyl part of Aeneas' plea to the Sibyl at *Aen.* 6.108–9 *ire ad conspectum cari genitoris et ora | contingat.*

113 inuia uirtuti nulla est uia: a clever *sententia* with wordplay and alliteration. The Sibyl quotes Helenus from Virg. *Aen.* 3.383 *longa procul longis uia diuidit inuia terris* (Wills 1996: 455). Ovid also responds to the Sibyl's description of the difficulty of Aeneas' task of entering the Underworld at *Aen.* 6.154–5 *regna inuia uiuis | aspicies* and her similar claim at *Aen.* 6.129–31: *pauci, quos aequus amauit | Iuppiter aut ardens euexit ad aethera uirtus, | dis geniti potuere.* **uirtuti:** see 581n. on *Aeneia uirtus.*

113–14 auro | fulgentem ramum: the Golden Bough; Ovid's diction is again indebted to Virgil, *Aen.* 6.204 *discolor unde auri per ramos aura refulsit.* At *Aen.* 6.136–48 the Sibyl warns Aeneas that before he is allowed to enter the Underworld he must first obtain the Golden Bough, a sacred talisman demanded as a gift by Proserpina, which can be picked only by those called by destiny (146–8, see Austin on *Aen.* 6.138f.). Aeneas is led by Venus' doves to the Golden Bough and removes it with some effort (6.190–211); it is shown to Charon in order to gain entrance to the Underworld (6.405–10) and later is set at Proserpina's door (6.636). Ovid downplays the difficulty of Aeneas' task throughout the passage, removing the Virgilian air of solemnity surrounding Aeneas' feat, and reserving his emphasis for the Sibyl herself (see Galinsky 1975: 224). A humorous allusion to Virgil's Golden Bough has been detected in Midas' transformation of a branch to gold at 11.109 *ilice detraxit uirgam: uirga aurea facta est* (see Curran 1972: 83).

114–15 The description abridges Virgil's more evocative lines at *Aen.* 6.136–8 *latet arbore opaca | aureus et foliis et lento uimine ramus, | Iunoni Infernae dictus sacer; hunc tegit omnis | lucus.* **Iunonis Auernae:** epic periphrasis for Proserpina, a variation on Virgil's *Iunoni Infernae*: cf. Sil. *Pun.* 13.601 *Iunonis Auernae,* Stat. *Silv.* 2.1.147 *infera Iuno* (see Van Dam ad loc. on the popularity of such paraphrases in Flavian poetry); so Hades is called at *F.* 5.448 *Stygii . . . Iouis* (=*Aen.* 4.638 *Ioui Stygio*). The story of Hades' rape of Proserpina is told by Ovid at 5.341–661 and *F.* 4.420–620.

115 diuellere: cf. of the golden bough *Aen.* 6.143 *auolso,* 148 *nec duro poteris conuellere ferro.*

116–19 In another four-line summary, Ovid condenses Aeneas' visit to the Underworld in *Aen.* 6.262–898. In Virgil's catabasis numerous regions of the Underworld are described, characters from Aeneas' past are met (Palinurus, Dido, Deiphobus, Anchises) and, most importantly, Aeneas is given a vision of his future Roman descendants and a pageant of Roman history down to the time of Augustus. Other passages in Roman literature where the Sibyl delivers prophecies about Rome include Tib. 2.5.39–66, Prop. 4.1.53–4, Stat. *Silv.* 4.3.114–63. Ovid gives a fuller description of the Underworld at 4.432–63, in which he also draws heavily on Virgil's scene (see Bernbeck 1967: 11–24), and cf. 11.592–615 (House of Sleep), 12. 39–63 (House of Fame).

116–17 formidabilis: evidently an Ovidian invention, elsewhere only at 2.174, 857 and later at e.g. Stat. *Theb.* 4.473, 9.544, Sen. *Ep.* 104.25; cf. *Aen.* 6.290–1 (Aeneas' reaction to the monsters at the entrance to the Underworld) *corripit hic subita trepidus formidine ferrum | Aeneas.* Ovid follows Virgil in his frequent use of adjs. in *-bilis* at the fifth foot (Murphy on 2.145), cf. 225, 406, 590, 748. The pentasyllabic word creates a ponderous and portentous four-word hexameter (*et* is proclitic), cf. 87, 161, 211, 249; on such lines (frequent in Ovid, rarer in Virgil), see Courtney on Cinna fr.1.2 *FLP* pp. 214–15, Mayer on Lucan 8.407, Dewar on Stat. *Theb.* 9.146, Winbolt 1903: 227–8, Basset 1919. **Orci | . . . opes** 'the realm of Orcus'. *Orcus* (only here in Ovid) refers to the ruler of the Underworld and often the Underworld itself; cf. *Aen.* 6.273 *uestibulum ante ipsum primisque in faucibus Orci.* There may be word play here with *opes,* hinting at the etymological association of another name for Hades, *Dis,* with *diues* (Cic. *ND* 2.66 *Diti patri . . . , qui diues, ut apud Graecos* Πλούτων), see Bömer ad loc., Solodow 1988: 149; cf. Courtney on *FLP* p. 48 ('epitaph of Naevius') *Orci . . . thesauro,* Jocelyn on Enn. *Trag.* 192, [Tib.] 3.3.8 *diues . . . Orcus.* **atauosque suos:** Aeneas sees his ancestors (cf. *Aen.* 6.648 *genus antiquum Teucri*), but Ovid omits the corresponding (much longer) vision of Aeneas' descendants given in the *Aeneid* at 6.756–846: (756–7) *Nunc age, Dardaniam prolem quae deinde sequatur | gloria, qui maneant Itala de gente nepotes*; see Stitz 1962: 78. For Aeneas' ancestry (Dardanus, Erichthonius, Tros, Assaracus, Capys, Anchises), see *F.* 4.31–8, *Aen.* 6.648–50, 8.134–5, and Hom. *Il.* 20.213–41. **umbramque**

senilem: enallage: *senilem* refers to *Anchisae* (the adjs. are shared between the two nouns when one noun is already qualified).

118 magnanimi: the epithet belongs to high epic style (based on the Homeric epithet μεγάθυμος or μεγάλας φρένας; perhaps Ennian, see Norden on *Aen.* 6.305, Skutsch 1985: 784) and in the *Aeneid* (12x) is used most often of Aeneas (e.g. 1.260, 5.17, 407 *Anchisiades*), but never of Anchises. Ovid makes a similar surprising use of a Virgilian epithet at 13.640 *pius Anchises* (see Hopkinson ad loc.) and 644 (see 108n.). The moving scene of Aeneas' reunion with his dead father is related at *Aen.* 6.679–702. **iura locorum:** a reference to Anchises' long and complex account of the cycle of the rebirth of human souls (metempsychosis), leading to philosophical eschatology, in *Aen.* 6.703 -51 (see Hardie 1986: 66–83). Cf. Sen. *HF* 660–1 (also of the Underworld) *iura abdita* | *et operta terris.*

119 quaeque . . . essent adeunda 'what dangers would have to be met' sc. by the Trojans; indirect question introduced by *didicit.* **nouis . . . bellis** 'in new wars' (locatival abl.). At the end of his long speech to Aeneas about the Roman future, Anchises warns him in similar phraseology of the upcoming wars in Italy, which will form the subject of the second half of the *Aeneid*: *Aen.* 6.890–2 *exin bella uiro memorat quae deinde gerenda,* | *Laurentisque docet populos urbemque Latini,* | *et quo quemque modo fugiatque feratque laborem.*

120–1 These lines effect a transition to the following story of the Sibyl and Apollo. At *Aen.* 6.897–901 Anchises sends Aeneas and the Sibyl to the world above by the ivory gate of false dreams: *his ubi tum natum Anchises unaque Sibyllam* | *prosequitur dictis portaque emittit eburna* (897–8). Despite the Sibyl's earlier warnings (*Aen.* 6.126–9, see 121n.), we hear nothing more about the upward trip in Virgil. Upon emerging from the Underworld, Aeneas immediately returns to his ships and moves on from Cumae to the coast of Caieta (see below 157n.). Although he perhaps takes a hint from Virgil's *prosequitur dictis,* Ovid cleverly takes advantage of this temporal and textual gap in Virgil's narrative as an opportunity for the insertion of his own story, thus reversing the focus of the Virgilian episode by expanding on Aeneas' return from, rather than his entrance to the Underworld (see 121–2, 123–8nn.). **inde** 'from there'. **aduerso tramite** 'on the uphill path back' (*OLD aduersus*[1] 6); cf. 154 *conuexum per iter,* and the similar lines on Orpheus' exit from the Underworld at 10.53–4 *carpitur adcliuis per muta silentia trames,* | *arduus, obscurus, caligine densus opaca* (during which he must, in contrast to Aeneas, keep completely silent (10.53 *per muta silentia*)). **cum duce Cumaea:** cf. 135 *uirgo Cumaea*; for *dux* of the Sibyl, cf. 112, *Aen.* 6.253. **mollit sermone laborem:** Ovid exploits in his typically humorous literal manner the Sibyl's claim at *Aen.* 6.126–9 that Aeneas' greatest task will be to win his way back out of the Underworld: *facilis descensus Auerno:* | *noctes atque dies patet atri ianua Ditis;* | *sed reuocare gradum superasque euadere ad auras,* | *hoc opus, hic labor est.* Cf. Sen. *HF* 675–8 *nec ire labor est; ipsa deducit uia:* | . . . *gradumque retro flectere haud umquam sinunt* | *umbrae tenaces.* Virgil's Aeneas had found it in fact much easier to get out of the

Underworld than to descend into it and Ovid perhaps implicitly 'corrects' Virgil's seemingly effortless anabasis at the end of *Aen.* 6. On Aeneas' *labor*, cf. *Aen.* 6.103–4.

122 iter horrendum . . . carpit 'he picks his way along the terrifying path' (*OLD carpo* 8, cf. 2.549, 10.709). This sombre description contrasts with the lighter tone introduced by the previous line and recalls the Sibyl's words to Aeneas upon their arrival at Elysium at *Aen.* 6.629 *sed iam age, carpe uiam* (see Austin ad loc.). *horrendus* is also used of the Virgilian Underworld at *Aen.* 6.298, 327. **per opaca crepuscula** 'through the dark gloom': *crepuscula* is poetic pl. and here signifies the spooky dusk of the Underworld; cf. 11.596 (the cave of Somnus), and see Varro's definition of *crepusculum* (a rare word earlier only in Plautus, see Varro *LL* 7.77) at *LL* 6.5: *crepusculum significat dubium; ab eo res dictae dubiae creperae, quod crepusculum dies etiam nunc sit an iam nox multis dubium.* The line alludes again to Virgil's description at *Aen.* 6.268–9 *ibant obscuri sola sub nocte per umbram | perque domos Ditis* and 270 *per incertam lunam sub luce maligna.*

123–8 Aeneas thanks the Sibyl for her guidance and pledges future worship. Ovid bases these vows on the promises Aeneas makes in his supplication of the Sibyl to allow him *into* the Underworld at *Aen.* 6.69–74. There he vows a temple to Apollo and Hecate, festal days for Apollo, and a shrine for the Sibyl's prophecies. Ovid's exclusive focus on the Sibyl removes the Virgilian references to contemporary events and institutions, namely Augustus' dedication of temples to Apollo at Actium and on the Palatine, the *ludi Apollinares*, and the removal of the Sibylline oracles to the Apollo temple on the Palatine (see Austin on *Aen.* 6.71). In the light of the Sibyl's story, praise of Apollo would be out of place here.

123 dea . . . praesens 'goddess in the flesh' (*OLD praesens* 3); *praesens* is the standard term for the helping presence of a god (N-H on Hor. *C.* 1.35.2), cf. *Aen.* 9.404 (Nisus to Diana–Luna) *tu, dea, tu praesens nostro succurre labori.* In the *Aeneid* Aeneas addresses the Sibyl as *'tuque, o sanctissima uates | praescia uenturi'* (6.65–6). Ovid seems to draw here and in the Sibyl's response (130n.) on Aeneas' address to Venus when she is in disguise as a maiden huntress at *Aen.* 1.327–8 *'o quam te memorem, uirgo? namque haud tibi uultus | mortalis, nec uox hominem sonat; o, dea certe'*, lines which are in turn based on Odysseus' addresses to Nausicaa at *Od.* 6.149–69, and 8.461–9 (see Ellsworth 1988: 338–9). Cf. 4.320–2 (Salmacis to Hermaphroditus) *puer o dignissime credi | esse deus es, siue tu deus est, . . . | siue es mortalis.* **dis gratissima:** cf. *F.* 1.585 (Carmentis) *felix uates, ut dis gratissima uixit.*

124 numinis instar eris semper mihi: the promise of divine honours to a benefactor goes back to Homer (e.g. *Od.* 8.467–8 Odysseus to Nausicaa 'so will I pray to you there as a god for all my days; for you, girl, saved me'), cf. Lucretius' eulogy of Epicurus at 5.8 *deus ille fuit, deus, inclute Memmi*, Virg. *Ecl.* 1.6–7 *o Meliboee, deus nobis haec otia fecit. | namque erit ille mihi semper deus.* See Nock 1972: 145 on the qualification of *mihi*, with examples. The equation of a beloved to a god is also an erotic topos, e. g. *Am.* 3.11.47 *perque tuam faciem, magni mihi numinis instar*, *F.* 2.842 (Brutus to Lucretia) *perque tuos manes, qui mihi numen erunt.*

125 muneris esse tui 'exist by your favour', i.e. 'owe my life to you'; for the expression, cf. *Am.* 2.13.22, *Tr.* 1.6.6 *si quid adhuc ego sum, muneris omne tui est* (based on Hor. *C.* 4.3.21–4), Tac. *Ann.* 15.52.3.

125–6 In these lines Ovid is picking up some of Virgil's language from *Aen.* 6.534 *ut tristis sine sole domos, loca turbida, adires?*, 128–9 *sed reuocare gradum superasque euadere ad auras,* | *hoc opus, hic labor est.* **quae . . . | quae** 'who allowed me to approach the regions of death, and to escape them after I looked upon them'; repetition (anaphora) with variation in the lines for emphasis. *uoluisti* (*OLD uolo*[1] 13b) is to be taken with both infinitives, which are chiastically arranged at the ends of both lines with *mortis.*

127 'in return for these services, when I have been conveyed to the upper air'. The variant *uiuenti* for *meritis*, which has MS support (*M*), seems to contradict Aeneas' claims for the Sibyl's immortality at 123, yet could be understood to contain a compliment to the Sibyl, as most heroes at that dramatic date had to wait for a temple until after their death (cf. *numinis instar*). But cf. *Pont.* 4.5.39 *pro quibus ut meritis referatur gratia.*

128 Cf. Aeneas' vows to Apollo at *Aen.* 6.69–70 *Phoebo et Triuiae solido de marmore templum* | *instituam,* and to the Sibyl at 71–4 *te quoque magna manent regnis penetralia nostris:* | *hic ego namque tuas sortis arcanaque fata* | *dicta meae genti ponam, lectosque sacrabo,* | *alma, uiros.* A carefully crafted line imparting solemnity: it is framed by the two nouns, with the verbs (placed on either side of the main caesura), objects, and indirect objects arranged chiastically, and is heavily alliterative. **tibī́ . . . tibĭ́:** so-called 'prosodic variation', where the same word is scanned differently in a short space, was a popular figure in Hellenistic and Latin poetry (see Hopkinson 1982 and on 13.100, Wills 1996: 461–9); here the final syllable of the first *tibi* is scanned long (as it originally was), of the second, short (the law of iambic shortening made this the commoner pronunciation).

129–53 *Apollo and the Sibyl.* The Sibyl narrates the story of Apollo's earlier passion for her, which led to her present situation through her disastrous request for longevity. As in the first erotic tale in the poem, that of Daphne and Apollo (1.452–567), Apollo's last suit is unsuccessful. The story is not attested before Ovid and may have been invented by him on the analogy of other similar myths, especially that of Apollo and the prophetess Cassandra, who, having been granted the gift of prophecy, was punished for rejecting Apollo by forever being disbelieved (Aesch. *Ag.* 1202–12), and the myth of Aurora and her mortal lover Tithonus, who was also granted immortality without eternal youth and wasted away with age (*Hom. Hymn* 5.218–38). Only Servius on *Aen.* 6.321 preserves a similar version of the Sibyl's tale. In a move typical of his treatment of the Virgilian and Homeric poems in this whole section, Ovid goes back in time to a pre-*Aeneid* period to explain the Sibyl's presence as a prophetess in the *Aeneid* (cf. Scylla's metamorphosis and Polyphemus in love at 13.740–897).

The Sibyl was not always regarded as inspired by Apollo; other versions make the gift of prophecy her own and in one version she is shot down by an envious Apollo (Phlegon, *FGH* 257 F 37). The Sibyl's association with Apollo was reinforced by Augustus when he transferred the Sibylline oracles from the temple of Capitoline Jupiter to that of Palatine Apollo (dedicated in 28 BCE, Suet. *Aug.* 31.1), and was adopted by Virgil and Tibullus (2.5); see Parke 1988: 77–8, Potter 1994: 82–3. The suggestion that the Sibyl's long career is a result of her rejection of Apollo's sexual advances may thus strike an odd note (see Lundström 1980: 59–61), although the tale forms a parallel with the laurel trees positioned at Augustus' doors, which derive from Daphne (1.562–3), another victim of Apollo's failed seduction.

129 suspiratibus: *suspiratus* is a hapax legomenon for the more usual *suspirium*; cf. the prophetess Ocyroe 2.655–6 *suspirat ab imis* | *pectoribus*, and Aeneas' response to the disguised Venus at *Aen.* 1.370–1 *quaerenti talibus ille* | *suspirans imoque trahens e pectore uocem.* On Ovid's formation of fourth decl. abstract nouns see Kenney 2002: 69.

130–1 nec sacri turis honore | humanum dignare caput: cf. the similar answer the disguised Venus delivers to Aeneas at *Aen.* 1.334 *haud equidem tali me dignor honore.* Here, however, the Sibyl's rejection of divine honours for a human sounds a potentially odd note in a book full of apotheoses. **nec . . . | . . . dignare:** imperative. **neu nescius erres** 'and so that you do not err out of ignorance', final subj. (*neu* = *et, ne,* cf. 32n.). As Hardie (forthcoming) observes, these words encapsulate much of Aeneas' experience in the *Aeneid*: see e.g. *Aen.* 4.71–2 *pastor . . . nescius,* 8.730 *rerumque ignarus,* 1.755 *erroresque tuos.*

132 lux aeterna 'eternal life' (*OLD lux* 6a). **dabatur** 'was offered', imperfect indicative in the apodosis of an 'unreal' condition (*NLS* §200).

133 si . . . patuisset amanti 'had my virginity been open to Phoebus' passion'; the Sibyl's words report in *oratio obliqua* (secondary sequence) Apollo's stipulation (where the verb (*pateo*) in *oratio recta* would be the future perfect indic.), cf. 140–1.

134 dum tamen hanc sperat: cf. Apollo's desire for Daphne 1.490 *quodque cupit, sperat.* **praecorrumpere:** the verb appears elsewhere only at 9.295 (on *prae-* compounds in Ovid, see 55n.). *corrumpo* is used frequently with reference to erotic seduction of women (*OLD* 5b), with the suggestion of bribery (*OLD* 5a), cf. *Am.* 2.4.35, 3.8.30, *AA* 1.714 *F.* 2.765, Prop. 2.32.58, *TLL* IV 1056.35ff. The prefix here perhaps emphasizes the difference between Apollo's attitude before and after his unsuccessful suit. **donis:** gift-giving is another topos of amatory persuasion, cf. 13.839 *iam, Galatea, ueni, nec munera despice nostra,* 7.739–40, *AA* 1.453 *hoc opus, hic labor est, primo sine munere iungi,* 3.654 *placatur donis Iuppiter ipse datis.*

135–9 For the theme of the 'Binding Promise and Foolish Wish', cf. 3.289 (Jupiter to Semele) *cui deus 'elige' ait 'nullam patiere repulsam',* 2.43–5 (Phaethon), 11.100–5 (Midas); see Kenney 1986: 438.

135 uirgo: although the Sibyl is often called *uirgo* in the *Aen.* (3.445, 6.45, 104, 318, 560), the word here has special force in the context of the choice the Sibyl is given (cf. 133 *uirginitas,* 142n.).

135–6 optes: | optatis: polyptoton (for the type, see 44n.) for emphasis.

136–7 pulueris hausti | ostendens cumulum 'showing him a pile of dust I had scooped up'. Ovid tweaks the topos of dust and sand as proverbially innumerable by giving the precise number of one thousand (cf. 11.614–15, Hom. *Il.* 9.385, Catull. 7.3–6, 61.199–201, see McCartney 1960: 81). **corpora** 'particles' (*OLD* 12, *TLL* IV 1024.43–4), cf. *Tr.* 1.5.47–8 *tot mala sum passus, quot in aethere lucent | paruaque quot siccus corpora puluis habet.*

138 contingere . . . rogaui: *rogare* with the infin. is rare, cf. *AA* 1.433, *Her.* 6.144, Catull. 35.10. **uana** 'fool that I was', in effect adverbial.

139 excidit, ut peterem 'I forgot to ask', an unusual construction with *ut* + consecutive subj.; with this meaning the infin. is usual with *excido* (*OLD excido*[1] 9b; cf. *TLL* V 2.1239.79–81 (citing only this passage)). The Sibyl remembered perhaps too late the myth of Tithonus and Aurora (Eos). Aurora asked Zeus that her mortal lover Tithonus be granted immortality, but she forgot to request eternal youth for him as well (*Hom. Hymn* 5. 223–4), cf. 9.421–2, *Am.* 1.13.35–8. **iuuenes . . . annos** 'years of youth', i.e. 'that my years should be youthful', *iuuenes* has an emphatic and predicative force, cf. 7.295, and contrast 9.421–2 (Aurora complains of Tithonus' decrepitude) *queritur ueteres Pallantias annos | coniugis esse sui.* **protinus** 'forthwith' (*OLD* 3), suggesting simultaneity.

140–2 Apollo renews his proposition of the Sibyl, offering now to correct her flawed wish. **hos . . . dabat** 'these he would have given me', see 132n. **aeternamque iuuentam** 'eternal youth', an improved form of the *lux aeterna* above at 132. **Venerem:** a common metonym for sex, cf. *Rem.* 357, *Am.* 1.10.33, *F.* 4.657 *usus . . . Veneris*, etc.; see Adams 1982: 189, Quint. *Inst.* 8.6.24 *et 'Venerem' quam 'coitum' dixisse magis decet.* **paterer:** imp. subj. in historic *oratio obliqua* (representing the original *patiere*); cf. 133n. For *patior* used as a sexual term, see *OLD* 2c, Adams 1982: 189–90. **innuba permaneo:** on the Sibyl's virginity, cf. Tib. 2.5.64 '*aeternum sit mihi uirginitas*', and compare also Daphne's plea to her father at 1.486–7 '*da mihi perpetua . . . | uirginitate frui*'. Sibyls were uniformly considered women who remained virgins. *innuba* is attested before Ovid only at Varro, *Men.* 44; cf. 10.92 *innuba laurus*, 567 (Atalanta), Sen. *Ag.* 314, Luc. 9.665 (*TLL* VII 1.1722.50–73).

142–54 The Sibyl laments the effects of old age (which constitutes the metamorphosis of the episode) with an oddly misplaced vanity. It is an erotic topos, for which see *AA* 2.113–20, Prop. 3.24, Galinsky 1975: 229, Stitz 1962: 71, Murgatroyd on Tib. 1.4.27.

143 terga dedit 'has taken flight', for the phrase (a military metaphor) see Bömer on 7.73; for the topos of fleeing youth, cf. Hor. *C.* 2.11.5–6 *fugit retro | leuis iuuentus et decor*, N-H on Hor. *C.* 2.5.13.

144–6 For the Sibyl's age of a thousand years Ovid is probably following a Greek source (Plut. *Mor.* 397A (Heraclitus), Parke 1988: 20 n.15, Potter 1990: 116). At *Aen.*

6.748 one thousand years is given as the period of time before the rebirth of human souls (see Austin ad loc. for the Platonic and Orphic associations); see 148n.

144–45 mihi saecula septem | acta uides 'you see in me a woman seven hundred years old'. Instead of *uides* Clausen 1963: 416–17 conjectured *tamen*, to be taken with *superest*, supposing *tn* (a scribal abbreviation of *tamen*) to have been lost after *–ta*, but *uides* imparts an immediacy ('what you are looking at [believe it or not] . . . ') which seems right.

145–6 superest, numeros ut pulueris aequem, | . . . uidere, 'in order to equal the numbers of (the grains of, *OLD numerus* 1a) dust, it remains for me to see . . . '. For a similar manner of temporal reckoning, see *F.* 3.557–8 *tertia nudandas acceperat area messes,| inque cauos ierant tertia musta lacus: | pellitur Anna domo.* The heavily spondaic line 146 underlines the slow passage of time for the Sibyl. **centúm . . . céntum:** repetition of word with varying metrical ictus, cf. 128, 153, 308–10, etc. (see Bömer on 15.856).

147 tempus erit, cum: the Sibyl prophesies her own future, cf. *F.* 1.529 (Carmentis) *tempus erit cum . . .*, *Med. Fac.* 47 *tempus erit, quo uos speculum uidisse pigebit*, *AA* 3.69 *tempus erit, quo tu, quae nunc excludis amantes, | frigida deserta nocte iacebis anus.*

148 longa dies 'a long length of time'; *dies* is regularly fem. when used of time in general (*OLD* 10), cf. 1.346, *Tr.* 1.5.14, 4.6.38, *Pont.* 4.11.19 *cum longa dies sedauit uulnera mentis*, Sen. *Ben.* 4.32.4. Virgil uses the expression at *Aen.* 6.745–7 to define the same cycle of time (748 *mille . . . per annos*, cf. above 144–6n.), needed for the soul's purification: *donec longa dies perfecto temporis orbe | concretam exemit labem, purumque relinquit | aetherium sensum atque aurai simplicis ignem*; after which time, the souls *incipiant in corpora uelle reuerti* (751). The contrast with the Sibyl's fate is clear and critics have observed the marked difference in the tone of the two passages; see Solodow 1988:150, Baldo 1995: 87–8.

148–9 consumptaque . . . | . . . onus 'and my limbs consumed by old age will be reduced to the very lightest weight'; pathetic repetition with variation and amplification of *paruam . . . minimum* for effect. **senecta:** metrically convenient variation, cf. 143 *senectus.* **nec amata uidebor:** the Sibyl's complaints here take on a distinctly elegiac (and erotic) tone as she laments the loss of the beauty which had attracted Apollo's (previously unwanted) advances. Aurora was no longer attracted to Tithonus once he showed signs of aging, see 9.421–2, *Am.* 1.13.37–8 *illum dum refugis, longo quia grandior aeuo, | surgis ad inuisas a sene mane rotas*, *Hom. Hymn* 5.225–30. At 9.424–5 Venus worries about Anchises' aging.

150–1 forsitan . . . | . . . cognoscet: Ovid less often uses the indicative rather than the subj. with *forsitan;* in the *Met.* only here and at 10.467, cf. *Am.* 1.6.45, *F.* 2.97, *Her.* 2.14 (with Knox).

152–3 The Sibyl is to share the fate of Echo (3.397–401) and Tithonus (*Hom. Hymn* 5.231–38); cf. Serv. on *Aen.* 6.321 *defecta corporis uiribus uitam in sola uoce retinuit.* Tarrant brackets these lines as interpolations providing the missing metamorphosis (*mutata*): cf. the similar (more certainly) spurious lines at 3.400–1 (Echo). But there are both stylistic and contextual arguments for retaining them. In a divergent tradition, the Sibyl's bones were said to be preserved in an urn in the sanctuary of Apollo at Cumae (Paus. 10.12.8) and Parke conjectures that this object may have inspired the tale related by Petronius about the Sibyl, her voice remaining, hanging in a bottle wishing to die (48.8 *in ampulla pendere*); see Parke 1988: 41, Courtney 2001: 97. However, it is the Sibyl's voice that Virgil emphasizes on her first appearance at *Aen.* 6.43–4 *ostia centum, | unde ruunt totidem uoces, responsa Sibyllae.* The entirely different fate of the prophetess Ocyroe at 2.657–8 *'praeuertunt' inquit 'me fata uetorque | plura loqui uocisque meae praecluditur usus'* (see Keith 1992: 81–4) seems to form an important contrast with the Sibyl. The Sirens keep their human voices at 5.563 *uox humana remansit,* as, of course, does Echo at 3.398–9 *uox tamen atque ossa supersunt: | uox manet,* where her invisibility admittedly has more point. Versions of the story of Tithonus also lay emphasis on the retention of his voice in his old age as a cicada (Call. *Ait.* 1 fr. 1.29–36 Mass./Pf., cf. Theocr. *Id.* 7.139); on the poetic and programmatic motif see Crane 1986, King, 1986: 21–3, Forbes-Irving 1990: 318–19. Thematically in book 14 the Sibyl's fate forms a contrast to those of the Cercopians (90–100), Diomedes' men (494–507), and the Apulian shepherd (512–26), whose loss of human voice is stressed. Critics have also observed that the lines recall Ovid's own claims for immortality at 15.875–6 *parte tamen meliore mei super alta perennis | astra ferar, nomenque erit indelibile nostrum* (Ellsworth 1988a: 53). **usque adeo mutata ferar** 'to such an extent shall I be said to have changed'; cf. Catull. 67.7 *dic agedum nobis, quare <u>mutata feraris</u> | in dominum ueterem deseruisse fidem.* **ferar . . . | . . . fata:** 'Ovid here situates *fata* in a context in which the etymological relationship between *fata* and *fari* is emphasized' (Keith 1992: 83, see *LALE* s.v. *fatum*). Murgatroyd on Tib. 2.5.16 (*fata canit*) discusses the same etymology and suggests an allusion to *Libri Fatales*, an alternative title for the Sibylline books, cf. *F.* 4.257 *carminis Euboici fatalia uerba, TLL* VI 332.78–80. **nullique uidenda** 'though visible to no one'; *nulli* is dat. of agent. For the gerundive, cf. 15.844 *constitit alma Venus nulli cernenda,* 13.947 (with Hopkinson), Bömer on 12.251. **uóce . . . uocém:** the shift of the metrical ictus emphasizes the repetition (polyptoton) at the beginning of each half of the hexameter (cf. 146n.), which serves a closural function.

154 talia . . . memorante Sibylla: epic formula, cf. Enn. *Ann.* 35 Sk. *talia tum memorat lacrimans, Aen.* 2.650 *talia perstabat memorans,* 6.699 *sic memorans largo fletu, Met.* 7.863, 8.396, 10.209; see Döpp 1968: 109. **conuexum per iter** 'on the arched path'; cf. 6.697 *conuexa foramina terrae.*

155 Euboicam . . . in urbem: i.e. Cumae; *Euboicus* (cf. 4n.) is applied by Virgil to the Euboean colony of Cumae at *Aen.* 6.2 *Euboicis Cumarum . . . oris,* 42, 9.710; cf. *F.* 4.257 (of the Sibylline books) *carminis Euboici fatalia uerba.* Cumae, the earliest Greek colony in Italy, was founded from Chalcis in Euboea in about 750–730 BCE, making the references in Virgil and Ovid anachronistic; see Frederiksen 1984: 52–84.

156 Troius Aeneas = *Aen.*1.596, 6.403, 7.221 (in the same metrical position always). **sacrisque . . . litatis** 'after making holy offerings'; the transitive use of the ritual term *litare* is modelled on *Aen.* 4.50 *sacrisque litatis indulge hospitio* (*TLL* VII 2.1512.55–69). Ovid limits the use of *litare* to Roman contexts, as here; cf. 15.794, *F.* 4.630. The Trojans perform sacrifices to Apollo and Trivia before arriving at the entrance of the Sibyl's cave at *Aen.* 6.38–41, but the line recalls Aeneas' performance of rites for Caieta at 7.5 *at pius exsequiis Aeneas rite solutis.*

157 'he approached the shores which did not yet have the name of his nurse'. In the final lines of *Aen.* 6 Aeneas' fleet lands at Caieta (mod. Gaeta): 900–1 *tum se ad Caietae recto fert litore portum.* | *ancora de prora iacitur; stant litore puppes.* In a tone of mock-pedantry Ovid corrects with *nondum* and the 'gloss' on Caieta Virgil's chronological 'mistake' of prematurely naming the port before explaining how it came to be so called (cf. Serv. on *Aen.* 6.900 *a persona poetae prolepsis: nam Caieta nondum dicebatur*), see Hinds 1998: 107–11. At the opening of *Aen.* 7.1–4 Virgil supplies the etymological explanation in the burial of Aeneas' old nurse there: *tu quoque litoribus nostris, Aeneia nutrix,* | *aeternam moriens famam, Caieta, dedisti;* | *et nunc seruat honos sedem tuus, ossaque nomen* | *Hesperia in magna, si qua est ea gloria, signat.* At 441–5 Ovid will give us the episode of Caieta's burial, thereby completing the narrative expectation set up here.

In the *Aeneid*, the Trojans reach Caieta at the end of book 6, bury Aeneas' nurse there at the opening of the next book (7.1–7), and, after passing by Circe's shores (8–24), arrive at the mouth of the Tiber (25–36). In the *Metamorphoses*, the almost three hundred line interpolation between the two Caieta passages creates a gap between the two halves of the *Aeneid* (Hinds 1998: 110–11); thus *nondum* also serves as a cue for Ovid's own narrative deferral of her burial and his treatment of the second half of the *Aeneid.* For Ovid's frequent use of *nondum* and similar expressions throughout the poem to create aetiological and narratological anticipation within the time-sequence of the poem, cf. e.g. 789, 1.450 *(nondum laurus erat)*, 2.219 *nondum Oeagrius Haemus*, 7.232–3 *gramen* | *nondum mutato uulgatum corpore Glauci*, 8.372 *at gemini, nondum caelestia sidera, fratres*, 11.87–8 *non aureus illo* | *tempore*, *F.* 4.855 *tum iuuenem nondum facti fleuere Quirites*; see Solodow 1988: 63–4.

158–440 Achaemenides and Macareus

Upon their arrival in Italy at the site of Caieta the Trojans meet a character named Macareus, a shipmate of Ulysses who had stayed behind after the Greeks left Circe's island (435–40). He recognizes among the Trojan crew another Greek companion of Ulysses, Achaemenides, and the two exchange stories about their adventures, which constitute a retelling of events from *Odyssey* 9–10, with the inclusion as well of the first tale in the poem set in Italy, that of Picus and Canens. Ovid's episode is a reworking and duplication of Virgil's own famous 'remake-with-sequel' in *Aeneid* 3. 613–54 of Homer's Cyclops episode, which had been reported by Odysseus in *Odyssey* 9.105–564 (see Hinds 1998: 111). It is the one place in the *Aeneid* where a definite link is established between the concurrent travels of the Trojan and Greek heroes and Virgil directly reworks a Homeric scene, bringing his poem in spatial and temporal proximity to the *Odyssey* (Barchiesi 2001: 16). At the corresponding point in his narrative of the Trojans' journey, Ovid had replaced this scene with the story of Polyphemus and Galatea (13.740–897), where Polyphemus appears in his Theocritean form as a suitor of the nymph Galatea before the arrival of Ulysses. Ovid's long narrative delays (*nondum*) the Trojans' journey, returning only at 441 to Caieta and the continuation of Aeneas' voyage as recounted in *Aen.* 7. There is no metamorphosis in this section until the episode of Circe, which begins at 242; the point is rather the rewriting of Virgil and Homer.

In the third book of the *Aeneid*, immediately after their narrow escape from the dangers of Charybdis (554–69), the Trojans land again on the island of Sicily and meet the squalid and unfortunate Achaemenides at the foot of Aetna (570–95), where he had been inadvertently marooned three months earlier by Ulysses and his crew when they fled after blinding the Cyclops (on the chronological conflict between the *Aeneid* and *Odyssey* in this scene (Aeneas is only three months later than Ulysses, although Ulysses encountered the Cyclops early in his travels and Aeneas has been travelling almost seven years), see Williams on *Aen.* 3.588f., Horsfall on *Aen.* 3.645, Serv. *auct.* on *Aen.* 3.590). Achaemenides tells the Trojans of his encounter with the Cyclops and subsequent abandonment (*Aen.* 3.588–683). After hearing his sad tale, the Trojans take Achaemenides aboard, and narrowly escape when the giant Cyclopes suddenly reappear on the shore. Virgil's scene is a bold variation on Homer, where there is no mention of any companions left behind after Ulysses' escape (*Od.* 9.424–64, see Harrison 1986). As far as we know, the episode was not part of the Aeneas myth before Virgil (see Lloyd 1957); on Virgil's use of a number of Homeric and Apollonian sources for the episode, see Ramminger 1991 and Nelis 2001: 51–60.

In his sequel to Virgil's sequel Ovid shows Achaemenides at a later point in the voyage than in the *Aeneid*. He is already aboard the Trojan ships, and Ovid explicitly contrasts his appearance in this poem with his earlier appearance in the *Aeneid* (165–6nn.). Achaemenides retells (with variation) his version of the Cyclops episode that he had already offered in the *Aeneid*. Macareus, seemingly an Ovidian invention, then responds by continuing the highlights of Odysseus' voyage from Aeolus' abode to Circe's island (*Od.* 10.1–468), to which he appends an Italian tale (Picus, Circe, and Canens). Persistent reduplication in the episode (a second crewmate of Ulysses, Achaemenides' retelling of his Virgilian narrative, a second Homeric narrative, and the return of the Cyclops and Circe (the latter 2x)) underlines Ovid's imitation of his two epic models; see Stitz 1962: 80–7. Due 1974: 84, Ellsworth 1988, Döpp 1991: 338–9, Esposito 1994: 11–36, Baldo 1995: 120–41, Hinds 1998: 11–15, Andrae 2003: 198–207, Papaioannou 2005: 75–142.

158 quoque: Macareus (as well as Caieta); 'Wackernagel's law' (Wackernagel 1969: 86) is that unaccented particles (and pronouns) seek second place, even if this separates words which go together syntactically. Perhaps we are meant to hear an echo of the opening of *Aen.* 7.1 *tu quoque*, cf. *Met.* 14.221 *tu quoque*. **substiterat** 'had stayed behind' (*OLD subsisto* 5). Cf. 440n. on Macareus' presence at Caieta. **per taedia**

longa laborum 'out of weariness from his long labours' (through enallage); cf. 10.482 *taedia uitae*. The causal use of *per* (*NLS* §45, *OLD* 13), is more to the point than *post*, the reading of most of the main MSS, cf. 324 *per annos*.

159 Neritius Macareus: the epithet *Neritius* here serves as a synonym for 'Ithacan' and associates Macareus with Ulysses' contingent; cf. 563, 13.712 *Neritiasque domus, regnum fallacis Vlixis*, *F.* 4.69 (Ulysses) *dux* . . . *Neritius*. Neriton was a mountain on Ithaca in Homer (*Od.* 9.21–2), but Ovid follows Virgil in conceiving of it as a near-by island, cf. *Aen.* 3.271 *Neritos ardua saxis* (see Fantham on *F.* 4.69). The name Macareus does not appear in Homer and the pointed echo here of Virgil's description of Achaemenides at the beginning and end of the episode at *Aen.* 3.613 and 691, as *comes infelicis Vlixi* suggests that Ovid is underlining his own invention of the character on the Virgilian analogy (possibly with wordplay on Macareus (Greek μάκαρ 'happy') as the etymological antonym of Achaemenides (ἄχος 'pain, grief', see Hinds 1998: 112n.22) or of the replaced Virgilian epithet *infelix*). The same name appears earlier in the poem in association with different tales, at 6.124 *Macareida* . . . *Issen*, 12.452 (a Lapith) *Pelethronius Macareus*, and in *Her.* 11 (the incestuous affair between a Macareus and Canace, children of Aeolus); cf. *Am.* 2.18.23. **comes experientis Vlixei:** Ovid's variation of Virgil's *comes infelicis Vlixi* at *Aen.* 3.613 and 691 (see above). *Vlixis* (the reading here of most MSS) is the form of the gen. sing. preferred by Ovid (cf. 180, 671), while Virgil uses only *Vlixi* (see Leumann 1945); however, the testimony of Priscian (*G. L.* 2.277) suggests that here Ovid may have signalled his allusion to Virgil by using *Vlixei* (the old spelling of *Vlixi*): see Bömer ad loc. and on 13.304, Goold 1967: 121, and on the forms of *Vlixes*, see 71n. In Virgil's *Aeneid*, Ulysses is twice called *infelix* (3.613. 691), where the epithet is meant to underscore Ulysses' suffering. When repeated by Aeneas at the end of the episode (*Aen.* 3.691), it highlights the Trojans' magnanimity towards this former enemy (see Williams on Virg. *Aen.* 3.613) and, more broadly, an empathy and reconciliation between Trojans and Greeks based on a communality of suffering; see Kinsey 1979, Cairns 1989: 93, Putnam 1995: 63, Baldo 1986: 118. The epithet *experiens* removes the pathos of the Virgilian scene of rescue (which is now in the past); see Esposito 1994: 32–5. The sense of *experiens* seems to be 'enterprising', suggesting such well-known Homeric epithets for Ulysses as πολύτροπος 'much-travelled', or πολύτλας 'much enduring' (Bömer ad loc., McKeown on *Am.* 1.9.32, *TLL* v 2.1682.84–1683.3), cf. 1.414 *genus durum sumus experiensque laborum*, 671 *audacis*, *Pont.* 4.10.9 *animi nimium patientis Vlixes*, Hor. *Epod.* 17.16 *laboriosi* . . . *Vlixei*, *Epist.* 1.7.40 *Telemachus proles sapientis Vlixei*. In book 13 the character of the clever and resourceful Odysseus is developed in the judgement of arms between Odysseus and Ajax (1–398). For the (largely negative) epithets applied to Ulysses in Latin poetry, see Stanford 1963 and N–H on Hor. *C.* 1.6.7. In his exile poetry, Ovid draws on Ulysses as an exemplar of suffering against whom he compares his own hardships (see Williams 1994: 108–14).

160–1 desertum . . . Achaemeniden: the delayed name (Gk acc.) surely comes as a surprise to the reader, since the original Virgilian episode had been localized in Sicily and at an earlier point in the Trojans' voyage. With *improuisoque repertum* in the following line Ovid underlines the intertextual joke. This isn't the place in the poem where Ovid's readers might have expected to find him. In *Aeneid* 3 Achaemenides explains how he was deserted by the Greeks (616–18) *hic me, dum trepidi crudelia limina linquunt, | immemores socii uasto Cyclopis in antro | deseruere.* The claim contradicts Homer, where Ulysses sees to the escape of all of his men before himself leaving the Cyclops' cave (*Od.* 9.424–64). Among the numerous etymologies suggested for Achaemenides, O'Hara 1996a: 147 observes that the associations of *Achae-* (= Achaean) and *–men* (= μένω), which produce 'the left-behind Greek', may be reinforced by *deseruere* at *Aen.* 3.618; cf. Bömer on 14.158–444 (p. 65), Cova, *EV* I 22a–23a, Horsfall on *Aen.* 3.614. Cf. *Pont.* 2.2.25 *puppis Achaemeniden Graium Troiana recepit, Ib.* 413 *qualis Achaemenidae, Sicula desertus in Aetna.* **quondam:** a temporal marker which may also serve as an allusive reminder of Achaemenides' earlier appearance in the *Aeneid;* cf. 165–6n. and *F.* 3.613–14 (Aeneas and Anna Perenna) *Anna, per hanc iuro, quam quondam audire solebas | tellurem fato properiore dari.* Cf. also *Met.* 1.487 *dedit hoc pater ante Dianae,* where Daphne recalls to her father Artemis' earlier request for eternal virginity from Zeus, as recounted in Callimachus' sixth *Hymn.* **mediis . . . rupibus Aetnae:** although in the *Aeneid* Achaemenides claims that he was left behind *uasto Cyclopis in antro* (3.617), he had since escaped and approaches the Trojans *e siluis* (3.590) and explains that for three months he has been hiding there and eking out a meagre existence 3.645–8 *tertia iam lunae se cornua lumine complent, | uitam in siluis inter deserta ferarum | lustra domosque traho uastosque ab rupe Cyclopas | prospicio.* **noscit:** Macareus' recognition of Achaemenides (cf. *Aen.* 3.591 *ignoti noua forma uiri*) may signal another intertextual reference to Virgil's earlier treatment.

161–2 improuisoque repertum | uiuere miratus 'marvelling at finding him so unexpectedly still alive'. Ovid uses the adv. *improuiso* only here (Virg. 2x). Compare the introduction of Achaemenides at *Aen.* 3.590–2 *subito e siluis . . . procedit.* **casusue deusue:** a Virgilian ending; cf. *Aen.* 9.211 *si quis in aduersum rapiat casusue deusue,* 12.320–2.

163–4 barbara . . . | prora 'foreign ship'; for the Greek view of the Trojans as barbarians or foreigners (the juxtaposition with *Graium* heightens the implied contrast), cf. 574 *barbarus ignis* (see n.), *Her.* 1.26 (Penelope) *barbara praeda,* 17.64 (Helen to Paris) *at certe barbara terra tua est,* Hor. *C.* 2.4.9, Prop. 3.8.31 *barbarus Hector*; see Galinsky 1969a: 93–8. Virgil uses *barbaricus* of the Trojans at *Aen.* 2.504 *barbarico . . . auro* and 11.777 *barbara tegmina crurum,* in the sense foreign or 'oriental' (see Austin on 2.504 and cf. *Aen.* 7.38–9 *aduena . . . exercitus*), but does not oppose the term to 'Greek'; Horace, however, does so at *Epist.* 1.2.7 *Graecia barbariae lento collisa duello.* Homer never uses the word βάρβαρος. **prora . . . carina:** both words stand for 'ship' by synecdoche; *prora* (prow) in this sense is rare (*OLD* b, only here in Ovid), *carina* very common (72n.).

165–6 When the Trojans first meet Achaemenides in the *Aeneid,* he is emaciated and filthy. Ovid's lines underline the temporal distance between this and Achaemenides' earlier appearance in the *Aeneid* by contrasting it through verbal allusion with his current much improved condition (*iam non . . . iam . . . nullis*); cf. *Aen.* 3.590–4 *subito e* *siluis macie confecta suprema | ignoti noua forma uiri miserandaque cultu | procedit supplexque manus ad litora tendit. | respicimus. dira inluuies immissaque barba, | consertum tegimen spinis. iam . . . iam* thus has both temporal and textual implications, reminding us of this character's previous appearance in Virgil's text at a previous stage of the story; see Morison 1995: 106–9, Hinds 1998: 113–14. On such intertextual figures, see Conte's 1986: 60–2 classic exposition of Ovidian characters' consciousness of their literary antecedents, where he discusses Ariadne's quotation of her earlier laments in Catullus 64 at *F.* 3.469–75 (quoted below 167n.), and see below 622–771n. on Vertumnus. **non hirsutus amictu, | iam suus** 'not roughly attired, now his own man' (*OLD suus* 4b). Ovid perhaps here acknowledges the literary establishment (through his own imitation) of Virgil's invented character, introduced at *Aen.* 3.591 as *ignoti noua forma uiri miserandaque cultu* (Hinds 1998: 114). **spinis conserto tegmine nullis** 'his clothing no longer held together by thorns'. The phrase clearly makes sense only as an amusing negation of the earlier Virgilian passage at *Aen.* 3. 594 *consertum tegimen spinis* (in oblique cases of *tegimen,* the shorter form is metrically necessary). *nullis* as elsewhere is an emphatic negative (Bömer on 152). Cf. Tacitus *Germ.* 17.1 (on the primitivism of the German clothing) *tegumen omnibus sagum fibula aut, si desit, spina consertum.*

167–220 *Achaemenides and the Cyclops.* Achaemenides narrates the disastrous Greek encounter with the monstrous Cyclops Polyphemus, as Odysseus had done at *Od.* 9.105–564, and then continues with his own adventures after the Greeks departed. Polyphemus, a savage cannibal giant, attacked Odysseus and twelve of his companions when they became trapped in his cave. After Polyphemus devours six of his men in three gruesome meals, Odysseus gets him drunk on wine and burns out his single eye with a hot pointed stake. He and his men escape from the cave by clinging to the undersides of sheep being led out to pasture, evading detection by the blind Polyphemus, who is still guarding the entrance and feeling the sheep's backs. As he sails away, Odysseus twice exults in his triumph and reveals his true name, whereupon Polyphemus realizes that an ancient prophecy given him by Telemus has been fulfilled. In response to Odysseus' taunting he throws first a huge mountain crag and then an even larger rock at his ship and calls on his father Poseidon to curse Odysseus' homeward voyage. In *Aeneid* 3.613–54 Achaemenides graphically describes the events in the cave when Polyphemus consumed two of Ulysses' men and his subsequent blinding by the Greeks as he lay in a drunken stupor. He ends his narrative with a warning to the Trojans to flee, and thereupon Polyphemus himself comes into view (655–83). Ovid's narrative deftly combines elements of both Homer's and Virgil's versions of these events. His Achaemenides continues, as it were, his earlier narration in Virgil with an eye-witness account of the departure of Ulysses' crew without him, *after* their escape from the cave. He describes the Cyclops' hurling of the giant crag and his laments at the escape of Ulysses and hopes for future revenge. Much of the significance of the Virgilian scene is removed by the change in location; the Cyclopes no longer pose any threat. Throughout the narrative numerous verbal allusions recall the Virgilian episode.

The contrast in this episode with Polyphemus' earlier appearance in book 13 (740–897) in Alexandrian guise as the suitor of the nymph Galatea is striking, although the earlier scene foreshadows his reappearance here as Homeric monster (Hopkinson 2000: 35–40). He refers to Telemus' prophecy of Odysseus' arrival (770–3) and by the end of the episode has been transformed to his epic monstrosity and crushes Galatea's lover Acis with a rock. On the Cyclopes and Polyphemus, see Barchiesi, *EV* I 778a–9a, Flores, *EV* IV 164b–66b, Glenn 1972, Hutchinson 2007.

167–76 Achaemenides first expresses his gratitude to Aeneas for rescuing him from the Cyclops. Through this speech, Ovid, in effect, encapsulates the overall import of the Virgilian scene in its expression of Trojan magnanimity; cf. its conclusion at 220 *Graiumque ratis Troiana recepit.*

167 iterum metapoetically underlines Achaemenides' second literary appearance in this same scene (it is also Polyphemus' second appearance in the poem), see Hinds 1998: 114. On the use of *iterum* as an 'external marker' of allusion, see Wills 1996: 31, cf. 183, *F.* 3.471–2 (Ariadne) *en iterum, fluctus, similes audite querellas* | *en iterum lacrimas accipe, harena, meas* (with Conte 1986: 60–2), *Am.* 2.12.21–2 *femina Troianos iterum noua bella mouere* | *impulit,* Virg. *Aen.* 10.26–9 *muris iterum imminet hostis* | *nascentis Troiae nec non exercitus alter,* | *atque iterum in Teucros Aetolis surgit ab Arpis* | *Tydides* (with Barchiesi 2001: 18–19). **Polyphemon:** Gk acc. for metrical convenience.

168 aspiciam: optative subjunctive. **fluidos humano sanguine** 'dripping with human blood' (*OLD fluidus* 2, *TLL* VI 1.952.82–953.5, the first occurrence with this meaning); cf. *Aen.* 3.663 *fluidum . . . cruorem.*

169 'if my home and Ithaca are more precious to me than this ship'. *Ithace* (gen. *-es*) is a Gk nom. form of *Ithaca* (Ἰθάκη, cf. 13.711 *Ithacam, Tr.* 1.5.67 *Ithaceue*). For the enclosed line construction of adj. and noun, see Pearce 1966, Bömer on *M.* 14.218.

170 In Virgil it is actually Anchises who takes the lead in offering Achaemenides sympathy: *Aen.* 3.610–11 *ipse pater dextram Anchises haud multa moratus* | *dat iuueni atque animum praesenti pignore firmat.* In Ovid's narrative Anchises is no longer alive (cf. 84).

171 praestem licet omnia 'though I offer him everything I can' ('give my all'); *licet* with the subordinate subjunctive in a concessive sense (*OLD licet* 4, *NLS* §248). The enclosing syntax underlines the sense.

172–3 quod 'seeing that', 'in view of the fact that' (*OLD* 10). Cf. 9.779–80 (Telethusa to Isis) *quod uidet haec lucem . . .* | *consilium munusque tuum est,* Hor. *C.* 4.3.21–4 *totum muneris hoc tui est; . . . quod spiro et placeo, si placeo, tuum est.* **sidera solis** 'the light of the sun'; *sidus* can refer to any 'heavenly body' (Lyne on *Ciris* 37–8 *lunae* | *sidera, OLD sidus* 2c); cf. 1.424 *aetherioque . . . sidere,* 1.778–9 *sub ignibus . . .* | *sidereis,* 4.169 *siderea . . . luce,* 9.286 *decimum premeretur sidere signum.* The echoes of Achaemenides' plea to the Trojans at *Aen.* 3.599–61 are unmistakable: *cum fletu precibusque tulit: 'per sidera testor,* | *per superos atque hoc caeli spirabile lumen,* | *tollite me, Teucri'* (see Stitz 1962: 82). **possimne:** potential subj. The word creates an unusual elision at the third-foot caesura (after the first *longum*), see Clausen 1979: 247–9. Here the effect is qualified by the fact that *in-gratus* can be felt as quasi-divided (cf. Kenney on Lucr. 3.174, 258). **immemor:** the alternative reading *impius* is perhaps the more obvious, linking with Achaemenides' expressed desire to regard Aeneas as a father (170), and contrasting with Aeneas' famous *pietas*. In the *Aeneid*, however, Achaemenides' charge against Ulysses is precisely that he was *immemor* (3.617 *immemores socii uasto Cyclopis in antro | deseruere*); cf. *Met.* 10.682 *nec grates immemor egit*, Cic. *Phil.* 2.33 *quae uero tam immemor posteritas, quae tam ingratae litterae reperientur* (*TLL* vii 1.447.21–6).

174 ille dedit, quod 'it was he who granted that'; an unusual construction (*dare* usually takes *ut/ne*, or infin.; see *TLL* v 1.1691.8–9). **anima haec** 'this life of mine', rhetorical emphasis, cf. *Aen.* 3.654 (Achaemenides) *uos animam hanc potius quocumque absumite leto* (with Horsfall ad loc.).

175 ut iam nunc lumen uitale relinquam 'though I die right now'; *ut* is concessive. The lofty expression *lumen uitale relinquam* has a long tradition: see Skutsch on Enn. *Ann.* 137 *postquam lumina . . . Ancus reliquit*, cf. Cic. *Cons.* fr. 10.24 *FLP* (p. 160) *uitalia lumina liquit*, Lucr. 3.542 *lumina qui linquuunt*, *Aen.* 4.452 *lucemque relinquat*; *Tr.* 5.9.37 *dum lumen uitale uidebo*, cf. *lux* 132n.

176 'I shall be buried in a grave or at any rate not in that belly'; *condar* and *in* are both to be understood ἀπὸ κοινοῦ with *tumulo* (*condo* + *in aluo* is a Virgilian line-end at *Aen.* 2.401, 9.152). This refers to the Cyclops' cannibalism described below (203–4); cf. 209 *semianimesque artus auidam condebat in aluum*. Virgil's Achaemenides also tells the Trojans that any death would be preferable to being left with the Cyclops: *Aen.* 3.652–4 *huic me, quaecumque fuisset, | addixi: satis est gentem effugisse nefandum. | uos animam hanc potius quocumque absumite leto*. The idea of an animal as the 'living tomb' of its victim is old; e.g. Gorgias fr. 5a D–K, Aesch. *Sept.* 1020, Ennius *Ann.* 125–6 Sk. *uolturus . . . miserum mandebat homonem: | heu quam crudeli condebat membra sepulcro*, Lucr. 5.993. Cf. 6.665 (Tereus) and Pythagoras against carnivorism at *Met.* 15.88 *heu quantum scelus est in uiscere uiscera condi*.

177–222 Achaemenides now turns to the events immediately following the launching of Ulysses' fleet, before his rescue by the Trojans. The multiple enjambments in the lines enhance the drama by imparting urgency and impetus.

177 Quid mihi tunc animi 'what then did I feel?'; *animi* is partitive gen., cf. e.g. 5.626 (Arethusa) *quid mihi tunc animi miserae fuit?* **nisi si** = *nisi* (*OLD nisi* 7a); cf. 561, 5.20, 615, 10.200, *Her.* 4.111 (not. in Virg., Hor., Prop., Tib.).

178–9 uos: Achaemenides refers to Macareus and his Greek shipmates, cf. 180–1 *uestrae . . . rati*, 187 *uos*. **petere alta . . . | aequora** 'making for the high/open seas'.

180–2 Achaemenides refers to the scene in Homer, *Od.* 9.473–542, where Odysseus cannot resist deriding the blinded Cyclops from his ship. In response to Odysseus' first taunt that he deserved his punishment, Polyphemus hurls a mountain peak at his ship (473–86). Odysseus then calls out a second time, despite the protests of his men, and reveals his name, upon which the Cyclops throws another and greater stone and barely misses the ship (491–542). Earlier at *Met.* 13.882–3 the Cyclops rehearsed his future attempt to sink Odysseus' ship when he threw a huge rock at Acis and crushed him with it: *insequitur Cyclops partemque e monte reuulsam | mittit*; cf. also 12.341–2. See Baldo 1995: 125–36.

180 quoque 'in the same way'.

181–2 Cf. *Od.* 9.481–3 'he broke off the peak of a high mountain and threw it at us' (481 ἧκε δ' ἀπορρήξας κορυφὴν ὄρεος μεγάλοιο). **uidi, cum** 'I looked on when'; a cue (along with the repetition of *uidi* at 183 below) to recall the Homeric scene (narrated by Odysseus), and simultaneously Virgil's imitation in Achaemenides' similar claims of witnessing the Cyclops eat Ulysses' men at *Aen.* 3.623 *uidi egomet,* 626 *uidi . . . cum*. Ocular testimony is traditional in epic, see Horsfall on *Aen.* 3.623. **permisit** 'hurled', *OLD* 1.

183–4 'I saw him a second time casting a huge boulder with his Giant-like arm as if it had been driven by the force of a catapult'. *saxa* is poetic pl. **iterum:** in Homer, after Odysseus taunts him for a second time with the revelation of his name, Polyphemus throws another mass of rock (9.537 αὐτὰρ ὅ γ' ἐξαῦτις πολὺ μείζονα λᾶαν ἀείρας 'But again he lifted up a much greater stone'). **tormenti:** *tormentum,* an anachronism here, is a general term for catapults and other war-engines for discharging missiles; the same simile is used at 9.217–18 *terque quaterque rotatum | mittit in Euboicas tormento fortius undas* (where Hercules hurls Lichas into the sea), cf. 8.357. It is taken from Virgil, *Aen.* 11.615–17 *excussus Aconteus | fulminis in morem aut tormento ponderis acti | praecipitat longe,* 12.921–2 *murali concita numquam | tormento sic saxa fremunt.* Line 184, which marks the climax of Polyphemus' violent actions, is a highly mannered 'golden line', with its ornate pattern of two adjectives, verb, and two nouns abVAB: cf. the chiastic so-called 'silver line', abVBA). On such symmetrical lines, see Wilkinson 1963: 215–17, Kenney 2002: 60, Navarro Antolín on Lyg. 3.5. Homer too stresses the Cyclops' strength at *Od.* 9.539 'he swung and hurled it, putting into the throw measureless strength'. **Giganteo:** the adj. is usually used of the Giants themselves; cf. 1, 5.346, *F.* 5.435, *Tr.* 2.71. See Hardie 1986: 101 on Gigantomachic mountain throwing, and 265, 274 on the Cyclopes' associations with the Giants.

185 deprimeret: technical language for the sinking of ships, only in prose except for this passage (*TLL* v 1.613.60–7). **fluctusue lapisue:** the variant *uentusue* for *lapisue* would refer to the current of air raised by the rock (a perhaps unlikely exaggeration). For the waves produced by the throwing of the rocks see *Od.* 9.484–6, 541–2.

186 iam . . . illa 'having forgotten that I was no longer in it'.

187–213 Achaemenides stresses the contrast between the escape of Greeks (*uos*) and his own harsh fate. Ovid constructs this new scene out of reminiscences of Homer and Virgil. The closest parallel is the view of the blinded Polyphemus wandering with his flocks that Aeneas and his men catch sight of before fleeing at *Aen.* 3.655–65. Achaemenides' Cyclops is more terrifying than the somewhat pitiable figure depicted in Virgil.

187 ut uero 'but when' (*OLD ut* 26). **a certa morte reduxit:** the language is Virgilian: *Aen.* 2.62 *certae occumbere morti*, 4.375 *socios a morte reduxi.*

188 gemebundus 'groaning'; the word occurs first here (*TLL* VI 2.1734.70–9); cf. *Aen.* 3.664 *dentibus infrendens gemitu.* **obambulat:** rare in verse; cf. 2.851, *Tr.* 2.459, Virg. *G.* 3.538, Plautus 4x (*TLL* IX 2.35.21–61).

189 praetemptatque manu siluas 'he gropes his way through the woods with his hands'. In *Aen.* 3 the Trojans see Polyphemus using a trimmed pine tree as a cane (659 *trunca manum pinus regit*). **luminis orbus** 'bereft of sight'; for the gen. with adjs. denoting fullness or lack, see *NLS* §73 (3), K–S 1.441; cf. *Aen.* 3.658 *lumen ademptum.*

190–1 Ovid combines elements from both Virgil and Homer; in Virgil Polyphemus goes down to the shore to bathe his bloody eye-socket (*Aen.* 3.662–3 *ad aequora uenit, | luminis effossi fluidum lauit inde cruorem*) and at *Od.* 9.526–36 Polyphemus prays for vengeance to his father Poseidon (9.527 εὔχετο χεῖρ' ὀρέγων εἰς οὐρανὸν ἀστερόεντα 'he prayed stretching out both hands to the starry heaven'); see Baldo 1986: 129–30. **rupibus incursat** 'he bumps against rocks'. **foedataque bracchia tabo:** the strong language suggests that this probably refers to the Cyclops' killing of Ulysses' men, rather than the blood from his eye-socket; cf. *Aen.* 3.626–7 *uidi atro cum membra fluentia tabo | manderet.* **gentem . . . Achiuam** 'Greek race'.

192–7 Achaemenides quotes Polyphemus' wishes for future revenge. His speech recalls a number of Homeric and Virgilian passages, a strategy discussed by Barchiesi 1993 as 'future-reflexive allusion', wherein the older literary tradition, here both Virgil's *Aeneid* and Homer's *Odyssey*, enters a new text as a view of the future, cf. 563–5. The gruesome events are from Homer's *Odyssey* 9.289–91, where Polyphemus devours Odysseus' men: 'in one stride he clutched at my companions and caught them in his hands like squirming puppies to beat their brains out, spattering the floor. Then he dismembered them and made his meal, gaping and crunching like a mountain lion – everything: innards, flesh, and marrow bones' (trans. Fitzgerald). At *Od.* 9.526–35 Polyphemus prays for future troubles for Odysseus. Finally, Ovid's scene may also be indebted to *Od.* 9.447–60, where Polyphemus tells his ram (under which Odysseus is hiding) that if he could find Odysseus he would dash his brains to the ground (558–60). Ovid's passage closely recalls the eye-witness account of the episode given by the Virgilian Achaemenides at *Aen.* 3.622–7; see Hinds 1998: 114–15.

193 aut aliquem e sociis reminds the audience of Achaemenides' (past) danger as he overheard this speech, cf. 199ff. **saeuiat:** this and the following four verbs of the clause are final subjs.

194–6 The lines constitute a rising tricolon, with anaphora of *cuius*, building in horror. This stylistic excess is typical of Polyphemus; cf. his inflated song to Galatea at 13.789–807 (see Bömer on 13.789–869).

194 Ovid elaborates Virgil, who is following Homer's description (*Od.* 9.293 ἔγκατα = *uiscera*); cf. *Aen.* 3.622 *uisceribus miserorum et sanguine uescitur atro* (with similar alliteration of *u*); cf. the Cyclops' earlier threat against Acis at 13.865 *uiscera uiua traham,* and see Lucr. 5.993 *uiua uidens uiuo sepeliri uiscera busto.*

195–6 The lines are closely based on *Aen.* 3.626–7 *uidi atro cum membra fluentia tabo | manderet et tepidi tremerent sub dentibus artus* ('I saw when he chewed limbs dripping with black matter and those still-warm members quivered under his teeth', trans. Horsfall). *trepident* neatly recalls both *tepidi* and *tremerent* (Hinds 1998: 115).

197 'how unimportant and slight would be the loss of my stolen sight'; a nod to Virgil's famous line on the blinded Cyclops *Aen.* 3.658 *monstrum horrendum, informe, ingens, cui lumen ademptum,* cf. *Met.* 13.772–3. Homer's Cyclops also claims that his heart would be lightened if he could have revenge on Odysseus (*Od.* 9.459–60).

198 haec et plura ferox: sc. *dixit.* On the ferocity of Polyphemus, cf. 13.767 *feros . . . uultus,* 768 *feritas,* 780 *ferus . . . Cyclops,* 772 *terribilem Polyphemon.* **luridus . . . horror** = χλωρὸν δέος, Hom. *Il.* 7.479, *Od.* 11.43, *al.*; i.e. fear which turns one pale.

199 uultus: poetic pl.

200 inanem luminis orbem 'his eye devoid of sight'; for the gen. with *inanis,* cf. 189n.

201 Tarrant questions the authenticity of this line on the basis of the vagueness of *membra* and the contrast of *concretam . . . barbam* with the fresh gore of 199 (*humano . . . sanguine* is repeated from 168). *concretam sanguine* also has to be taken ἀπὸ κοινοῦ, with *concreta* understood to agree with *membra*; but the fact that *concretus* is *uox propria* only of hair argues against the line as well. Cf. *Aen.* 2.277 (Hector) *squalentem barbam et concretos sanguine crinis,* a line imitated also at *Met.* 12.270 *pars (sc. oculorum) fluit in barbam concretaque sanguine pendet.* For Polyphemus' beard cf. 13.766.

202 Tarrant excises this line. The theme of death anticipates its appearance at 215 and the line interrupts the flow of the syntax and contrasts with the vivid and detailed description in the surrounding lines. The possible jest of using *ante oculos* immediately after the repeated reference to the Cyclops' blindness (see Galinsky 1975: 233) is perhaps not a strong argument in its favour. **mors erat ante oculos** = *Her.* 11.55. **minimum tamen ipsa doloris:** sc. *erat,* 'it (death) was, however, the very smallest part of my grief' (the biggest part being eaten alive!). *minimum* is a neut. subst. with part. gen. *doloris*.

203–212 Achaemenides now recalls Polyphemus' cannibalistic attack in the cave, which draws much from his earlier account of the same event in *Aeneid* 3.623–7, the lines which were already allusively evoked above in the Cyclops' speech.

203–4 et iam prensurum: sc. *esse* (the unstated subject of both future infinitives is the Cyclops); cf. *Aen.* 3.623–4 *corpora . . . | prensa manu.* **mea uiscera . . . | in sua mersurum:** for the use of *mergo* = 'devour/swallow', cf. 6.664 (Tereus is served his son Itys) *egerere inde dapes immersaque uiscera gestit* (cf. 651 *uescitur inque suam sua uiscera congerit aluum*), *F.* 4.199–200 (Rhea swallows her children) *prolem | deuorat, immersam uisceribusque tenet.* The passages all suggest the unnaturalness of the act; so also in book 15 Pythagoras rails against the evils of meat-eating and compares it to the Cyclops' cannibalism: 92–3 *nil te nisi tristia mandere saeuo | uulnera dente iuuat ritusque referre Cyclopum,* cf. 176n.

204–5 mentique haerebat imago | temporis illius, quo uidi 'and the image stuck in my mind of that time when I saw'; 'a cue for still more allusions to Virgil and to Homer' (Hinds 1998: 115), cf. 13.280–1 *quanto cogor meminisse dolore | temporis illius, quo.*

205–6 cf. *Aen.* 3.623–5 *uidi egomet duo de numero cum corpora nostro | prensa manu magna medio resupinus in antro | frangeret ad saxum.* Ovid is also following Homer's account at *Od.* 9.287–93 (289–91 quoted above 192–7n.); cf. 289–90 ποτὶ γαίῃ | κόπτ' (*terrae*). With *bina*, Ovid perhaps 'corrects' Virgil's passage (*duo*) by referring to the Homeric version where six of Odysseus' companions are eaten at three meals 'two at a time' (*Od.* 9.289, 311, 344); see H–E–A ad loc. Luck 2006: 119–20 argues that instead of *bina* we read *uiua* (as in some MSS), citing Lucr. 5.993 *uiua uidens uiuo sepeliri uiscera busto,* but see 209n. below on *semianimesque* for the same notion. **affligi:** *affligere* is rare in epic (*Met.* 2x, *Aen.* 2x).

207 The simile is from Homer's scene of the Cyclops: *Od.* 9.292 ἤσθιε δ' ὥς τε λέων ὀρεσίτροφος 'he ate them like a mountain lion'. Virgil had omitted it, although *resupinus* at *Aen.* 3.624 may gesture toward it. **super . . . iacens** is either tmesis of the very rare verb *superiaceo*, where the prepositional prefix of a verb is separated from its stem, or *super* is simply an adverb 'on top'. The archaic flavor of tmesis (H–S 217) suits the elevated context of a Homeric simile.

208–9 que et . . . que . . . que: polysyndeton contributes to the mounting horror of the long list. **carnes cumque albis ossa medullis:** cf. Hom. *Od.* 9.293 ἔγκατά τε σάρκας τε καὶ ὀστέα μυελόεντα 'entrails and flesh and bones and marrow'. **semianimesque artus** 'half-alive limbs'; cf. the similar suggestion in Virgil's *tepidi tremerent sub dentibus artus* (*Aen.* 3.627). *semianimis* is regularly scanned as a quadrisyllable by treating the first *i* of *semi* as a consonant. The adj. goes back to Ennius 484 Sk. *semianimesque micant oculi lucemque requirunt*; cf. *Aen.* 10.396 *semianimesque* *micant digiti.* **auidam condebat in aluum:** cf. the similar expression at 176 and in Pythagoras' attack on the inventor of carnivorism at 15.101–6 *corporeasque dapes auidam demersit in aluum, | fecit iter sceleri.* Alliteration and word-patterning (aAbVB) signal a climax.

210 sine sanguine 'bloodless', here perhaps, 'lacking strength' (substituting for *exsanguis*); cf. 7.136 *palluit et subito sine sanguine frigida sedit.* Bömer observes the fondness in contemporary poetry for the use of *sine* with a noun as an equivalent to an alpha-privative adjective.

211–12 Ovid models his lines on Virgil, *Aen.* 3.630–3 *nam simul expletus dapibus uinoque sepultus | ceruicem inflexam posuit, iacuitque per antrum | immensus saniem eructans et frusta cruento | per somnum commixta mero,* which elaborate in turn Homer's gruesome description at *Od.* 9.292f. (cf. *Od.* 9.373–4 φάρυγος δ' ἐξέσσυτο οἶνος | ψωμοί τ' ἀνδρόμεοι. ὁ δ' ἐρεύγετο οἰνοβαρείων 'the wine gurgled up from his gullet with gobs of human meat. This was his drunken vomiting.' (transl. Lattimore)). 211 is a weighty four-word hexameter, see 116–17n. The three present participles add to the build-up of horror, cf. Barchiesi–Rosati on 4.237–9. **mandentemque:** 'the verb stresses the visual aspect of eating and therefore tends to be used in scenes of horror' (Skutsch on Enn. *Ann.* 125 Sk.); cf. 15.92 (Cyclops, above 203–4n.), *Aen.* 3.627, 'Liuius Refictus' *FLP* p. 45 *cum socios nostros mandisset impius Cyclops.* **eiectantemque:** a predominantly poetic word, occurring first in Virgil *Aen.* 5.469–70 (Dares after being beaten by Entellus) *crassumque cruorem | ore eiectantem*; cf. *Met.* 2.231, 5.352–3, *TLL* v 2.312.42–53. **frusta mero glomerata** 'lumps massed together with wine'; cf. *Aen.* 3.632–3 (above); *frusta* are Homer's ψωμοί. Cf. also *Aen.* 3.576–7 (Enceladus/Aetna) *liquefactaque saxa sub auras | cum gemitu glomerat.*

214–19 Achaemenides breathlessly (enjambment, asyndeton) describes his terrifying days as a castaway on the Cyclops' island. Virgil specifies that Achaemenides was alone for three months at *Aen.* 3.645–6.

214–15 omnemque tremescens | ad strepitum: Ovid varies Virgil, *Aen.* 3.648 *sonitumque pedum uocemque tremesco* (he also repeats the assonance of *–um* and *–em* in 215). **cupidusque moriri:** Ovid has *cupidus* with the inf. only here, if the reading is correct (some MSS have *cupiensque*). Furthermore, the archaic fourth conjugation form of the infinitive *moriri* (*TLL* VIII 1492.42–7 Plautus (7x), Pompon. *Atell.* 31) is remarkable. On the whole, genuine archaisms are very rare in the *Met.* (see Kenney 2002: 61).

216 Achaemenides subsists on the same sort of primitive fare at *Aen.* 3.649–50 *uictum infelicem, bacas lapidosaque corna, | dant rami, et uulsis pascunt radicibus herbae. glans* 'acorns' (*glande* is collective sing., K–S 1.68, as also *herba*) and *herbae* 'wild plants' appear traditionally as part of the diet of primitive pre-agricultural man, see e.g. 1.106, 4.401–2 *prima Ceres homine ad meliora alimenta uocato | mutauit glandes utiliore cibo,* 395 *panis erat primis uirides mortalibus herbae, Am.* 3.10.9–10, Lucr. 5.935–6, Virg. *G.* 1.7–8, Juv. 13.57 (with Courtney ad loc. for further references). *frondes et herba* are also often fodder for animals, cf. 1.632, 4.767, Virg. *G.* 3.528. **famem pellens:** cf. Tib. 2.1.37–8 *his uita magistris | desueuit querna pellere glande famem.*

217 solus inops exspes: cf. 13.510 (Hecuba) *nunc trahor exul, inops, Her.* 6.162 (Hypsipyle curses Medea) *erret inops, exspes, Ib.* 113. The phrasing recalls tragic speeches, e.g. Eur. *Hec.* 809–11, Accius, *Medea* 415 Ribbeck *exul inter hostes, exspes exspers desertus uagus* (see Knox on *Her.* 6.162). **leto poenaeque relictus** 'left to death and suffering'; for the dat. see *OLD relinquo* 12b.

218 Cf. *Aen.* 3.651–2 *hanc primum ad litora classem | conspexi uenientem*; for the enclosed word order see 169n. **longo post tempore** 'after a long time'; *post* is an adverb, *tempore* an abl. of the measure of difference (*NLS* §82 (iii)); cf. 7.494, 9.570, 10.180, Virg. *Ecl.* 1.29, 67, *Aen.* 6.409, *Ciris* 74. By this general temporal indication Ovid may 'correct' the chronological problem involved in Virgil's statement that Achaemenides was rescued after only three months at *Aen.* 3.645–6, see 158–440n.

219 'I begged for escape by my gestures and I ran to the shore'. *Imitatio cum uariatione* of Achaemenides' rescue in Virg. *Aen.* 3.598–9 *mox sese ad litora praeceps | cum fletu precibusque tulit.* The resulting sequence serves as an example of the so-called '*hysteron proteron*' construction (see H–S 698–9), which seemingly reverses the logical order of the actions, but in Latin sentences, through the flexibility allowed in word order, was understood in the correct sequence (see Kenney on *Her.* 21.32). **ad litusque:** the placement of *-que* is standard (prose) usage in such prepositional phrases (K–S I 583), cf. 11.131, 12.136, 15.545, *Her.* 20.138.

220 et moui 'and I touched their hearts' (Miller-Goold, *OLD moueo* 15a). **Graiumque ratis Troiana recepit:** Achaemenides concludes his narration with an epigrammatic line, which sums up the main thrust of the episode through the pointed juxtaposition of Greek and Trojan (Baldo 1995: 135–6, Galinsky 1975: 231), cf. *Pont.* 2.2.25 *puppis Achaemeniden Graium Troiana recepit.* Bömer points out that Ovid uses *Graius* as a sing. masc. substantive only here, perhaps in imitation of Virgil's sole use of the sing. adj. in this manner (also of Achaemenides) at *Aen.* 3.594.

221–2 Typical transitional story-telling formula for the continuation of Ovid's narrative in the poem; cf. 162–3, 4.680 (Perseus to Andromeda) *pande requirenti nomen terraeque tuumque*, 13.747–8 (Scylla to Galatea) '*refer, o carissima,' dixit* | '*neue tui causam tege (sic sum fida) doloris', Aen.* 3.609 (motivation for Achaemenides' speech) *hortamur, quae deinde agitet fortuna fateri.* **tu quoque** ~ *Aen.* 7.1 (see 158n.).

223–440 *Macareus' narration.* Macareus' long narrative continues the adventures of Odysseus and his crew immediately following the episode of the Cyclops up to and including their meeting with Circe, which encompass the whole of *Odyssey* 10. The Greeks' visit with Aeolus and the disastrous encounter with the Laestrygonians are each abbreviated in around ten lines (223–32, 233–41); the encounter with Circe is the most fully elaborated (242–440), although the majority of this section is taken up with an inserted and original Italian tale involving Circe, which was narrated to Macareus during his stay by one of Circe's attendants (308–434).

223–32 The first section of Macareus' narrative is summarized in *oratio obliqua* and refers to the arrival of Odysseus and his crew at the floating island of Aeolia, home of Aeolus, after their escape from the Cyclops at the beginning of *Od.* 10 (1–79). Upon their departure after a month's stay they are given an ox-hide in which Aeolus has imprisoned the storm winds and are sent with a fair west wind on their journey home. After nine days Odysseus is within sight of Ithaca, when his comrades open the bag in the hopes that it contains treasure and they are all blown back to the island of Aeolus. Upon this unexpected second visit, Aeolus harshly sends them away.

The passage is carefully structured in a pattern of two introductory lines, two sets of three lines, and two concluding lines (with 232 *Aeoliique* recalling the opening *Aeolon*). There is variation of syntax between perfect infinitives, participles, and subordinate clauses. At 225 and 231 the clauses are coordinated through connecting relatives. The mixture of indirect and direct speech allows Ovid to speed up his narrative and then slow it down again for emphasis on his expanded metamorphic narratives when Macareus resumes direct speech at line 233; cf. Diomedes at 461–511.

223–4 Aeolon . . . | Aeolon Hippotaden: with this epanalepsis (the mannered repetition of a word from a marked position in a line to a position at or near the beginning of the next; see Wills 1996: 124, on Ovid 161–3) Ovid 'directly recalls the names at the opening of *Od.* 10, keeping them in their same position' (Wills 1996: 162): *Od.* 10.1–2 Αἰολίην δ' ἐς νῆσον ἀφικόμεθ'. ἔνθα δ' ἔναιεν | Αἴολος Ἱπποτάδης ('we came next to the Aeolian island, where lived Aeolos, Hippotas' son'), and at the same time he acknowledges Apollonius' earlier adaptation of Homer's lines at *Arg.* 4.764–5 ἀτὰρ καὶ ἐς Αἴολον ἐλθεῖν, | Αἴολον ὅς τ' ἀνέμοις αἰθρηγενέεσσιν ἀνάσσει ('then go to Aeolus too, Aeolus, who rules the sky-born winds'), cf. *Aen.* 6.162–4 *Misenum . . . Misenum Aeoliden.* For the patronymic *Hippotaden* (Gk acc. sing.) see 86n. **Tusco regnare profundo** 'reigned as king in the Tuscan deep'; locatival abl. For the location of Aeolia (Lipara) in the Tyrrhenian sea, see 86n. **cohibentem carcere uentos:** Ovid imitates Virgil's description of Aeolus and his cave of winds at *Aen.* 1.53–4 *luctantes uentos . . . | imperio premit ac uinclis et carcere frenat,* 141 *clauso uentorum carcere regnet,* cf. *Met.* 4.663 *clauserat Hippotades Aetnaeo carcere uentos,* 11.431–2 *Hippotades . . . qui carcere fortes | contineat uentos.*

225 quos bouis inclusos tergo: cf. *Od.* 10.19–20 'He gave me a bag made from the hide of a nine-year old ox and in it he bound the howling winds blowing in different directions'. *quos* (= *et eos*) coordinates the two clauses; on the connective relative see *NLS* § 230.6. **memorabile munus:** an allusive reminder that the tale is following Homer's account or an ironic comment on the marvellous nature of the gift (Kenney 1986: 455); the phrase occurs earlier at Tib. 2.1.57, see Maltby ad loc. for etymological and literary implications.

226 Dulichium . . . ducem = Odysseus; Odysseus ruled over Dulichium, Same, Zacynthus, and Ithaca (*Od.* 1.246–7, 9.24, *Aen.* 3.270–3, cf. *Met.* 13.711–12) and the adj. *Dulichius* was used in poetry as a recherché way to refer to Ulysses and his followers, cf. 13.107, 425, 711, Prop. 2.2.7, Virg. *Ecl.* 6.76, *TLL Onomasticon* III 1.268.57–74. Dulichium may perhaps be identified with the island of Leucas (see West on *Od.* 1.246–7). **secundo** 'favourable', i.e. a 'following wind' (*secundus* is in origin the gerundive of *sequor* used as a (passive in form) pres. part., cf. Leumann 331), in Homer the West Wind (Zephyrus) *Od.* 10.25.

227 'he had sailed for nine days and had caught sight of the land he sought'; *lucibus* is abl. of duration of time (*NLS* § 54 (1), K–S 1.360–1). Cf. *Od.* 10.28–9 'For nine days we sailed without stopping, both night and day, and now on the tenth the native land of our fathers came in sight'. The elision of the final *-m* of an iambic word (*nou(em) et*) is rare, occuring commonly before a monosyllable (see Soubiran 1966: 236, 526–9, Platnauer 1951: 84n.5), here it appears at the first *longum* of the third foot at the main (strong) caesura.

228 'When the tenth morning dawned'; cf. 6.48 *cum primum Aurora mouetur*. On the epic dawn motif, cf. 416n.

229–30 Indirect speech continues, with *socios* as acc. subject, and the infinitive *dempsisse* as main verb. Cf. *Od.* 10.35–45 where Odysseus falls asleep and his men decide that the bag must contain gold and silver as gifts from Aeolus, which Odysseus plans to keep for himself.

230 'having thought that there was gold (in the bag), they had removed the fastenings from the winds'; cf. *Od.* 10.47 ἀσκὸν μὲν λῦσαν, ἄνεμοι δ' ἐκ πάντες ὄρουσαν ('they opened the bag and the winds all burst out'). Hardie (forthcoming) observes ad loc. that *uentis* hints at *aura*, creating wordplay with *aurum*, the men find not *aurum* but *aurae* (cf. *Aen.* 6.204 *auri . . . aura*, 209 *uento*).

231 cum quibus = *et cum eis (uentis),* connective rel. (225n). **retro per quas modo uenerat undas** 'back over the waves it had just crossed'. *per* does double duty (brachylogy) = '*per undas, per quas . . .* ', cf. 11.632 (with Bömer). *uenerat* is indicative in a subordinate clause in *O. O.*, because the clause expresses an objective fact (*NLS* § 287).

232 Aeoliique . . . tyranni: adj. and noun frame the final line of the passage. Macareus omits the sequel to this scene. After his ships are driven back to Aeolus' island by the escaped storm wind, Odysseus again approaches the king, who refuses further help and dismisses him with a curse (*Od.* 10.56–75). Bömer conjectures that *tyranni* may contain a hint of Aeolus' harsh reception of the Greeks. **portus:** poetic pl.

233–42 Seven days after leaving Aeolus' island Odysseus and his companions arrive at the land of the Laestrygonians, a race of man-eating giants, and are attacked (*Od.* 10.80–132). Odysseus manages to escape with only his own ship, losing the eleven ships of his companions. Ovid's version is extremely abbreviated and requires a knowledge of the Homeric episode. Variously localized, the Laestrygonians were believed to have founded Formiae (Formia) in Latium, in close proximity to Caieta where Macareus tells his tale (cf. *F.* 4.69 *testes Laestrygones exstant,* Cic. *Att.* 2.13.2, Hor. *C.* 3.16.34). **Lami . . . Laestrygonis:** Lamos (Λάμος) is the name of the city founder (cf. *Od.* 10.81), a son of Neptune. **inquit:** Macareus now moves into direct speech for the rest of his narration.

234 Antiphates: named by Homer as the king of the Laestrygonians (*Od.* 10.106, 114).

235 numero comitante duorum 'with two companions'. The details of the embassy sent to discover the inhabitants of the land follow Homer: *Od.* 10.102 ἄνδρε δύο κρίνας, τρίτατον κήρυχ' ἅμ' ὀπάσσας 'I chose two men, and sent a third with them, as herald'.

236–8 In Homer, when the embassy sent by Odysseus arrives at the palace of Antiphates, the king immediately seizes one of the men and prepares to eat him. The other two Greeks escape back to the ships (*Od.* 10.103–17).

236 fuga: cf. *Od.* 10.117 τὼ δὲ δύ' ἀίξαντε φυγῆι ἐπὶ νῆας ἱκέσθην 'the other two darted away in flight, and got back to my ships' (Lattimore). **comitique mihique:** on the double *-que* see 78n.

237–8 Laestrygonis impia . . . | ora 'the impious mouth of the Laestrygonian' (i.e. Antiphates). *ora* is poet. pl. Cf. 15.98 *nec polluit ora cruore,* 478 *ora cruore uacent, Aen.* 10.348 *crassum uomit ore cruorem,* [Tib.] 3.5.13–14 *nec nos . . . | impia in aduersos soluimus ora deos.*

238–9 fugientibus . . . Antiphates 'Antiphates pursued us as we fled and summoned his troops against us'(*OLD concito* 3). Cf. *Od.* 10.118–24 the Laestrygonians assemble at a cry from Antiphates and hurl huge rocks at the Greeks and their ships in the harbour. **coeunt:** cf. *Od.* 10.118–19 οἱ δ' ἀίοντες | φοίτων ἴφθιμοι Λαιστρυγόνες ἄλλοθεν ἄλλος, 'Hearing him the powerful Laistrygones came swarming up from every direction' (Lattimore). The three alliterative verbs beginning with *c-* add to the drama of the lines.

240 merguntque . . . franguntque: the Homeric model for this line (*Od.* 10.123 ἀνδρῶν ὀλλυμένων νηῶν θ' ἅμα ἀγνυμενάων 'men being killed and ships smashed to pieces') led Kenney 2003: 620 to propose *frangunt* for the second *mergunt* in the MSS (a repetition 'feeble by Ovidian standards'), thus producing another seeming case of *hysteron proteron,* see 219n.

241–2 una . . . | effugit: sc. *carina;* Odysseus' ship alone is able to escape the onslaught of the Laestrygonians because he had moored it outside the harbour (*Od.* 10.95–6, 125–32). The phrasing is reminiscent of Virg. *Aen.* 1.113 unam, *quae Lycios fidumque uehebat Oronten.*

242–3 Cf. *Od.* 10.133–5 'From there we sailed on further along, glad to have escaped death, but grieving still at heart for the loss of our dear companions. We came to Aiaia, which is an island' (Lattimore). **multaque conquesti** 'lamenting greatly', *multa* is an adverbial acc., like the Greek πολλά (see K–S 1.280f.). **adlabimur:** cf. *Aen.* 3.569 *ignarique uiae Cyclopum adlabimur oris.*

243–307 *Odysseus and Circe.* Odysseus' encounter with Circe occupies the remainder of *Odyssey* 10 (133–574). While Ovid follows Homer in the general outline of the story, he again abbreviates the episode and changes the perspective of the story through the use of Macareus as narrator instead of Odysseus. Virgil famously only mentions Circe at the beginning of *Aen.* 7 (10–24), describing briefly her singing (12), the smell of cedar (13), the whistling of her shuttle (14) and the howling of beasts (15–18) coming from her home, only to have Neptune keep the Trojans from reaching her shores: *Aen.* 7.21–4 *quae ne monstra pii paterentur talia Troes | delati in portus neu litora dira subirent, | Neptunus uentis impleuit uela secundis, | atque fugam dedit et praeter uada feruida uexit.* Through *praeteritio,* Virgil allows the dangers represented by Circe to resonate upon the Trojans' arrival in Italy, while he avoids treating the Homeric tale of metamorphosis (*Aen.* 7.10 *proxima Circaeae raduntur litora terrae*, see Putnam 1995: 103–7). Ovid reinserts the omitted episode and even appends to it a further amatory tale involving Circe, that of Picus and Canens (308–434), which had been briefly alluded to in the *Aeneid* (7.189–91). In his treatment of this episode, Ovid makes explicit the symbolic significance of Circe's transformative powers which are only briefly mentioned in Virgil (*Aen.* 7.19–20). See Hardie 1992, Segal 1968.

244–5 quas . . . crede mihi!: the lines are based on a series of parallelisms and doublings: *procul hinc – procul hinc, cernis – uidenda, mihi crede – crede mihi* (with prosodic variation in *míhĭ* . . . *mihī́*, see 128n.) which give emphasis to Macareus' warning. *crede* in 245 is Shackleton Bailey's conjecture (1981: 336). *uisa,* the reading of the main MSS, creates wordplay with *uidenda* and would emphasize Macareus' own experience 'the island seen by me', but fails to establish the required contrast with *procul uidenda*, as Shackleton Bailey explains, 'an island seen from a distance can be contrasted with the same seen at close quarters, but not with the same seen'. Courtney 2005: 39 suggests instead *pressa* in place of the second *crede.* **insula:** see 9–10n. on the localization of Circe's home. **iustissime:** for this uncommon epithet for Aeneas, cf. *Aen.* 1.544–5 *rex erat Aeneas nobis, quo iustior alter | nec pietate fuit, nec bello maior et armis.* At *Met.* 15.833 Augustus is *iustissimus auctor.*

246 nate dea 'born of a goddess'; a frequent term of respect used of Aeneas in the *Aeneid* (1.582, 615, 2.289, 3.374, *al.*), cf. *Met.* 15.439. Here, as Macareus explains, it signals his change of heart (from 163–4 *barbara Graium | prora uehit?)* about his former enemy. **neque enim:** these words mark a transition, and frequently introduce a parenthesis, cf. 25n., 679, 13.270, 564, *al.*; see Hardie on *Aen.* 9.617. **Marte** 'war'; a common metonymy in epic, cf. 450, 746, Quint. *Inst.* 8.6.24 *eruditus est sermo.* Greek epic uses Ares, the god of war, in the same way.

247 fuge litora Circes! This recalls Achaemenides' warning to the Trojans to flee from the Cyclopes at *Aen.* 3.639–40 *sed fugite, o miseri, fugite atque ab litore funem | rumpite.* Ovid gestures toward Virgil's narrative manoeuvre in the *Aeneid* of having the Trojans avoid a meeting with Circe at *Aen.* 7.21–4, cf. 446–7.

248 Circaeo . . . in litore echoes Virgil's similar use of the ennobling personal adj. (see 1n., cf. 253, 348) at *Aen.* 7.10 *Circaeae . . . litora terrae* (which in turn imitates Ap. Rh. 2.400, see Horsfall *ad Aen.* 7.10).

249 An impressive four-word line, abbreviating Hom. *Od.* 10.198–200 'So I spoke, and the inward heart in them was broken, as they remembered Antiphates the Laestrygonian and the violence of the great-hearted cannibal Cyclops, and they wept loud and shrill' (Lattimore). **Antiphatae:** (Gk first decl., gen. sing.), cf. 234. **immansuetique:** 'such compounds (*in* + pf. part.) are characteristic of Ovid, and this may have been coined by him' (Kenney on *Her.* 18.37); here perhaps it should be taken ἀπὸ κοινοῦ with Antiphates. Cf. 15.85–7 *at quibus ingenium est immansuetumque ferumque, | Armeniae tigres iracundique leones | cumque lupis ursi, dapibus cum sanguine gaudent.* **Cyclopis:** the first syllable is here left short (a syllable with a vowel short by nature before a mute and a liquid can either be lengthened or left short), cf. 3.305, *Aen.* 3.647 and contrast *Met.* 14.2, 174 where the syllable is long.

250 'we refused to go further and to enter unknown dwellings'; on this poetic construction of *negare* see McKeown on *Am.* 2.15.19, *OLD* 4. The line is framed by *ire* and the compound *subire* (*OLD* 10c). *et* construes *subire* with *negabamus*, but requires the lengthening of the final syllable of *negabamus*, which is allowed in arsis (the metrical ictus of the foot) at a main third foot caesura (diastole); see Winbolt 1903: 203–4, Fordyce on *Aen.* 7.174. Courtney 1965: 64 quotes *Met.* 7.61), cf. 491, 809. Tarrant (*per litteras*) suggests that this may have prompted other textual variants as metrical corrections.

251–3 In Homer's account (*Od.* 10.203–9) Odysseus divides his men into two bands and appoints himself the leader of one group and Eurylochus leader of the other. Lots are then taken for which group will be sent out and Eurylochus' lot springs out of the helmet and he sets out with twenty-two men.

251 fidumque Politen: Polites takes the lead in addressing Circe upon arriving at her home in Homer (*Od.* 10.224–8) and *fidum* closely renders his Homeric epithet κεδνότατος 'most dear/trusted' (225).

252 nimiique Elpenora uini 'Elpenor, too fond of wine', genitive of description (*NLS* §84). Ovid alludes to the very end of Homer's Circe episode when Elpenor, drunk (οἰνοβαρείων), falls off Circe's roof and breaks his neck (*Od.* 10.551–60). Later his shade meets Odysseus in the Underworld and asks for burial (*Od.* 11.51–83).

253 Eighteen companions join Macareus, Polites, Eurylochus, and Elpenor, making twenty-two in all, while in Homer Eurylochus led a division of twenty-two men (*Od.* 10.208), making twenty-three.

254 Cf. *Od.* 10.220 ἔσταν δ' ἐν προθύροισι θεᾶς 'they stood there at the palace-doors of the goddess'.

255–70 For the depiction of Circe's home Ovid follows Homer's account at *Od.* 10.210–23, while also drawing on Virgil's brief description at *Aen.* 7.10–24. In Homer there are only lions and wolves in Circe's forecourt (*Od.* 10.212, 218–19), while later Circe transforms Odysseus' men into swine (10.239ff.). Virgil mentions the sounds of lions, wolves, swine, and, surprisingly, bears, coming from Circe's home (*Aen.* 7.15–18); Horsfall ad loc. explains the bears as 'a piece of peculiarly Italian colour', while Thomas 1986: 66–7 refers to Hom. *Od.* 11.611 (bears, lions, boars on Heracles' belt). Ovid picks up Virgil's bears, while saving mention of the pigs for the upcoming scene of transformation (276–84), as in Homer. For the grouping wolves, bears, and lions cf. 10.540–1, 15.86–7. The line is elevated by homoeoteleuton, polysyndeton (see 78n.), alliteration, and polyptoton. For illustrations of Circe's abode see Canciani, *LIMC* VI.2.24–31 (plates). **mille lupi:** Ovid perhaps tops Virgil's *formae magnorum . . . luporum* (*Aen.* 7.18).

256–9 In his description of the fawning animals at Circe's home Ovid draws on Homer's account at *Od.* 10.214–19. Here Homer compares the behaviour of the lions and wolves to that of dogs welcoming home their master. While Ovid omits the simile, much of his language gestures towards it.

256 occursu fecere metum 'frightened us by their onset', cf. Hom. *Od.* 10.219 τοὶ δ' ἔδεισαν, ἐπεὶ ἴδον αἰνὰ πέλωρα 'they were afraid when they saw the terrible big beasts'.

256–7 nulla . . . | nullaque agree in gender with *leae*, but qualify all the animals in the sense, 'not one of them was to be feared, not one of them was to give us a single scratch on our bodies'.

258–9 The details recall Homer's description of Circe's beasts as 'waving their long tails and fawning, in the way that dogs go fawning about their master' (*Od.* 10.215–16). *blandus* is a transferred epithet that describes the animals' behaviour.

260 atria marmore tecta: cf. Virg. *Aen.* 7.12 (Circe's home) *tectisque superbis*, Hom. *Od.* 10.210–11 τετυγμένα δώματα Κίρκης | ξεστοῖσιν λάεσσι 'the home of Circe built from stones, well-polished.' *atria* is a Roman touch, cf. 9–10, 13.968.

261 pulchro . . . recessu 'in an attractive inner room' loc. abl. (89–90n.); cf. of a dwelling 1.177 (Jupiter's palace) *marmoreo . . . recessu*, 7.670 (palace of Aeacus) *pulchrosque recessus*.

262 sublimi solio: suggests Circe's royal and divine status (Bömer), cf. 2.24 (Phoebus), 3.273 (Juno), 6.650 (Tereus), *Aen.*1.506 (Dido) *solioque alte subnixa resedit*, 7.169

(Latinus) *solio medius consedit auito. sublimi* (Kenney 1959: 243 'fort. recte') seems preferable to the alternative *sollemni* found in some MSS, cf. 6.650 *ipse sedens solio Tereus sublimis auito.* **pallamque induta nitentem:** *induta* is to be understood as middle voice, with *pallam* as object, see 45n. (Courtney 2004: 426 (1), Harrison 1991: 290–1 (iv)). A *palla* is a rectangular mantle worn as an outdoor garment especially by women; in Latin poetry it is associated particularly with deities, singers, and poets (McKeown on *Am.* 1.8.59–60), cf. 2.672 (Ocyroe), 3.167 (Diana), 11.166 (Apollo).

263 'she was in addition covered with a golden mantle'. Another four-word hexameter (116n.) rounds out the description. *circumuelatur* is a hapax legomenon (cf. Varro *LL* 5.132 '*amictui' dictum quod ambiectum est, id est circumiectum*); for the line end cf. Catull. 64.265 *uelabat amictu*, *Aen.* 3.545 *uelamur amictu*, 8.33.

264–5 Ovid here pointedly departs from the Homeric and Virgilian texts which depict Circe engaged in the typically feminine task of weaving (*Od.* 10.221–3, 226, 254; *Aen.* 7.14), while acknowledging the deviation through the negation of the earlier versions. Ovid instead emphasizes Circe's magical powers by representing her home as an herbal pharmacy. **Nereides** = Νηρείδες 'sea nymphs' (daughters of Nereus), Gk. nom. pl. The second syllable of *Nereis* may be scanned long or short (here it is short), a variation derived from the Greek forms Νηρείς or Νηρηίς (see McKeown on *Am.* 2.11.36). In Homer *Od.* 10.348–51 Circe's attendants are said to be 'daughters born of the springs and from the coppices and the sacred rivers which flow down to the sea' (Lattimore, see Segal 1968: 440), in Apollonius they are Naiads (*Arg.* 4.711). **quae . . . | . . . ducunt** 'who card no fleece and spin no threads with nimble fingers'; cf. 4.36 *leui deducens pollice filum*, 54 *lana sua fila sequente*, Catull. 64.311–19. *uellera* are the masses of unspun fleece (6.19 *rudem . . . lanam*). *fila sequentia* refers to the process of drawing out and forming the threads (which then seem to follow, see *OLD sequor* 8a). For a similar negation of conventional female activities see Callisto at 2.411 *non erat huius opus lanam mollire trahendo*, cf. Pomona 626–36.

265–7 Knox 1986a: 85–6 observes that these lines create an unusual sequence of the violation of Hermann's Bridge (avoidance of a trochaic caesura in the fourth foot of the hexameter, a rhythm used freely by Ovid and Propertius after Tibullus' example, see Kenney 2002: 32n.29), creating a deliberately swift cadence for the activity of Circe's servants (other such triplets occur in similar sequences at 8.307–9, 13.877–9).

266–70 Circe oversees the preparation of herbs for her potions.

266 sine ordine 'at random', an Ovidian 'formula' (Knox on *Her.* 10.19, *TLL* IX 2.952.32).

267 uariasque coloribus herbas 'herbs varied in color' (*OLD uarius* 4), ablative of respect *NLS* § 55.

268 ipsa . . . ipsa: the anaphora emphasizes Circe's mastery of the magical properties of the plants, cf. Hom. *Od.* 10.276 Κίρκης . . . πολυφαρμάκου ('Circe, skilled in medicines'), see Tupet 1976: 397–8. **opus exigit** 'she oversees the performance of the work' (*OLD exigo* 8b).

270 aduertens 'paying close attention' (*OLD* 6). **pensas . . . herbas** 'the apportioned herbs'; the choice of language here hints at Circe's original activity of weaving (*OLD pensum* 1 'a quantity of wool given to be spun or woven'), cf. 4.10 *calathosque infectaque pensa reponunt*, see Frécaut 1972: 106.

271 dicta acceptaque salute: repeated from 11, in a context perhaps ominously similar.

272 'she smiled and returned favorable responses to our greetings'; for *diffundo* see (*OLD* 5); *uultus* is poetic pl.

273–76 Circe mixes the drink (consisting of barley, cheese, honey, and wine) in which she places the magical juices to transform Odysseus' men, as at *Od.* 10.234–6.

273 nec mora: a formula especially popular in epic, cf. 362, 845; see Gibson on *AA* 3.709. **tosti . . . hordea grani** 'toasted barley grains', elevated poetic locution, with the inversion of normal construction (*tosta hordei grana*), for the ingredient (ἄλφιτα) in Homer (Bömer).

274 uimque meri 'powerful wine', on the model of Greek epic and tragic periphrases with βία ('strength') + genitive (Kenney on Lucr. 3.8). **lacte coagula passo** 'milk that has been subjected to (i.e.'curdled by') rennet', i.e. cheese, cf. 8.666 *lactis massa coacti*, 13.829–30, *F.* 4.545. Rennet is a coagulant taken from the stomach of lambs or goats; a technical term used earlier in verse only at Tib. 2.3.14b. Poetry usually avoids the prosaic *caseus* (but see *F.* 4.371, 769, Virg. *Ecl.* 1.34, Tib. 2.5.38) and prefers such poetic periphrases (see Coleman 1999: 59, Maltby 1999: 236, Bömer on 8.666), cf. Virg. *Ecl.* 1.81 *pressi copia lactis.*

278 uirga: Ovid's Circe uses both herbal potions and her wand to transform Odysseus' men (cf. 299–300, 412–15, 387), as in Homer (ῥάβδος *Od.* 10.238). So also in Virgil Picus' transformation is ascribed to Circe's *uirga* and *uenena* (*Aen.* 7.190–1, cf. *Ecl.* 8.70 *carminibus Circe socios mutauit Vlixi*). **dea dira:** at *Aen.* 7.22 Circe's shores are called *litora dira*, cf. Hom. *Od.*10.136 (of Circe) δεινὴ θεός. For the epithet *dirus* of dark magic, cf. *Her.* 6.84 *dira pabula*, Hor. *Epod.* 5.61–2, Luc. 6.501, 580.

279–86 Macareus narrates his own metamorphoses, from man to pig and back again. Other narrators of their own transformation in the poem include Glaucus 13.917–65 and Virbius 15.497–547. In Homer Odysseus is, of course, the narrator and he describes the transformations of his men to and from pigs. Ancient allegorical interpretations (cf. 25n.) saw Circe's metamorphoses as a result of her victims' own vices of gluttony or lust, see Xen. *Mem.* 1.3.6, Plut. *Mor.* 52d, Hor. *Epist.* 1.2.22–6. See Horsfall on *Aen.* 7.16, Kaiser 1964: 202–3, Segal 1968: 442.

279 (et pudet et referam) 'I am shamed to relate it but I will', for the almost adversative force of *et* see *OLD et* 10, *TLL* v 2.893.4ff., cf. *Rem.* 407 *et pudet et dicam*, Tibull. 1.5.42 *et pudet et narrat.*

280–1 nec iam posse . . . : with *posse, edere,* and *procumbere* we are to understand *coepi* from 279. On the loss of speech through metamorphosis, see 98–9n. Cf. Hom. *Od.* 10.239–40 'they took on the look of pigs, with the heads and voices (φωνήν) and bristles of pigs' (Lattimore). **in terram toto procumbere uultu:** proverbially definitive of animals, see 1.84 *pronaque cum spectent animalia cetera terram,* and contrast 302–3.

282 sensi: suggests, as in Homer (*Od.* 10.240 'the minds within them stayed as they had been before'), that the metamorphosis is only one of outward appearance (cf. Io 1.635–57, Callisto 2.485, Actaon 3.198–203). **pando occallescere rostro** 'hardening into a curved snout'; an extension of the instrumental ablative. For *pando . . . rostro* of swine cf. 10.713, 15.112–13. *occallescere* appears before Ovid only at Plaut. *As.* 419, and Cic. *Att.* 2.18.4 (*TLL* IX 2.330.27–52).

283 qua . . . parte: the antecedent is incorporated in the relative clause, see 85n. On *pars* as 'body part' or 'limb' see *OLD* 6a.

285 passis: sc. *sociis.* **(tantum medicamina possunt)** = 7.116 (of Medea, Circe's aunt, the sister of Aeetes, Medea's father), cf. 34 *carmine cum tantum, tantum quoque gramine possim,* Juv. 6.595.

286 claudor hara: cf. Hom. *Od.* 10.283. **suis** is gen. sing. of *sus* 'pig'.

286–7 In Homer it is explained that Eurylochus suspected Circe's hospitality and waited outside her home as his companions entered and were transformed (*Od.* 10.232–3, 258). He was therefore able to return to the ships and tell Odysseus what happened (244–60).

289 saetigeri: borrowed from Virg. *Aen.* 7.17 *saetigerique sues,* drawn from Lucr. 5.970 *saetigerisque subus,* 6.974.

290 certior: sc. *factus.* **Circen:** Gk acc., cf. 376, 399. Here, as often, the Greek form is metrically convenient.

291 pacifer . . . Cyllenius: Mercury is called *Cyllenius* from the Arcadian mountain Cyllene, on which he was said to be born, cf. 1.713, *Od.* 24.1, *Aen.* 8.138–9 *Mercurius . . . quem candida Maia* | *Cyllenae gelido conceptum uertice fudit.* The epithet *pacifer* (the adj. is found first in Virg. *Aen.* 8.116 *paciferae . . . oliuae*) derives from Mercury's role as a messenger and negotiator, cf. *F.* 5.665 *pacis et armorum . . . arbiter,* Plaut. *Amph.* 32, Eitrem *RE* VIII 782.62–783.25.

292 moly uocant superi: the name of this magical plant is 'an example of the so-called "language of the gods"' (Hom. *Od.* 10.305 μῶλυ δέ μιν καλέουσι θεοί, with Heubeck and Hoekstra ad loc., who note that it may be related to the Sanskrit *mulam* 'root', see also Clay 1972). For an ancient attempt at botanical identification, see Plin. *Nat.* 25.26. *moly* is one of the very small number of Greek words in the *Met.*; see Kenney 2002: 68n.244.

293 monitisque . . . caelestibus: at Hom. *Od.* 10.275–301 Hermes appears to Odysseus and not only gives him the *moly* but instructs him in detail on how to deal with Circe when he encounters her.

294–6 In Homer Odysseus is able to drink Circe's potion (*pocula* poetic pl.) because of the immunity the *moly* has given him (10.290–2, 316–17). When Circe tries to strike him with her wand, he rushes forward with his sword as if to attack her and she surrenders to him (321–35).

297–8 Ovid again only briefly touches on the main story elaborated in Homer's account where, as Hermes had advised (10.297–301), Odysseus accepts Circe's invitation to go to bed with her after she has sworn an oath to him that she intends him no further evil (10.336–44). Afterwards, Circe serves him a lavish banquet which he refuses to eat until she changes his companions back to men (375–87). Ovid neatly compresses this exchange, and his Ulysses withholds his sexual favours with a witty play on Roman marriage convention. **fides dextraeque datae:** formula (Bömer ad loc.), cf. e.g. 6.506, *Aen.* 4.597 *en dextra fidesque.* **coniugii dotem:** marriage terminology, perhaps here loosely of Ulysses and Circe's affair; cf. *coniunx* used of Circe's relationship with Picus (Serv. on *Aen.* 7.189 '*coniunx' uero non quae erat sed quae esse cupiebat*), see Moorton 1988: 254.

299–305 Circe reverses the metamorphosis of 273–84 and returns the men to their own forms. Reverse transformation is rare. Compare the same scene at *Od.* 10.388–96 and Io at *Met.* 1.738–46.

299 ignotae sucis melioribus herbae 'more benign juices of a mysterious plant', reverses the action of 275; cf. 250 *tecta ignota*, 366 *ignoto carmine*, 13.944 *ignotos . . . sucos.*

300 percutimurque caput 'we are struck on the head'; *caput* is acc. with the passive verb, denoting the body-part affected, see 97n., Courtney 2004: 428 (6), cf. Virg. *G.* 4.357 *percussa noua mentem formidine.* **conuersae** denotes the reversal of the spell.

301 'words are spoken reversing the words that had been spoken.' An elaborately structured line framed by emphatic repetition with variation (*uerba/uerbis*, cf. 300 *uerbere*), with the caesura also marked by polyptoton (*dicuntur/dictis*), while the repetition is arranged chiastically. The complex ordering of the line (the opposition of repeated vocabulary) mirrors the reverse effect being described and evokes Circe's magical incantations (Wilkinson 1963: 168 'suitable abracadabra', cf. the marked alliteration of the preceding line and see 34n.); for the notion of spells in reverse nullifying previous effects, cf. Hor. *Epod.* 17.7 *citumque retro solue, solue turbinem*, Val. Fl. 1.782–3 (Stygian rites) *iamiam exorabile retro | carmen agens.* There had been, however, no mention of spells earlier when the men were transformed. Wills 1996: 202n.36 compares *Aen.* 10.448 *talibus et dictis it contra dicta tyranni.*

302–3 leuati | erigimur: a quintessential human characteristic (cf. 1.85–6 *os homini sublime dedit caelumque uidere | iussit et erectos ad sidera tollere uultus*), which reverses 281.

303–4 bifidosque relinquit | rima pedes 'the cleft left our cloven feet', i.e. they are no longer cloven (*bifidus* first here, cf. 2.325 *trifidus*). **redeunt umeri:** cf. Io's return to human form 1.741 *redeunt umerique manusque.*

304–5 subiecta lacertis | bracchia sunt 'forearms were placed beneath the upper arms'; a humorously literal detail, cf. 283–4. **illis:** (referring to *bracchia*) seems to place witty emphasis on the men's recently restored arms, while *ipsi* (supported by Bömer) seems unnecessary after the polyptoton of *flentem flentes.* The MS reading *illum* provides a heightened closure (with enclosed word order) to the scene, but fits awkwardly with *ducis* in the following line. Cf. the same scene at Hom. *Od.* 10.397–9.

306–7 nec uerba . . . gratos = (by brachylogy) *nec ulla priora uerba locuti sumus quam ea testantia nos gratos esse*, 'nor did we say anything before declaring how grateful we were' (Bömer). *priora* is adverbial.

308–434 *Circe, Picus, and Canens.* With the Italian tale of Circe, Picus, and Canens the poem now veers from events in *Odyssey* 10, which continue with Circe's reception of Odysseus and his men and their eventual departure after a year (*Od.* 10.397–574). Taking advantage of a 'narrative gap' (308 *annua mora*, 312, 435 *longum . . . per annum*), where Homer had simply stated the expiration of a year (*Od.* 10.467–8 'There for all our days until a year was completed we sat there feasting on unlimited meat and sweet wine'), Ovid inserts his own tale of metamorphosis. This story constitutes a particularly complex example of narratological construction: Macareus repeats to Achaemenides the Italian story, which had been told to him earlier by one of Circe's attendants (Arethusa's narrative in book 5.572–642 is the most complex example of embedded narrative (Muse-Calliope-Arethusa), see Barchiesi 2002b: 188–9, Rosati 2002: 272). Ovid's focus stays on lesser characters: while waiting for Odysseus to leave Circe's island, his crew evidently socialized with her housemaids. After Macareus finishes this tale, the Homeric Circe episode is quickly summarized and completed (435–8).

The story of Picus, Canens, and Circe marks a significant transitional point in the poem as the first Italian episode, introducing the new Italian material and Ovid's aetiological approach. It is prompted by Virgil's description of a statue of Picus standing in the forecourt of the ancient Laurentine palace (*Aen.* 7.171 *Laurentis regia Pici*), amidst the other statues of the ancestors of king Latinus, eponym of the Latins (*Aen.* 7.187–91 *ipse Quirinali lituo paruaque sedebat | succinctus trabea laeuaque ancile gerebat | Picus, equum domitor, quem capta cupidine coniunx | aurea percussum uirga uersumque uenenis | fecit auem Circe sparsitque coloribus alas*). Following probably a Varronian genealogy (Varro, *De gente pop. Rom.* fr. 27 Fracc., *Res div.* 217 Cardauns), Virgil makes Picus the grandfather of Latinus (*Aen.* 7.47–9, Faunus and the nymph Marica are said to be Latinus' parents); for the problem of Circe as Picus' *coniunx* see Moorton 1988. An earlier Greek tradition had located Circe in Italy and made her the mother by Odysseus of Latinus ([Hes.] *Th.* 1011–13, see West ad loc., Jameson and Malkin 1998, Rosivach 1980). In contrast to Virgil's genealogical and national context, Ovid's Picus appears as an attractive youth, whose tale is introduced by a description of his cult statue set up by Circe. Ovid's erotic triangle involving Picus, Circe, and Canens seems original (we know nothing of Aemilius Macer's treatment of Picus' (Picumnus') metamorphosis in his *Ornithogonia* (*FLP* p. 293)). It is the third of the series of love triangles within the '*Aeneid*' section of the poem, the second in this book involving Circe (see the notes below for parallels with the story of Circe, Glaucus, and Scylla at 13.898–14.74), which share thematic (as well as verbal) affinities with the triangle of Aeneas, Turnus, and Lavinia in Virgil (see Nagle 1988c, Ellsworth 1986). Chronologically the tale functions as another 'prequel' to the *Aeneid.*

Picus is a rustic *numen* from Italian religious folklore, rather than contemporary cult (cf. *F.* 3.292 *Romani numen . . . soli*). He was identified with the woodpecker, an augural bird sacred to Mars (*F.* 3.37 *Martia picus auis,* cf. Plin. *Nat.* 10.41) and possibly with an agricultural deity Picumnus (Radke 1979: 255–6), in addition to being considered as one of the ancient Italian kings (321 *rex*) and a deity with augural powers (Val. Ant. fr. 6 Peter, Varr. *Res div.* fr. 35 Cardauns, see Horsfall on *Aen.* 7.171, Rohde *RE* xx 1214ff.). In the *Fasti* Ovid tells a story of Picus' and Faunus' assistance to Numa in the reception of the *ancilia* from Jupiter Elicius (*F.* 3.259–392, cf. Virg. *Aen.* 7.188); the chronological problem of his appearance at this much later date in non-avian form obviously did not bother Ovid. Silius Italicus associates Picus with the *Picentes* and at *Pun.* 8.439–42 tells of his transformation. The nymph Canens appears nowhere else (Servius on *Aen.* 7.190 mentions a version in which Pomona (soon to appear in a different tale at *Met.* 14.622–771) was Picus' wife). See Myers 1994a: 104–13, Tissol 1997: 210–14, Nagle 1988c, Ellsworth 1986, Casali 1995a, Papaianou 2005: 113–39, A. Hardie (forthcoming).

308 mora is a signal, as often, for narrative excursus/digression, cf. 312.

308–10 múltaque . . . múlta . . . cum multís: anaphora with variation of metrical ictus. Macareus ends his narrative similarly at 435 *talia multa mihi longum narrata per annum | uisaque sunt.* **multaque praesens | tempore tam longo uidi, multa auribus hausi** 'in so long a period of time I saw many things with my own eyes and I drank in many tales with my ears'. For the epic and aetiological story-telling motif of autopsy and report, cf. 181–2n., 13.787 *procul auribus hausi, F.* 4.689 *is mihi multa quidem. sed et haec narrare solebat,* Hom. *Od.* 3.92–5, 4.323–5, Virg. *Aen.* 4.358–9 *ipse deum . . . uidi . . . uocemque auribus hausi.* **hoc quoque cum multis** 'this (story) too, along with many others . . .' For the motif of multiple story choice cf. 4.43–53, 276–84, Tarrant 2005.

311 quattuor e famulis: the detail derives from Homer *Od.* 10.348–59, where Circe's four nymph maidservants prepare a meal for Circe and Odysseus. A discreet hint that Homer is still in the background. **ad talia sacra:** these rites are presumably those for Picus which are explained in 315–16.

313–15 Picus' statue presents him as a handsome youth with a woodpecker on his head as a symbol of his transformed state. Virgil instead depicts Picus as an Italian king, or augur (*Aen.* 7.187–9, cited 308–434n.). Circe's statue is anachronistically made of marble, whereas primitive Italian statues were traditionally made of wood, as is Picus' statue in the *Aeneid* (7.177–8 *ueterum effigies ex ordine auorum* | *antiqua e cedro*, cf. *Met.* 10.694 *lignea . . . ueterum simulacra deorum*, Tib.1.10.19–20, Prop. 4.2.59–60). Dido, however, has a marble shrine to Sychaeus at *Aen.* 4.457–9 *praeterea fuit in tectis de marmore templum* | *coniugis antiqui, miro quod honore colebat,* | *uelleribus niueis et festa fronde reuinctum*, cf. her image of Aeneas (*Aen.* 4.508 *effigiemque toro locat*). In *Her.* 7.99 Dido's shrine includes an image of Sychaeus.

313–14 signum | . . . iuuenale 'a statue of a youth'. **gerens in uertice picum:** an odd representation, but cf. the statue of M. Valerius Corvus with a raven on his head set up by Augustus in his forum (Aul. Gell. *NA* 9.11.10). Bömer also cites stories told of woodpeckers landing on the heads of Roman statesmen, such as Aelius Tubero, *praetor urbanus*, in Varro, *De vita pop. Rom.* fr. 94 (Non. p. 518M), Plin. *Nat.* 10.41.

315–16 Circe has placed Picus' statue in a shrine and has made it an object of cult worship, a fact emphasized by the placement of *aede* framing the two lines (with *sacra* in chiastic order).

316–19 Macareus' questions (*quis . . . quare . . . cur*) prompt the narration of the story as an explanation of Picus' cult statue. The language and situation are reminiscent of the many aetiological queries in the *Fasti* that in turn imitate Callimachus' interrogations (some about cult statues) in the first two books of the *Aitia* (see Miller 1982, Myers 1994a: 61–94, 105–7), cf. 4.704 *accipe quaesitam causam*, 7.757–8, *F.* 1.115 (Janus) *accipe quaesitae quae causa sit altera formae.* In *Aitia* 1 (frr. 35–8 Massimilla = frr. 31b–e Pf.) Callimachus asked a Muse about a statue of Artemis in Leucadia with a mortar on its head.

316 foret for *esset,* in the first of three indirect questions dependent on *quaerenti.*

318 dominaeque potentia: the tale is introduced as an example of Circe's dangerous power, cf. 34. **quae sit:** for lines ending with two monosyllables (far more common than a one-monosyllable ending), see Hellegouarc'h 1964: 52–5 (2% *Met.* 13–14, of which a form of *esse* is the most common final word, cf. 318, 361); cf. Helzle on *Pont.* 4.2.47.

319 The language is didactic, cf. 4.287, *F.* 1.102 (Janus) *uoces percipe mente meas*, 3.177–8, Kenney 1958: 203.

320 proles Saturnia: cf. *Aen.* 7.48–9 *Fauno Picus pater, isque parentem* | *te, Saturne, refert, tu sanguinis ultimus auctor*; the genealogy may be Virgilian in origin (see Horsfall on *Aen.* 7.48). Italy is *Saturnia tellus* from the story of Saturn's arrival and rule in Latium, cf. *F.* 1.233–7, 6.31 *a patre dicta meo quondam Saturnia Roma est*, Ennius, *Ann.* 21 Sk., Virg. *Aen.* 8.319–25, *G.* 2.173. *proles* is a poetic archaism (Cic. *De orat.* 3.153), here further elevated by the adj. for genitive *Saturnia* indicating his ancestry: for parallels see Bömer on 2.19 *Clymeneia . . . proles*, Harrison on *Aen.* 10.353–4. **in Ausoniis . . . terris:** cf. 7n.; reminders of the story's Italian locale are frequent in this tale, cf. 326, 390, 422.

321 studiosus equorum: cf. *Aen.* 7.189 *Picus, equum domitor* (the Homeric heroic epithet ἱππόδαμος, Fordyce ad loc.). *studiosus* is colloquial, appearing in poetry before only at Hor. *Sat.* 2.5.80, see Knox 1986b: 100, Kenney 2002: 37–8. Cf. *Am.* 3.2.1 *non ego nobilium sedeo studiosus equorum.*

322–3 'The appearance of the man was as you see it: you can observe his beauty for yourself and from the constructed image you may esteem the true'. Barchiesi 2002b: 185 suggests that this comment by the internal narrator breaks epic convention whereby 'internal addressee and general addressee together enjoy shared information and shared access to the storyworld'. *ficta . . . ueram* suggests the nymph's concern with credibility, cf. 433–4n.; see Feeney 1991: 224–32 on Ovid's sophisticated play with fiction and reality, and the suspension of disbelief and belief.

324–5 'He could not yet in the course of his years have watched four quinquennial contests at Grecian Elis', i.e. the Olympic Games, celebrated every four years (five in inclusive counting) at Olympia in Elis in the north-west Peloponnese. *Elide pugnam* is attested by Heinsius, possibly as a conjecture; the main MSS have *edere pugna.* Picus could be between 12 and 15, (or 19, if, as elsewhere, five years is actually meant, cf. 4.292, *Tr.* 4.10.95, Bömer); cf. other attractive youths 2.497 (Arcas) *ter quinque fere natalibus actis*, 3.351–2 (Narcissus) *ter ad quinos unum Cephisius annum* | *addiderat*, 4.292 (Hermaphroditus) *is tria cum primum fecit quinquennia.* The nymph's method of dating constitutes an anachronism (Eratosthenes dated the first Olympiad to 776/5, Varro to 773 BCE (fr. 3 Peter), i.e. about four hundred years later, see Feeney 1999: 21) and sits oddly in this Italian context (although the nymph is presumably Greek, as is her auditor Macareus). Courtney (*per litteras*) observes that the reference may suit Picus' equestrian passion (see 321).

326–32 A catalogue of Picus' nymph admirers (Dryads are tree nymphs, Naiads river nymphs, cf. 327–8 *fontana . . . numina*). For the topos of erotic desirability, see 673n. and cf. the description of Lavinia at Virg. *Aen.* 7.54–5 *multi illam magno e Latio totaque petebant* | *Ausonia.* Geographical catalogues are a learned feature of the epic tradition (cf. 2.217–26 (mountains), 241–59 (springs and rivers), 7.350–93, 15.273–360, *Am.* 3.6 (rivers), see Reitz 1999); for river catalogues, cf. Call. *H. Del.* 70ff., Virg. *G.* 4.365–73, Jones 2005: 81–91. Through this list of nymphs and their rivers, all of which appear also in the second half of the *Aeneid* (some in Virgil's catalogue of the Italian forces at 7.641ff.),

Ovid localizes his story in Italy and foreshadows Aeneas' arrival in Latium, which is only mentioned in passing at 447–9. The list 'fills the place of an actual description of landscape' (Segal 1969: 64) and, simultaneously, eroticizes the Italian setting. Ovid notably avoids military catalogues in his treatment of the Trojan legend (see 452–3n.). See Gassner 1972: 111 on geographical catalogues at the openings of stories in the *Met.*, cf. 1.579–82 (rivers), 6.414–21, 10.529–31. Typical of catalogue language is the multiple anaphora (and polyptoton) of *quas . . . quasque . . . quas . . . quaeque* (Homeric οἵτε . . . οἵτε cf. e.g. *Il.* 2.496, 499, 500, 681), cf. Virg. *Aen.* 7.682ff. *quique . . . quique . . . quos . . . quos*, 712ff., 10.167ff.

326–7 ille suos . . . | uerterat in uultus 'he had attracted to his appearance the Dryads born on the mountains of Latium'. **Latiis in montibus ortas:** localization (cf. 390, 422) and a Virgilian echo (*Aen.* 9.92 (of the ship-nymphs) *prosit nostris in montibus ortas*), cf. 557n. **illum fontana petebant:** cf. 1.478 (Daphne) *multi illam petiere.*

327–8 fontana . . . | numina Naiades: etymological wordplay on the derivation of *Naiades* from νάω (flow), νᾶμα (stream) (Servius on *Ecl.* 10.62 *a fluminibus naides . . . nominantur,* cf. 557 *Naides aequoreae*), see Helzle on *Pont.* 4.16.35. *Naiades* is Gk. nom. pl. Ovid varies for metrical convenience the forms *Nais/Naias*, but prefers the former (cf. 557, 786 *Naides*), see Bömer on 6.329. **Albula** is the 'original' name of the Tiber, cf. *F.* 5.646 *Albula, si memini, tunc mihi nomen erat* (see Bömer 1957: 134), *Aen.* 8.330–2 (333 *amisit uerum uetus Albula nomen*), Varro *LL* 5.30 *priscum nomen Latinum.* See further 614–16nn. for the etymology of *Tiber* from *Tiberinus/Thybris.* **Numici:** the Numicus (or Numicius), a stream in Latium (mod. Rio Torto or Fosso di Pratica, see Horsfall on *Aen.* 7.797 for the debate about its identification and location), which figures prominently in the story of Aeneas' deification at 598–9 (see nn.). In Virgil, it is always paired with the Tiber (e.g. *Aen.* 7.150, 242, 797). Ovid varies the syntax with the genitives *Numici* and *Anienis* (to be taken with *aquae*).

329 Anienis: the river Anio (mod. Aniene) rises NW of Rome near Trevi and enters the Tiber at Antemnae. On the alternative declensions *Anio/Anien*, see *NW* 1.290, Radke 1977: 195–6, Meister 1916: 2–10. *Anio* is more common than *Anien* in the nom., the forms in *-en-* are normal in the oblique cases (Fordyce on *Aen.* 7.683). This and the following rivers are all tributaries of the Tiber. **cursuque breuissimus Almo:** a tributary of Tiber (mod. Acquataccio), which rises from the Alban hills and flows NW to Rome (see Richardson 1992 s.v. *Almo Flumen*), cf. *F.* 4.337–8 (*lauatio* of Cybele) *est locus, in Tiberim qua lubricus influit Almo | et nomen magno perdit in amne minor.* Virgil draws on the name of the river for a Latin hero *Almo* in *Aen.* 7.532, 575. The syntax returns to the use of nominatives for the next three rivers (now varied also with descriptive modifiers).

330 Narue: the sulphurous river Nar (mod. Nera) rises N of Rome in Umbria and flows down into the Tiber SE of modern Orte (cf. Virg. *Aen.* 7.517, Enn.

Ann. 222 Sk.). **Farfarus:** (mod. Farfa) ; Virgil uses a Latinized form of the name, *Fabarim*, at *Aen.* 7.715 (on the forms of the name, see Ernout 1957: 209–10). The stream rises near Monteleone Sabino and enters the Tiber opposite Soracte.

331 quaeque colunt: catalogue language, cf. Virg. *Aen.* 7.713–14 *qui Tetricae horrentis rupes montemque Seuerum | Casperiamque colunt Forulosque et flumen Himellae*, 7.682–4 *quique arua Gabinae | Iunonis gelidumque Anienem et roscida riuis | Hernica saxa colunt.* **Scythicae stagnum nemorale Dianae:** the precinct and sanctuary of Diana Nemorensis (with its *lacus Nemorensis*, mod. Lago di Nemi) was located near Aricia sixteen miles SE of Rome. On the famous cult, see Ovid's account of Hippolytus/Virbius, Egeria, and the Arician grove at 15.487–551 (cf. *F.* 3.261–74, Virg. *Aen.* 7.761–82), see Coarelli 1987: 165–85, Green 2007. *Scythicae . . . Dianae* refers to a version of the cult's mythical foundation by Orestes, who is said to have carried off the cult image of Tauric Artemis from the Scythian Chersonese (near the Black Sea) and brought it to Aricia (cf. 15.488–9 *Oresteae . . . Dianae*, Lucan 1.446 *Scythicae non mitior ara Dianae*, 3.86, Serv. on *Aen.* 2.116, 6.136, Strabo 5.3.12).

332–3 unam | . . . nymphen: her name, Canens, is delayed until 338. Both the nymph and her genealogy seem to be original to Ovid. Greek forms of *nymphe* are common, cf. 762, 771, 1.744, 3.357, 4.277, *al.* **omnibus unam:** on such numerical juxtaposition, cf. 36n. **colit** 'he is devoted to' (*OLD* 7a), contrast with 331 *colunt* (*OLD* 1).

333–4 quondam . . . | dicitur: typical learned formula for introducing a traditional tale, cf. 5.539, *AA* 3.175, *Tr.* 4.3.7 (see Clausen 1986: 164–5 on the frequency of the phrase in epyllia), and see also Latinus' genealogy at *Aen.* 7.47–8 *hunc Fauno et nympha genitum Laurente Marica | accipimus.* Here, as at 5.539 (Ascalaphus and his mother Orphne), the appeal to tradition (*dicitur*) may instead humorously signal an Ovidian innovation (Bömer ad loc.), cf. 434n. **in colle Palati:** Canens' birth is located at the future site of Rome. The reference to the Palatine hill (first mentioned in the *Met.* at 1.175–6, where Jupiter's palace is compared with the Palatine of Ovid's day) is anachronistic, as the name was commonly derived from Evander's Pallanteum (see Fordyce on *Aen.* 8.51), cf. 622n., 822, 15.560. **Ionio:** objections to the obvious etymological play (*Ionio/Iano*) perhaps gave rise to the variant *ancipiti*, found in a number of MSS, cf. *F.* 1.95 *ancipiti mirandus imagine Janus*, Virg., *Aen.* 7.180 *Ianique bifrontis.* Canens' dual Greek/Italian heritage fits within the pattern of cultural assimilation in Ovid's Italian stories, cf. Pomona 623–4n. A Greek origin for Janus, however, appears only in the later tradition (Plut. *Quaest. Rom.* 22 [*Mor.* 269A]), while Ovid claims Janus exclusively for Italy at *Fasti* 1.90 *nam tibi par nullum Graecia numen habet*, cf. 381n. Janus is associated with water as the father of Fons and Tiberinus (see Porte 1985a: 172) and his appearance here may foreshadow his upcoming role in the book involving a fountain at 785–99. **Venilia:** an old Italian deity, apparently a sea nymph, also mentioned as the mother of Turnus in the *Aeneid* at 10.76; cf. Varro, *LL* 5.72, Serv. on *Aen.* 10.76, Radke *RE* VIII A 787–8.

335 Cf. Virgil's description of Lavinia at *Aen.* 7.53 *iam matura uiro, iam plenis nubilis annis.* **ubi . . . primum:** (*OLD ubi* 9c) only here in Ovid (once at *Aen.* 11.19, 2x Stat. *Theb.* 1.123, 3.34); more commonly *cum . . . primum* or *ut . . . primum* (352).

336 'she was given in marriage to Laurentine Picus, preferred above all other suitors'. **Laurenti . . . Pico:** cf. Virg. *Aen.* 7.171 *Laurentis regia Pici* (where the application of *Laurens* contradicts the aetiological legend of Latinus' naming of his Laurentine settlers from a sacred laurel tree at *Aen.* 7.59–63); cf. 342 *Laurentes . . . agros*, 598 *litus . . . Laurens. Laurentes* designates the people that lived near Lavinium (see Horsfall, *EV* III 141). **tradita:** *tradere* is technical for the act of next of kin 'giving away the bride' (*OLD* 5c).

337 rara . . . rarior 'rare indeed was her beauty, but rarer still her art of singing'. For *rarus* 'incomparable' (Camps on Prop. 1.8.42, *OLD* 6) cf. *Her.* 17.93 *facies tibi rara, Am.* 2.4.17 *places raras dotata per artes*, Prop. 1.8.42 *Cynthia rara mea est,* 1.17.16. The adjective also hints at Canens' upcoming double rarefaction (from liquid to air 431–2). The polyptoton may recall Virg. *Ecl.* 5.44 *formosi pecoris custos, formosior ipse*, describing another pastoral singer, Daphnis (see Wills 1996: 234).

338 unde Canens dicta est: cf. the similar etymology for Carmentis at *F.* 1.467 [*Carmentis*] *nomen habes a carmine ductum.* For the etymological/aetiological phraseology cf. 626, 10.223 *unde etiam nomen traxere Cerastae, F.* 1.237 *inde diu genti mansit Saturnia nomen*, Virg. *Aen.* 7.778, [*Aen.*] 6.242, see Myers 1994a: 67.

338–40 Canens' singing has the same power over nature as that traditionally ascribed to the legendary bards Orpheus (10.86–105, 11.1–49, Hor. *C.* 1.12.7–10 *unde uocalem . . . Orphea . . . arte materna rapidos morantem | fluminum lapsus*) and Arion (*F.* 2.84–90, 116 *aequoreas carmine mulcet aquas*). Magicians also have power over water (see 7.154, 200–1 (Medea), *Am.* 1.8.5–6 (*lena*), Virg. *Aen.* 4.489 (with Pease ad loc. for further examples). Circe's malevolent abilities in song (cf. esp. 20, 34, 357) compete and contrast with those of her rival Canens (Segal 1969a: 65).

341 feminea . . . uoce: such adjectives in *-eus* are more poetic than a modifying genitive and are metrically convenient (see Ross 1975: 60–3). **modulatur carmina:** besides this passage and 428 (Canens' dying song), *modulor* appears elsewhere in Ovid only at 11.154 (*leue cerata modulatur harundine carmen*), where it describes Pan's pastoral piping, and at *Rem.* 181 where again it describes the bucolic song of a *pastor.* Both passages echo Virgil's similarly restricted use of the verb to signify bucolic verse at *Ecl.* 5.14 and 10.51 *carmina pastoris Siculi modulabor auena.* Canens' poetic sympathies associate her both with pastoral poetry appropriate to her rustic landscape and with neoteric elegy (cf. 428–34, and Pomona at 623–4); see A. Hardie (forthcoming) for possible Gallan associations uniting the two traditions.

342–5 Picus sets out to hunt in the forest. For the motif of hunting in the *Metamorphoses* and its association with *amor* ('hunter hunted' topos), see Davis 1983, Parry 1964: 269–74.

343 indigenas . . . apros: these are real boars, not artificial, like the one created by Circe which Picus will in fact hunt (358–60).

344–5 Picus' hunting attire denotes regal status (cf. Dido hunting at *Aen.* 4.134–9 *Sidoniam picto chlamydem circumdata limbo;* | . . . *aurea purpuream subnectit fibula uestem*), but also presages his transformation into a like-colored bird at 393–5 (see nn.). In Virgil Picus is clad in a *trabea*, a ceremonial garment worn by kings, augurs, and magistrates (also purple-red, see Serv. on *Aen.* 7.612). **acris equi:** heroic, cf. 321, 3.704, 7.542, Virg. *Aen.* 1.444. **poeniceam fuluo chlamydem constrictus ab auro** 'having fastened his purple cloak with tawny gold' (i.e. with a pin, cf. 394 *fibula*). *constrictus* (*OLD* 1a) is in the middle voice, *chlamydem* its object, see 45n. (Courtney 2004: 426 (1)). On Ovid's use of *ab* with instrumental ablatives see 15n.

346 filia Solis: cf. 33, Virg. *Aen.* 7.11 *Solis filia.*

347 utque: *-que*, although placed in the subordinate clause, connects the two main clauses.

348 'she had left the Circean fields named after herself'. On the location of Circei see 9–10n.; on the etymology see O'Hara 1996a: 97, 183–4.

349–50 uidit, | **obstipuit:** for the *topos* of love at first sight and its immediate physical effects, cf. 4.676–7 (Perseus and Andromeda) *stupet et uisae correptus imagine formae* | *paene suas quatere est oblitus in aere pennas,* Prop. 4.4.19–22 (Tarpeia) *uidit . . . obstipuit regis facie et regalibus armis,* | *interque oblitas excidit urna manus.* Love at first sight is a topos of the literary treatment of love since at least the Alexandrians and frequent in the *Met.*; cf. 698–700 (Iphis), 7.727 (Cephalus) *et uidi, obstipui, Am.* 1.9.37–8, *Her.* 16.135. See Kenney on Ovid, *Her.* 20.205–8 and Fordyce on Catull. 64.86 for further examples.

351 flamma: on Circe's passionate nature see 25n. **medullas:** for the 'marrow' as the seat of love (*OLD* 2b), cf. e.g. 1.473 (Cupid shoots Apollo) *laesit Apollineas traiecta per ossa medullas, Am.* 2.19.43–4, Catull. 45.15–16, 64.92–3 *cuncto concepit corpore flammam* | *funditus atque imis exarsit medullis*, Virg. *Aen.* 4.66 *est mollis flamma medullas* (see Rosenmeyer 1999).

352 'as soon as she recovered her mind from her strong passion' (*OLD colligo*' 17b); for *aestus* as 'passion (of love)', see 52–3n.; cf. 7.815 *releuare uelis quibus urimur aestus*, [*Am.* 3.5.36] *aestus amoris erat, AA* 3.543, 697, *Her.* 16.25, Prop. 2.33.43, *Ciris* 340.

353 ne posset adire: after *facio* etc. no strict distinction is drawn between intended and actual result; with the former, which is commoner, the negative would be *ne* (as here), as in a purpose clause, with the latter it would be *ut non,* as in a consecutive clause (*NLS* §168).

354 cursus equi . . . circumfususque satelles 'the speed of his horse and the circle of his attendants'. *circumfusus* is a predicative participle, which, in agreement with a noun (*satelles*, collective sing.), forms an abstract noun phrase (*NLS* §95, G–L §664.2, K–S I 766–8, H–S 393–4).

355 licebit is concessive (cf. 171n.) 'you will not escape, though you be snatched away by the wind'. Cf. 4.370–1 (Salmacis to Hermaphroditus) '*pugnes licet . . . | non tamen effugies*', 10.565–6 (Atalanta) *fuge coniugis usum. | nec tamen effugies.*

356–7 On Circe's confidence in her powers, cf. 34 *carmine cum tantum, tantum quoque gramine possim.* **uirtus** 'potency' (*OLD* 5c).

358–64 Circe creates a phantom boar to attract Picus into the dense forest in order to get him alone. Jupiter similarly attempts to lure Io into the woods at 1.589–93 with the offer of shade. The scene recalls the phantom Aeneases found both in *Il.* 5.449–50 (to deceive Diomedes) and *Aen.* 10.636–64 (Juno distracts Turnus) (640 *dat sine mente sonum gressumque effingit euntis*).

358–9 effigiem . . . | finxit is a *figura etymologica.*

360 uideri is logically pleonastic, but reinforces the sense of illusion.

361 plurima qua silua est 'where the wood is densest'; *plurima* (*OLD* 6) is predicative.

362 haud mora, continuo = *Aen.* 3.548 (Servius ad loc. comments '*unum de his uacat*'), *G.* 4.548, cf. *Aen.* 5.368 *nec mora, continuo.* **praedae . . . umbram** 'the semblance of a quarry', or 'phantom prey', cf. 3.434 (Narcissus) *repercussae . . . imaginis umbra*, Virg. *Aen.* 10.636 (phantom Aeneas) 636 *tum dea nube caua tenuem sine uiribus umbram.*

363 celer: 'quickly', adverbial. **spumantia terga:** poetic plural. 'Epic horses . . . tend to "foam"' (Austin on Virg. *Aen.* 6.881).

364 spemque . . . uanam: cf. *Aen.* 10.648 (Turnus pursues the phantom Aeneas) *spem . . . inanem.* **pedes** 'on foot'.

365 concipit 'utters' (*OLD* 12a). **preces et uerba precantia:** the repetition (also at 2.482 *neue preces animos et uerba precantia flectant*) has found its critics (some MSS have *uenefica* for *precantia*), but *uerba precantia* is frequent in Ovid (8x), cf. Virg. *Aen.* 7.237.

366 ignotosque deos ignoto carmine: Macareus continually stresses the mysterious quality of Circe's powers, so also 57–8 *obscurum uerborum ambage nouorum | . . . carmen*, 250 *tecta ignota*, 299 *spargimur ignotae sucis melioribus herbae*, cf. Luc. 6.576–7 (the witch Erictho) *illa magis magicisque deis incognita uerba | temptabat carmenque nouos fingebat in usus*, Stat. *Ach.* 1.139 *ignotis . . . diuis*, *Theb.* 3.497 *plura ignotaque iungit | numina.* For *ignotus*, Norden 1913: 116 suggested 'barbarian', from the native Italian perspective, but here we should understand the more general quality of strangeness (cf. Tupet 1976: 176).

367–71 Circe's magic creates a fog which isolates Picus from his men, cf. Jupiter and Io at 1.599–600 *cum deus inducta latas caligine terras | occuluit, tenuitque fugam, rapuitque pudorem.* Her magical powers over nature, specifically the moon and sun and the weather, are those conventionally ascribed to magic and witchcraft; for similar lists of magical powers, cf. 7.199ff. (Medea), *Her.* 6.85–6 (Medea) *illa reluctantem cursu deducere lunam | nititur et tenebris abdere solis equos, Am.* 1.8.9–12, 2.1.23–8, *Med. Fac.* 35–42, Virg. *Ecl.* 8.68–71, Tib. 1.2.45–54, 1.8.19–21, Luc. 6.461–506, Ap. Rh. 3.533.

367 niueae uultum confundere lunae 'to obscure the face of the white moon'. For magical powers over the moon, drawing it down or changing its appearance (often a technique of erotic magic), see Bömer on 7.207–8, Hill 1973, Tupet 1976: 92–103.

368–70 The language in these lines recalls Lucretius on cloud formation in storms: *DRN* 6.481–2 *urget enim quoque signiferi super aetheris aestus | et quasi densendo subtexit caerula nimbis* (Hill, H–E–A ad loc.) and on mist (as an illustration of atoms lighter than those of the earth) at *DRN* 5.463 *exhalantque lacus nebulam,* 466 *subtexunt nubila caelum,* cf. 13.602–3, Virg. *Aen.* 3.582. Ovid frequently likes to give his transformations a 'scientific' feel (see Myers 1994a: 27–60).

368 'weave a curtain of dank clouds beneath her father's head (the sun)', *OLD subtexo* 2a. Cf. 7.201–2 (Medea) *nubila pello | nubilaque induco* (with Bömer), 208–9 *currus quoque carmine nostro | pallet aui, Rem.* 256–8, Tib. 1.2.51 *cum libet, haec tristi depellit nubila caelo.*

370 nebulas exhalat humus: for further intimations of the Underworld see 410–11, cf. 4.434 *Styx nebulas exhalat iners,* 11.595–6 (cave of Sleep) *nebulae caligine mixtae | exhalantur humo dubiaeque crepuscula lucis.*

370–71 caecisque uagantur | limitibus comites 'his companions wander about on unknown paths'.

371 abest custodia regis: on the isolation (and consequent vulnerability) of the *uenator* in the 'amatory' hunt, cf. 3.379 (Narcissus) *forte puer comitum seductus ab agmine fido,* 2.422 (Callisto) *Iuppiter ut uidit fessam et custode uacantem* (see Davis 1983: 91).

372–77 Circe's second speech of supplication is as unsuccessful as her first to Glaucus at 28–36; cf. her vain pleas for Odysseus to remain with her in *Rem.* 271–86. Her language and Picus' response draw from the vocabulary of amatory poetry: see 373n., 376, 378, 380n.

372 nacta locum tempusque: cf. *AA* 2.367 *cogis adulterium dando tempusque locumque.* **'per o tua lumina':** phrases introduced by *per* frequently preface prayers, cf. 13.375–7, *Am.* 3.11.45 *parce per o lecti socialia iura,* Wackernagel 1953–79: II 194, Pease on *Aen.* 4.314, Dewar on Stat. *Theb.* 9.632. For swearing by (someone else's) eyes, cf. *Am.* 3.11.48 *perque tuos oculos, qui rapuere meos,* 2.16.44.

373 quae mea ceperunt: for this erotic topos, cf. e.g. *Am.* 1.10.10, 3.11.48 (above), *Her.* 12.36 *abstulerant oculi lumina nostra tui,* Prop. 1.1.1 *Cynthia prima suis miserum me cepit ocellis* (with Fedeli ad loc. and Shackleton Bailey 1956: 268).

374 supplex: the conventional attitude of the lover to the beloved, see 702n. **dea:** concessive 'although I am a goddess'. Circe also boasts of her lineage to Glaucus (33–4n.) and to Odysseus at *Rem.* 275–6.

374–5 nostris . . . | ignibus: cf. 25n.

376 durus 'cruelly', adj. used adverbially; cf. 377 *ferox.* The conventional language of amatory poetry for the hard-hearted lover (*OLD* 5b), cf. 693n. **Titanida . . . Circen:** two Gk accusatives elevate Circe's boast (for *Titanis* see 14n.).

377 ferox 'defiantly', cf. of amatory rejection 715, *Her.* 3.133, 4.165, Catull. 64.71 (Pichon 1966: 145). **ipsamque precesque** 'he disregarded both her and her prayers', mild syllepsis (Tissol 1997: 221), see 78n.

380 Venere externa: perhaps not merely 'adulterous' (*TLL* v 2.2023.61ff., Shackleton Bailey 1956: 270 '*alienus*'), but also 'foreign' or 'of an interloper'; cf. 9.19 (Achelous' suit for Deianira) *nec gener externis hospes tibi missus ab oris, Her.* 5.101–2 (Oenone to Paris) *ut minor Atrides temerati foedera lecti | clamat et externo laesus amore dolet,* 17.96, Prop. 2.32.31 (Helen). An intertextual association with the relationship of Aeneas and Lavinia may be activated with the echo of the complaints against Aeneas by Allecto and Amata in the *Aeneid* at 7.424 (Allecto) *externus . . . heres* and 7.367 (Amata) *gener externa petitur de gente Latinis* (see Casali 1995a: 70–1); cf. *Aen.* 6.94 (the Sibyl) *externi . . . thalami,* 7.98 (Latinus) *externi uenient generi,* 255, 270, Horsfall 1991. Cf. 574–5n. **laedam** 'violate' *OLD* 5.

381 The claim is reminiscent of Glaucus' rejection of Circe at 37–9 (*sospite . . . Scylla*). Janus' Italian ancestry (see 334n.) might give more point here to the repetition of Canens' genealogy. **Ianigenam:** a hapax legomenon, cf. 449 *Faunigena* (Kenney 2002: 63).

382 retemptatis: first in Ovid: see McKeown on *Am.* 1.8.75–6 for a list of verbs compounded with *re-* occuring first or only in Ovid, also Kenney 2002: 39. **Titania:** a metrically convenient alternative adjectival form (also of Circe at 438, cf. 1.395 (Pyrrha), 3.173 (Diana), 6.346 (Latona)), cf. *Titanis* at 14, 376, 13.968. **frustra:** the failure of persuasive speech, especially by a lover, is a major theme in the poem, cf. Vertumnus at 765n. and see Tarrant 1995.

383 non impune feres 'you will not escape punishment' (*OLD fero* 37) = 11.207 (Neptune to Laomedon), cf. 2.274 (Juno to Callisto) *haud impune feres,* Catull. 78b.4, Prop. 1.4.17 (with Fedeli ad loc.). **reddere:** future passive. **Canenti:** Circe repeats emphatically the last word of Picus' response in the same position.

384 For the theme of the fury of the scorned female, cf. 9.150–1 (Deianira), *AA* 2.373–84, Virg. *Aen.* 5.6 *notumque furens quid femina possit.* Cf. Circe's jealous revenge on Scylla, 36n., 40–67.

385 This line is probably an interpolation (del. Korn): *rebus* seems ineptly connected to *disces* (cf. 13.382–3 *quid facundia posset* | *re patuit*, 3.368, with the expected words–deeds contrast) and the repetition of *ait* from line 383 cannot be defended (see Kenney 1988: 248).

386–96 Ovid imaginatively amplifies Virgil's description of Picus' transformation into a woodpecker (*picus*) at *Aen.* 7.190–1 *aurea percussum uirga uersumque uenenis* | *fecit auem Circe sparsitque coloribus alas.* The *picus Martius* (mod. *Dryocopus martius*) is usually identified with the great black woodpecker, but Ovid's colourful description of the *picus* seems to resemble more the *picus uiridis* (see photo in Capanna 2000: 225) or to be purely fantastical (Mackay 1975: 274, André 1967: 128–30); cf. Sil. It. *Pun.* 8.442 *sparsit croceum plumis fugientis honorem.* Picus' fate reverses the outcome of Circe's earlier love for Glaucus, where she had taken out her anger on Scylla instead (see 41n.).

386 'Then she turned twice to the west, twice to the east'; cf. 2.190. Circe's actions are (perhaps deliberately) mysterious, cf. 7.189 (Medea) *ter se conuertit.* H-E-A. suggest that the two directions represent, respectively, her invocation of both chthonic and heavenly gods. For prayer to the east, cf. *F.* 4.777–8 (a shepherd at the Parilia) *haec tu conuersus ad ortus* | *dic quater*), Virg. *Aen.* 8.68–9 (Aeneas) *aetherii spectans orientia solis* | *lumina*, 12.172 (with Serv. ad loc).

387 For magical threefold repetition, cf. 58n. and *F.* 4.551 (Ceres and Triptolemus) *terque manu permulsit eum, tria carmina dixit.*

388 solito uelocius 'faster than usual' (i.e. 'than he usually ran'). For this type of brachylogy, cf. 7.84, 9.105, *F.* 5.547 *solito citius*, G–L §398n.1, K–S II 469–71, H–S 108–9.

389 miratur: Actaeon has a similar reaction to his transformation into a stag at 3.198–9 *fugit Autonoeius heros* | *et se tam celerem cursu miratur in ipso. miror* is common in metamorphoses, cf. 505, 2.353, 5.206, *al.*

390–1 seque nouam . . . | **indignatus auem** 'and, angry that he was being added suddenly to the Latin woods as a new bird', cf. 5.674 (the Emathides) *uidet uolucresque nouas accedere siluis.* In descriptions of metamorphosis *nouus* means both 'strange' (a new state) as well as 'new' (signalling an aetion), see Hopkinson on 13.894, Bömer on 2.377. *subito/subitus* are frequent in descriptions of metamorphosis: cf., e.g., 2.535 <u>*subito*</u> *nigrantes uersus in alas*, 7.281, 7.372 <u>*subitus*</u> . . . *olor*, 13.893–4 (Acis) *miraque res,* <u>*subito*</u> *media tenus exstitit aluo* | *incinctus iuuenis flexis* <u>*noua*</u> *cornua cannis.*

391–2 For psychological continuity into the metamorphosed state, which explains a natural characteristic, cf. e.g. 524–6, 6.374–8, 11.344–5 *et nunc accipiter, nulli satis aequus, in omnes* | *saeuit aues aliisque dolens fit causa dolendi*, 787 *indignatur*; see Solodow 1988: 175–86. Both of Circe's victims, Scylla (cf. 70–1) and Picus, continue to vent their anger after metamorphosis, although it had been a characteristic of neither before their transformations. **duro fera robora rostro** | **figit:** the unusual choice of the adj. *ferus* to modify *robur* (Bömer ad loc. points out *durus* is more common and suggests a double enallage here (transference of epithets, see 112n., Kenney 2002: 73)) is perhaps meant to suggest the *ferae* which Picus used to hunt and transfix (*figit, dat uulnera*), but cf. Catull. 63.89 *nemora fera*, Hor. *Sat.* 2.6.92 *feris . . . siluis*. Picus' beak now replaces his spears (cf. 6.666–73 (Tereus) 673 *prominet immodicum pro cuspide rostrum*).

393–5 The appearance of the bird derives from the description of Picus' apparel at 345 *poeniceam fuluo chlamyden contractus ab auro*.

394–5 'the gold which had been a fibula and had gripped his garment became plumage and his neck was encircled by tawny gold'; cf. 8.318 *mordebat fibula uestem*, Virg. *Aen.* 12.274 *fibula mordet*. The continuity between his previous and new appearance is underlined by the repetition of *aurum/auro* (polyptoton) at the end of the two lines.

396 The transformation ends with the etymology of the name of the woodpecker (*picus*), which is signalled by *nomina* (poetic pl., cf. 612, 616, 5.524, 7.654, 8.508, 10.739); cf. on *nomen* 90n. **antiquum** 'of his former self'.

397–415 Ovid expands the story still further by recounting the metamorphoses of Picus' companions (last seen at 370–1). This apparently original scene supplies a culminating illustration of Circe's fearful magical powers (cf. 318–19 *dominaeque potentia quae sit | hinc quoque disce meae*) and corresponds (another doublet) to her earlier transformation of Odysseus' men. The conventional list of magical powers seems especially indebted to Virgil's *Aeneid* 4, in which Dido and the Massylian (Numidian) *sacerdos* undertake magic rites, and *Aeneid* 6, where Aeneas and the Sibyl make sacrifices to the gods of the Underworld in preparation for their descent. Ovid may be developing in these lines the Underworld associations of Circe hinted at in Virgil's brief description in *Aen.* 7, see Hardie 1992: 67–8, and Putnam 1995: 296. There are also parallels with the portents before Julius Caesar's death described at *Met.* 15.782–98.

399–400 Circe reverses her earlier actions at 368–70: *tenuauerat auras* ~ 369 *densetur carmine caelum*, *passaque erat nebulas . . . recludi* ~ 370 *nebulas exhalat humus*.

401 criminibusque premunt ueris 'they attack her with charges of real crimes' (*OLD premo*[1] 8a).

402 uimque ferunt 'they threaten to use force'.

403 nocens . . . uirus sucosque ueneni: cf. 43 *horrendis . . . sucis*, 55–6 *portentificisque uenenis . . . radice nocenti*, 275–6 *sucos | adicit*, 2.800 *nocens uirus* (with Moore-Blunt).

404–5 In lines drawing liberally from Virgil, Circe invokes the conventional gods called upon for magic rituals, cf. Medea at 7.192 *Nox, ait, arcanis fidissima*, 194–5 *triceps Hecate, . . . adiutrixque uenis cantusque artisque †magorum†*, 198 *dique omnes noctis*. The Virgilian passages include the Numidian priestess at Virg. *Aen.* 4.510–11 *ter centum tonat ore deos, Erebumque Chaosque | tergeminamque Hecaten* (which has clearly influenced this line), the Sibyl at *Aen.* 6.247 *uoce uocans Hecaten caeloque Ereboque potentem*, and Aeneas at *Aen.* 7.136–40. **Noctem Noctisque deos:** Ovid imitates Virg. *Aen.* 7.138 *Noctem Noctisque orientia signa* (Wills 1996: 260). **Ereboque Chaoque:** both terms connote the Underworld (cf. 5.543, 10.30, 76, Virg, *G.* 4.471–2, *Aen.* 4.26, 6.247, 265, Luc. 6.513, 696). *Erebos* is found in Homer and Hesiod as a term for the darkness of the Underworld and often also represents a god of darkness (see West on *Th.* 123, Pease on Cic. *ND* 3.44). *Chaos* (*OLD* 2 'Underworld') is also a philosophical term which recalls the cosmological opening of the poem (7 *quem dixere Chaos*) and here presages the discord of elements brought about by Circe's magic (Bömer on 403ff.). For the double *–que*, see 78n. **Hecaten:** See 44n. **longis . . . ululatibus:** the various forms of the onomatopoeic verb *ululare* are often used for the cries of exotic or frightening rituals, esp. of the dogs associated with Hecate, cf. 7.190–1 (Medea) *ternisque ululatibus ora* | *soluit*, 15.797 (portents) *nocturnos ululasse canes*, Virg. *Aen.* 4.609 *nocturnisque Hecate triuiis ululata per urbes*, 6.257–8 *uisaeque canes ululare per umbram* | *aduentante dea*, 7.18 (of Circe's animals) *magnorum ululare luporum*, Theocr. 2.35, Sen. *Oed.* 569, (see Smith on Tib. 1.2.52).

406 The power to move trees and rocks is most often associated with Orpheus (cf. 338–40n., 11.1–2, Virg. *Ecl.* 3.46, 6.70–1), but is also attributed to magicians such as Medea at 7.205 *siluas moueo* and *Her.* 6.88 (Hypsipyle about Medea) *illa loco siluas uiuaque saxa mouet*, and the Massylian priestess at Virg. *Aen.* 4.491 *descendere montibus ornos*. Cf. *Aen.* 6.256–7 (Aeneas and the Sibyl sacrifice to the chthonic gods) *iuga coepta moueri* | *siluarum*. **(dictu mirabile):** this supine construction, which functions as an emotional heightening device, is found only here in Ovid (cf. 3.326 *mirabile*, *F.* 3.31 *uisu mirabile*), but is relatively common in Virgil and here may provide further Virgilian colouring (cf. e.g. *G.* 2.30, *Aen.* 1.439, 2.174, 3.26, 4.182, 7.64). Austin's note on *Aen.* 2.174 is apt: 'not just a tag, but part of the ritual description of a *prodigium* . . . then of other supernatural occurrences', see also von Albrecht 1964: 120–1 on 'marvelling' parentheses.

407 ingemuitque solum: cf. 409n., 15.798 (portents) *ferunt motamque tremoribus Vrbem*, Cic. *Cons.* fr.10.25 (*FLP* p. 161). **uicinaque palluit arbor:** *arbor* is collect. sing. (*OLD* 2); cf. 7.208–9 (of Medea's magic) *currus quoque carmine nostro* | *pallet aui, pallet nostris Aurora uenenis*, Tib. 1.8.17 (magic) *pallentibus herbis*. For paleness of trees, cf. 8.759–60 *et pariter frondes, pariter pallescere glandes* | *coepere ac longi pallorem ducere rami*, *AA* 3.704–5 *pallescunt frondes, quas noua laesit hiems*.

408 A 'golden line' (abVAB) marks a gruesome highlight. For such bloody portents, cf. 15.788 (prodigies) *saepe inter nimbos guttae cecidere cruentae*, and see Pease on Cicero, *Div.* 1.98.

409 uisi: (sc. *sunt*) the verb (to be taken with the following four infinitives) regularly introduces supernatural phenomena and serves to emphasize the uncanniness and strangeness of the scene (cf. Virg. *Aen.* 6.256ff. with Norden, 'der stehende Ausdruck des Prodigienstils', Austin on *Aen.* 2.256, and *Aen.* 7.73–7). **mugitus:** another typical portent caused by magic or supernatural powers, cf. Medea at 7.205–6 *iubeoque tremescere montes | et mugire solum*, Virg. *Aen.* 4.490–1 *mugire uidebis | sub pedibus terram*, 6.256 *sub pedibus mugire solum*, Sen. *Oed.* 173, 576ff., Luc. 3.417–18, Cicero, *Div.* 1.35; see Pease on *Aen.* 4.490.

410 canes . . . serpentibus atris: dogs and snakes belong to the standard imagery associated with the Underworld and witchcraft (especially in association with nekyomantia), cf. 405n., Hor. *Sat.* 1.8.34 (on the summoning of Hecate by the witch Canidia) *serpentis atque uideres infernas errare canes, Epod.* 5.15–16, Ap. Rh. 3.1214–17 (Jason's supplication of Hecate) where Hecate appears crowned with serpents and escorted by χθόνιοι κύνες, Virg. *Aen.* 6.257 (cit. 405n.). Snakes were especially associated with the Furies and black is the colour associated with the Underworld, cf. 4.454 (Furies) *atros . . . angues*, 10.349, *Aen.* 4.472 (Clytaemnestra as Fury) *armatam facibus matrem et serpentibus atris* (with Austin's comment ad loc. 'not merely "black" but "ghastly"'). For the power of magicians to affect snakes, cf. 7.203 (Medea) *uipereas rumpo uerbis et carmine fauces, Am.* 2.1.25, *Med. Fac.* 39, Virg. *Ecl.* 8.71, Sen. *Med.* 684–90, Luc. 6.488–91; see Tupet 1976: 64–5, 187–95. The infernal dogs also recall Circe's transformation of Scylla, cf. 44 *Hecateia carmina*, 60 *latrantibus . . . monstris*, 63 *ora proterua canum*, 66.

411 tenues animae uolitare: necromancy is another typical activity associated with magic and witchcraft: cf. Medea at 7.206 *manesque exire sepulcris, Am.* 1.8.17–18, *Rem.* 253–4, Tib. 1.2.45–8, 1.5.51, Virg. *Aen.* 4.490 *nocturnosque mouet manis,* Luc. 6.419–830. Ovid is again imitating Virgil, cf. *Aen.* 6.292–3 (of the monstrous forms at the entrance to the Underworld) *tenuis sine corpore uitas | . . . uolitare caua sub imagine formae*, 'flimsy, disembodied creatures, fluttering in hollow phantom shape' (transl. Austin ad loc.). **silentum** 'of those silent in death', so called by Virgil at *Aen.* 6.264 *umbraeque silentes*, 432–3 *silentum | concilium*, cf. *Met.* 15.797 *umbrasque silentum.*

412 monstris: ironic, considering in 414 they themselves become *monstra.* **pauet . . . pauentum:** polyptoton underlines the fear of the men.

413 Another 'golden line' signals the mode of Circe's magical transformation (cf. 278, 300, 387).

414 ab: causal (*OLD* 15), Guttmann 1890: 15–20. **attactu** 'touch', a rare compound variation of *tetigit* above (Wills 1996: 444). **uariarum monstra ferarum** = Virg. *Aen.* 6.285 *multaque praeterea uariarum monstra ferarum*, again of the mythological 'monsters' lurking *uestibulum ante ipsum primisque in faucibus Orci* (6.273), cf. 411n. The genitive is descriptive, defining what the 'monsters' consist of (cf. Kenney 1993: 458).

415 in iuuenes ueniunt: this unusual reversal of the usual process of metamorphosis, wherein bodies and body parts change *into* new forms (cf. 499 *comaeque in plumas abeunt*, 549–51, 13.674 *in uolucres, niueas abiere columbas*), perhaps underlines the suddenness and violence of the transformation, vividly concluding the long series of Circe's elaborately described metamorphoses which have dominated the book. **sua . . . imago** 'his own original appearance'.

416–34 The fate of Picus' wife Canens is introduced through a temporal transition (cf. 53–4, 2.417–18, 3.50, 6.587, 10.446–51) and surprisingly does not involve the agency of Circe or an actual metamorphosis; Canens wastes away into nothingness through her excessive grief over the loss of her husband. For grief and metamorphosis cf. 2.340–6 (Heliades), 3.393–8 (Echo), 6.301–12 (Niobe), 9.663–5 (Byblis). Egeria's metamorphosis into water over grief at her husband's death (15.547–51) provides the closest parallels. Canens, Hersilie, and Egeria all represent mourning Italian widows (cf. their respective metamorphoses into air, fire, water); see Myers 2004–5, Hollenburger-Rusch 2001, Cole 2008: 146–7.

416 An ornate indication of time in the epic tradition, the 'dawn and dusk motif', introduces the new episode, cf. (dawn) Lucr. 2.144 *primum Aurora nouo cum spargit lumine terras*, Virg. *Aen.* 4.584–5 *et iam primum nouo spargebat lumine terras* | . . . *Aurora*, see Austin on *Aen.* 6.535. Horace parodied the tradition in *Satires* 1.5.9–10, and 2.6.100–1 (both night) and Quintilian discusses the use of temporal periphrasis at *Inst.* 8.6.60: *ornatum petit solum, qui est apud poetas frequentissimus.* Ovid is particularly addicted to variations on this theme (Kenney 2002: 53). **sparserat:** sc. *lumine* (H–E–A). **Tartessia:** of Tartessus, the legendary name for Baetis (Guadalquivir), a river in sw Spain, indicates the extreme west (Kenney 1986: 456).

417 oculis animoque: on Ovid's fondness for syllepsis see 78n., cf. 4.129 (Thisbe seeks Pyramus) *oculis animoque requirit.* For the association of eyes and love, cf. 373n., Prop. 2.15.12 *oculi sunt in amore duces.*

419 obuia 'to meet him'.

421 dare plangorem: refers to the ritual beating of the breast in grief, but also means 'lamentation' (*OLD* 2), cf. 580, 749, 4.554 *solito temptat plangore ferire,* 13.611. **(facit haec tamen omnia):** arch Ovidian parenthetical aside; for such 'footnoting parentheses' or 'stage directions', cf., e.g., 6.359, 9.782, 10.557, Kenney 2002: 53.

421–2 seque | proripit 'she rushed forth'.

423–4 Hardie (forthcoming) detects echoes of Virgil's depiction of Orpheus' grief over the loss of his wfe in *G.* 4.507 *septem illum totos perhibent ex ordine mensis*, cf. Ovid's Orpheus earlier at 10.73–4 *septem tamen ille diebus* | *squalidus in ripa Cereris sine munere sedit.* **inopem somnique cibique** 'without sleep or food'. Cf. 4.262 (Clytie's wasting away) *perque nouem luces expers undaeque cibique.*

426–7 ultimus aspexit Thybris 'the Tiber was the last to see her' (adverbial adj.); cf. 1.728–30 (Io) <u>*ultimus*</u> *immenso restabas, Nile, labori;* | *quem simul ac tetigit,* <u>*positisque*</u> *in margine* <u>*ripae*</u> | *procubuit. Thybris* is a Hellenized form (cf. Varro *LL* 5.30 'Etruscan') for the name of the Tiber (*Tiberis*), which was introduced into Latin poetry by Virgil (Meister 1916: 53–60) and is the preferred form for the river's name in the *Met.* After the etymology of *Tiberinus* appears at 614, it used as an adj. at 15.728 *Tiberinaque* *ad ostia*. The nomenclature of the river was a scholarly 'problem' (see Cairns 2002) and the names *Thybris/ Tiberis/ Tiberinus* all appear in the *Fasti* and in the *Aeneid*; see Fordyce on *Aen.* 7.30, Horsfall, *EV* v 156–7, *LALE* s.v.v. *Thybris* (2), *Tiberinus, Tiberis*, and cf. 448 *Thybris*, 328n. *Albula*. Canens' journey from Circeii to the Tiber corresponds to that of Aeneas, see Ludwig 1965: 68. **luctuque uiaque | fessam** 'worn out from grief and from her journey', syllepsis. Canens' wild grief, wandering, and metamorphosis replay themes from the Byblis episode at 9.635–65, cf. 431–2n. Byblis similarly collapses onto the ground before her metamorphosis at 9.649–51 *cum tu lassata sequendo | concidis et dura positis tellure capillis, | Bybli, iaces.* **in gelida . . . ripa:** for the coolness of the bank, cf. Hor. *Sat.* 2.3.294 *in gelida . . . ripa*, Stat. *Silv.* 2.3.17 *niueae posuit se margine ripae* (which Carole Newlands suggests *per litteras* may be drawing on this scene). Hardie (forthcoming) cites *G.* 4.509 *gelidis . . . sub astris.* Tarrant has *iam longa* for *in gelida*, which could mean 'distant' (*OLD longus* 6), indicating the length of her journey (cf. Apul. *Met.* 6.11 *ripisque longis,* Sil. 9.617–18). **corpora:** poetic plural.

428 modulata: fem. nom. sing.; cf. for possible programmatic implications 341n. **ipsos . . . dolores:** this reading adopted by Tarrant is a variant found as a correction in several later MSS (*ipso . . . dolore* is the reading of the main MSS). It has the advantage of providing *modulata* with an object, paralleling pathetically the earlier construction of *modulor* with the object *carmina* in 341.

429–30 sono tenui: cf. 2.373 (Cycnus' transformation into a swan) *uox est tenuata. tenuis* (cf. 431 *tenues . . . medullas*) is used often of wasting away in metamorphosis, but is also a literary-critical term denoting the refinement of Callimachean poetry, see Keith 1992: 140–6, Myers 1994a: 111n.71, A. Hardie (forthcoming); on similar programmatic terms in the episode of the Minyeides (4.32–415) and Arachne (6.5–145) see Rosati 2006. **ut olim . . . cycnus:** *olim* here means 'on occasion' (*OLD* 4). The belief in the dying swan's especially beautiful song of mourning is found as early as Aeschylus, *Ag.* 1444–5 and was widespread (cf. Plato, *Phaedo* 84e–85a, Cic. *Tusc.* 1.30.73, Sen. *Phaed.* 303), see Thompson 1936: 179–86, Arnott 1977, van Dam on Stat. *Silv.* 2.4.10. Canens' association with poetry is suggested through the widepsread use of the swan metaphor for poets and poetic deaths in ancient literature, see Ahl 1982, Hinds 1987: 44–8, Keith 1992: 137–46, N-H on Hor. *C.* 2.20.10. Swans also hint at apotheosis, cf. Hor. C. 2.20, Hardie 1987a. The 'swan song' is elsewhere used by Ovid for Arion at *Fasti* 2.109–10, for Dido in *Heroides* 7.1–2, and finally for himself in *Tristia* 5.1.11–14. Cycnus' metamorphosis into a swan is recounted at 2.367–80, but Ovid here seems to be drawing on Virgil's version of the story at *Aen.* 10.185–9, which stresses Cycnus' grief for the loss of his beloved Phaethon (10.189 *luctu Cycnum Phaethontis amati*). Like Canens, Cycnus sings of his grief at *Aen.* 10.191 *dum canit et maestum Musa solatur amorem* (cf. Canens' *ipsos . . . dolores* at 428); see Harrison on *Aen.* 10.190–1 for echoes of the Orpheus tale. Other versions of swan metamorphosis are recounted at *Met.* 7.371–81, and 12.71–145. On etymological play between *canit . . . cycnus*, see Michalopoulos 2001: 64 (Isid. *Etym.* 12.7.19 *cygnus autem a canendo est appellatus*).

430 carmina . . . exequialia 'funeral songs', the adjective is used here for the first time (then in Statius, *Theb.* 6.123, 7.90, 11.610, *TLL* v 2.1849.5–15), cf. 2.371–2 (Cycnus) *querelis* | *Eridanum implerat.* Canens' mourning connects thematically with the upcoming death and commemoration of Caieta at 441–4 and the later scene of Ardea's end at 573–80.

431–2 Canens wastes away from grief and dissolves into the air in a unique transformation closer to death or apotheosis (see 432n.) than metamorphosis. Antoninus Liberalis preserves a number of tales that similarly end in an ἀφανισμός and the subsequent establishment of a cult (see Ant. Lib. 1 (Ctesylla), 13 (Aspalis), 26 (Hylas), etc., with Papathomopoulos 1968 on 1.21). Cf. the wasting away of Echo at 3.397 *in aera sucus* | *corporis omnis abit*, Hercules at 9.174–5 *caecaque medullis* | *tabe liquefactis*, Byblis at 9.663–4 *sic lacrimis consumpta suis Phoebeia Byblis* | *uertitur in fontem*, Hyrie at 7.380–1 *flendo* | *delicuit*, and Egeria at 15.549–51 *liquitur in lacrimas, donec pietate dolentis* | *mota soror Phoebi gelidum de corpore fontem* | *fecit et aeternas artus tenuauit in undas.* **tenues liquefacta medullas** | **tabuit** 'she wasted away, her thin marrow melted'. *medullas* is an acc. of respect, see 97n. (Courtney 2004: 428–9 (5)). On the erotic associations of *medullas* see 351n. Cf. 3.489–90 (Narcissus) *sic attenuatus amore* | *liquitur*, 5.431 (Cyane is transformed into water) *primaque de tota tenuissima quaeque liquescunt*, and compare Pythagoras' scientific theory of the four elements at 15.245–7 *resolutaque tellus* | *in liquidas rarescit aquas, tenuatus in auras* | *aeraque umor abit* (see Myers 1994a: 46). *tabescere* (suggesting a wasting disease) is often used of the effects of unrequited love, cf. 4.259 (Clytie) *tabuit ex illo dementer amoribus usa*, 3.445 (Narcissus), Catull. 68.55, Prop. 1.15.20, 3.6.23, and cf. Lucretius on the damaging passion of love *DRN* 4.1120 *usque adeo incerti tabescunt uulnere caeco*, and of grief *DRN* 3.911 *cur quisquam aeterno possit tabescere luctu.* Here the metaphorical meaning overlaps with physical reality. **extremum** 'finally, at last', adverbial neuter accusative (cf. *Tr.* 1.3.15); but this usage is rare and the variant *extremis* (attested in the important MS *M*), which recalls similar phrases (e.g. 2.665 *pars . . . extrema querelae*, 13.469–70 *ultima . . . uerba*, 14.717 *uerba nouissima*), may be right. **inque leues paulatim euanuit auras:** such expressions usually occur in the context of death or apotheosis, cf. *F.* 2.509 (Romulus' deification) *in tenues oculis euanuit auras*, *AA* 3.741 (Procris' death) *iam spiritus exit in auras*, *Her.* 12.85 *spiritus ante meus tenues uanescit in auras*, Virg. *Aen.* 4.278 (Mercury vanishes) *in tenuem ex oculis euanuit auram* (for further parallels see Bömer 1957: 129). *paulatim* is frequent in metamorphosis, underlining the process of change, cf. 757, 2.827, 4.580, 9.353, *al.*

433–4 The tale ends with an aetion for a *locus Canens*, which is mentioned nowhere else and seems to be an Ovidian invention. **fama . . . signata loco est** 'her story has been made known by the place'; the nymph-attendant's claim for authority only underlines the fact that both the place and character are otherwise unknown and receive commemoration solely through their narration in this poem, cf. 730–1n., 7.353 *euentu ueteris loca nota Cerambi.* Echoes of *Aen.* 7.1–4 (*tu quoque litoribus nostris, Aeneia nutrix,* | *aeternam moriens famam, Caieta, dedisti* | . . . *ossaque nomen* | . . . *signat*) both connect and contrast Canens' *fama* with Caieta's famous toponym in the following lines. For the use of the verb, cf. Luc. 4.64–5 *hinc . . . famosa uestustas* | . . . *signauit nomine terras*, Tac. *Germ.* 28.2 *manet adhuc Bohaemi nomen signatque loci ueterem memoriam*. See A. Hardie (forthcoming), who argues for the scene as an allegory of *fama*. *signata* corresponds to *signum* (313) at the beginning of the story. **nymphae ueteres . . . Camenae:** an etymological link is suggested between *Canens* and the *Camenae*, the ancient Italian muses, in their association with song (cf. Serv. on *Ecl.* 3.59 *Camenae musae, quibus a cantu nomen est inditum, LALE* s.v. *Camena*). Bömer points out that the pairing of these two names at the end of the two successive lines marks the conclusion of the episode (on consecutive line-ends as 'etymological markers', see Maltby 1993: 269–70, 272). *Camenae* has good MS authority (*M*), although *coloni* (the consensus of the main MSS), combined with *ueteres*, is an example of language typical of tradition and etymology (cf. 6.318 *non impune deam ueteres spreuere coloni*, 15.289, see Myers 1994a: 109, Cairns 1996: 31, A. Hardie (forthcoming)). The *Camenae* might recall their (different) grove near the Porta Capena, which was associated with the nymph Egeria, another mourning wife (Livy 1.21.3, Richardson 1992 s.v.), see H–E–A ad loc., Nagle 1988c: 89. **dixere:** Ovid is using the conventional language of authentication (along with *ueteres*, *fama* and *rite*) for an aetion of his own invention, cf. 333–4n.

435–6 Talia multa . . . | uisaque sunt 'Many such tales were told to me during that long year, many such things I saw'. *mihi* to be taken both as indirect object with *narrata* and as dative of agent with *uisa*. The end of the story of Picus and Canens echoes its beginning at 308–9.

436–7 In Homer Odysseus' men approach him after a year with a request to depart (*Od.* 10.467–75). **resides et desuetudine tardi:** the line is modelled on a Virgilian pattern, cf. *Aen.* 1.722 (of Dido's affections) <u>*resides*</u> *animos* <u>*desuetaque*</u> *corda*, 6.813–15, 7.693–4 (the Italians are roused to war) *iam pridem* <u>*resides*</u> *populos* <u>*desuetaque*</u> *bello* | *agmina in arma uocat*. *desuetudo* is found elsewhere in Latin poetry only at *Tr.* 5.7.57–8 (*TLL* v 1.777.55–73).

438–40 Ovid summarizes in two swift lines the elaborate advice the Homeric Circe gives to Odysseus and his men about their journey on two separate occasions. At *Od.* 10.488–540 she tells them they must go the Underworld and upon their return to Aeaea at 12.36–141 she warns them of the many further dangers, ranging from the Sirens and Scylla and Charybdis to the Cattle of the Sun. Macareus' version stresses the dispiriting effect her list of trials had on him (*ancipitesque uias, iter . . . uastum, saeui . . . pericula ponti*), leading him to abandon the journey (*pertimui*). **nactusque hoc litus:** the Trojans meet Macareus at Caieta (cf. 154–9).

441–573 The second half of the '*Aeneid*'

441–4 *Caieta's burial.* Ovid now returns to the frame of the *Aeneid* and fulfills the expectation created by the narrative deferral of line 157 when the Trojans first arrive at the port of Caieta (*litora adit nondum nutricis habentia nomen*) with the narration of the burial of Aeneas' nurse Caieta (based on Virg. *Aen.* 7.1–7). The reader is meant to recall the toponym, here merely implied, from the earlier passage and from *Aen.* 7.3–4 *et nunc seruat honos sedem tuus, ossaque nomen | Hesperia in magna, si qua est ea gloria, signat.* Cf. also mention of the landmark at 15.716 (Asclepius' journey) *quam tumulauit alumnus.* The themes of death, mourning, and commemoration continue from the preceding episode. The second half of the *Aeneid* is now reached and selected events from books 7–12 will be treated in the next 140 lines. The episodes of the Latin embassy to Diomedes, involving the narration of the metamorphosis of his men, (457–511, *Aen.* 11.225–95) and the metamorphosis of the Trojan ships (530–65, *Aen.* 9.77–122) take up the majority of the lines, along with a non-Virgilian tale of an Apulian shepherd (512–26). See Hinds 1998: 107–11.

441 Aeneia nutrix = Virg. *Aen.* 7.1 (in the same *sedes*). With this echo Ovid marks the opening of the second half of the *Aeneid.* For quadrisyllabic *Aeneia* (– – ∪ ∪) in this *sedes* cf. 581, *Aen.* 10.156, 494.

442 marmoreo tumulo: cf. *Her.* 7.194 *hoc tantum in tumuli marmore carmen erit, F.* 3.547–8 *tumulique in marmore carmen | hoc breue . . . erat* (both of Dido's epitaph), *Tr.* 3.3.72, Prop. 2.1.72. Ovid recalls Virg. *Aen.* 7.6 *aggere composito tumuli.* Bömer points out that a marble tomb is anachronistic. **breue carmen:** as the introduction to the direct quotation of an inscription, cf. 2.325–8 (the epitaph for Phaethon), 9.793 (Iphis' offering to Isis) *titulus breue carmen habebat, Am.* 2.6. 59–60 *lapis exiguus par sibi carmen habet,* Prop. 4.7.83–4 *hic carmen media dignum me scribe columna, | sed breue,* Virg. *Ecl.* 5.42 *tumulo super addite carmen.* The quotation or embedding of sepulchral epitaphs is widespread in Augustan poetry, especially in elegy (the appropriate metre for such inscriptions, cf. e.g. *Am.* 2.6.61–2, *Her.* 2.147–8, *F.* 3.547–50, *Tr.* 3.3.73–6, Tib. 1.3.55–6, Prop. 2.13B.35–6, 4.7.85–6), but also is common in epic, see Lausberg 1982: 285, Thomas 1998, Ramsby 2005. Ovid transforms Virgil's epigrammatic praise of Caieta at *Aen.* 7.1–4 into an actual epitaph (see Barchiesi 1979: 9 n.18).

443 HIC: conventional at beginning of an epitaph, cf. 3.327, *Tr.* 3.3.73, Tib. 1.3.55, *CIL* 9.3184, 6281, *TLL* VI 2745.76ff.

443–4 CAIETAM . . . CREMAVIT: Ovid is probably playing on an etymological link between Caieta and her cremation, suggested by Servius on *Aen.* 7.1, where he gives an alternative derivation for the name of the port from the burning of the Trojan ships based on the Greek for 'to burn' (ἀπὸ τοῦ καίειν): see O'Hara 1996a: 183, Barchiesi *EV* I 604; Tissol 2002: 321. **NOTAE PIETATIS:** Hinds 1998: 110, suggests *notae* 'perhaps "annotates" the inevitable *at pius . . . Aeneas* found at the equivalent moment in the Virgilian model passage, *Aen.* 7.5'; cf. *Aen.* 1.10 *insignem pietate uirum.* **ARGOLICO:** 'Argive', the reference is to the flight from Troy, cf. Virg. *Aen.* 10.56 *Argolicos medium fugisse per ignis.* With *ereptam* understand *igni* (with which *Argolico* agrees) from *igne* 'snatched [me] from the fire (set by) the Greeks and cremated [me] in a fitting fire'.

445 'The mooring rope tied up to the grassy bank is set loose'. The wording of this line recalls a number of passages from *Aen.* 7. Bömer adduces Virg. *Aen.* 7.106 *gramineo ripae religauit ab aggere classem* (the Trojans land and end their journey in Latium), while Hinds 1998: 110 suggests that the 'subliminally funereal' *aggere funis* recalls Caieta's burial mound at *Aen.* 7.6 (*aggere composito tumuli*; for the etymological association of *funis* 'rope' and *funus* 'funeral' see *LALE* s.v. *funis*, McKeown 1987: 60). *herboso* (the Homeric ποιήεις, see Knox 1986b: 95) varies the Virgilian *gramineo*, but also recalls the importance of Circe's magical herbs (cf. 9 *herbiferos . . . colles*, 14, 21–2, *al.*). On the lexicographical question of the meaning of *religare* ('tie up' or, rarely, 'untie'), see Gratwick 1979: 114–16.

446 procul: the word recalls Macareus' warning to stay away from Circe's shores at 244–5 *procul . . . procul hinc, mihi crede, uidenda* | *insula.* **relinquunt:** cf. *Aen.* 7.7 *tendit iter uelis portumque relinquit.*

447–8 ubi . . . harena 'where the Tiber dark with shade bursts into the sea with its yellow sand'. This passage is based on Virgil's description of Aeneas' first view of the Tiber at *Aen.* 7.29–32 *atque hic Aeneas ingentem ex aequore lucum* | *prospicit. hunc inter fluuio Tiberinus amoeno* | *uerticibus rapidis et multa flauus harena* | *in mare prorumpit* (see Stitz 1962: 96); cf. *Aen.* 7.36 *fluuio . . . opaco. flauus* is a conventional euphemism in descriptions of the Tiber (see N–H on Hor. *C.* 1.2.13, 'perhaps from Ennius'), cf. *F.* 6.228, *Tr.* 5.1.31. **Thybris:** *variatio* of the Virgilian model, see 426n.

449–53 In another masterpiece of miniaturization, five lines condense *Aeneid* 7–12. First a line and a half essentially summarize the main plot of the second half of Virgil's *Aeneid*, then the following four lines describe the terms of battle. The *Aeneid* in fact is threatened with premature closure in line 449 in a 'happy ending', until the following half line is added (*non sine . . .*). The impersonal and passive constructions seem to strip the battle of human agency or will.

449 Faunigenaeque . . . Latini: Virgil names Faunus as Latinus' father at *Aen.* 7.47–8, 81–2 (for the genealogy see above on 308–434); cf. Acis' genealogy at 13.750 *Fauno . . . creatus.* Faunus was a native Italian woodland deity, sometimes conflated with Pan, cf. *Her.* 5.137–8, *F.* 2.267–452 (the Lupercalia), 4.641–72, 5.99–102; see Bömer on *F.* 2.271, Radke 1979: 119–21. At *Aen.* 7. 81–103 Faunus delivers an oracle to Latinus which warns him to accept Aeneas as his son-in-law. The adjective (original, later in Sil. 5.7, 8.356) and noun frame the line. **domo potitur nataque** 'obtains both Latinus' hospitality and his daughter', syllepsis. Cf. *Aen.* 7.52 (Lavinia) *sola domum et tantas seruabat filia sedes*, Livy 1.1.9 *ibi Latinum apud penates deos domesticum publico adiunxisse foedus filia Aeneae in matrimonium data.*

450 non sine Marte tamen: see 246n. for the metonymy Mars = war. With this curt understatement, underlined by litotes and metonymy, Ovid coolly and offhandedly introduces the major theme of the 'Iliadic' half of the *Aeneid*, signalling his own avoidance of martial narrative throughout the section, cf. 452–3, 529–30 *multumque ab* *utraque cruoris | parte datur.* **bellum cum gente feroci:** cf. Jupiter's prophecy to Venus at *Aen.* 1.263–4 *bellum ingens geret Italia populosque ferocis | contundet. feroci* 'spirited' (Austin on *Aen.* 1.264) is used also of the Italians at *Aen.* 7.384, 724–5.

451 pactaque . . . pro coniuge 'for his promised wife'; *pangere* is common in the context of marital arrangements (*TLL* x 1.206.82ff.). Ovid cites as the cause of the war the view of Turnus' side in the *Aeneid* that Lavinia has been formally engaged to Turnus, cf. *Aen.* 9.138 (Turnus) *coniuge praerepta,* 10.79 (Juno) *gremiis abducere pactas,* 423–4 (Allecto), 12.440. Unlike Livy (1.2.1 *Turnus rex Rutulorum, cui pacta Lauinia ante aduentum Aeneae fuerat*), however, Virgil himself as narrator never vouches for this claim (see *Aen.* 7.56–7, 259–73, 314, 12.31 (with Servius ad loc.: *licet multi dicant, ante eam Turno fuisse promissam: quod falsum est*)). For similar narrative 'focalizing' through oppositional figures in Ovid's '*Aeneid*', cf. 79n. and see Thomas 2001: 80–3, and Casali 1995a: 70–1. **furit:** Bömer observes that *furor* is a characteristic of Turnus in the *Aeneid* (Hardie on *Aen.* 9.691 *Turno . . . furenti* translates 'battle-frenzy', cf. *Aen.* 11.486, 901).

452–7 As the war between the Trojans and Italians escalates, both sides seek allies in episodes which stretch from *Aeneid* 7 to 11. The lines recall most closely the beginning of *Aeneid* 8.1ff., where Turnus displays the signal for war against the Trojans (8.4–10 *simul omne tumultu | coniurat trepido Latium saeuitque iuuentus | effera. ductores primi . . . undique cogunt | auxilia . . . mittitur et magni Venulus Diomedis ad urbem | qui petat auxilium*).

452–3 'All of Etruria rushes to fight against Latium, and for a long time a hard-won victory is sought in anxious struggle.' Ovid rounds off his summary of the major action of the second half of the *Aeneid* with 453, a quasi-golden line (abAVB), see 184n. **Tyrrhenia tota:** Ovid recalls the first line of Virgil's catalogue of Italian forces (*Aen.* 7.647 *primus init bellum Tyrrhenis asper ab oris*), where, however, the adj. describes Mezentius and his forces, who fight on the side of the Latins. Cf. *Aen.* 8.4–5 *omne . . . Latium,* 8.494 *omnis furiis surrexit Etruria iustis* (where Evander promises that the Etruscans (under Tarchon) will join forces with Aeneas), 10.153–6. **sollicitis:** enallage. *sollicitus* is not usually used of objects, but of people or places, cf. 706 *sollicita . . . uoce,* Sall. *Hist.* 1.77.8 *Hispaniae armis sollicitae.*

455 Rutulos: these are Turnus' people, from Latium and linked with Ardea, see 573n.

456 Euandri ad moenia: Evander, an Arcadian king, founded the city of Pallanteum on the future site of Rome (*moenia* is never used of Pallanteum in Virgil, but cf. *Aen.* 1.7 *altae moenia Romae*). One line alludes to the important and extensive episode of Aeneas' visit to Evander in *Aeneid* 8 (lines 66–369, 454–607), where Aeneas successfully gains the assistance of the Etruscans and Evander's son Pallas.

456–7 frústra . . . frustrá: variation of metrical ictus.

457–511 *Diomedes.* Ovid directly reworks a Virgilian episode from the *Aeneid.* In Homer's *Iliad* Diomedes, leader of the Argives at Troy, fights and wounds Aeneas in single combat and attacks and wounds Aphrodite when she comes to her son's rescue (*Il.* 5.297–349). According to (some versions of) the post-Homeric tradition, Diomedes returned after the war to Argos (cf. *Od.* 3.180–3), but in punishment for his wounding of Aphrodite was subsequently driven into exile by his faithless wife and her lover. After many adventures he finally landed in Italy, joined the local king Daunus in a war against the Messapians, after which he received from the king the reward of land and his daughter as wife (459 *dotalia arua,* 511 *gener*) and founded a number of cities in Apulia (Timaeus, *FGrH* 566 F 53, Lycoph. *Alex.* 592–632, Ant. Lib. 37 (possibly Nicander); see Horsfall on *Aen.* 11.225–42, Malkin 1998: 234–57). In the *Aeneid* (10.28–30, 11.246) Diomedes is settled in northern Apulia at Argyripa, where the Italians send an embassy to ask him for help against the Trojans (8.9–17). It is not until *Aen.* 11 that Venulus reports Diomedes' refusal of an alliance at the Council of the Latins (226–95). Diomedes' important speech in Virgil acknowledges the guilt of the Greek side, declares the justification of his own punishments as retribution for his wounding of Venus, praises Aeneas, and urges the Italians to make peace with the Trojans (*Aen.* 11.253–95).

Ovid recalls the Virgilian scene through numerous verbal reminiscences, but changes the import of the episode by focusing on the expanded tale of the metamorphosis of Diomedes' men into birds (484–509, cf. *Aen.* 11.271–4), which constitutes Diomedes' sole excuse for not fighting the Trojans (see Solodow 1988: 151–2). Ovid's Diomedes is made to recall Aeneas in his similar role as exile and founder of a new city (see Wiltshire and Krickel 1982, Hinds 1998: 116–19, Papaioannou 2000).

457 profugi: famously of Aeneas at *Aen.* 1.2 *fato profugus,* cf. *Met.* 13.627–8 (Aeneas) *profugaque per aequora classe | fertur.* **urbem:** *Arpi* (cf. Virg. *Aen.* 10.28–9, 11.250, 428, called *Argyripa* at 11.246, also *Argos Hippion* (Strabo 5.1.9 p. 215, 6.3.9 p. 284, Serv. on *Aen.* 11.246)), a town in northern Apulia, near Mt Gargano (Talbert s.v., Horsfall on *Aen.* 11. 246). This line recalls *Aen.* 8.9 *mittitur et magni Venulus Diomedis ad urbem.*

458–60 These lines echo *Aen.* 11.246–7 *ille urbem Argyripam patriae cognomine gentis | uictor Gargani condebat Iapygis agris.* **ille quidem . . . sed:** the common construction (colloquial/prosaic) alerts the reader to an antithesis; on its frequency in Ovid see Bömer on 6.679, Knox 1986a: 39, McKeown on *Am.* 1.8.35. **sub Iapyge . . . Dauno:** Daunus (cf. 510), traditionally an immigrant from Illyria, was the legendary eponymous king of Daunia, the northern part of Apulia (Hor. *C.* 3.30.11–12, Ant. Lib. 31.1–2, Serv. on *Aen.* 8.9). He is Diomedes' father-in-law, according to the later tradition (cf. *F.* 4.76 with Bömer). Virgil instead transplants him to Ardea and is the first to make him the father of Turnus (e.g. *Aen.* 10.616). *Iapyge,* 'Iapygian' (or 'Apulian'), borrowed from Virgil (*Aen.* 11.247 quoted above), is a 'learned anachronism, in that V.'s use of the adj., used in the poet's time for Messapia or Calabria, had once been applied to all of the E. coast up to Gargano' (Horsfall on *Aen.* 11.247, cf. Serv. on *Aen.* 11.247, Holland 1935: 208). Iapygia is mentioned again in the routes of Myscelus and Aesculapius at *Met.*15.52 *Iapygis arua,* and 703. **maxima . . . | moenia condiderat:** cf. *Aen.* 11.226 *magna Diomedis ab urbe.* For *moenia condere,* cf. 775

(Rome), 3.13 (Boeotia), 15.56–7 (Croton), Virg. *Aen.* 1.276–7 (Rome). **dotaliaque arua:** cf. (of Aeneas) 569 *dotalia regna* and *F.* 3.603 *litore dotali solo comitatus Achate.*

460–1 sed Venulus Turni postquam mandata peregit | auxiliumque petit 'but when Venulus had carried out Turnus' commands and sought help'. The two actions are one and the same; *-que* is epexegetic (*OLD* 6). Cf. *Aen.* 8.9–10 *mittitur . . . Venulus . . . | qui petat auxilium.*

461–4 Diomedes' response is first given in indirect speech and then the narrative switches abruptly to direct speech in the middle of 464. In the *Aeneid* Latinus hears first the report of Diomedes' refusal (11.225–30) and then calls a council at which Venulus quotes Diomedes' speech in direct speech (251–93, cf. 251 *auditis ille haec placido sic reddidit ore*).

461–2 uires Aetolius heros | excusat 'the Aetolian hero alleges his lack of resources as an excuse'. Diomedes, although king of Argos, was Aetolian through his father Tydeus (12.622 Diomedes = *Tydides*), son of Oeneus (cf. 512 Diomedes = *Oenides*), king of Calydon, in Aetolia (*Aen.* 11.270). This form of the adj. appears only here (and cf. *Ilias Latina* 556, 698), elsewhere *Aetolus*, cf. 528 *arma Aetola, Rem.* 159, Virg. *Aen.* 10.28, 11.239, 308. On such learned epic geographical periphrasis, see Kroll 1988: 45; cf. 80, 230, 468, 584, 694. In the *Aeneid* Diomedes makes no such excuse, but cf. Evander's reply to Aeneas at *Aen.* 8.472–3 *nobis ad belli auxilium pro nomine tanto | exiguae uires.* The following infinitives, *uelle* and *habere*, also depend on *excusare* in a slightly different sense, 'he explains'.

463–4 aut quos . . . ullos = *aut habere ullos e gente suorum quos armet* 'nor does he have any of his own people to arm'; the relative clause of purpose precedes the main clause. Cf. *Aen.* 11.272 *socii amissi.* **'neue . . .** = *et, ne*: cf. 16n. For the abrupt switch from indirect to direct speech (here with no verb of speaking), cf. 223–32n. **commenta:** Ovid's internal narrators often express a concern with belief; for this as a motivation for the narration of a story, cf. 759 *neue ea ficta putes,* 8.620 *quodque minus dubites,* 13.935 *quid mihi fingere prodest?* see Feeney 1991: 224–32. Ovid here may be slyly drawing attention to his Virgilian source, cf. 13.733–4, 15.878–9.

465–6 Diomedes recalls his own words at *Aen.*11.280 '*nec ueterum memini laetorque malorum*', and, even more closely, the introduction of Aeneas' speech to Dido at *Aen.* 2.3 '*infandum, regina, iubes renouare dolorem*', and 12–13 '*quamquam animus meminisse horret luctuque refugit, | incipiam*'. **quamquam luctus renouentur:** Ovid is the first poet to adopt the general use of *quamquam* with the subj., probably on the analogy of *quamuis* (Austin on *Aen.* 6.394, H–S 602–3, *NLS* § 245), cf. 15.244 (*distent* U, *distant* Tarrant, *codd. pler.*), *Pont.* 4.9.103. The verb is relatively rare in verse: cf. the close parallel in Tib. 2.6.41 *ne dominae luctus renouentur acerbi;* see Navarro Antolín on Lyg.3.5. **memorare:** we may detect in the verb another reminder of Ovid's allusive reworking of Virgil (on the use of verbs of memory to signal textual reminiscences, see Conte 1986: 57–69, Miller 1993, Hinds 1998: 3–4, 14–16), cf. 813n.

466–7 postquam . . . flammas 'after high Ilion had been burned and Pergama had glutted the furious passions of the Greeks' (Miller-Goold). *flammas* gives better sense than the variant *dextras* found in some MSS and provides characteristic Ovidian play by picking up the imagery of the literal *cremata est* of the previous line and giving it a metaphorical twist (*OLD flamma* 8b). As Bömer observes, Ovid continues to recall the opening of book two of the *Aeneid*: 2.4–5 *Troianas ut opes et lamentabile regnum | eruerint Danai*; cf. also *Aen.* 3.1–3 *postquam res Asiae Priamique euertere gentem | immeritam uisum superis ceciditque superbum | Ilium et omnis humo fumat Neptunia Troia* (Baldo 1995: 73). **alta . . . Ilion:** cf. 13.197 *altae . . . Troiae*, 374 *altaque . . . Pergama*. 'Troy is called "lofty" (αἰπεινός) in the *Iliad* (e.g. *Il.* 9.419, 13.773), but *altus* is found typically in descriptions of great cities in epic' (Hopkinson on 13.197); cf. *Aen.* 2.56 *Priamique arx alta*). *Ilion* (the reading of the majority of MSS) is usually neuter, cf. *Her.* 16.49, 17.240, while the form *Ilios* (the Gk form of the noun) is feminine (and so should perhaps be read here instead), as at *Her.* 1.48, *AA* 1.363, Hor. *Epod.* 14.14, *C.* 4.9.18–19. Virgil always uses the neuter *Ilium.* **Danaas pauerunt Pergama flammas** 'Pergamum had fed the Greek fires', *OLD pasco* 4c. *Danaus* is the Homeric synonym for 'Greek' used most often by Virgil: see e.g. *Aen.* 2.5. *Pergama*, the acropolis or citadel of Troy, is a frequent synonym for the city. Homer has only the fem. singular *Pergamos* (see Hopkinson on 13.169), while later Greek and Latin writers use the metrically convenient neuter plural. *flammas* may here also have a figurative meaning 'fury' (*OLD* 8b).

468 Naryciusque heros: the 'lesser'Ajax, son of Oileus (cf. 13.356 *moderatior Aiax*, *Il.* 2.527–8), king of the Locrians. Naryx/Naryc(i)um was a city in Opuntian Locris (in Greece, near Euboea), cf. 8.312 *Narycius Lelex*, Virg. *Aen.* 3.399 *Narycii . . . Locri.* **a Virgine uirgine rapta** 'from the Virgin (Minerva), because a virgin had been raped'; Locrian Ajax raped Cassandra, priestess of Apollo and daughter of Priam, in the Temple of Minerva at Troy (cf. 13.410–11 *raptata comis antistita Phoebi | non profecturas tendebat ad aethera palmas*, Virg. *Aen.* 2.403–52 (413 *ereptae uirginis ira*) with Austin ad loc., Apollod. 5.22, 23) and for this he was killed by the goddess (*Aen.* 1.39–45, *Od.* 4.499–511). On the tradition in the Epic Cycle, see Davies 1989: 75–6. See Wills 1996: 215–16 on Ovid's fondness for repetition of *uirgo*, cf. 2.579 [Minerva] *mota est pro uirgine uirgo*, 9.725, 12.28, *F.* 6.289–90, *Her.* 21.11.

469 'had brought on us all the punishment which he alone deserved'. This claim directly repudiates the Virgilian Diomedes' assertion of general Greek guilt as a cause for the many unhappy homecomings from Troy (*nostoi*) at *Aen.* 11.257–58 *infanda per orbem | supplicia et scelerum poenas expendimus omnes* (cf. 255 *Iliacos ferro uiolauimus agros*). Ovid instead recalls the angry tone of Juno's complaint about Minerva's power to revenge herself on Ajax at *Aen.* 1.39–45 '*Pallasne exurere classem | Argiuum atque ipsos potuit summergere ponto | unius ob noxam et furias Aiacis Oilei?*' (39–41), where the emphatic *unius* corresponds to *solus* here (Simmons on *Met.* 14.469). At *Aen.* 11.259–60 Diomedes alludes to Ajax's fate (*triste Mineruae | sidus*, cf. 265).

470 uentis inimica per aequora rapti: cf. 8n., Virg. *Aen.* 1.42–3 *ipsa Iouis rapidum iaculata e nubibus ignem | disiecitque rates euertitque aequora uentis*, 123 *accipiunt inimicum imbrem rimisque fatiscunt*, Val. Fl. 8.326ff. *inimica Colchis aequora.*

471 A remarkable line of six substantives, the first four in asyndeton, which emphasizes the terrors facing the Greeks (Bömer ad loc.). **caelique marisque:** cf. Virg. *Aen.* 10.695 *minas perfert caelique marisque* (which Harrison ad loc. suggests recalls the Homeric line-ending οὐρανὸς ἠδὲ θάλασσα), *Aen.* 6.113 *omnis pelagique minas caelique ferebat.*

472 Capherea: Gk acc., a promontory at the SE end of Euboea (mod. Kavo Doro, Talbert s.v.), where the Greek fleet was driven on to the rocks by Nauplius, who, to avenge the unjust murder of his son Palamedes instigated by Ulysses (see 13.34–40, 55–60, *Aen.* 2.81–5), lit false beacons to lure them ashore; cf. Diomedes at *Aen.*11.260 *Euboicae cautes ultorque Caphereus.* Homer instead speaks of Ajax's death on the rocks of Gyrae (*Od.* 4.499–511). **cumulumque . . . cladis** 'the culmination (*OLD* 4) of our disaster', in apposition to *Capherea*; cf. 11.205–6 *addit, | perfidiae cumulum, falsis periuria uerbis.* 'The corresponding Greek metaphor is from the coping-stone of a wall, cf. Eur. *Tro.* 489' (Simmons ad loc.). For the elaborate word order, with a noun and its modifier surrounding a noun (*Capherea*) in apposition to it, a favourite Ovidian mannerism, cf. 833, McKeown on *Am.* 1.12.7, Solodow 1986.

473 A witty extra-narrative rejection of a repetition of the list of the fates of the other Greek heroes after the fall of Troy that the Virgilian Diomedes gives at *Aen.* 11.261–7, immediately following mention of Caphereus. Thus the author, through an internal narrator, comments on his own narrative strategies, see Rosati 2002: 284. Cf. other internal narrator's attention to narrative economy: 1.214–15 (Jupiter) *longa mora est . . . | enumerare,* 3.225, 5.207–8, 462–3, 7.520 (Aeacus) *ordine nunc repetam, neu longa ambage morer uos,* 13.205 (Ulysses) *longa referre mora est,* 15.453; on *mora* as 'digression' see 308n. Diomedes executes a similar rhetorical manoeuvre at *Aen.* 11.256–7 *mitto ea quae muris bellando exhausta sub altis, | quos Simois premat ille uiros*, a *praeteritio* which effectively bypasses a repetition of the events of the *Iliad* (see Horsfall ad loc.). **ex ordine** 'from first to last', cf. 9.5 *referam tamen ordine*, 5.335 *refer ordine carmen*, *Her.* 20.203 *ordine fac referas.* At *Aen.* 11. 240–1 Latinus demands that Venulus give a full and clear report of his meeting with Diomedes: *responsa reposcit | ordine cuncta suo.*

474 The sentiment is drawn from Diomedes' speech at *Aen.* 11.259 *uel Priamo miseranda manus* (Serv. ad loc. quotes Pacuvius as the model (*trag.* 391 Ribbeck) *Priamus si adesset, ipse eius commiseresceret*), cf. Sen. *Ag.* 521 (with Tarrant), Currie 1981: 2721–2. **potuit** 'might have', cf. 30n.

475 armiferae . . . Mineruae: cf. *F.* 3.681 *armifer armiferae correptus amore Mineruae*, 6.421, *Am.* 2.6.35, *Tr.* 4.10.13. The adjective occurs first in Ovid (for lists of original compounds of this type, see Kenney 2002: 63–4 and McKeown on *Am.* 2.6.35).

Minerva saves Diomedes from the storm she raised; cf. Athena's protection of Diomedes in Hom. *Il.* 5.121–32, 846–63.

476–9 These four lines are reminiscent of the opening five lines of Virgil's *Aeneid* (see Hinds 1998: 117, Baldo 1995: 74). The motif of the vengeful Venus has been met with a number of times earlier in the poem (cf. 27, 4.190–2, 10.681–5) and will reappear in this book at 693–7. Venus assumes a noticeable prominence in the latter portion of the *Met.*, figuring in the deification of Aeneas at 14.581–608, in the tale of Pomona and Vertumnus (622–771), and in the story of Tatius which immediately follows (775–804), as well as in the deification of Julius Caesar at 15.760ff. See Döpp 1968: 121, von Albrecht 1982, Barchiesi 1999.

477 antiquo . . . de uulnere: a reference to Diomedes' wounding of Aphrodite in Homer *Il.* 5.311–54; cf. 15.769 (where Venus still remembers) *quam modo Tydidae Calydonia uulneret hasta, Am.* 1.7.31–4, *Rem.* 5–6, *F.* 4.119–20. Diomedes here considerably downplays his crime in comparison with the much stronger assertion of guilt at *Aen.* 11.276–7 '*cum ferro caelestia corpora demens* | *appetii et Veneris uiolaui uulnere dextram*', cf. 10.29. Venus' anger recalls the Virgilian Juno at *Aen.* 1.36 *Iuno aeternum seruans sub pectore uulnus* (see Hardie 1990 on the displacement of Juno's anger to *Met.* 3).

477–8 memores . . . poenas | **exigit:** cf. 694n., 4.190 *exigit indicii memorem Cythereia poenam*, which all evoke Virg. *Aen.* 1.4 *saeuae memorem Iunonis ob iram;* see Bömer 1959: 275–7. For *poenas exigere* (not attested before Livy and Ovid, see Knox on *Her.* 7.58), cf. 8.125, 532, *F.* 4.230 (also of the avenging Venus) *poenas exigit ira deae, Tr.* 5.8.9 *exigit . . . dignas Rhamnusia poenas.* In Ant. Lib. 37 (but not in Virgil, cf. *Aen.* 11.269–70) Diomedes was betrayed by his wife as punishment for wounding Venus. **alma Venus:** a conventional epithet for Venus, cf. 10.230, Lucr. 1.2, here used ironically.

478–9 tantosque . . . armis: cf. *Aen.* 1.3 *multum ille et terris iactatus et alto,* 1.10 *tot adire labores.* With *terrestribus armis* Ovid varies the traditional formula and creates a lack of symmetry with *per alta . . . aequora,* cf. 483 *belloque fretoque.*

480–2 Diomedes continues to shadow Aeneas, here echoing the death-wish of Aeneas' first speech at *Aen.* 1.94–101, where he wishes he had died in the Iliadic encounter with Diomedes: '*o terque quaterque beati,* | *quis ante ora patrum Troiae sub moenibus altis* | *contigit oppetere! o Danaum fortissime gentis* | *Tydide! mene Iliacis occumbere campis* | *non potuisse tuaque animam hanc effundere dextra . . . !*' (see Hinds 1998: 117–18). Virgil's model is the speech of the Homeric Odysseus at *Od.* 5.306–10 (306–8 τρισμάκαρες Δαναοὶ καὶ τετράκις οἳ τότ' ὄλοντο | Τροίηι ἐν εὐρείηι χάριν Ἀτρείδηισι φέροντες. | ὡς δὴ ἐγώ γ' ὄφελον θανέειν καὶ πότμον ἐπισπεῖν 'three times and four times happy those Danaans were who died then in wide Troy land, bringing favor to the sons of Atreus, as I wish I too had died at that time and met my destiny' (Lattimore)); see Bömer 1959: 271–3, Ellsworth 1988: 339. The motif in Ovid has, however, undergone a significant change: here Diomedes wishes he *had* died in a shipwreck (see Stitz 1962: 103, Hinds 1998: 118).

481 communis 'universal, affecting everyone' (*OLD communis* 6), perhaps emphasizing the shared fate of the majority of the Greeks, cf. 469. **importunusque Caphereus:** *importunus* can here mean 'relentless' or 'threatening', but Ovid may also recall the origin of the adj. as a a nautical metaphor (lit. 'which does not carry to harbour': see Horsfall on *Aen.* 11.305, *LALE* s.v.). Cf. the similar personification of *Caphereus* at *Aen.* 11.260 *ultor . . . Caphereus. Caphereus* is scanned as a trisyllable (Gk diphthong).

483–4 Diomedes' lines now pick up the opening of Aeneas' second speech at *Aen.* 1.199 '*o passi grauiora, dabit deus his quoque finem*'. *finem* for Aeneas' men is Italy, for Diomedes' men it will instead be metamorphosis (Hinds 1998: 118–19), cf. 503 *finemque in acumine ponunt.*

483 ultima 'extremes (of experience)', neut. pl. as substantive (*OLD* 7b); cf. *Aen.* 1.219 *extrema pati* (of death). **belloque fretoque:** cf. 478n.

484–509 Ovid expands the Virgilian Diomedes' account of Venus' metamorphosis of his men into birds at *Aen.* 11.271–7. Virgil's Diomedes blames the transformation (11.273–4 *dira meorum | supplicia*) on his earlier wounding of Venus (275–7), while the Ovidian Diomedes shifts the blame to one of his companions who insults Venus during their homecoming. The story in various forms is attested from the 4th century (Lycos *FGrH* 570 F6 = Ant. Car. *Hist. Mirab.* 172 (= Call. fr. 407.172 Pf.), Lycophr. *Alex.* 594–611, Ant. Lib. 37, [Arist.] *Mir. ausc.* 79 p. 836a 7ff., Varro, *De gente pop. Rom.* fr. 17 Peter, Plin. *Nat.* 10.126–7; see Malkin 1998: 238–9, Bömer on 14.445ff.). Ovid follows Virgil's alteration of the traditional version in which Diomedes' comrades change *after* his death (as Servius observes on *Aen.* 11.271), thus allowing for Diomedes' vivid first-hand account (see Papaioannou 2000: 214–15), but otherwise his account seems original. The birds are not identified either in Virgil or Ovid (see 508–9n.), while other sources variously identify the birds as a type of seabird (Mediterranean shearwaters?) or herons (cf. the following tale of Ardea 573–80), see Celoria 1992: 209–10, André 1967: 39–40, Thompson 1918. The conventional location of the transformation was on the Adriatic Islands of Diomedeia (Isole Trèmiti, offshore islands facing the Gargano promontory in Apulia (Strab. 6.3.9 p. 284)), cf. *Aen.* 11.274 *scopulos.* Ovid and Virgil omit any reference to the frequently mentioned curiosity that these birds were friendly only to Greek visitors (e.g. Lycophr. *Alex.* 605–11, Ant. Lib. 37.6, Aelian, *NA* 1.1, Serv. on *Aen.* 11.271), cf. 562n.

484 Acmon: cf. 494 *Pleuronius Acmon,* not elsewhere named as a companion of Diomedes (the name appears as a Trojan ally at *Aen.* 10.128).

485 tum uero et cladibus asper 'then indeed exasperated by our disasters also' (Hill). *tum uero* is 'largely confined in poetry to the higher genres' (*Met.* 16x, see McKeown on *Am.* 2.5.23–4, Axelson 1945: 86f.).

486–93 Acmon complains of Venus' harsh treatment of the Greeks, employing the rhetorical devices of anaphora, indignant rhetorical questions, parallelism, parenthesis, and *sententia*. Ellsworth 1988: 339–40 compares it to the speech of Eurylochus on Thrinacia to induce Odysseus' men to eat the cattle of the Sun at *Od.* 12.340–51. Bömer detects an echo of Aeneas' speech to his men at *Aen.* 1.198ff. *o socii . . . o passi grauiora*. Like the Cercopes and the Apulian shepherd in this book, Acmon is a *contemptor deorum*. For the motif of blasphemy and punishment, cf. 3.511ff. (Pentheus), 4.389ff. (Minyades), 5. 669–70 (Pierides), 6.317ff. (Lycian peasants), 10.684ff. (Atalanta and Hippomenes).

486–7 quod . . . recuset | ferre: subj. in a rel. clause of characteristic, as below in a parallel construction (with anaphora) at 487 *quod . . . faciat.*

487–8 quid . . . faciat? 'what more can Venus do (assuming she wants to)?' For *puta* see *OLD puto* 9. **Cytherea:** a frequent epithet of Venus, from her famous cult-site on Cythera, an island off Cape Malea in the Peloponnese, where she was born; cf. 584 *Cythereius heros, Od.* 8.288, Hes. *Th.* 195, *Aen.* 1.257, 657.

488–90 A pointed *sententia* underlines the crew's desperate plight.

489 est locus in uotum 'there is still some point in praying'; *uotum* (a conjecture by Magnus) gives better sense than the MS *est . . . in uoto* (which would mean 'is prayed for' *OLD uotum* 3c), but the construction has no parallel (see *TLL* VII 2.1596.59) and the problem may lie elsewhere (Courtney *per litteras* suggests for *in uoto* '*hinc uoto*'). For the sentiment, cf. *Pont.* 2.2.31–2 *fortuna miserrima tuta est, | nam timor euentus deterioris abest.* **pessima rerum** 'the worst in the world'; *rerum* (partitive gen.) augments the force of the superlative, see *OLD res* 4b, Bömer on 12.502–3, Hor. *Sat.* 1.9.4. Alternatively, one might translate *sors . . . rerum* as 'the general situation'.

490 sub pedibus: the position of a conquered enemy (*OLD pes* 7c), cf. *Rem.* 530, *Tr.* 1.8.15–16 *illud amicitiae sanctum et uenerabile nomen | re tibi pro uili sub pedibusque iacet?*, Lucr. 1.78. **securaque summa malorum** 'the height of misery has no care' (Simmons).

491–3 audiat . . . spernimus 'though she herself may hear and hate (and hate she does) all those who serve under Diomedes; nevertheless we all despise her hate.' Acmon brings home his point with the repetition of *omnes* at the end of two successive lines and wordplay in *oderit/odium*. **licet:** with the subjunctive, see 171n. For the scansion of the final syllable ('irregular' lengthening in arsis), see 250n. **et †magno stat magna† potentia nobis:** the sense is hard to construe and the text is surely corrupt. The context requires something like 'even granting that her great power costs us dearly', which would be given by the conjecture (*apud* Simmons) of *ut* (*OLD* 35) . . . *stet*. Heinsius' reading *et paruo* for *et magno* makes Acmon say something blatantly untrue; see also Shackleton Bailey 1981: 336–7.

494–5 iratam . . . | instimulat . . . stimulisque iram: two highly mannered lines sum up the effect of Acmon's speech. Verbal repetition continues in the derivational polyptoton of adjective and noun (*iratam . . . iram*) and verb and noun (*instimulat . . . stimulisque*) arranged in chiastic order. *stimulus* is, literally, a goad (Gk κέντρον), cf. 647; here it is used metaphorically. **Pleuronius Acmon:** Pleuron is in Aetolia, cf. 461n. Ovid adds 'authenticating detail' to his invented character.

496 numeri maioris amici 'we, the greater number of his companions'. Diomedes again denies collective guilt.

497–8 The metamorphosis process begins abruptly, starting with Acmon's voice, which had instigated the punishment. Ovid describes the transformation from head to toes, returning finally to his mouth, which now has a beak; cf. the similar details in the transformation of Cycnus (the first bird transformation in the poem) at 3.367–80. **corripimus** 'rebuke' (*OLD* 6). **uox pariter uocisque uia est tenuata:** syllepsis, *tenuata* is to be taken literally and metaphorically 'his voice became bird-like/shrill and his throat was made long and slender'; cf. 429n., 2.373 (Cycnus' transformation into a swan) *uox est tenuata*. For *uocis uia*, cf. 6.355, 2.830 *uocis iter*, Lucr. 6.1148 *uocis iter*, Virg. *Aen.* 7.534. Loss of voice is a frequent motif in the poem, especially, as here, in the punishment of the misuse of speech, cf. 98–9n.

498–9 comaeque | in plumas abeunt 'his hair changes into feathers' (*OLD* s.v. *abeo* 11), cf. 551, 1.236 *in uillos abeunt uestes*, 13.674 *in uolucres niueas abiere. plumas . . . plumis*: polyptoton marks both this line and the previous (*uox . . . uocis*), accentuating the process of the transformation (on repetition in metamorphosis descriptions, see Moore-Blunt on 2.7). Cf. 2.373–5 (Cycnus) *canaeque capillos | dissimulant plumae collumque a pectore longe | porrigitur.* **noua:** for *nouus* as a term in metamorphoses, see 390–1n.

499–500 colla . . . pectoraque: both are poetic plurals, like *ora* in 502.

500 maiores . . . pennas: the metamorphosis is naturalistically detailed, moving from the upper to the lower arm, cf. 8.189–91 (Daedalus) *ponit in ordine pennas, | . . . ut cliuo creuisse putes.*

501 cubitique leues sinuantur in alas 'his elbows curved into light wings'.

502 magna pedis digitos pars occupat 'a great part of what is foot takes possession of his toes', i.e. instead of toes a solid webbed foot is formed, cf. 2.375 *digitosque ligat iunctura rubentes. pedis* is a collective or representative sing. for the new nature overtaking him, cf. 502.

502–3 oraque . . . ponunt 'his mouth having hardened in a beak grows stiff and ends in a point'; ornithological detail, cf., by contrast, 2.376 (Cycnus) *tenet os sine acumine rostrum. cornu* (instrumental ablative, cf. 282n.) is used of a bird's beak only here and Stat. *Silv.* 2.4.13.

504–5 Anaphora links this series of names of Diomedes' companions, all borrowed from elsewhere and new to this tale. Lycus (cf. 12.332), Idas (cf. 5.90, 8.305), and Abas (cf. 4.607) appear in Virgil (*Aen.* 1.222, 9.575, 1.121); for Nycteus, cf. Prop. 1.4.5, 3.15.12; Rhexenor, cf. Hom. *Od.* 7.63–4. **miratur . . . mirantur:** cf. 389n.

506 faciem 'form', the word is regular in descriptions of metamorphosis, cf. 550: *TLL* VI 1.45.77ff. **numerusque ex agmine maior:** this seems hardly fair, since Diomedes claimed at 496–7 that the majority of the crew (*numeri maioris amici*) had opposed Acmon.

507 'fly upwards and circle the oars with flapping wings', cf. 577 (Ardea) *subuolat et cineres plausis euerberat alis*, 8.238 (*perdix*) *plausit pennis*, Hor. *Sat.* 2.1.58 *Mors atris circumuolat alis.*

508–9 Ovid playfully alludes to the obscurity surrounding the ornithological identification of these birds (see 484–509n.). Their species is not mentioned by Virgil in his brief account of the metamorphosis at *Aen.* 11.272–4 *socii amissi petierunt aethera pennis* | *fluminibusque uagantur aues . . . et scopulos lacrimosis uocibus implent* (cf. Servius ad loc.: *hae aues hodieque Latine Diomedeae uocantur, Graeci eas* ἐρωδιούς [heron or shearwater] *dicunt*). Ovid is closest to Lycoph. *Alex.* 599 κύκνοισιν ἰνδαλθέντες εὐγλήνοις 'like in form to bright-eyed swans'; cf. Plin. *Nat.* 10.127 *fulicarum* [coots?] *similes.* While Ovid draws on language of the earlier transformation of Cycnus in Acmon's metamorphosis, he distinguishes the two species of birds here and at 502–3. **subitarum** is Heinsius' conjecture (attested as a variant in one MS; *dubiarum* is the reading of the major MSS). *subitus* is a frequent term in descriptions of metamorphosis: cf. 390–1n., 7.372 *subitus . . . olor*, 2.349, 5.559–60, 13.617, and see *OLD* 4. *dubiarum* would unnecessarily anticipate the riddling description of the birds in the following lines. **ut . . . sic** 'though it is not that of swans, yet it is closest to white swans'; *ut* is concessive, *NLS* §259, G–L §608.

510–511 Iapygis arida Dauni | **arua:** cf. 458n. Apulia was proverbially parched, cf. Hor. *C.* 3.30.11 *pauper aquae Daunus*, *Epod.* 2.41–2, 3.16 *siticulosae Apuliae* (with Watson).

511 minima cum parte meorum: Diomedes ends as he began (461–4), stressing his lack of resources, cf. 496 *numeri maioris amici*, 506 *numerusque ex agmine maior.*

512–26 *The Apulian shepherd and the nymphs.* Venulus' return journey by an unlikely southerly route offers another occasion for a metamorphosis tale, this one not in the *Aeneid.* Ovid thus adds more local Italian colour and splits the embassy into two parts, as in Virgil (*Aen.* 8.9–17, 11. 225–95). A similar story is found in Antoninus Liberalis 31 (attributed to Nicander, fr. 47 Gow-Scholfield), in which Messapian shepherds challenge nymphs to a dance contest and, upon losing, are turned into trees that still emit sounds of complaint. In Ovid's version the Apulian shepherd wilfully frightens and mocks the nymphs, for which he is punished by being transformed into an oleaster. The shepherd's rustic and obscene imitation of the dance of the nymphs possibly hints at theories of the origins of Italian drama (cf. Livy 7.2.4–13, Hor. *Epist.* 2.1.139–76), see Baier 1997: 182–3. The tale is linked with the previous episode (and the Cercopians at 91–100) in the similar motivation for metamorphosis (verbal abuse) and the following metamorphosis of the Trojan ships will reverse the arboreal metamorphosis, see Galinsky 1975: 237, Myers 2004–5. Tree metamorphoses are frequent in the poem, cf. 1.548–67 Daphne, 2.340–66 Heliades, 10.106–42 Cyparissus.

512 Oenides: Diomedes, grandson of Oeneus of Calydon (cf. *F.* 4.76); the papponymic being, as often in the Latin poets, loosely used: cf. (eg.) in Homer for Diomedes' father Tydeus (*Il.* 10.497) and in Ovid for Meleager (*Met.* 8.414 and *Her.* 4.99). **Calydonia regna:** for Diomedes as Calydonian, cf. 15.769, *Aen.* 11.270.

513 Peucetiosque . . . Messapiaque arua: Ant. Lib. 31 begins with mention of the eponymous founders of the region of Apulia: Iapyx, Peucetius, Daunius, and Messapius. Venulus' return journey from Arpi to Latium takes him unnecessarily far south (cf. 102–3n.). The Messapians were furthest south, in Italy's heel (the Salento peninsula), the Peucetii just above them along the coast (in the Bari region), see Strab. 6.3.8 p. 283.

514 antra: the proverbial haunt of nymphs (cf., e.g. 3.314–15, 4.289, Virg. *Aen.* 1.166–8, Hom. *Od.*12.318), and Pan (cf. 11.147 *Panaque montanis habitantem semper in antris*). **nubila** 'shaded', cf. 447, 4.432.

515 leuibus guttis manantia 'wet with lightly dripping water'. Caves were conventionally represented as damp; cf. e.g. 2.269, 3.31, 177, *al.* (Bömer) **semicaper Pan** 'half-goat Pan', i.e. goat-footed; the adj. is an Ovidian coinage (Kenney 2002: 64), cf. *F.* 4.752 *semicaperque deus*, 5.101. Pan, an Arcadian woodland deity, was identified with the Italian Faunus, see 449n. Only seven lines in the *Met.* end in a monosyllable preceded by a polysyllable, a 'pattern long recognized as archaic' (Knox 1986a: 70); here perhaps a nod towards the rustic early Italian setting of the tale. The Apulian's rude behaviour towards the nymphs resembles Pan's typical lewdness.

516 nunc . . . quodam . . . tempore: aetiological formula, introducing a transformation cf. 834 *ante . . . nunc*, 4.281 *nunc . . . quondam*, 6.88, 12.531; for *nunc* see 73n.

517–18 'An Apulian shepherd caused them to run away in terror from that region, filling them at first with sudden fear'. *fugatas* is, as often with the pf. part., contemporaneous in aspect with the finite verb (Kenney on Lucr. 3.171, *NLS* §103), while *et* has epexegetic force (*OLD* 11).

519 rediit: on *-it* scanned long, see 101n.

520 'they performed their dance, moving their feet in rhythm'.

521 imitatus: perhaps some suggestion of meta-literary subtext, cf. 5.299 (Pierides) *imitantes omnia picae,* Livy 7.2.5 (origins of the *ludi scaenici*) *imitari deinde eos iuuentus, simul inconditis inter se iocularia fundentes uersibus.*

522 addidit . . . dictis 'he added rustic insults to obscene words'; cf. the similarly cloddish behaviour of the Lycian peasants (344 *agrestes*, 348 *rustica turba*) who insult Latona at 6.362 *conuiciaque insuper addunt,* also 5.664–5 (Pierides) *conuicia uictae | cum iacerent*, 10.238 *obscenae . . . Propoetides.*

523–6 The rustic shepherd is transformed into a wild olive tree (oleaster). The type of tree is not specified in Ant. Lib. 31 and the association of the character of the shepherd with his metamorphosed form is an Ovidian touch (524 *sucoque licet cognoscere mores*), cf. Solodow 1988: 174–86 and Anderson 1963: 4–5 on continuity in metamorphosis.

523 'nor was his mouth silent until tree-trunk buried his throat'; for metamorphosis and the interruption of speech, cf. 8.719–20 *simul abdita texit* | *ora frutex*, 9.392 *desierant simul ora loqui, simul esse. guttura* is poetic pl.; stress is placed on the punishment of the offending organ, cf. 9.322–3 (Galanthis) *quae quia mendaci parientem iuuerat ore,* | *ore parit.*

525–6 quippe . . . | **exhibet** 'for the wild-olive displays the identifying mark of his tongue in its bitter berries'. Ovid varies his sources, which locate the bitterness of the plants in its leaves, cf. *Aen.* 12.766 *foliis oleaster amaris*, *G.* 2.314, Lucr. 6.972. An oleaster sacred to Faunus also appears prominently in *Aen.* 12.766ff. For *nota* in metamorphosis, cf. 6.670, *F.* 1.113. **asperitas uerborum cessit in illas** 'the harshness of his words passed into them', cf. 485 (Acmon) *cladibus asper*, 11.142–3 *uis aurea tinxit* | *flumen et humano de corpore cessit in amnem. asperitas* and the adj. *asper* are rhetorical terms signifying stylistic coarseness and lack of refinement (*OLD asperitas* 6, *asper* 8b), cf. Hor. *Epist.* 1.18.6 *asperitas agrestis*, Cic. *De orat.* 3.44 *rusticam asperitatem*, Vell. 1.17.1 (early Roman tragedy) *aspera ac rudia*.

527–30 A swift transitional passage sums up the return of the embassy to Diomedes (corresponding to *Aen.* 11.226–95).

527–8 Hinc ubi legati rediere negata ferentes | **arma Aetola sibi** 'when the envoys returned from here, reporting that Aetolian aid had been refused to them'. Tony Woodman observes (*per litteras*) the line's historiographical colour, e.g. Livy 9.1.3 *ubi legati . . . . redierunt.*

528–9 sine uiribus illis | **bella instructa gerunt** 'they waged battles <though> not equipped with those forces' (Kenney 1988: 248), or perhaps 'without those forces they <nevertheless> waged organized war'.

529–30 multumque ab utraque cruoris | **parte datur:** another off-hand mention, and evasion, of the major martial theme of the second half of Virgil's *Aeneid*, cf. 450n.

530–65 *The transformation of the Trojan ships into Naiads.* Ovid returns to *Aen.* 9, where Turnus' attempt to set fire to the Trojan fleet is thwarted by Cybele's transformation of them into sea nymphs at 69–122 (a scene indebted in turn to the Homeric Hector's attempts to burn the Greek fleet in *Iliad* 8, 15, and 16). Ovid follows the chronology of Virgil's 'story', not the narrative, in placing the Diomedes episode first. While Diomedes' response is not reported to the Latins until *Aeneid* 11.225ff., the embassy had been sent out in book 8. Ovid's placement of the ship metamorphosis near the end of his reworking of the *Aeneid* also acknowledges the closural function of the episode in Virgil (the end of Aeneas' wanderings, see Knauer 1964: 271). Virgil's episode begins with a flashback scene between Jupiter and Cybele, where we learn that Cybele claimed protection over the ships when they first were constructed from trees cut from her sacred grove on Mt Ida, and received a promise from Jupiter that any ships that reached Italy safely would be transformed into sea goddesses (*Aen.* 9.80–106); see *Met.* 14.535n. on *memor.* When Turnus, following Allecto's command (*Aen.* 7.431), tries to burn the fleet, Cybele arrives to exact her promise (107–22). The metamorphosis of the ships occupies only four lines (118–22), and the Naiads reappear in their new forms later at *Aen.* 10.219–50, when they arise from the sea to urge Aeneas on. Virgil's claim of authority for the tale (9.79 *prisca fides facto, sed fama perennis*) only underlines his invention of it (see Hardie on *Aen.* 9.77–122); cf. Ovid's mention of the metamorphosis in *Am.* 3.12.38. From the time of Servius (on *Aen.* 9.81) critics reproached Virgil for his inclusion of the fantastic metamorphosis; see Fantham 1990. Ovid compresses the Virgilian episode, characteristically concentrating his narrative on an expanded version of the metamorphosis (see Solodow 1988: 127–36, Papaioannou 2005: 167–80, Baldo 1995: 89–100). At the end of this episode (564–5) he refers to one of Virgil's most important models for his scene, the Homeric tale of the Phaeacian ship that returned Odysseus to Ithaca and was turned to stone by Poseidon at *Od.* 13.125–64 (see Fantham 1990: 105–6). The remainder of Ovid's treatment of the second half of the *Aeneid* is characterized by the foregrounding of Turnus.

530–1 ecce introduces the new episode, cf. *Aen.*11 .226–7 where the envoys' return from Diomedes is announced *ecce super maesti magna Diomedis ab urbe | legati responsa ferunt* and *Aen.* 10.219–20 where the transformed nymphs first appear to Aeneas *atque illi medio in spatio chorus, ecce, suarum | occurrit comitum nymphae.* Hardie (forthcoming) notes a parallel at 13.91–2 *ecce ferunt Troes ferrumque ignesque Iouemque | in Danaas classes* (the episode from *Iliad* 15 and 16 on which Turnus' attack is based). The lines are carefully constructed; both open with the identical metrical unit (trithemimeral caesura), with paired adjs and nouns in chiasmus (*auidas in pinea . . . texta faces*). **pinea . . . texta** 'pine-framed ships' (Hill), cf. *F.*1.506, *Tr.* 1.4.9, Catull. 64.10 (another model for Virgil's episode, see Fordyce ad loc. for the use of *texo* for ship-building). Cf. 535n. *pinus . . . caesas.*

531 ignesque timent quibus unda pepercit 'those the waves spared fear the fire'; a reference to Jupiter's promise to Cybele at *Aen.* 9.98–103 to transform whatever ships arrive safely at Laurentum (99–102 *quaecumque euaserit undis . . . mortalem eripiam formam magnique iubebo | aequoris esse deas*). The contrast of elements (fire, water, earth/wood) is a persistent feature of this episode (also in the opening of Catull. 64.1–15, see Bramble 1970: 35–7). **timent:** the ships are already anthropomorphized.

532–4 Ovid details the progression of the fire on the ships, while in Virgil Turnus only threatens the ships. **iamque** qualifies the series of imperfects for the inverted *cum* at 535. **picem et ceras:** used for sealing and waterproofing the ships, cf. 11.514–15, *Her.* 5.42, *Rem.* 447, Casson 1994: 106. For their flammability, cf. Virgil's corresponding scene at *Aen.* 9.75 *piceum . . . lumen* (of Turnus' burning torches). **alimenta** 'fuel' (*OLD* 3a).

533 Mulciber is a rarer name of Vulcan, here 'fire' metonymically, cf. 2.5, 9.263, 423, Virg. *Aen.* 8.724 (in Virgil only here). Ovid has chosen the name for dramatic personification and for variety (cf. *Aen.* 9.75–6 *fert . . . commixtam Volcanus ad astra fauillam*), and perhaps to suggest etymologically the melting of the pitch and wax (*LALE* s.v. *Mulciber: a molliendo scilicet ferro dictus*).

534 incuruae . . . transtra carinae 'the rowers' benches of the curving keel'. Ovid draws from the scene in *Aen.* 5.654ff., where the Trojan women set fire to the fleet: 662–3 *furit immissis Volcanus habenis | transtra per et remos et pictas abiete puppis.*

535–8 The goddess Cybele arrives to rescue the ships through transformation. With the inverted *cum*-clause (in which the grammatically subordinate *cum*-clause is more important than the main clause, see *NLS* §237, Williams on *Aen.* 5.84–5) Ovid recalls *Aen.* 9.107–9 *ergo aderat promissa dies et tempora Parcae | debita complerant, cum Turni iniuria Matrem | admonuit ratis sacris depellere taedas.* In the *Fasti* (4.251–4, 273–6) Ovid associates the importation of Cybele's cult from Pergamon to Rome in 204 BCE with the earlier building of Aeneas' fleet. On the cult of the Magna Mater at Rome, see Gruen 1990: 5–34, Roller 1999: 263ff.; on her importance to the Julians and her prominent role in the *Aeneid*, see Wiseman 1984, Roller 1999: 299–304, Knox 2002.

535 memor: with acc. and inf. (*OLD* 1c). Perhaps another self-referential gesture towards Ovid's adaptation of Virgil and his models (see 466n.): Cybele recalls not only the sacred origins of the pines, but also the interview between her and Jupiter at *Aen.* 9.82–106, during which he had promised that Aeneas' remaining ships would be transformed into nymphs. **has pinus Idaeo uertice caesas:** sc. *esse. pinus* is often used poetically for 'ship' (see 88n.), but here we should translate 'pines', stressing their earlier form and Cybele's association with the tree (her favourite Attis is transformed into a pine at 10.103–5). Cf. the description of the grove at *Aen.* 9.85–9 (85–6 *pinea silua mihi multos dilecta per annos | lucus in arce fuit summa*), and 10.230 *Idaeae sacro de uertice pinus*, passages which recall Catull. 64.1 *Peliaco quondam prognatae uertice pinus* (on Catullus as a model for Virgil's scene, see Hardie 1987b, Harrison on *Aen.* 10.230). From her association with her cult site on Mt Ida in Phrygia, Cybele is known as *Magna Deum Mater Idaea* in the public *Fasti* (see Fantham on *F.* 4.182, *ILS* 4099, 4100), cf. *F.* 4.182, 263–4, Lucr. 2.611 *Idaeam uocitant matrem*, Catull. 63.30, *Aen.* 10.252. The language also recalls Cybele's request to Jupiter at *Aen.* 9.88–9 *has ego Dardanio iuueni, cum classis egeret, | laeta dedi.*

536–8 Cybele's appearance is heralded by the cacophonous sounds of her traditional exotic entourage (cf. *F.* 4.181–6, Lucr. 2.618–21, Catull. 63.21–4). By contrast, in the *Aeneid* Virgil marks her epiphany by only a brief mention of her *Idaeique chori* (*Aen.* 9.112, referring to the Corybantes, Cybele's ecstatic followers) and emphasizes instead the ominous heavenly signs that accompany her *uox horrenda* (110–11 *noua lux oculis offulsit et ingens . . . nimbus*).

536 sancta deum genetrix: Cybele was identified with Rhea, mother of Zeus, cf. *F.* 4.201–2, *Aen.* 9.82 *ipsa deum . . . genetrix Berecynthia,* 2.788 *magna deum genetrix,* Lucr. 2.598–9. Neither Virgil nor Ovid actually names the goddess.

536–7 tinnitibus . . . pulsi | aeris 'ringing of clashing bronze cymbals'; cymbals were associated with Cybele and Bacchus, cf. 3.532–3 (Liber's throng) *aerane tantum | aere repulsa,* 4.29–30, 6.589, *F.* 4.184 *aeraque tinnitus aere repulsa dabunt,* 213 *cymbala,* Lucr. 2.618–19, 637 *pulsarent aeribus aera,* Catull. 64.262 *tereti tenues tinnitus aere ciebant,* Virg. *G.* 4.64, Prop. 3.17.35, 4.7.61 *aera rotunda Cybeles.* **aera . . . compleuit** '[Cybele] filled the air'. *aera . . . aeris* is wordplay, varying the usual repetition of *aes* (see above examples). **inflati . . . murmure buxi** 'the sound of the blowing of the box-wood pipe', the famous Phrygian pipes (*buxus* a metonymy *OLD* 3b), cf. 3.533, 12.158 *longaue multifori tibia buxi, F.* 4.181, *Aen.* 9.619–20 *buxusque uocat Berecynthia Matris | Idaeae,* Prop. 4.8.42, *Ciris* 166, Val. Fl. 1.319, Stat. *Theb.* 9.479–80. For the instrument, see Fantham on *F.* 4.181, Summers 1996: 358–60. For the loud, deep noise of woodwinds, cf. Lucr. 4.545 *cum tuba depresso grauiter sub murmure mugit.*

538 domitis inuecta leonibus: Cybele is routinely represented in art, coins, and literature as riding in a chariot drawn by lions, e.g. Virg. *Aen.* 3.113, 10.157, 252–3, Lucr. 2.600–1, Catull. 63.76, *LIMC* VIII 2.513–16; see Summers 1996 for the chariot in Cybele's ritual procession in Rome (cf. *Aen.* 6.785 *inuehitur curru Phrygias turrita per urbes*). At *Met.* 10.686–704 Hippomenes and Atalanta are transformed into Cybele's lions in punishment for their violation of her shrine, while at *F.* 4.215–18 Erato explains that the tamed lions represent Cybele's civilizing power over wild animals, cf. Lucr. 2.600–5. This 'silver' line and the next are the first of four such lines in this episode (cf. 543, 556). They add another ornamental touch to a highly descriptive scene.

539 A golden line opens Cybele's address to Turnus, adding solemnity. At *Aen.* 9.114–17 she instead speaks to the Trojans, telling them that they need not defend their ships. **sacrilega . . . dextra:** Cybele's words are stronger than Virgil's *Turni inuria* at *Aen.* 9.108, and may recall Latinus' condemnation of Turnus and the Latins' attack on the Trojans at 7.595 *ipsi has sacrilego pendetis sanguine poenas* (cf. Stitz 1962: 107).

540 me patiente 'with my consent'.

541 nemorum partes et membra meorum 'parts and limbs of my forests'. *membra* (frequent in metamorphosis descriptions) is anthropomorphizing, cf. of ships, 11.559 *partes et membra carinae, AA* 1.412 *naufraga membra ratis, TLL* VIII 643.24ff.; of trees, Plin. *Nat.* 17.218.

542–5 The storm which ensues may amplify Virgil's heavenly signs at Cybele's appearance (cf. *Aen.* 9.110–11 *ingens . . . nimbus*), but also recalls the tempest called forth by Jupiter to save the ships from fire at *Aen.* 5.693–9 (694–6 *tonitruque tremescunt | ardua terrarum et campi; ruit aethere toto | turbidus imber aqua densisque nigerrimus Austris*), an episode mentioned at *Met.* 14.85. Cf. the winds let loose in the opening storm in *Aen.* 1.81ff. and the storm at *Aen.* 4.161 *insequitur commixta grandine nimbus.*

542 intonuit 'it thundered', a traditional sign of Jupiter's divine authority since Homer (*Il.* 1.528–30), cf. 816–17, 2.311, *F.* 4.833–4, Virg. *Aen.* 9.104 (the end of Jupiter's promise to Cybele) *adnuit, et totum nutu tremefecit Olympum,* 631, 2.693 *intonuit laeuum.*

543 grandine nimbi is a line end at Virg. *Aen.* 5.458, 9.669, 10.803.

545 Astraei . . . fratres 'Astraean brothers', i.e. 'the winds'; Zephyrus, Boreas, and Notus were the sons of Astraeus and Aurora; see Hes. *Th.* 378–80. The adj. *Astraeus* is elsewhere only at Germ. fr. 4.125. Adj. and noun frame the line, see 169n. **eunt in proelia:** the use of military language (cf. 544 *concursibus*) to depict storms is also Virgilian, cf. *G.* 1.318 *omnia uentorum concurrere proelia uidi,* cf. Hor. *C.* 1.9.10–11 *uentos . . . deproeliantis.*

546–58 Cybele takes an active role in Ovid's version of Virgil's much shorter scene at *Aen.* 9.117–22, where the process of metamorphosis is glossed over as the ships dive into the water and resurface as sea goddesses: 120–2 *hinc uirgineae (mirabile monstrum) | reddunt se totidem facies pontoque feruntur.* Ovid enumerates in anatomical detail the change of ship- to body-parts, starting from the stern of the ship, the highest part, which becomes the head. The passage is a veritable *tour de force* of ship terminology. Verbal repetition underlines the correspondence between the new and previous forms. This transformation of inanimate (ships) to animate (nymphs) is unusual in the poem (while metamorphoses of humans into trees is common, cf. the Apulian shepherd 512–26), and recalls one of the first metamorphoses, that of rocks into humans in book 1.395–415. In both scenes Ovid reverses the usual process of transformation, detailing the assumption of human forms from the properties of the earlier objects (see Barkan 1986: 85, Myers 1994a: 45–6). In this case, the original numinous quality of Cybele's trees (on the bond between nymphs and trees, cf. 623–4n., 8.757–6, *F.* 4.231–2, Herter *RE* XVII 1542) is in a sense restored to them from their intermediate ship-form (cf. *Aen.* 10.234 *hanc genetrix faciem miserata refecit,* see Fantham 1990: 108). The transformation also has associations with the surrounding tales of deification (cf. esp. Acis 13.886–97, Glaucus 13.917–55 (both of which involve the sea). See also Galinsky 1975: 238–41, Lamacchia 1969: 9–12.

546 e quibus . . . unius uiribus usa 'making use of the strength of one of these', connective relative. *unius* is scanned with a long middle syllable (see McKeown on *Am.* 1.14.14). **alma** is a common epithet of goddesses (esp. Venus, see 478n.), here aptly describing the nurturing Great Mother as she rescues her ships/trees, cf. *F.* 4.319 (Cybele), *Aen.* 10.220 *alma Cybebe* (with Harrison ad loc.), 252 *alma parens.*

547 In Virgil, by contrast, the ships break loose themselves at Cybele's command: *Aen.* 9.117–18 *et sua quaeque | continuo puppes abrumpunt uincula ripis* (this passage may be the source of *puppis* in most primary MSS, which would have to be a collective sing.

here), cf. *Aen.* 10.233 *rupimus inuitae tua uincula.* **stuppea . . . retinacula** 'hempen ship cables'. *stuppeus* is a rare word, found first in Virgil at *Aen.* 2.236 *stuppea uincula* (see Austin ad loc.); cf. Lucan 10.493, Stat. *Silv.* 3.2.26–7.

548 'she carries off the ships and plunges them headfirst deep beneath the sea'. Ovid varies Virgil's use of a dolphin-simile to describe the first stage of metamorphosis at *Aen.* 9.119 *delphinumque modo demersis aequore rostris | ima petunt,* but also verbally recalls *Aen.* 6.342 (Palinurus' drowning) *medioque sub aequore mersit*; cf. 13.878 (Galatea) *sub aequore mergor,* 948 (Glaucus) *sub aequora mersi,* 11.791–2 *furit Aesacos inque profundum | pronus abit.*

549 'when the timber had softened and the wood had turned into flesh'. For *mollire* of metamorphosis, cf. 1.402, 4.381–2, 5.427–9. By contrast, hardening is a recurrent feature of the many transformations of people into trees, e.g. 10.494 (Myrrha) *duratur cortice pellis.*

552 quodque latus fuerat latus est 'and what had been side is still side'. The major MSS have *sinus* for the first *latus,* but *sinus* seems only to refer to ships' sails swelled out by winds (*OLD* 7); for *latus* of ships, e.g. *Tr.* 1.4.24, Virg. *Aen.* 1.104–5. On *latus* in metamorphoses see Bömer on 2.376. For the close correspondence between the nymphs and their old forms, see also 554–5, cf. 1.410 (Deucalion and Pyrrha) *quae modo uena fuit, sub eodem nomine mansit.*

552–3 mediisque . . . usum 'and the keel that lay below the middle of the ships is changed to serve as spine'; cf. 1.408 *uersa est in corporis usum.*

554 'the cables become soft hair, the sailyards arms'. Sailyards are the spars slung across the masts from which the sails were hung. At *Aen.* 5.829 *bracchia* = *antemnae* (see Williams ad loc.).

555 caerulus: 45n., an appropriate colour for sea deities, e.g. 2.8 *caeruleos habet unda deos,* 5.432 (Cyane), 13.288 (Thetis), 962 (Glaucus), but used also of ships, e.g. *F.* 2.112 *caerula puppis, Aen.* 6.410 *caeruleam . . . puppim.*

555–8 A series of lines exploiting the paradoxes of the contrast between the Naiads' old and new forms (*timebant/exercent, duris montibus/molle fretum*), stressing the contrast between the elements of water and earth, soft and hard (cf. 1.19–20 *pugnabant . . . umentia siccis, | mollia cum duris*).

556 uirgineis . . . lusibus recalls *Aen.* 9.119–20 *uirgineae . . . facies.* **exercent . . . undas** 'they stir up the waves', cf. 8.166.

557 Naides aequoreae recalls Virgil's model Catull. 64.15 *aequoreae . . . Nereides.* The placement emphasizes the result of the metamorphosis. On the form and etymology of *Naides,* see 328n. **durisque in montibus ortae:** cf. *Aen.* 9.92 *prosit nostris in montibus ortas* (with Hardie ad loc. '*ortas* suggests the birth or sprouting of living things'), cf. 326.

558 'they frequent the yielding waters untouched by (any memory of) their birthplace'. *molle* conrasts with *durisque* in the previous line. **eas:** the oblique cases of *is/ea/id* are generally avoided by the Roman poets as unpoetic (Axelson 1945: 70–3; Platnauer 116–17), but are more freely admitted in the *Met.* and Ovid's later elegies (see Kenney on *Her.* 20.29); this is the only example of pl. acc. fem.

559–65 The Naiads assist ships in trouble at sea – unless they are Greek. Their assistance recalls *Aen.* 10.246–7, where, after addressing Aeneas, the new sea goddess Cymodocea propels his ship forward: *dixerat et dextra discedens impulit altam | haud ignara modi puppim.* The anti-Greek attitude of the nymphs signifies their patriotism for the Trojan/Italian side (cf. also their own Trojan origins), but also seems to reverse pointedly the omitted traditional pro-Greek position of the *aues Diomedeae* (see 484–509n.), see Bömer on 559–61, Myers 1994a: 103n.36. The metamorphosed Scylla was eager to sink both Greek and Trojan ships (14.70–4).

560–1 iactatis . . . manus 'they often have placed their hands under ships which have been tossed about'. *supposuere manus* is a phrase used of rescue from drowning, cf. *Am.* 3.6.81–2 (with McKeown ad loc), *F.* 2.113–14, *Pont.* 2.6.14, Prop. 3.7.69. **nisi si** = *nisi* (see 177n.).

561–2 Achiuos . . . Pelasgos are both 'Greeks'. In Homer *Achaioi* also was used for Greeks in general (e.g. *Il.* 2.235). The Pelasgians, however, are in Homer allies of the Trojans (*Il.* 2.840, 17.301); later the name was used for Greeks as a whole (the Augustan poets probably borrowed the word from Ennius, see Skutsch on *Ann.* 14). **cladis . . . Phrygiae:** the destruction of Troy.

563–5 In a rare flash-forward, Ovid ends with mention of two episodes from Homer's *Odyssey*. The first is the wreck of Odysseus' ship (see 563n.), which most editors take to refer to that at *Od.* 12.403–46, after his men kill the cattle of Helios on Thrinacia. Barchiesi 2001: 17, 166n.18, however, suggests that the scene recalled is *Od.* 5.368ff., where Odysseus' raft is destroyed and he is washed ashore at Scheria/Phaeacia (pointedly, with the help of the naiad Leucothea). Not only does the latter episode fit geographically with the following Homeric metamorphosis of the Phaeacians' ship (564–5), it would also be chronologically 'plausible', occurring after the Virgilian ship-metamorphosis (i.e. after Odysseus' seven years with Calypso vs. the earlier wreck in book 12). Ovid plays again with the relative chronologies of the *Aeneid* and the *Odyssey* with this example of 'future reflexive allusion', wherein Homer's text represents a view of the future (cf. 192–7n., 158–222, Baldo 1995: 99, Cole 2004: 409). Ovid acknowledges Virgil's Homeric model by having his nymphs witness the petrifaction of Alcinous' ship, which at *Od.* 13.63–164 marked the end of Odysseus' journey (see Fantham 1990: 18, Baldo 1995: 100). The ship-petrifaction contrasts with the softening of the Trojan ships, while recalling Scylla (70–4), and anticipating the upcoming petrifaction of Anaxarete (753–60).

The tale ends with three highly patterned lines exhibiting parallelism, with repetition (*uultibus* repeated in the same position in consecutive lines, polyptoton *uiderunt/uidere*), variation (*laetis uultibus* repeated with variation in metrical ictus (*láetis/laetís*) and word position), rhyme (*rigescere/increscere*), and enjambment.

563 Neritiaeque ratis . . . fragmina 'the broken pieces of the craft of Odysseus'. On *Neritiae*, cf. 159n. *ratis* can mean either 'raft' (cf. the δούρατα μακρά of Odysseus' σχεδίη) or 'ship'; the ambiguity may be part of Ovid's chronological game. Barchiesi 2001: 166n.18 observes the phonetic wordplay in the line (*NeRITI-aeque RATIs . . . fRAgmina*).

564–5 uultibus . . . uultibus again recalls Catull. 64.14 *emersere feri candenti e gurgite uultus*. **saxumque increscere ligno** 'and rock grow over its timber', *ligno* is dat. Alcinous, king of the Phaeacians, hosted Odysseus and sent him home in one of his boats, which on its return was turned to stone by Poseidon in the mouth of the harbour (*Od.* 13.63–164).

566–7 Spes erat: no similar hope is held out at *Aeneid* 9.123ff., where the horrified reaction of Turnus' followers to the metamorphosis of the ships (123–4 *obstipuere animis Rutuli, conterritus ipse | turbatis Messapus equis*) contrasts with Turnus' own misguided interpretation of the omen as a sign that Jupiter has denied the Trojans the hope of flight by sea (9.128–9). Ovid brings out, however, Virgil's emphasis on Turnus' role in continuing warfare (see Galinsky 1976: 12–13). **in nymphas . . . marinas** 'now that the fleet had been brought to life as sea nymphs'. *animare* is used of metamorphosis only in the creation of life, cf. 1.158 (early humans), 4.619 (snakes) *animauit in angues*. **posse . . . desistere** 'might cease'; on the potential function of *possum* see *NLS* §125. **metu monstri** 'out of fear at the portent'. *monstrum*, which applies to supernatural or unnatural phenomena, here retains its original religious meaning of 'sign' (see Hardie on *Aen.* 9.119–22). Ovid recalls the characterization of the metamorphosis as a *mirabile monstrum* at *Aen.* 9.120, a phrase which derives in turn from Catull. 64.15 *aequoreae monstrum Nereides admirantes*. Cf. Turnus' reaction to the portent at *Aen.* 9.133 *nil me fatalia terrent*.

568–73 At 450–3 Ovid introduced the war between Turnus and Aeneas for Lavinia. Now the climax of the battle is reached, only to be treated in a compressed and oblique manner in only five and a half lines. Notable throughout the passage is the focus on Turnus (as in *Aeneid* 12); Aeneas is never mentioned by name. The stark summary of the plot of *Aen.* 7–12 reduces the conflict to mere violence, stripping away all but the combatants' fury, see Quint 1993: 82–3, Barchiesi 2002a: 12, Hardie 1993: 25. Ovid's equating of Aeneas' and Turnus' motivation in their final duel erases crucial differences between the two protagonists in the *Aeneid*, where Aeneas is defined primarily by his devotion to duty and Turnus by his pride and passion; see Döpp 1991: 341. Earlier Turnus' motivation was for marriage with Lavinia (451, cf. *F.* 4.879–80 *Turnus an Aeneas Latiae gener esset Amatae | bellum erat*, Virg. *Aen.* 12.80 *illo quaeratur coniunx Lauinia campo*), now, however, (*nec iam*) the combatants have lost sight of any goals beyond victory in battle. Virgil expresses a similar view of the dehumanizing effects of warfare on both armies at *Aen.* 12.282 *sic omnis amor unus habet decernere ferro*. Cf.

Mettius Fufetius on 'greed for empire' as the real cause of war between Rome and Alba at Livy 1.23.7 *si uera potius quam dictu speciosa dicenda sunt, cupido imperii duos cognatos uicinosque populos ad arma stimulat,* see Barchiesi 2002a: 12, and Hardie (forthcoming) ad loc. compares Stat. *Theb.* 1.150–1 *nuda potestas* | *armauit fratres.* At *Met.* 15.773–4 Venus views the conflict from the divine perspective: *bellaque cum Turno gerere, aut, si uera fatemur,* | *cum Iunone magis.*

568–9 perstat: asyndeton and emphatic placement of the verb underline Turnus' resolve, cf. *Aen.* 9.126 *at non audaci Turno fiducia cessit.* **habetque deos pars utraque:** most obviously in the *Aeneid,* Venus supports Aeneas, Juno Turnus (cf. Venus' complaint at *Met.* 15.771–4), but it is stressed throughout that Jupiter as enforcer of fate guarantees Aeneas' success. In his speech responding to the metamorphosis of the Trojan fleet in the *Aeneid* Turnus dismisses the Trojans' claims of divine support (9.135 *sat fatis Venerique datum*) and speaks of his own fates: 136–8 *sunt et mea contra* | *fata mihi, ferro sceleratam exscindere gentem* | *coniuge praerepta.* For the idea of conflicting fates in the *Aeneid,* see Hardie on *Aen.* 9.136–7. **quodque . . . animos:** *animos* is used in the sense of θυμός, 'proud spirit' (Horsfall on *Aen.* 11.366). The sentiment comes close to the sacrilegious words of Mezentius at *Aen.* 10.773–4, where he invokes the aid of his own hand and spear along with his god: *dextra mihi deus et telum . . .* | *nunc adsint.* Also relevant may be the 'famous dilemma' between supernatural and human motivation evoked by Nisus' alternatives at *Aen.* 9.185 *an sua cuique deus fit dira cupido?* (see Hardie ad loc.). **dotalia regna:** cf. 459 *dotaliaque arua*; Virg. *Aen.* 7.423 *coniugium et quaesitas sanguine dotes,* 9.737 *dotalia regia Amatae,* 11.369 *dotalis regia.*

570 sceptrum: an 'impeccably Homeric' ancient symbol of royal power (see Horsfall on *Aen.* 7.173). **Lauinia uirgo:** a Virgilian clausula, cf. *Aen.* 7.72, 11.479; the epithet defines her main role in the poem as a female of marriageable age, cf. *Aen.* 7.318, 362, 389. The prosody of the first syllable of *Lauinia* (here long) varies, see Austin on *Aen.* 1.2.

571–2 sed . . . gerunt 'they seek victory and wage war out of shame of giving up'. *peto* takes a complementary infin. (*OLD* 7c). *petunt* governs the three negated acc. objects in 569–70 (with the triple anaphora of *nec* driving home the point), as well as the infinitive *uicisse.* All three rejected goals involve marriage to Lavinia, who is herself highlighted by apostrophe at the end of the tricolon. **pudore:** for *pudor* used as shame in quitting battle (the Homeric αἰδώς), cf. Virg. *Aen.* 12.666–8 [of Turnus] *aestuat ingens* | *uno in corde pudor mixtoque insania luctu* | *et furiis agitatus amor et conscia uirtus,* cf. *Aen.* 5.455, 9.44, 787, 10.398, 871. Bömer compares Livy 8.7.8 (T. Manilius) *mouet ferocem animum iuuenis seu ira seu detractandi certaminis pudor.*

572–3 tandem neatly supplants actual battle narrative. **Venus uictricia nati** | **arma uidet:** cf. 453 *sollicitis uictoria quaeritur armis.* Aeneas' victory is viewed from the divine level, with imperial terminology recalling Prop. 4.1.46–7 *uexit et ipsa sui Caesaris arma Venus,* | *arma resurgentis portans uictricia Troiae* and Virg. *Aen.* 3.54 *uictriciaque arma.* *uictricia* glosses the goddess' cult-title *Venus Victrix* (see Michalopoulos 2001: 171 and

Varro, *LL* 5.61, who rejects the etymology from *uincere*). Pompey dedicated a temple to *Venus Victrix* in 55 BCE as part of his theatre complex (Richardson 1992 s.v. *Venus Victrix, aedes*) and the cult was promoted by Caesar and Augustus (Weinstock 1971: 83–112). Venus gives Aeneas his weapons at Virg. *Aen.* 8.608ff., but she plays no role in the final scene of Virgil's epic. Her personal involvement in her son's fate continues in the account of his deification at 581ff., suggesting her Julian role as *Venus Genetrix* (see 605n.).

573 Turnusque cadit : in mid-line Ovid marks the end of Virgil's *Aeneid* – but not his own – with a brief mention of Turnus' death, which functions as a transition to another story of metamorphosis. Omitted (see 574–5n.) is any reference to Aeneas' role in his killing as Virgil relates at *Aen.* 12.950–1 *ferrum aduerso sub pectore condit* | *feruidus*, cf. 12. 926–7 *incidit ictus* | *ingens ad terram duplicato poplite Turnus* (I owe this parallel to P. Hardie). With this transition Ovid perhaps comments on the *Aeneid*'s famously abrupt ending. While Ovid avoids closure, the following story of Ardea supplies the ritual of lament lacking to the *Aeneid*'s conclusion. The doubling of *cadit* (with prosodic variation, see 128n.) and the repetition of *Turnus* . . . *Turno* in chiastic structure creates narrative continuity and sounds an elegiac note of mourning (on 'pathetic' repetition, see Wills 1996: 7n.17, 138–42, *Rhet. Her.* 4.38, Macr. *Sat.* 4.6.23 *nascitur pathos et de repetitione*).

573–580 Ardea

The tragedy of the death of Turnus is deflected by the swift transition to the story of the creation of the heron (*ardea*) from the ashes of Turnus' town of Ardea, while the motifs of destruction and mourning provide the narrative with thematic continuity. The tale seems to be Ovid's own creation, possibly inspired by an etymological hint at Virg. *Aen.* 7.411–13 *locus Ardea quondam* | *dictus auis, et nunc magnum manet Ardea nomen,* | *sed fortuna fuit* 'the place was once called Ardea by our forefathers and Ardea still remains a mighty name, but her fortune is gone' (Horsfall's translation); see Ahl 1985: 265 n.29, Hardie 1992: 77 n.16, Casali 2006: 162–4. Ardea's decline may suggest a parallel with the destruction of Troy (cf. *Aen.* 2.325 *fuimus Troes, fuit Ilium*), see Casali 1995a: 73., cf. 13.404 [*Troia simul Priamusque cadunt*]. Servius on *Aen.* 7.412 supplies a reverse etymology from C. Iulius Hyginus (fr. 11 Peter), deriving the name of the town from the name of the bird (*ab augurio auis ardeae*), while Virgil's *magnum* . . . *nomen* at *Aen.* 7.412 seems to endorse the etymological association with the adj. *arduus* (cf. Serv. ad loc.: *bene allusit: nam Ardea quasi ardua dicta est, id est magna et nobilis,* Virg. *G.* 1.364 *altam supra uolat ardea nubem*, see O'Hara 1996a: 70, 190).

The harbour-town of Ardea (25 m./35.5 km south of Rome), famous as cult-centre of Juno, was by the late Republic an insignificant tourist site (Cic. *ND* 3.47). The closest parallel for this metamorphosis is that of the Memnonides (ruffs) from the smoke of Memnon's funeral pyre at 13.604–19, which serves as a coda to the fall of Troy and bridges the end of the section of the poem deriving from Homer and the

Epic Cycle, and the commencement of Ovid's '*Aeneid*' (see Hopkinson 2000: 27); on the ring-composition see Papaioannou 2005: 187–97. Cf. the Coroni, who arise from a pyre at 13.692–9 and the birds of Diomedes (484–509).

573–4 Turno | sospite 'as long as Turnus was unscathed/alive', cf. 15.440 (Helenus to Aeneas) *non tota cadet te sospite Troia*, Virg. *Aen.* 8.470–1. **dicta potens:** cf. Virg. *Aen.* 7.411–12 *Ardea quondam | dictus auis.*

574–5 quam postquam barbarus ignis | abstulit: the text and interpretation are much disputed. The choice between *quam/quem* and *ignis/ensis* depends on whether the reference is to the destruction of Ardea or the death of Turnus. *ensis* (the reading of the primary MSS) would suggest Turnus' death by Aeneas' sword, but the narrative seems to demand that the subject has changed from Turnus to Ardea's fate, which requires *quam*. With *ignis*, Ovid may be picking up another Virgilian etymological hint at the association between Ardea and *ardere* at *Aen.* 7.623–31; see O'Hara 1996a: 106. *aufero* is frequently 'kill' (*TLL* II 1336.83ff., *OLD* 8), but a meaning closer to the required sense 'capture' or 'destroy' perhaps recurs at *F.* 4.873 *utque Syracusas Arethusidas abstulit armis* (see, however, Fantham ad loc.); cf. Skutsch on Enn. 244 *auferre domos* ('a synonym of *cepit*').

In place of *barbarus* Heinsius suggested *Dardanus*, but *barbarus* refers to the Trojans also at 163–4 (from the Greek perspective, see n.), cf. 380n. (see on Turnus as the defender of Italy against the foreigner Virg. *Aen.* 7.468–9, 723, 10.74–8, 516 *aduena*, 12.261). Here the epithet may reflect negatively on the Trojan destructiveness in Italy (reversing the prophecy of the Sibyl to Aeneas in Tibullus 2.5.48 *iam, tibi praedico, barbare Turne, necem*); see Casali 1995a: 76, cf. Hor. *Epod.* 16.11 (fear of Rome's future destruction) *barbarus, heu, cineres insistet uictor.* For arguments against 'neutralizing' *quem postquam barbarus ensis*, see Casali 2006: 164–5, Thomas 2001: 83, Junod 1991: 73–4.

575 tepida latuerunt tecta fauilla 'her buildings lay hidden by the warm ash'. For *fauilla*, cf. the metamorphoses of the Memnonides (13.604 *atra fauilla uolat)* and the Coronides (13.697 *exire fauilla*).

576–80 The creation of the heron (*ardea*, Gk ἐρωιδιός) from Ardea's ashes is another inanimate to animate metamorphosis (see 546–58n.). For the multiple etymologies of the bird's name, see *LALE* s.v., André 1967: 33. Ovid's story may be a pointed reversal of the usual associations of herons as good omens for cities and households (Hutchinson 2002: 4), see Call. *Ait.* fr. 50.62 Massimilla (= fr. 43.62 Pf.), Posidippus 4.36–9 = *Ep.* 26 Austin-Bastianini.

576 congerie e media 'from the middle of the heap'; *congeries* elsewhere in Ovid only at 1.32–3 (chaos), 9.235–6 (Hercules' funeral pyre). **tum primum cognita praepes** 'a bird known then for the first time'; Ovid lays stress on his aetiological invention (for similar terminology, see Myers 1994a: 65). *praepes* as a noun is found first in Livy 7.26.4 and Ovid (cf. 4.714, *F.* 6.196).

577 'flies up and beats the ashes with flapping wings', cf. 507. *euerberat alis* is taken from Virg. *Aen.* 12.865–6 (the *Dira* in the shape of a screech owl harasses Turnus) *Turni se pestis ob ora | fertque refertque sonans clipeumque euerberat alis* (*euerbero* first attested here), see Baldo 1995: 44.

578–80 The appearance and name of the heron (its sad cry, thinness, and ashen colour) are explained in this list of the qualities remaining in the bird from the destroyed city (all subjects of the verb *mansit*), culminating in its name. **macies:** cf. 11.793 (Aesacos transformed into a *mergus*) *fecit amor maciem.* **nomen quoque mansit in illa | urbis:** etymological formulae, see 90n.; cf. *Aen.* 7.412 *nunc magnum manet Ardea nomen.* **ipsa suis deplangitur Ardea pennis:** the phrase plays with a 'sylleptic pun on *deplangere,* "to beat the breast" and, less physically, "to mourn for", whereas *suus* extends to Ardea both before and after her transformation: "Ardea (the city) is lamented / Ardea (the bird) beats her breast with her own wings"' (Tissol 1997: 61n.93). The flapping of the bird's wings imitates the ritual breast-beating of mourners, cf. 13.610–11 (the Memnonides) *consonus exit in auras | ter plangor,* 4.545–6 *palmis | deplanxere, Am.* 2.6.3 (bird mourners again) *ite, piae uolucres, et plangite pectora pinnis.*

581–608 The deification of Aeneas

The apotheosis of Aeneas after a three-year rule in Latium is an event foretold by Jupiter twice in the *Aeneid,* at 1.259–60 (to Venus) *sublimemque feres ad sidera caeli | magnanimum Aenean* and at 12.794–5 (to Juno) *indigitem Aenean scis ipsa et scire fateris | deberi caelo fatisque ad sidera tolli.* Aeneas was said to have been killed or to have disappeared in a second battle with the Rutulians by or in the river Numicius and to have received worship near Lavinium (mod. Pratica di Mare) under the cult-name of either 'Pater Indiges', 'Indiges', or 'Jupiter Indiges' (an earlier deity later identified with Aeneas, see 608n., Radke 1979: 149–50). The literary tradition of his apotheosis reaches back at least to Varro, *Ant.* fr. 214 Cardauns (cf. *De gente populi romani* fr. 17 Peter (= Aug. *Civ.* 18.19) and was possibly related in Ennius (= Serv. on *Aen.* 6.777, see Skutsch on *Ann.* 1.lxii (p. 261)); cf. Cassius Hemina, fr. 7 Peter, Tib. 2.5.43–4, Liv. 1.2.6, Dion. Hal. *Ant. Rom.* 1.64.4–5, Serv. on *Aen.* 7.150, *Orig. gent. Rom.* 14.4; see Bömer on *Met.* 14.445–608 (pp. 153–8). The development of Aeneas' association with the ancient cults of Lavinium is controversial (Liou-Gille 1980: 85ff., Dury-Moyaers 1981: 211ff., Castagnoli 1982, Schilling 1979). Evidence of the association of a cult of Aeneas during the Empire with the annual sacrifices to the Penates at Lavinium is dubious (Serv. *auct.* on *Aen.* 1.260; see Galinsky 1969: 147–60, Poucet 1983). Dionysius of Halicarnassus describes a hero-shrine to Aeneas in Latium as a tumulus on the bank of the river Numicius (1.64.5), which has been identified by some with a seventh-century BCE tomb surmounted by a fourth-century building excavated at Lavinium (illustrated in Fulminante 2000: 213–15). A fourth- or third-century inscription at Tor Tignosa near Lavinium is supposed to record a dedication to 'Lar Aeneas' (*CIL* 1.2843). This archaeological evidence, however, is disputed and too inconclusive to assume either the establishment of the Aeneas legend in central Italy before the fourth century or the existence of an actual Aeneas cult (see Bremmer and Horsfall 1987: 17, Cornell 1977: 79–81, 1995: 68, Gruen 1992: 24–5, Galinsky 1983: 42–5).

The episode follows that of Aeneas' ships turning into nymphs as the second in a series of apotheoses in the Italian tales of the *Metamorphoses* (cf. Picus), which continue with Romulus and Hersilia in book 14, and Hippolytus, Aesculapius, Julius Caesar, Augustus, and Ovid in book 15 (see the Introduction pp. 8–10). Among earlier apotheoses in the poem, that of Hercules at 9.250–72. offers the most significant parallels, reflecting Hercules' prominence as a paradigm for human apotheosis (for his presence in the traditional canon of deified human benefactors, e.g. Horace, *C.* 3.3.9ff., Cicero, *ND* 2.62 with Pease, see Feeney 1991: 161–2, Galinsky 1972: 136–49, Anderson 1928. Davis 1980: 126 observes that the successive apotheoses of Hercules, Aeneas, Romulus, and Caesar occur in four elemental media: fire, water, air, and *aether* (cf. Juv. 11.63 *alter* [Aeneas] *aquis, alter* [Hercules] *flammis ad sidera missus*), see Norden 1926: 28 on elemental purgation. In his own apotheosis (predicted at 15.871–89) Ovid will be raised above all others *super alta . . . astra* (Feeney 1991: 249). On deification in the *Met.*, see also Lieberg 1970, Due 1974: 85, Petersmann 1976, Schmidt 1991: 133–8, Salzman 1998: 325, Tissol 2002: 322–7. Venus' active role in Aeneas' apotheosis prefigures her actions on behalf of Julius Caesar in book 15 (cf. her earlier appeals to Neptune for the deification of Ino and Melicertes at 4.531–42) and fulfils Jupiter's prediction of her welcome of Augustus in heaven at *Aen.* 1.289–90. On Venus' prominence at the end of the *Met.*, see 476–9n.

581–3 Iamque . . . cum: an inverted *cum*-clause, see 532–8n.

581–2 ipsamque . . . iras: in Virgil Juno's abandonment of her anger against Aeneas and the Trojans (*Aen.* 1.4,, *al.*) is predicted by Jupiter at *Aen.* 1.279–82 (*quin aspera Iuno . . . mecumque fouebit* | *Romanos*), but falls outside the poem's events. Juno's reconciliation with Jupiter at *Aen.* 12.806–42, after Jupiter's second mention of Aeneas' future apotheosis (793–6), has been seen as limited or qualified, considering her future role in the Punic Wars. Ennius placed her renunciation of hostility to Rome during the second Punic War (*Ann.* 8.xv–xvi Sk. (= Serv. on. *Aen.* 1.281). The goddess' acceptance of Aeneas' deification in Ovid may share a common Ennian model with Horace's association of Juno's conciliation with the death and deification of Romulus at *C.* 3.3.30–6 *protinus et grauis* | *iras et inuisam nepotem . . . Marti redonabo . . . adscribi quietis* | *ordinibus patiar deorum* (see Enn. *Ann.* 53–5 Sk., Feeney 1984: 185–91, Nisbet and Rudd 2004: 36). The Ennian *concilium deorum* is alluded to by Mars at 808–15 (see 805–17n., 812n.) and is also relevant to the council before Hercules' deification at 9.242–61. In Ovid's poem, only one hundred lines later (778ff.), Juno is again Rome's enemy; see Tissol 2002: 329–30. **Aeneia uirtus:** Aeneas is famous for his *pietas* (cf. *F.* 4.799 *pietas Aeneia*), but his *uirtus* is also an important feature of his heroic stature in the *Aeneid*, see *Aen.* 1.566, 4.3, 8.131; cf. *Met.* 14.113 (the Sibyl to Aeneas) *inuia uirtuti nulla est uia*. Ovid has probably chosen the term because of its association with Stoic and

Euhemeristic doctrines concerning the deification of human benefactors of mankind: cf. 9.163 (Hercules) *solita . . . uirtute*, *Pont.* 4.8.63 *Caesar, auum, quem uirtus addidit astris*, Cicero, *Rep.* 1.25.4 *Romulum . . . etiamsi natura ad humanum exitum abripuit, uirtus tamen in caelum dicitur sustulisse*, Virg. *Aen.* 6.129–31 *pauci, quos aequus amauit | Iuppiter aut ardens euexit ad aethera uirtus, | dis geniti potuere*, 806 *uirtutem extendere factis*, 9.641 (Apollo to Ascanius) *macte noua uirtute, puer, sic itur ad astra*, 10.468–9 *sed famam extendere factis | hoc uirtutis opus*, Hor. *C.* 3.2.21–2 *uirtus recludens immeritis mori | caelum*, Livy 1.7.15. On political *uirtus*, see Weinstock 1971: 230–3. For quadrisyllabic *Aeneia*, see 441n. **ueteres:** cf. *Aen.* 1.23 *ueterisque memor Saturnia belli.*

583 bene fundatis opibus crescentis Iuli 'since the dominion (*OLD ops* 2a) of growing Iulus was well established'; cf. 808–9 (justification for Romulus' ascension) *quoniam fundamine magno | res Romana ualet.* Cf. Virg. *Aen.* 6.364 *spes surgentis Iuli*, 4.274 *Ascanium surgentem*, 10.524. *Iuli* (from *Iulus*, another name for Aeneas' son Ascanius, see 609n.) is scanned with vocalic *i* as three syllables.

584 tempestiuus erat caelo 'he was ready for heaven'; cf. 808 (Romulus' deification) *tempus adest*, 15.816–17 (on Julius Caesar's apotheosis) *hic sua compleuit pro quo, Cytherea, laboras | tempora, perfectis quos terrae debuit annis*, *F.* 1.583–4 (Hercules), Hor. *Epist.* 2.1.15 (on Augustus) *praesenti tibi maturos largimur honores.* **Cythereius heros** 'the heroic son of Venus'; the epithet (not in Virgil) signals Venus' prominent role in supporting her son and is also used of Aeneas at at 13.625, the beginning of the '*Aeneid*' section of the poem. For Venus' association with Cythera, see 487n. For variations of the adj., see Kenney 2002: 68–9.

585–96 Ovid recalls the Virgilian scene of Venus' entreaty of Jupiter at *Aen.* 1.223ff., where she receives reassurances of Aeneas' future apotheosis, a scene more fully recalled in the next book in Venus' campaigning for Caesar's deification (15.803–42); cf. her earlier plea to Neptune for the deification of her granddaughter Ino at 4. 531–42, and Aurora's pleas to Jupiter for her son Memnon at 13.583–99. Venus' appeals are emphatically personal and familial.

585 ambieratque Venus: *ambire* is the technical term for political canvassing (*OLD* 2 and 3), cf. 13.289 *Thetis ambitiosa.* See Feeney 1991: 207 on Ovid's 'parody of senatorial procedure' in his epic narratives of deification, and cf. Weinstock 1971: 388–91 on the Senate's meetings concerning the cults of Julius Caesar and Augustus.

585–6 colloque parentis | circumfusa 'hanging on her father's neck'. The detail recalls the relaxed intimacy of the scene between Artemis and Zeus in Callimachus' third Hymn (1–40), Due 1974: 85; cf. also the physical blandishments Venus uses on Vulcan at *Aen.* 8.387–8 *niueis hinc atque hinc diua lacertis | cunctantem amplexu molli fouet.*

588–9 Aeneaeque meo ~ Virg. *Aen.* 1.231 *meus Aeneas*; cf. *Met.* 4.534 (Venus) *tu miserere meorum.* **qui te de sanguine nostro | fecit auum** 'who through my bloodline made you a grandfather'. Venus' 'family agenda' is again stressed; cf. the scene between Jupiter and Mars about Romulus' deification at 807–16 and the conversation between Jupiter and Venus concerning Caesar at 15.814–21 (with Barchiesi 1999: 119–20).

589–90 quamuis paruum . . . aliquod 'may you grant, o most excellent one, some divinity [to my Aeneas], however small, as long as you give him some', cf. Aurora 13.598 *da, precor, huic aliquem, solacia mortis, honorem.* For *di minores,* cf. 15.545 (the newly deified Hippolytus/Virbius) *de disque minoribus unus | numine sub dominae lateo,* 1.173 *plebs, F.* 5.20 *de media plebe . . . deus.* On the mock-humble tone of this request see Galinsky 1975: 170, Due 1974: 85; contrast Venus' pleas for Ino and her son at 4.534 *magna quidem posco.*

590–1 satis est . . . per amnes: Hill ad loc. observes Ovid's correction of Virgil, who has the Sibyl, seemingly unaware of Aeneas' apotheosis to come, assume a second trip for him to the Underworld after his death (*Aen.* 6.133–6). Ovid's *semél . . . sémel* (duplication with prosodic variation) responds to Virgil's lines at 6.133–5 *si tanta cupido est | bis Stygios innare lacus, bis nigra uidere | Tartara.* **inamabile regnum:** cf. 4.477, Virg. *Aen.* 6.438 *tristisque palus inamabilis unda* ~ *G.* 4.479.

592–3 nec coniunx . . . placatoque adnuit ore: Juno's consent to Aeneas' deification is again singled out (see 581–2n.), cf. 9.259–61 (Juno on Hercules' deification) *adsensere dei; coniunx quoque regia uisa est | cetera non duro, duro tamen ultima uultu | dicta tulisse Iouis.* Ovid recalls Juno's reaction in Virgil's *Aeneid* to Jupiter's promise to make the Romans Latin in name and language at 12.841 *adnuit his Iuno et mentem laetata retorsit. regia coniunx* is used in the *Aeneid* of Amata (7.56) and Lavinia (2.783, 11.371); see Bömer on *Met.* 6.332, cf. 829 *regia Iuno.*

594 munere: some MSS have *numine,* but it would be out of place to compliment Venus by calling her 'worthy of her divinity'; with *munere* Jupiter compliments both Venus and Aeneas (and emphasizes his own benefaction).

595 pro quoque = *(is)que pro quo.*

597 iunctis . . . columbis: doves were sacred to Venus, cf. 13.673–4 where Anius' daughters are turned into doves, Virg. *Aen.* 6.192–3 (see Thompson 1936: 244–6), *Am.* 1.2.23 *maternas iunge columbas,* Apul. *Met.* 6.6, Claud. 22.354. Venus' chariot is elsewhere drawn by swans, cf. *Met.* 10.708–9 (with Bömer's discussion ad loc.), Hor. *C.* 3.28.14–15, 4.1.10.

598–608 Aeneas is made immortal by the purification of his mortal qualities in the river Numicius. Ovid makes no mention of the traditional circumstances of his death or disappearance by the river in battle. Ritual purification by water (*lustratio*) was a common feature of Greek and Roman cult practice, cf. Glaucus 13. 951–3 (with Hopkinson ad loc.), Virg. *Aen.* 6.741–2 (on the cleansing of souls after death) *aliis sub gurgite uasto | infectum eluitur scelus aut exuritur igni.* Drowning also was a means of divine ascension, see Weinstock 1971: 356; cf. the marine deifications of Ino and Melicertes

(4.531–42), Glaucus 13.917–55, the Trojan ship-nymphs. The separation of the divine or immaterial soul from the prison of the body was a philosophical (and poetic) commonplace, cf. Cicero's *Somnium Scipionis, Rep.* 6.14 *hi uiuunt qui e corporum uinclis tamquam e carcere euolauerunt, Met.* 14.824–8 (Romulus), 15.840–1 (Caesar's apotheosis) *hanc animam interea caeso de corpore raptam | fac iubar, Pont.* 4.13.25–6 *nam patris Augusti docui mortale fuisse | corpus, in aetherias numen abisse domos.*

598 litus . . . Laurens: see 336n. **tectus harundine** recalls Virgil's Tiber at *Aen.* 8.34 *crinis umbrosa tegebat harundo.*

599 flumineis . . . undis 'with its fresh waters'. The line exhibits elegant intertwining word order (AbaB), **Numicius:** see 328n. Although Virgil makes no explicit reference to the Numicius' association with the death or worship of Aeneas, he proleptically calls its waters sacred: *Aen.* 7.242 *fontis uada sacra Numici,* 797–8 *sacrumque Numici | litus.* Tibullus stresses the river's role in Aeneas' deification: 2.5.43–4 *illic sanctus eris cum te veneranda Numici | unda deum caelo miserit indigetem.* In the *Fasti* Dido's sister Anna becomes a nymph in the Numicius (3.647–56).

600 Aeneae is dat. with *abluere.* **quaecumque obnoxia morti** 'any mortal parts' (*OLD* s.v. *quicumque* 8).

602 corniger: river deities were often associated with bulls and depicted with horns, cf. 8.881–9.87 where the river Achelous explains the loss of one of his horns, 13.894 (Acis' new horns), *F.* 3.647 *corniger . . . Numicius,* Virg. *G.* 4.371–2 (with Thomas ad loc.), Hor. *C.* 4.14.25 *sic tauriformis uoluitur Aufidus.*

603 quidquid . . . mortale: cf. the elimination of the mortal in other apotheoses: 4.539–40 (Ino and Melicertes, by sea-water) *Neptunus . . . abstulit illis | quod mortale fuit,* 9.262–3 (Hercules, by fire) *quodcumque fuit populabile flammae | Mulciber abstulerat,* 13.949–55 (Glaucus, by water) *mihi quaecumque feram mortalia demant* (950), 14.824–8 (Romulus, in the air).

604 pars optima cf. 9.268–9 (Hercules) *sic, ubi mortales Tirynthius exuit artus, parte sui meliore uiget,* 15.875–6 (Ovid), *parte tamen meliore mei super alta perennis | astra ferar.*

605–7 Nectar and ambrosia, the food of the gods, often figure in scenes of apotheosis. In Theocr. 15.106–8 Aphrodite deifies Queen Berenice by anointing her with ambrosia, cf. Pind. *P.* 9.62f. (Aristaeus is fed nectar and ambrosia), *Hom. H. Dem.* 237 (Demeter anoints Demophoon), Ap. Rh. 4.870–2 (Thetis anoints Achilles). At *Met.* 4.250 Apollo dissolves Leucothoe's dead body and causes incense to grow up in its place: *nectare odorato sparsit corpusque locumque,* and at *Met.* 10.731–2 Venus creates a flower from Adonis' blood: *sic fata cruorem | nectare odorato sparsit.*

605 genetrix: the cult of Venus Genetrix, as ancestress of the *gens Iulia,* was an important element of Julius Caesar's (and after him Augustus') religious programme, cf. 15.762 *Aeneae genetrix* and see Wlosok 1967: 62–3, 119–20, Weinstock 1971: 15–18, 23–6, 80–90, Feeney 1991: 213. **diuino . . . odore:** the fragrance of ambrosia and nectar is often noted, cf. Venus' first appearance to Aeneas at *Aen.* 1.403–4 *ambrosiaeque comae diuinum uertice odorem | spirauere*, 12.419, Theocr. 17.29 νέκταρος εὐόδμοιο.

607 contigit os: cf. Apollo's attempt to fireproof Phaethon at 2.122–3 *tum pater ora sui sacro medicamine nati | contigit.* **turba Quirini** 'the Roman crowd'. The Sabine god *Quirinus* was the name under which Romulus was worshipped, see 828n. Ovid anticipates the deification of Romulus at 14. 828 (see n.), cf. 15.572 *populoque Quirini*, 756.

608 nuncupat: a formal and archaizing verb of naming, in Ovid only here and at *F.* 1.246 'ebenfalls in einem Aition' (Bömer ad loc.), cf. Varro, *Ant.* fr. 15, 16 Cardauns, Cic. *ND* 1.38, *De orat.* 3.153, Tac. *Ann.* 3.71.1. **Indigetem:** the title under which Aeneas was said to be worshipped in Lavinium, probably through assimilation to an earlier native cult (see on 581–608). An *elogium* was inscribed for a statue of Aeneas at Pompeii (*CIL* 1^2 p. 189.1 = *ILS* 63): *appel[latus] q.est Indigens [pa]ter et in deo[rum n]umero relatus.* The precise meaning of this obscure term (also applied to other deities, cf. 15.861–2 *Di, precor, Aeneae comites, quibus ensis et ignis | cesserunt, dique Indigetes, genitorque Quirine*, Virg. *G.* 1.498 *di patrii, Indigetes et Romule Vestaque mater*, Lucan, *BC* 1.556), usually translated as 'native' or 'ancestral', was in dispute in ancient, as modern, times. See *LALE* s.v., for ancient etymologies; for some modern theories see Bömer on *Met.* 14.445ff., Radke 1979: 150–1, Latte 1960: 43–5, Dury-Moyaers 1981: 211ff., Schilling 1979. **temploque arisque recepit** 'honoured him with a temple and altars'.

609–621 The Alban kings

The Alban king list was created by Hellenistic historians to fill the chronological gap (*c.* 432 years, Cato fr. 17 Peter = 20 Cugusi and Sblendorio Cugusi) between the fall of Troy set by the Hellenistic historians in the late twelfth century BCE and the date of the foundation of Rome in the eighth century (eventually set by Varro at 754/3 BCE). Virgil speaks more vaguely of three hundred years of Alban rule (*Aen.* 1.272); see Dion. Hal. *Ant. Rom.* 1.74–5, Horsfall 1974), Feeney 2007: 88–100 on the variant chronologies. Mention of the dynastic list is found as early as Fabius Pictor (fr. 7a Chassignet = Plut. *Rom.* 3.1–3), where Diocles of Paparethus (a late third-century BCE historian) is named as his source (see Gruen 1992: 20), cf. Fabius Pictor fr. 1 Chassignet, Cato, *Orig.* fr. 11 Peter (= 14 Cugusi and Sblendorio Cugusi = Serv. on *Aen.* 6.760), but the exact names of the kings are not quoted until the first century. Cf. the lists at Livy 1.3.1–11, *Aen.* 6.760–70 (abbreviated, only Silvius, Procas, Capys, Numitor, Silvius Aeneas), Diod. 7.5.1ff., Dio fr. 4, Dion. Hal. *Ant. Rom.* 1.70–1, Appian 1.1.2; see Trieber (1894), Brugnoli 1983, Forsythe 1994: 113–23. Naevius and Ennius, however, seemingly ignored the chronological difficulties and made Romulus the grandson of Aeneas (see Serv. *auct.* on *Aen.* 1.273, Enn. *Ann.* 34–60, 154–5 Sk., Skutsch 1985: 190, Feeney 2007: 99).

The catalogue is typically brief and punctuated by topographical aetiologies and etymologies, supplying local heroes and a 'symbolic pageant of Roman history'

(Ogilvie 1970: 44). The Julian ancestors were represented by statues beginning from Aeneas and the Alban kings in the NW portico of the Temple of Mars Ultor in the Forum of Augustus (*F.* 5.563–4 *hinc uidet Aenean oneratum pondere caro* | *et tot Iuleae nobilitatis auos*), see 109n., 772–851n.; fragmentary *elogia* survive = Degrassi XIII 3. pp. 1–11 (nos. 1–5). Propertius' *recusatio* at 3.3.1–4 (*reges, Alba, tuos*) suggests pressure on Augustan writers to include the patriotic subject of the Alban kings; see Fantham on *F.* 4.39. Tac. *Ann.* 4.9.2 reports that Drusus' procession included masks of Aeneas and 'all the kings of Alba Longa'.

Ovid gives essentially the same list at *Fasti* 4.39–56. The differences between the two lists, Capetus (*Met.* 14.613) = Calpetus (*F.* 4.46) and Acrota (*Met.* 14.617) = Agrippa (*F.* 4.49), seem to suggest that in the *Met.* Ovid has chosen the older and more obscure version. Ovid's lists follow the canonical versions given by Livy and Dionysius of Halicarnassus, with the notable exception of the omission in both poems of Silvius Aeneas, who usually appears between Silvius and Latinus (e.g. Livy 1.3.7, Dion. Hal. *Ant. Rom.* 1.71.4) and is even present in Virgil's brief list of five kings at *Aen.* 6.768–70; see Brugnoli 1996: 131–2 on the omission as an 'anti-Augustan' gesture, also Kyriakidis 2002. Ovid's interruption of the list at 622–771 (King Proca) for the tale of Pomona and Vertumnus and its inset tale is a highly unusual manoeuvre, but may reflect the fact that Amulius and Numitor were originally independent of the Alban king list (see 772–4n.). The list, marked by frequent enjambment, functions as a 'fast-forwarding' passage, moving the poem chronologically forward to the time of Romulus. Cf. the brief Trojan royal genealogy (754 *regia progenies*) at 11.754–6 (Ilus – Laomedon – Priam), which this catalogue in a sense continues (see Cole 2004: 365).

609 Ascanii . . . binominis: at Virg. *Aen.*1.267–8 Jupiter explains Aeneas' son's dual names to Venus: *at puer Ascanius, cui nunc cognomen Iulo* | *additur (Ilus erat, dum res stetit Ilia regno).* It was through the name Iulus that the *gens Iulia* promoted its connection to the Aeneas legend, see 15.447–8 *dominam rerum de sanguine natus Iuli* | *efficiet*, 767, *Aen.* 1.288 *Iulius, a magno demissum nomen Iulo,* Weinstock 1971: 5–12, Horsfall 1986: 10–11. *At F.* 4.39–40 the king list commences with Iulus: *nomen Iuli,* | *unde domus Teucros Iulia tangit auos*. Livy 1.3.2 records that there was some debate about Ascanius' maternity, with the Julian *gens* claiming a Trojan origin and a rival Italian version which made him the son of Lavinia instead (see Ogilvie ad loc. for a discussion of the political motives of the divergent traditions, also Bremmer and Horsfall 1987: 22–3, Bandiera 1986). Virgil famously seems to suggest in a number of passages that Ascanius will be the ancestor of the Alban kings (*Aen.* 1.267–71, 288, 8.628–9, *al.*), but elsewhere refers to the version that Aeneas' half-Italian son Silvius will be the ancestor instead (*Aen.* 6.760–6), see O'Hara 1990: 145–7. **Alba:** according to the tradition followed by Virgil, the legendary town of Alba Longa, in the region of the Alban hills SE of Rome in Latium, was founded by Ascanius/Iulus thirty years after the foundation of Lavinium by his father Aeneas (*Aen.* 1.267–71). The prodigy of a white sow with thirty piglets was said to have marked out the future site of the town and also given it its name, see *Aen.* 3.389–93, 8.41–8, Varro, *LL* 5.144, Prop. 4.1.35, Fabius Pictor fr. 4 Peter (= 5a Chassignet), Livy 1.3.3, Dion. Hal. *Ant. Rom.* 1.56.1–4. In Ennius, however, Aeneas arrived at an already existing Alba and married the daughter of Alba's king, Latinus (see Skutsch 1985: 190, D'Anna 1996). The town was said to have been defeated and razed by Rome in the seventh century and its population absorbed (Livy 1.27–30); hence the ancient sources had no clear idea of where precisely to locate the city, see Grandazzi 1986, Chiarucci 2000. Its role as mother city to Rome reflects its role as a religious centre for Italian peoples (see Alföldi 1965: 29–34); cf. the importance of Alban descent: Livy 1.52.2 *cum onmes Latini ab Alba oriundi sint*, Prop. 4.6.37–8 *o Longa mundi seruator ab Alba | Auguste*, cf. Galinsky 1969a: 144.

610 resque Latina 'the Latin state' (*OLD* s.v. *res* 16), Livy 1.3.1. **Siluius:** tradition again offered two different versions of the genealogy of Silvius, on which Ovid here avoids taking a position. At *F.* 4.41–2 Ovid identifies Silvius as the son of Ascanius (cf. Livy 1.3.6), but by calling him *Postumus . . . Siluius* he also alludes to the more widespread non-Julian 'Italian' version of the Alban king list followed by Virgil at *Aeneid* 6.763–66, in which Silvius was Iulus' Italian half-brother, born to Lavinia after Aeneas' death (*Aen.* 6.763 *Siluius, Albanum nomen, tua postuma proles*). Servius on *Aen.* 6.760 attributes this version to Cato (= *Orig.* fr. 11 Peter, 1.14 Cugusi and Sblendorio Cugusi), cf. Dion. Hal. *Ant. Rom.* 1.70.1, Diod. 7.5.8, see Ogilvie on Livy 1.3.2. The etymology of Silvius is given at *F.* 4.41–2 *quod siluis fuit ortus in altis*, cf. Virg. *Aen.* 6.763–5. In most versions Silvius' name was repeated as surname by succeeding Alban kings: Livy 1.3.7 *mansit Siluiis postea omnibus cognomen qui Albae regnarunt.*

611 quo satus 'his son', see 10n. on *satus.* **Latinus:** also known as Latinus Silvius (cf. Liv. 1.3.7, Dion. Hal. *Ant. Rom.* 1.71.1) was named after his grandfather, King Latinus (*repetita . . . nomina*). In most versions Aeneas Silvius comes between Silvius and Latinus (e.g. Livy 1.3.7, Dion. Hal. *Ant. Rom.* 1.71.1).

611–12 repetita . . . nomina: poetic pl. (or an allusion to the fact that he inherited two ancestral names as Latinus Silvius), cf. *F.* 4.45 *repetita uocabula.* The etymology is reproduced by the repetition of his name at the end of two successive lines. **clarus subit Alba Latinum** ~ *F.* 4.43, cf. Virg. *Aen.* 8.48 *Ascanius clari condet cognominis Albam* (for the wordplay see O'Hara 1996a: 98).

613 Epytus or Epitus (Diod. 7.5.10) is replaced in Livy 1.3.8 by Atys (see Ogilvie ad loc.). A Trojan is named Epytus at Virg. *Aen.* 2.340, cf. 5.547, 579. **Capetus:** as in Livy, cf. *F.* 4.46 *Calpetus.* Ogilvie on Livy 1.3.6 suggests Calpetus was invented 'to provide a pedigree for the Calpurnii', while Capetus is an eponym for the *Capitolium.* **Capys:** cf. *F.* 4.45 *ille dedit Capyi repetita uocabula Troiae,* Livy 1.3.7. A Trojan name; in Homer the name of Anchises' father (*Il.* 20.239, cf. *F.* 4.34, Enn. *Ann.* 28–9 Sk.). In Virgil Capys appears both in Anchises' Alban king list (6.768) and as a companion of Aeneas at *Aen.* 1.183, 2.35, 9.576, 10.145 (as founder of Capua). **-que . . . -que:** see 78n., cf. 616 below.

614 sed Capys ante fuit: the usual order (cf. *F.* 4.44–6); Ovid adopts a mock scholarly tone in correcting himself and plays with the chronological progression of the king list (see Granobs 1997: 25).

614–16 regnum Tiberinus . . . nomina fecit aquae: this etymology for the Tiber (earlier called Albula, see 327–8n.) from the drowning of king *Tiberinus* in the river is frequently mentioned in the Alban king lists, cf. *F.* 4.47–8, also 2.389–90, Livy 1.3.8 *Tiberinus, qui in traiectu Albulae amnis submersus celebre ad posteros nomen flumini dedit,* Diod. 7.5.10, Dion. Hal. *Ant. Rom.* 1.71.2, *Orig. gent. Rom.* 18.1. Virgil, however, has Evander derive the changed name of the river from an earlier individual named Thybris at *Aen.* 8.330–2 '*tum reges asperque immani corpore Thybris | a quo post Itali fluuium cognomina Thybrim | diximus; amisit uerum uetus Albula nomen*'. With *Tusci* in the following line Ovid may gesture towards this alternative etymology from king Thybris, usually specified as Etruscan (see *LALE* s.v. *Thybris* (2), Serv. on *Aen.* 8.330, Cairns 2002: 68). Ovid uses the term *Tiberinus* only one other time in the *Met.* (15.728 *Tiberinaque ad ostia*), while *Thybris* appears 5x, see 426n. *Tiberinus* was the name of the river in cult (Serv. on *Aen.* 8.31 *in sacris Tiberinus, in coenolexia Tiberis, in poemate Thybris uocatur*) and is found in Enn. *Ann.* 26 Sk., Cicero *ND* 3.52, Virgil *Aen.* 8/9x; see Bömer on *F.* 4.47). The river-god had a shrine and festival at Rome, see Latte 1960: 132. **Tusci . . . fluminis:** the river was in poetry conventionally 'Tuscan' because it flows south from Etruria and forms the boundary of Etruria and Latium, cf. e.g., *F.* 1.233, 4.48, *AA* 3.386, Virg. *Aen.* 8.473, 10.199, Hor. *C.* 3.7.28. **nomina fecit aquae:** *nomina* is poetic. pl., cf. *F.* 4.284 *Icarus, et uastae nomina fecit aquae,* 5.182, *Tr.* 1.1.90, Virg. *G.* 1.138. On this etymological formula, see 90n., O'Hara 1996b: 272.

616 Remulus: in the *Fasti* Remulus is instead the grandson of Tiberinus and succeeds Tiberinus' son Agrippa (*F.* 4.40–50), so also Livy 1.3.9 (where he is called Romulus Siluius), Dion. Hal. *Ant. Rom.* 1.71.3 (Allodius). Ogilvie on Livy 1.3.9 suggests that 'Remulus provides an attractive aetiology for the *ager Remurius* and the *Remoria*'. Virgil has a Numanus Remulus (*Aen.* 9.592–3), as well as two other Italians with the name Remulus at 9.360, 11.636.

617 Acrota: called Agrippa in the *Fasti* (4.50) and elsewhere, cf. Livy 1.3.9, Dion. Hal. *Ant. Rom.* 1.71.2. Ogilvie on Livy 1.3.9 argues that 'the original name is likely to have been Acrota (from ἀκρο alluding to the *arx* as Capetus alludes to the Capitol), which was rationalized to Agrippa'. Acrota is attested only here (Bömer notes that the reading is supported by *Mythogr. Vat.* 1.204.20).

618 'died from a stroke of lightning while he was imitating lightning'; cf. *F.* 4.50 *in Remulum fulmina missa ferunt,* Livy 1.3.9 *fulmine ipse ictus,* Dion. Hal. *Ant. Rom.* 1.71.3, Diod. 7.5.11. See Ogilvie on Livy 1.3.9 'there was a meteorite held in great veneration on the Aventine, which goes far to explaining this detail'. Frier 1979: 55 suggests the story was 'invented by the annalist L. Calpurnius Piso (F 33 Forsythe = *Orig. gent. Rom.* 18.2–3), on the analogy of the frequently recounted Greek myth of Salmoneus (cf. Virg. *Aen.* 6.586 (Salmoneus) *flammas Iouis et sonitus imitatur Olympi*), Bömer ad loc. This line is marked by alliteration of *f* (also the next line) and enclosed line structure of adj./noun (see 169n.).

619 moderatior: Acrota was *ferox* in 616, but here 'more restrained than his brother' he hands over the throne to *forti Auentino.*

620 Auentino: the derivation of the name of the Roman hill from the king's burial there is frequently mentioned in the Alban king lists, cf. *F.* 4.51–2 *uenit Auentinus post hos, locus unde uocatur,* | *mons quoque,* Dion. Hal. *Ant. Rom.* 1.71.4, Liv. 1.3.9. At Virg. *Aen.* 7.655–69 an Aventinus (son of Hercules), who gave his name to the hill (or derived it) from his birth there, not burial (660–1), appears in the Italian catalogue. Varro *LL* 5.43 offers multiple etymologies for the name of the hill (cf. Serv. on *Aen.* 8.231–5).

621 monte . . . monti: repetition (polyptoton) encloses the line and creates closure for this section of the catalogue. **positus** 'outstretched ' in death, of burial (*OLD* 7a *ad fin.*), cf. Livy 1.3.9 *is sepultus in eo colle qui nunc pars Romanae est urbis.* **uocabula:** (poetic pl., quoted by Leumann 1959: 145 as an extreme example of this trope); etymological terminology, only here in the *Met.*, cf. *F.* 3.511, 847, 4.45, 5.73. Cf. Liv. 1.3.9 *cognomen colli fecit.*

622–771 Pomona and Vertumnus

The Alban king list is unexpectedly interrupted by the amatory tale of the two ancient Italian agricultural deities Pomona and Vertumnus and does not resume until 772 with Amulius (*proximus . . .*). The story seems to be original to Ovid. The rustic Vertumnus, an Etruscan god brought to Rome from Volsinii after its defeat in the third century (cf. Prop. 4.2.3 *Tuscus ego et Tuscis orior*), attempts to enter the enclosed garden of Pomona, an ancient Roman deity of fruit trees, and to win her over, first through the use of numerous rustic disguises and then by persuasion, rather than resorting immediately to violence. He ultimately wins Pomona only when he reveals his true form. Ovid's description of Pomona at the beginning of the episode as a devotee of the garden gives us a clue that she will not follow the symbolic pattern of hunting and virginity which is established by the first amatory tale of Daphne and Apollo and is continued throughout the poem (see Davis 1983).

Important in this episode is Ovid's debt to Propertius' earlier poem 4.2, in which the statue of Vertumnus holds forth on his origins as a god and as a statue (see 644, 645–6, 648, 649, 684–5nn.). V.'s statue explains that three etymologies have been suggested for his name: (1) from his turning back of the flood waters of the Tiber (4.2.10 *Vertumnus uerso dicor ab amne deus*), (2) from the offerings of the first-fruits of the 'turning' year (4.2.11 *quia uertentis fructum praecepimus anni*), and (3) from his ability to turn himself into many forms (4.2.47–8 *at mihi, quod formas unus uertebar in omnes* | *nomen ab euentu patria lingua dedit*). The god insists the last etymology is correct: *de se narranti tu modo crede deo* (4.2.20). The appropriateness of Vertumnus as the narrator of an obscure Cypriot story about the hard-hearted Anaxarete transformed into a stone statue becomes apparent only when one considers his literary genealogy (see Myers 1994b). Ovid means us to recall this earlier appearance of Vertumnus as both a statue and an aetiological narrator in Propertius' poem (see 165–6n. on the intertextual awareness of Ovid's characters, cf. Hinds 1987: 19 on Achelous at *Met.* 8.545f., Kenney 2001a on Medea in *Met.* 7, Barchiesi 2001: 18–26, Knox 1995: 18–25 on the *Heroides*). At Propertius 4.2.51–2 we are told that Vertumnus was brought to Rome during the Sabine assimilation, an episode from which immediately follows this story in the *Met.* (775–804). On statue tales in book 14, see Myers 1994a: 104–28.

Vertumnus was known from a bronze statue that stood behind the temple of Castor on the *Vicus Tuscus*, between the edge of the Forum Romanum and the Velabrum (Richardson s.v. *Signum Vortumni*, Putnam 1967), which seems to have been a landmark of sorts in the city, see Varro, *LL* 5.46, Cic. *Verr.* 2.1.154, Livy, 44.16.10, Hor. *Epist.* 1.20.1. Varro explains that V.'s statue stood in the *Vicus Tuscus* because *is deus Etruriae princeps* (*LL* 5.46, see Marquis 1974). V. also had a temple on the Aventine (Fest. 228 L., Richardson s.v. *Vortumnus, Aedes*) with a state cult associated with the date 13 August (*Fasti* in Degrassi XIII.2, nos. 18, 24, 25); see Radke 1979: 317–20, Simon 1990: 111–12, Boldrer 1999, *LIMC* VIII 1.235 s.v. Vertumnus. Pomona had a *flamen* (Varro (*LL* 7.45) quotes three lines from Ennius' *Annales* (116–18 Sk.) listing six of the lesser-known *flamines* instituted by Numa among which is listed the *Pomonalis*), and possibly a sanctuary (*Pomonal*) outside Rome (Fest. 250 M, 296 L.); see Radke 1979: 257–8, Latte 1960: 37, 73–4. After Ennius, Ovid's passage is Pomona's earliest appearance in any known literary sources; she is found later in Calpurnius Siculus 2.33, Plin. *Nat.* 23.1ff., and Martial 1.49.8. Servius on Virg. *Aen.* 7.190 makes the surprising claim that Pomona was Picus' wife: *Picum amauit Pomona, pomorum dea, et eius uolentis est sortita coniugium*, but no other source reflects this tradition (see 308–434n.). Further bibliography on the episode: Littlefield 1965, Fantazzi 1976, Porte 1985b: 188, 190, Barkan 1986: 81–2, Fantham 1993, Gentilcore 1995, Johnson 1997, Lindheim 1998, Jones 2001. The episode was especially popular in seventeenth-century art, e.g. Hendrick Goltzius (Rijksmuseum), P. P. Rubens (Prado), Abraham Bloemaert (Princeton).

622 Iamque also opens the book (used similarly in an introduction to a story at 8.260, 15.506, 871). **Palatinae summam . . . gentis habebat** 'reigned over the Palatine race'; (*OLD habere* 6). *summam . . . gentis* finds no parallels in contemporary poetry (*TLL* VI 2406.13ff.), cf. 13.192 *summa mouet sceptri*, Livy 4.46.3 *summam imperii habere.* Virgil used the same anachronistic adj. *Palatinus* from *Palatium*, 'the Palatine hill', to refer to the future Roman race at *Aen.* 9.9 *sceptra Palatini sedemque petit Euandri* (see Hardie 1994 ad loc.). Cf. Canens' birth site *in colle Palati* (14.333) and 822n. The alliteration of *p* in this line and the next is paralleled in Virgil's abbreviated king-list at *Aen.* 6.767 *proximus . . . Procas.* **Proca** appears in the traditional Alban king list (his name here is an emendation of the corrupt MS tradition from the list at *Fasti* 4.52 *tradita regna Procae*), but no stories are otherwise associated with his reign (von Geisau *RE* XXIII 64–5), see Dion. Hal. *Ant. Rom.* 1.71.4 (where we are told that he reigned 23 years, 819–796 BCE); Virg. *Aen.* 6.767 *Procas, Troianae gloria gentis;* Livy 1.3.9.

At *Fasti* 6.131–68 the infant Proca is saved from *striges* by the Roman goddess Carna (as Hardie has observed *per litteras* the amatory story of Janus and Carna preceding this episode (101–30) has some interesting parallels with our episode in the nymph's (= huntress's) rejection of amatory advances: *F.* 6.108 *nequiquam multis saepe petita procis,* cf. *procis* 670, *procorum* 681; on other textual connections between *Met.* 14–15 and *F.* 6 see Myers 1994a: 127). Etymologically Proca's name may be connected with *proceres* (Walde–Hofmann 1965, s.v.), giving the meaning 'elder, leader, prince' (Ahl 1985: 316 sees a possible play with a false etymology at Livy 1.3.9 *Proca deinde regnat. Numitorem atque Amulium procreat*). For the Latinized form of the name, cf. 6.400 *Marsya,* 7.170 *Aeeta,* Quint. *Inst.* 1.5.61, Leumann 454.

623–36 The next fourteen lines describe the nymph Pomona, whose activities in her garden are centred on the cultivation of fruit trees (625) and involve such tasks as irrigation, pruning, and grafting. The vocabulary here and elsewhere in this passage is indebted to the technical language of agricultural treatises and Virgil's *Georgics*. Fantham's suggestion 1993: 34 that the episode also shares features with comic drama and mime (cf. Wiseman 2002: 283, who suggests a satyr play) might find support in the similarities of Pomona with Flora, whose festival, the *Floralia,* included comic performances (see *F.* 5.331–54, esp. the paraclausithyron motif at 337–9, and McKeown 1979: 77).

A remarkable series of negatives is used to characterize Pomona's pursuits antithetically (626–34). The description of P.'s vocation in contrast with hunting is a clue that she will not follow the pattern of the huntress-determined-virgin type (established earlier in the poem by the figures of Daphne, Syrinx, and Callisto) which she seems at first to resemble in her rejection of amatory advances (Davis 1983: 68–9; cf. Nagle 1988c: 42). The nymph Salmacis' role as a non-huntress is similarly negatively defined as a deviation from the norm at 4.302–15; contrast the huntress Callisto at 2.411–12 *non erat huius opus lanam mollire trahendo | nec positu uariare comas* (Davis 1983: 43–71; cf. Pindar on Cyrene at *Pyth.* 9.18ff. for the same rhetorical convention).

623–4 Latinas | inter Hamadryadas: Pomona, like Canens, and so many other heroines in the *Met.*, is a nymph, *hamadryas* (Serv. on *Ecl.* 10.62 *nymphae, quae cum arboribus et nascuntur et pereunt*), but she is also Latin. The juxtaposition of the two terms, *hamadryas* and *Latina,* emphasized by the enjambment and anastrophe, suggests that P., like Canens and Ovid's poetry, is a blend of the Greek and Roman (cf. 326 *dryadas Latiis in montibus ortas,* 334n.); see Fantham 1990 on the prominence of Italian nymphs in *Met.* 14–15. P.'s Italian origins perhaps also distinguish her from the 'Arcadian nymph virgin' stereotype (Davis 1983: 68). Ovid refers to Hamadryads only twice elsewhere in his poetry: *Met.* 1.690 (Syrinx), *F.* 2.155 (Callisto). Hamadryads are rare in Latin poetry (10x from Catullus 61.23 to Statius *Silv.* 1.3.63) and may share an association with the poetry of Gallus, see Virg. *Ecl.* 10.62, Prop. 1.20.32, 2.32.37, 2.34.76 (*inter hamadryadas*), and *Culex* 95; see Ross 1975: 95 n.4; Monteleone 1979; Kennedy 1982; O'Hara 1996b: 253–4. The ultimate source for the use of these nymphs as poetic symbols may be Callimachus (*Hy. Delos* 79–85), see Myers 1994a. **sollertius:** the adjective *sollers* (a favourite word of Ovid (14x), see McKeown on *Am.* 1.8.87–8) is used frequently of agricultural expertise (Bömer): Virg. *G.* 4.327 *frugum et pecudum custodia sollers*, Tib. 1.7.29 *primus aratra manu sollerti fecit Osiris.*

625 arborei . . . fetus: epic periphrasis for *poma* (glossing Pomona's name), from Virg. *G.* 1.55 *arborei fetus*, cf. 10.664–6 (Atalanta and Hippomenes) *de tribus unum | fetibus arboreis proles Neptunis misit. | obstipuit uirgo nitique cupidine pomi.* Adjs. in *-eus* are both poetic usage and often, as here, metrically convenient (see Thomas on *G.* 1.55 on the metrical intractability of *arborum*). **studiosior** 'nor more zealous in the care of fruitful trees' (Miller-Goold), cf. 5.578–9 (Arethusa) *nec me studiosius altera saltus | legit nec posuit studiosius altera casses*, Hor. *C.* 3.27.29 (Europa) *nuper in pratis studiosa florum.* The two comparisons follow a common formula with an epic ancestry, cf. 12.405–6 *qua nulla decentior inter | semiferos altis habitauit femina siluis*, 3.615–16, 5.130–1, Virg. *Aen.* 9.179–80 *quo pulchrior alter | non fuit* (with Hardie). On *studiosus*, see 321n.

626 unde tenet nomen: the etymology for Pomona (see Serv. on Virg. *Aen.* 7.190 *pomorum dea*, Fest. p. 144, 13 L. *praesidet pomis*, Walde–Hofmann 1965: 334f.); for similar etymological formulae, see 90n. (*nomen*), 338n. (*unde*). **siluas . . . amnes:** these are the usual haunts of nymphs (eg. 326–32, 1.690, 3.402–3, *F.* 1.512); contrast Ovid's description of Daphne at 1.475–6 *siluarum latebris captiuarumque ferarum | exuuiis gaudens innuptaeque aemula Phoebes.*

627 rus 'cultivated countryside' (*OLD* 1). The antithesis is conveyed by the emphatic placing of *rus* in asyndeton at the beginning of the line (Shackleton Bailey 1956: 67–8; K–S II 156–7). Cf. the description of Flora at *F.* 5.373–4 *non sibi respondit siluas cessisse, sed hortos | aruaque.* **felicia poma:** *felix* 'fruitful' (*OLD felix*[1] 1), cf. of the fruit itself 9.92, 13.719, Lucr. 5.1377–8, Virg. *Aen.* 6.230 *ramo felicis oliuae*, Sil. 15.532 *floret bacis felicibus arbor*, Mart. *Ep.* 8.68.6 *felix . . . uua* (see *TLL* VI 436.13–14). The epithet is also used of the gods themselves: [Tib.] 3.8.13 *felix Vertumnus*; Mart. *Ep.* 1.49.8 *Pomona . . . felix.*

628 iaculo . . . falce 'Her right hand was not laden with a javelin, but with a curved pruning hook.' The contrast between the two opposing occupations of hunting and horticulture is here encapsulated in the structure of the line, and stressed by the *apo koinou* placement of *grauis* and *dextera*, distributed between the two halves. Contrast Callisto at *Met.* 2.414 *modo leue manu iaculum, modo sumpserat arcum. falx* is the general name for a wide variety of iron implements, consisting of a curved blade with a single cutting edge (White 1967: 72–103).

629 luxuriem 'immoderate overgrowth' (*OLD* 1 (of plants)). Virgil warns of the harm caused to crops by *luxuria* of the stalks (*G.* 1.112) or foliage (*G.* 1.191), cf. *F.* 1.689–90, Col. 4.21.2. For the fifth-declension form of the acc. cf. Virg. *G.* 1.112 *luxuriem segetum*, Hor. *AP* 214; in other cases Ovid's MSS, like Virgil's, offer first-declension forms (*F.* 5.279 *luxuriae*, 6.444 *luxuria*, Virg. *G.*1.191 *luxuria foliorum*), see N–W I 561–4; *TLL* VII 2.1919.53ff. **premit** 'prunes', an agricultural technical term (*OLD* 19b);

cf. Hor. *C.* 1.31.9 *premant Calena falce . . . uitem*, Virg. *G.* 1.156–7 *ruris opaci | falce premes umbras*, Col. 4.27.6.

630 bracchia: of trees, as frequently (*OLD* 4), but the hint of anthropomorphizing may be activated here in this tale about a tree nymph named Pomona (cf. 1.550 (Daphne) *in ramos bracchia crescunt*). **compescit:** technical language again, cf. Virg. *G.* 2.370 *ramos compesce fluentis*, Col. 4.17.5.

630–1 fisso . . . cortice lignum | inserit 'she made a slit in the bark and inserted a cutting', cf. Prop. 4.2.17–18 where Vertumnus appears as an *insitor. TLL* VII 2.1387.50–3 offers no classical parallels for this sense of *lignum* (*de surculis, sim.*). *insero* is technical for grafting (*OLD* 2), cf. Thomas on Virg. *G.* 2.302 *neue oleae siluestris insere truncos.* **fisso . . . cortice:** the noun occurs in both the masculine and feminine (cf. Quint. *Inst.* 1.5.35, *TLL* IV 1069.11ff.). It seems to be treated consistently as masculine by Ovid, with the possible exception of 10.512 *fissa cortice*; cf. Lucr. 4.50 (fem.), Virg. *Ecl.* 6.63 (fem.), *Aen.* 7.742 (masc.). **sucos alieno praestat alumno** 'supplied fluids to the foreign nursling'; more use of technical terminology (*OLD alumnus* 1c, cf. Col. 4.27.4). For the use of *alienus* of grafting, cf. Virg. *G.* 2.76 *aliena ex arbore*, Col. 10.38 *aliena stirpe.*

632 recuruas: an unusual epithet applied to roots (some MSS have *repugnans*); Bömer's parallels are not quite apt: 3.664 *hederae . . . nexuque recuruo*, 11.70 *torta radix.*

633 irrigat: the verb, usually technical (*TLL* VII 2.418.44ff.), appears only here in Ovid (Virg. 4x, not in Hor., Tib., Prop., cf. *G.* 4.115 *irriget imbris;* Calp. *Ecl.* 2.97 *sitientes irriget hortos*). Cf. *F.* 5.209–10 (Flora) *est mihi facundus dotalibus hortus in agris; | aura fouet, liquidae fonte rigatur aquae.* For irrigation channels cf. Virg. *G.* 1.104–10, Hor. *C.* 1.7.14

634 hic amor, hoc studium = Virg. *Aen.* 11.739 (Etruscan dissipations), cf. *Aen.* 6.129 *hoc opus, hic labor est*, and Ovid *AA* 1.453 *hoc opus, hic labor est, primo sine munere iungi*, with Kenney 1958: 201, *F.* 3.709. Contextually Ovid's passage has more in common with a similar phrase in the *Georgics*, at 2.514–15 *hic anni labor, hinc patriam paruosque nepotes | sustinet, hinc . . .* (a passage describing the ideal Roman *agricola* which shares much vocabulary with our passage, 513 *incuruo . . . aratro*, 516 *pomis*, 521 *fetus autumnus*), cf. *G.* 3.288. Cf. 625 *studiosior*, 627 *amat.* **Veneris quoque nulla cupido est** 'for love she had besides no desire', adding an additional qualification of her single-mindedness and placing P. in the pattern of determined virginity which the above description so far has belied. Venus was, however, traditionally associated with gardens (Varro, *RR* 1.1.6, *LL* 6.16, see Grimal 1969: 49–54), which might hint at P.'s eventual susceptibility to love.

635 uim . . . agrestum: the adjective suggests boorishness (*OLD agrestis* 4). The solitude of Pomona's garden has already been threatened by the potential sexual violence always present in the landscape of the poem (*uis* in the *Met.* often implies rape, cf. 2.576, 3.344, 4.233, 239, 5.288, 6.525, etc., see Parry 1964, Segal 1969: 74–85, *OLD uis* 2a). The threat of *uis* reappears prominently at the end of the episode at 770. **pomaria claudit:** cf. 4.646–7 *id metuens solidis pomaria clauserat Atlas* | *moenibus*. The enclosed orchard/garden has symbolic sexual implications (κῆπος or *hortus* = *culus*, Adams 1982: 84) and is suggestive of P.'s virginity (cf. Segal 1969: 68–9, Parry 1964: 276). Erotic use of gardens and orchards is common, e.g. Catullus 62.39–48, Virg. Ecl. 8.37–41, *Priapea*, e.g. 5.3–4, 15; cf. *Met.* 13.797 (Polyphemus to Galatea) *et, si non fugias, riguo formosior horto;* see Littlewood 1968. On wordplay with P.'s name, cf. 627, 650, 687, 764.

636 accessus . . . uiriles: object of both verbs; the adjective *uirilis*, is used in place of a genitive, cf. e.g. 7.239–40 *uiriles* | *contactus*, 13.466–7 *uiriles* | . . . *manus*. The noun implies sexual advances, cf. *AA* 1.352, 604 (*TLL* I 288.21f.). *uiriles* at the end of the phrase may create an etymological balance with *uim* at its opening in the previous line (on the association of *uir* with *uis*, see *LALE* s.v. *uir*).

637–41 Pomona is beset by a sexually aggressive group of suitors: Pans, Satyrs, Silenus, and Priapus, cf. Syrinx at 1.692–4 *non semel et Satyros eluserat illa sequentes* | *et quoscumque deos umbrosaque silua feraxque* | *rus habet*, *Her.* 5.135–8 (Oenone) *me satyri celeres (siluis ego tecta latebam)* | *quaesierunt rapido, turba proterua, pede,* | *cornigerumque caput pinu praecinctus acuta* | *Faunus*. Satyrs and Pans were woodland deities (cf. P.'s aversion to *siluae* 626), see 1.192–3 *sunt mihi semidei, sunt rustica numina Nymphae* | *Faunique Satyrique et monticolae Siluani,* 6.392–3 *ruricolae, siluarum numina, Fauni* | *et Satyri fratres*, and were also, like Silenus and Priapus, associated with Bacchus, cf. *F.* 1.395–400 (with Green), *Tr.* 5.3.37. The lechery of Satyrs and Pan(s) was proverbial; see 1.698ff. (Pan and Syrinx), *F.* 1.397 *in Venerem satyrorum prona iuuentus*, 4.142 *satyri, turba proterua*, Hor. *AP* 233 *Satyris . . . proteruis*, *C.* 3.18.1 *Faune, nympharum fugientum amator*, Lissarrague 1990. Each deity is accompanied by mention of significant attributes (in a manner similar to hymnic formula, see Nisbet and Rudd on Hor. *C.* 3.18.1).

637 Satyri, saltatibus apta iuuentus: for Satyrs and dancing, cf. *AA* 1.542 *leues Satyri*, Virg. *Ecl.* 5.73 *saltantis Satyros*, Hor. *C.* 1.1.31. On satyrs, traditionally mostly human, but with some horse or goat features, see Seaford 1984: 5–10, *LIMC* III 2 s.v. 'Dionysos/Bacchus' plates 70–82.

638 pinu praecincti cornua 'their horns bound with pine', cf. 1.699 (Pan) *pinu caput praecinctus*, *Her.* 5.137–8 *cornigerumque caput pinu praecinctus acuta* | *Faunus*, *F.* 1.412 *pinu tempora nexa*. On the medial (middle reflexive) use of the perfect passive participle with an accusative of the body part functioning as an object (or 'retained' from an active form of the verb), see 45n., Courtney 2004: 427 (4). Pan was associated with the nymph Pitys, who was turned into a pine tree (Prop.1.18.20 *Arcadio pinus amica deo*, Lucian *Dial. deor.* 22.4, Nonn. 42.259–61). **Panes:** sometimes plural (*F.* 1.397, *Her.* 4.171), but in Ovid more often singular, as at 14.514–26 *semicaper Pan* (see 515n.), and 1.699, 705, 11.153.

639 Silenusque, suis semper iuuenalior annis: cf. *F.* 1.413–14 *te quoque, inexstinctae Silene libidinis, urunt:* | *nequitia est quae te non sinit esse senem*. Silenus is traditionally a regular attendant of Bacchus, father of the Satyrs, and old, bald, and drunk, cf. 4.26–7, *F.* 1.399, 3.745–60, *AA* 1.543–8, Virg. *Ecl.* 6.14–15. *LIMC* III 2.378 9 (plates 686–92).

640 quique deus = *et deus qui*: the relative precedes its grammatical antecedent. **falce uel inguine:** Pomona excludes the traditional horticultural guardian, Priapus, whose ithyphallic statue was set up as protector of the garden (see Grimal 1969: 46–9, *LIMC* VIII 2.680–94); cf. *F.* 1.400 *qui . . . ruber pauidas inguine terret aues*, 1.415 *ruber, hortorum decus et tutela*. 6.333, Virg. *G.* 4.110 *custos furum atque auium cum falce saligna, Ecl.* 7.34, Tib. 1.1.17–18, Hor. *Sat.* 1.8.5, Col. 10.32–4 *numen uenerare Priapi | terribilis membri, medio qui semper in horto | inguinibus puero, praedoni falce minetur.* The threat of rape is made explicit with *inguine*: cf. Ovid's stories of the libidinous Priapus at *F.* 1.391–440 (Priapus and Lotis, cf. *Met.* 9.347 *Lotis . . . nymphe fugiens obscena Priapi*), 6.319–48 (Vesta). Propertius' Vertumnus poem 4.2 is similar to a number of poems with talking Priapus statues (Call. *Iambi* 7 and 9, Tibullus 1.4, and Hor. *Sat.*1.8; see Suits 1969: 477); on Priapus, see O'Connor 1989.

641 poterentur: the verb *potior* uses both third and fourth conjugation forms in the imperfect subjunctive (*OLD potior*[1], *TLL* X 2.327.58–9), cf. 13.130 *poteremur*. For the erotic connotations of the verb, see Adams 1982: 188, *TLL* X 2.330.54ff; cf. *Met.* 3.405, 9.753, 9.797, *AA* 1.711. **ea:** on the rarity of oblique cases of *is/ea/id* see 558n. **sed enim superabat amando** 'but in fact Vertumnus surpassed even them in his passion'. In earlier Latin literature *enim* did not have the later meaning 'for,' but was asseverative, *OLD sed*[1] 5 K–S II 78; *sed enim* occurs 11x in the *Met.* and at *F.* 2.751, 5.529, *Am.* 3.2.73; see Norden on Virg. *Aen.* 6.28. Quint. *Inst.* 9.3.14 lists this expression as a Virgilian archaism (e.g. *Aen.* 1.19, 2.164).

642 neque 'but . . . not' (*OLD* 5, K-S II 42). **felicior** 'more successful in his suit' (*TLL* VI 442.63ff., cf. 2.809, Catull. 100.8, Hor. *Epod.* 12.25); this contrasts with Pomona's *felicia poma* at 627 above.

643–57 V. gains access to Pomona's garden through various disguises and tries to win her over. Ovid has cleverly created the motivation for these self-transformations which is lacking in Prop. 4.2. We may compare Ovid's erotic instructions to the male lover at *AA* 1.759–62 *pectoribus mores tot sunt, quot in ore figurae: | qui sapit, innumeris moribus aptus erit, | utque leues Proteus modo se tenuabit in undas, | nunc leo, nunc arbor, nunc erit hirtus aper* (see Myerowitz 1985: 134). While in Propertius' poem V. describes seventeen of the various forms he has taken, in Ovid he changes only eight (or six) times. Until the final form of an old woman, V.'s changes might more properly be considered impersonations, rather than actual transformations (some think his statue might have been given actual costume changes, see Fantham 1993: 31–2, cf. [Tib.] 3.8.13–14). V. adopts four of the guises described in Prop.: a reaper (*messor* 14.643–4 = Prop. 4.2.28), a mower (14.645–6 = 4.2.25–6), a soldier (*miles* 14.651 = 4.2.27) and a fisherman (*piscator* 14.651 = 4.2.37), and additionally becomes a ploughman (*arator* 647–8), a pruner (*frondator, putator* 649), an apple-picker (650), and an old woman (*anus* 654–6). Other gods who use self-transformation (8.730 *sunt quibus in plures ius est transire figures*) for erotic pursuit in the poem include Jupiter (2.425–33, 846–75) and Phoebus (4.217–33, 11.310–11); cf. Arachne's long incriminatory list (6.131 *caelestia crimina*) of such divine transformations at 6.103–26.

The descriptions in these 14 lines are carefully structured, with the variation of syntax typical of Ovid when he accumulates effects. The first three disguises each receive two lines, then the following two receive one line, two disguises share a line at 651, and the final disguise occupies three lines at 654–6. The different characters V. impersonates are described by Ovid through the clothing, tools, and products of each occupation. The verbs and tenses are varied, but balanced (see (tenses) 644 *fuit,* 646 *poterat,* 649 *erat,* 648 *iurares,* 650 *putares*; 646 *uersasse,* 648 *disiunxisse;* (verbs of carrying) 644 *tulit,* 645 *gerens,* 647 *manu . . . portabat,* 650 *induerat*). Clarke 1972: 59 points out the concentration of rhyming verses in these lines, which contributes to the effect of speed.

643–4 o quotiens is a dramatic opening for the following catalogue of descriptions, (elsewhere in the poem only at 3.375, 10.661; also *Her.* 16.187; *Pont.* 1.9.21ff., 4.1.9ff.). Ovid and other elegists use both *o quotiens* and *a quotiens* (*Met.* 2.489, 491, 15.490; *Am.* 2.19.11; *Her.* 5.49, 9.79, 16.241, 243; *AA* 1.313, 2.125, 567, 3.481; *Pont.* 1.1.7, *Tr.* 1.3.51, 53); attempts to distinguish semantic differences (and MS variants) quickly become subjective (see McKeown on *Am.* 2.19.11–12, Goold 1965: 68), though *a*, a word favoured by neoteric emotionalism, is generally rare in epic (on *a* see Ross 1975: 51–3, Knox 1986a: 31–2). Outside the *Met.*, *o quotiens* appears not to be found in heroic epic (in hexameter at Virg. *Ecl.* 3.72), *a quotiens* only at Lucan 5.615 and Val. Flacc. 1.447. **habitu duri messoris** 'in the costume of a hardy reaper'. This first disguise is based on Prop. 4.2.28 *corbis in imposito pondere messor eram. messor* is found only here in Ovid, cf. Virg. *Ecl.* 2.10, 3.42, *G.* 1.316. For *durus* as 'hardy, robust' (*OLD* 3), cf. *F.* 4.691–2 *hoc . . . in campo . . . habebat* | *rus breue cum duro parca colona uiro*, Virg. *G.* 1.160 *quae sint duris agrestibus arma*, Hor. *Epod.* 3.4 *o dura messorum ilia.* **messoris . . .** | **messoris:** repetition of the same word, here in the same metrical position in succeeding lines, emphasizes the verisimilitude of V.'s disguise 'and indeed he was the spitting image of a reaper'. **corbe** appears elsewhere in poetry after Plautus only at Prop. 4.2.28 (Fedeli ad loc.; *TLL* IV 948.10f.), cf. Varro, *RR* 1.50.1 *spicas coniciunt in corbem atque in aream mittunt*; *LL* 5.139), see White 1975: 56–9 (*corbis messoris*), Tränkle 1960: 115. **imago:** compare Jupiter's disguise at 3.1 *iamque deus posita fallacis imagine tauri,* cf. 1.754, 6.103–4, 110. The meaning 'statue' may here also be evoked as V. was known as a statue and is about to tell a story about a statue which concludes *dominae sub imagine signum* | *seruat adhuc Salamis* (759–60, cf. 14.323 Picus' statue), see Solodow 1988: 205–6 on *imago* in the *Met.*

645–6 This disguise of the hay mower is also indebted to Prop. 4.2.25–6 *da falcem et torto frontem mihi comprime faeno:*| *iurabis nostra gramina secta manu. uersare* has better MS support, but the perfect *uersasse* better stresses that his disguise is meant to look as though he has already tossed the hay (cf. 648 *disiunxisse*).

647–8 The ploughman (*arator*) is not mentioned in Prop. 4.2. **rigida** 'rugged', a transferred epithet, characterizing V. as an archetypal rural figure (*OLD* 4, Bömer ad loc.), cf. 797n. **iurares:** cf. Prop. 4.2.26 *iurabis.* The imperfect form (the primary MSS have *iurasses*) aligns with *poterat* in 646 and *putares* in 650 and is the usual tense for a past generalizing second person subjunctive (*NLS* § 121, H–S 334); here the verb functions simultaneously in a consecutive clause (cf. e.g. 8.191, 9.288).

649–50 Although the pruner and fruit-picker do not appear in Propertius, the passage continues to echo the earlier poem, cf. Prop. 4.2.25 *da falcem* (cit. 645, of the *messor*). Here V.'s activities parallel those of Pomona described above (627–31, *felicia poma* 627, *falce* 628). **frondator . . . putator:** Ovid has chosen two highly technical words; both occupations involve pruning (*falce*), so the disguise seems to be single. *frondator* occurs elsewhere only at Catull. 64.41 *non falx attenuat frondatorum arboris umbram,* Virg. *Ecl.* 1.56, and Plin. *Nat.* 18.314. *frondatio* involves the reduction of foliage to let sun in and at the same time to get fodder for livestock, see Servius on *Ecl.* 1.56: *nam tria genera sunt frondatorum: frondator, qui arbores amputat, et qui frondibus manipulos facit, hiemis tempore animalibus ad pastum offerendos, et qui manibus uitium folia auellit, quo ardor solis uuam maturiorem reddat. putator* appears in poetry elsewhere only at Virg. *G.* 2.28–9 *summumque putator | haud dubitat terrae referens mandare cacumen*; see Varro *LL* 6.63 *putator, quod arbores puras facit.* For the duties of vine pruning, see Varro, *RR* 1.6.5; Virg. *G.* 2.362–70, 397–419; Col. 4.17.5; 4.6–28. **induerat:** instead of subordinating the first sentence in a temporal clause, 'when he had put on a ladder' (i.e. to carry it *OLD* 2), Ovid uses parataxis (cf. 11.125–6 *miscuerat puris auctorem muneris undis: | fusile per rictus aurum fluitare uideres*). For parataxis cf. H–S 526–33, Lunelli 1988: 111 n. 52 (bibliography). Ovid uses asyndeton throughout the catalogue to give an impression of the speed of V.'s transformations. **putator | . . . putares:** for such line-final repetition of words (here cognates) Wills 1996: 422–3 gives a complete list of instances in the *Met.* (46x). Tissol 1997: 24–5 discusses this passage as an example of a 'sylleptic instance of paronomasia, or punning repetition of a word' where the semantic shift 'plays on the physical and conceptual meanings of *putare,* "to prune" and "to think"'. The original sense of the word is 'to prune', and 'to think' is a metaphor, cf. *LALE* s.v. *puto,* Austin on *Aen.* 6.332.

651 ~ Prop. 4.2.27 *arma tuli quondam et, memini, laudabar in illis*, 37 *piscis calamo praedabor.* Tarrant 2000: 425–7 suggests that the roles of soldier and fisherman 'are jarringly out of place' in this horticultural setting and that the line was interpolated by a reader familiar with Ovid's model (cf. Tarrant 1989a: on 'collaborative interpolation'). But the lack of logic and Vertumnus' implied desperation may instead be a touch of Ovidian humour; the *miles amator* is, after all, a stock amatory figure (cf. *Am.* 1.9) and both occupations are associated with pursuit and capture, see Galasso 2006: 119–20. **miles erat:** cf. 2.415 (Callisto) *miles erat Phoebes* (same *sedes*). **harundine sumpta** ~ Prop. 4.2.33–4 <u>*harundine sumpta*</u> | *fautor plumoso sum deus aucupio.* The syntactical ἀπὸ κοινοῦ (*sumpto* understood from *sumpta*) is characteristic of Ovid (see 109n.), but the unchanged repetition from Prop. is perhaps suspicious.

652 aditum: like *accessus* (635) quasi-technical amatory term, cf. *AA* 1.163, 229, 721, 3.442, Tib. 2.4.19–20.

653 ut caperet spectatae gaudia formae 'to gain the delights of admiring her beauty', the noun and predicative participle (here a perfect with a present aspect) replace an abstract noun with a dependent genitive (*spectata forma* = *spectatio formae*) *NLS* § 95, see 354n. For *spectare* in the sense 'admire' (*OLD* 5) cf. Moore-Blunt on *Met.* 2.366. Fantham 1993: 32n. 37 suggests there may be wordplay here on the erotic vocabulary of *gaudia capere*, used elsewhere for rape or intercourse, cf. 11.310, 12.198 (see Adams 1982: 197–8, Pichon 1966: 98–9), while Johnson 1997: 369 sees this as proof of V.'s lack of violent motive.

654–6 V.'s final guise (which possibly involves not merely a change of costume, but self-transformation) is that of an old woman, suitably harmless and trustworthy, and also well-known as a storyteller, cf. Catull. 68.46, Theocr. *Id.* 15, Herodas 1. Jupiter's and Phoebus' earlier use of cross-dressing for sexual predation at 2.425–33, 4.217–33, and 11.310 (*Phoebus anum simulat praereptaque gaudia sumit*) should remind the reader of V.'s erotic intent. Hints of the god's transvestism appear already in Prop. 4.2.23 *indue me Cois, fiam non dura puella*. It is also an old woman in *F.* 6.409–16 who explains V.'s name. See Harmon 1986: 1961–3, on the possibility that, like Pomona, there were both male and female (or bisexual?) versions of Vertumnus (cf. Latte 1960: 59–60, on early Italian male/female divine doublets). This final transformation may also involve a humorous etymology: '*uert-anus*', hinting at the etymology of Vertumnus from '*uert-annus*' given at Prop. 4.2.11; cf. *LALE* s.v. *anus*: (Paul. Fest. 6) *anus dicta est ab annorum multitudine, quoniam antiqui non geminabant consonantes*. For the disguise see 3.275 (Juno) *simulauit anum posuitque ad tempora canos*, 6.26–7 *Pallas anum simulat falsoque in tempora canos | addit et infirmos baculo quoque sustinet artus*, *F.* 4.517–18 (Ceres) *simularat anum, mitraque capillos| presserat*. **picta redimitus tempora mitra:** for the construction, see 638n. The *mitra* was a finely-woven headdress with Near-Eastern and Bacchic associations (and effeminacy), cf. *F.* 3.669 (Anna of Bovillae, a real old woman) *illa, leui mitra canos incincta capillos*, 4.517 (above), Prop. 4.2.31 (another of Vertumnus' disguises) *cinge caput mitra, speciem furabor Iacchi*, Juv. 3.66 *picta . . . mitra*, Virg. *Aen.* 4.216 *Maeonia . . . mitra*, Sen. *Herc. Fur.* 471 *mitra . . . barbara*. For an illustration of a Greek *mitra* by Polygnotos (praised at Plin. *Nat.* 35.58), see his volute krater Boston 33.56 (Caskey–Beazley, *Attic Vase Paintings* Boston II, pl. LIX).

655 baculo is found in Prop. only at 4.2.39, but is used by Ovid 16x (11x in *Met.*, cf. 6.27 (above)), otherwise it is rare in poetry (*TLL* II 1670.52ff.). **positis per tempora canis:** The phrasing here may imply that V. has merely put on a wig (Fantham 1993: 32 n.38), cf. 3.275 (Juno) *posuitque ad tempora canos* (where the close parallel suggests we perhaps consider here the less well attested variant *ad*), 6.26 (above). The substantival use of *cani* (= *cani capilli*) is Ovidian, cf. 3.517, Luc. 2.122, 5.274.

657–764 In a *suasoria*, V. employs *exempla* (661–74), flattery (669–74), (self-)praise and the promise of devotion (675–92), and finally an admonitory tale (693–765), in an attempt to induce Pomona to accept his suit. See Ovid's precepts on such erotic persuasion in the *AA*, e.g. 1.459–62, 709–10, cf. *Am.* 2.3.17 *aptius at fuerit temptasse precibus*. With V.'s persuasive speech one may compare Apollo's and Jove's attempts at seduction speeches (both failures), which aim at merely catching their intended victims (1.504–24, 589–96, see Nagle 1988a, Gross 1985: 62–5); cf. also Circe at 28–36, 372–6.

Throughout the passage there is extensive play with the use of a disguise and self-reference in the third person. V.'s narrative is characterized by vigorous colloquialisms, agricultural terminology, and (amusingly yet appropriately, considering his sophisticated literary genealogy) learned references to Greek myths and widespread use of the language of Roman amatory elegy. The figure of the old woman as romantic go-between is suggestive of the conventional nurse of elegy and drama, see 703n. (cf. *AA* 1.371–2 (on the maid's role) *tum de te narret, tum persuadentia uerba | addat, et insano iuret amore mori*). V.'s narrative does not convince Pomona (765 *nequiquam*) and, on the whole, seems to be characterized by some ineptness in its lines of argument.

657 mirata est: the gender change from 654 *redimitus* slyly signals the speed of V.'s transformation. **'tanto'que †'potentior!'† inquit** 'and', (s)he said, 'How much more capable are you'. H–S 421 characterize this type of verbal ellipse as often colloquial (cf. *OLD tantus* 5a). The attachment of the connective *-que* to the first word quoted in direct speech rather than to the verb of saying (the so-called '*-que Ovidianum*') is a linguistic device common in Ovid, see Bömer on 9.109, Kenney 2002: 44; Haupt 1967: 510–12; Marouzeau 1958: 104–5 (who lists numerous examples (not this one)), cf. e.g. 1.456, 4.263, 838, 848, 5.394, 7.487, 8.203, Val. Fl. 4.387, 474. *potentior* does not convey the appropriate compliment; the textual variant *peritior* 'more skilled' may have a more logical connection with the opening of the line and the way in which Pomona has been characterized earlier (e.g. *sollertius, studiosior*). Tarrant suggests *decentior*, Luck 1982: 61 *beatior* (cf. 4.325), Watt 1995: 103 *placentior*, Liberman 2004: 87 '*quanto'que es pulchrior*'. Tarrant conjectures that there may be a lacuna of one following verse. Such a line is inserted in some MSS, e.g. *omnibus es nymphis quas continet albula ripis*.

658 paucaque . . . oscula 'a kiss or two' (Kenney 1988: 248), cf. 2.430–1 (Jupiter disguised as Diana kisses Callisto): *et oscula iungit | nec moderata satis nec sic a uirgine danda*; *Am.* 2.5.23–5 *oscula . . . | qualia non fratri tulerit germana seuero*.

660 autumni 'autumnal fruit', (*OLD* 2, cf. 9.91–2) perhaps another play on V.'s name and his association with agricultural productivity. For Autumnus personified see 2.29, *F.* 4.897; cf. Hor. *Epod.* 2.17–18. *uel cum decorum mitibus pomis caput | Autumnus agris extulit* (in the similar company of Priapus and Silvanus).

661 ulmus erat: typical ecphrastic formula, cf. 51n. Plin. *Nat.* 17.200 explains that elm trees are the best for vine-growing, cf. Virg. *G.* 1.2, 2.221, Col. 5.6.3. **speciosa nitentibus uuis** 'standing out with its clusters of glistening grapes', cf. 3.20 *speciosam cornibus altis*, Hor. *Ep.* 1.16.45 *speciosum pelle decora*.

662 socia: frequently used by Ovid to describe marriage or the like (*OLD* 4b, only examples from Ovid), cf. 678 *tori socium*, *Her.* 2.33, 5.126, Kenney on *Her.* 21.155 (*socialis*), *AA* 2.377.

663–6 V.'s seemingly innocent actions prove to have a point; his strategy is to appeal to Pomona through an horticultural parallel (667 *exemplo . . . arboris huius*). The training of vines on trees is commonly referred to in terms of a marriage in Roman agricultural writers and in poetry (Cato, *Agr.* 32.2, Col. 5.6.18, Hor. *C.* 2.15.4–5, 4.5.30, see McKeown on *Am.* 2.16.41, Courtney 1985: 87). Ovid's use of this simile is especially reminiscent of Catullus 62.49–55, where it is similarly used by the men to persuade the women to give up their virginity and to embrace the virtues of marriage and procreation: *ut uidua in nudo uitis quae nascitur aruo | numquam se extollit, numquam mitem educat uuam, | sed tenerum prono deflectens pondere corpus | iam iam contingit summum radice flagellum; | at si forte eadem est ulmo coniuncta marito, | multi illam agricolae, multi coluere iuuenci* (cf. 61.102–6, with Fedeli 1983: 71–4). For the use of gardening and georgic imagery in amatory contexts, see *AA* 1.349, 757–8, 2.321–2, 513, 649–52 (grafting), 3.575–6 (*poma*); *Her.* 4.29–30 (*pomaria*).

663 at 'but', implies a contrast (K–S II 82–3, *OLD* 3) and suggests that the 'approval' of 662 may have been verbally expressed (continuation of speech rather than introduction, K–S II 81–8). **caelebs:** the vocabulary continues to draw on nuptial terminology, cf. Catull. 62.49 *uidua*, 56 *sic uirgo dum intacta manet, dum inculta senescit*, and the similar threats of senescence in elegy e.g. *Am.* 1.8.53 *forma, nisi admittas, nullo exercente senescit.* Cf. Hor. *C.* 2.15.4 *platanus . . . caelebs*, where the adjective signifies the plane tree's sterility and inability to support vines (see N–H ad loc. for further parallels).

664 nil praeter frondes quare peteretur haberet 'there would be no reason why it would be sought besides its leaves', for the construction (*OLD quare* 4a, K–S II 278–9), cf. *F.* 4.942 *et quare fiat nil nisi nomen habet.* Although elm leaves were used for fodder for sheep and cattle (Cato, *Agr.* 5.8, 6.3, Col. 5.6.3–4), and Plin. *Nat.* 24.48 lists numerous medicinal properties of elm leaves, bark, and branches, Kenney 1986: 458 observes that elms were favoured for training vines precisely because their foliage was not too thick.

665 requiescit can also have erotic associations, see 10.556–7, *Am.* 1.5.25–6 (with McKeown), Tib. 1.1.43, Lygd. [Tib.] 3.6.53–4.

666 nupta: cf. Cato, *Agr.* 32.2 *arbores facito uti bene maritae sint*, Hor. *Epod.* 2.9–10 *ergo aut adulta uitium propagine | altas maritat populos*, *OLD* 4. **terrae acclinata iaceret** 'would lie languishing on the ground' (*terrae* dative), i.e. useless and neglected (*OLD iaceo* 9c), cf. Catull. 62.51 *sed tenerum prono deflectens pondere corpus.* The rhyme of *iaceret* with *haberet* in 664 marks the end of the simile.

667 exemplo: Ovid underlines Vertumnus' strategic use of the simile.

669–74 In order to compliment and win over Pomona, V. offers three mythological *exempla* of famously beautiful heroines, Helen, Hippodamia, and Penelope, who were sought after by many suitors (Helen and Hippodamia appear in *Am.* 2.12.17ff. and Prop. 2.6.15ff. in catalogues of fighting caused by women). It does not seem that such an appeal would go over well with the reclusive hamadryad (634–6), and it is perhaps a further indication of V.'s characterization as an inept persuader. The strategy is indebted to amatory elegy, see Prop. 2.2.9–10 *qualis et Ischomache, Lapithae genus, heroine,*| *centauris medio grata rapina mero*, 2.9.3f. *Penelope . . .* | *tam multis femina digna procis*, 2.3.32ff. (Cynthia as a second Helen).

669 atque utinam: 'introduces with emphasis a wish consequential on the preceding context' (Owen on *Tr.* 2.557). **Helene:** Ovid more often uses the Greek form of her name, here for metrical convenience, (but cf. *Helenam* at 13.200, her only other occurrence in the *Met.*).

670 quae: Hippodame (12.210, 224, or Hippodamia *Her.* 17.250) in most, but not all, versions of the myth (cf. Prop. 2.2.9 *Ischomache,* quoted above), daughter of Adrastus. *Met.* 12.210–535 provides the fullest surviving version of the story of the battle between the Lapiths and the Centaurs at the wedding of Hippodame to Theseus' friend Pirithous (see Bömer's introduction to the episode ad loc., McKeown on *Am.* 1.4.7–8).

670–1 Lapitheia . . . | **proelia:** the adj. is first attested in Ovid and probably coined by him (see 44n.), cf. 12.417 *Lapitheia tecta.* **coniunx . . . Vlixis:** on Penelope's renowned desirabilty, cf. Ovid's famously tendentious description of Homer's *Odyssey* as an amatory poem at *Tr.* 2.375–6 *aut quid Odyssea est, nisi femina propter amorem,* | *dum uir abest, multis una petita procis?* For the gen. sing. *Vlixis,* see 159n. **†timidi aut audacis†** is the reading of the MSS, but an implausible combination. Although Ulysses is belittled by Ajax at 13.104 *furtis incautum decipit hostem,* the adj. *timidus* is illogical here. Among the numerous conjectures which have been suggested, Riese's *nimium tardantis* (printed by Miller-Goold), although not especially convincing, would seem to emphasize Penelope's desirability correctly by attributing the cause of her availability to Ulysses' delayed homecoming. On the other hand, it seems desirable to retain *audacis,* a quality often associated with Ulysses, cf. 13.196 *audax orator,* 378. Possanza 2002 has suggested that the line originally contained an epithet for Penelope (*proelia nec coniunx prudens audacis Vlixi*), thus drawing attention to her as the subject of the exemplum.

672 nunc quoque 'even as things are' **cum** 'though'. **auerserisque petentes:** cf. Daphne at 1.478–9 *illa auersata petentes* | *impatiens expersque uiri nemora auia lustrat.* The doubling of verbs echoes Pomona's repulsion at 636: *prohibet refugitque.*

673 mille uiri cupiunt et semideique deique: a variation on a typical formula of erotic desirability, reminiscent of Catullus 62.42 *multi illum pueri, multae optauere puellae,* which refers to an untouched flower in another enclosed garden in a simile describing an unmarried maiden. A closer echo in the story of Daphne and Apollo (1.478 *multi illam petiere*) provides another parallel between the first and last amatory episodes of the epic, cf. 14.327–8 (Picus) *illum fontana petebant* | *numina,* 3.353–5 (of Narcissus, perhaps suggested by Catullus' *ut flos* 62.39), 10.315–16 (Myrrha), 12.404 (Cyllarus), 13.735 (Scylla), *F.* 6.108 (Carna); Virg. *Aen.* 7.54–6 (Lavinia), 11.581–4 (Camilla); on expressions of this type see also Tissol 1992. **et semideique deique:** see Wills 1996: 436 n.2, on the repetition of word-parts in compounds, specifically here the variation of simple and compound forms, marking the climactic progression from men to gods. For the polysyndeton, cf. 13.257 *et Alastoraque Chromiumque*. Kenney 2002: 64 observes that *semideus* (subst.) occurs first in Ovid's *Met.* (also at 1.192).

674 Albanos . . . montes reminds us of the story's occurrence in the reign of the Alban king Procas. The Alban hills would be a recognizable locale, some 10 miles SE of Rome.

675–92 V. uses his disguise now to plead his own case openly, humorously referring to himself throughout the speech in the third person (see Doblhofer 1959–60: 89–90, von Albrecht 1968: 418). Other examples of this ploy in the *Met.* include Acoetes (perhaps) 3.572–691, Jupiter 2.428–30, Neptune 2.575–6, Cipus 15.590–602. Apollo and Jupiter had in contrast openly praised themselves in their entreaties. V.'s arguments and language are reminiscent of erotic elegy.

675 si sapies: a colloquial phrase in strong assertions, which appears frequently in Ovid (Bömer, Hofmann 1951: 134, 200, Tränkle 1960: 165). This long and blustering sentence perhaps characterizes V.'s ardour. **bene iungere** sc. *coniugio, conubio, vel sim.*; the expression may also share in the colloquial colouring with a quasi-technical ring 'make a good match' (Kenney *per litteras*), cf. *coniungere* (668), *iuncta* (665).

675–6 anum . . . | hanc 'me', colloquial reference to the first person in the third person (Bömer) and a crafty way of not actually saying '*me*'. **uoles** 'you will consent'.

677 plus quam credis, amo: a coy play with his disguise. **uulgares** 'common, belonging to the lower orders' (*OLD* 2). V. disparages the *rustica numina* listed earlier at 637–41, but Pomona has, of course, already rejected all advances. Cf. the arguments of Circe at 33, 375–6, Apollo 1.513–14, and Jupiter 1.595. At 1.171–3 Ovid similarly divides the gods into the two social categories of *nobiles* and *plebs*, cf. 1.192ff., *Ibis* 79–80 *uos quoque plebs superum Fauni Satyrique Laresque | fluminaque et nymphae semideumque genus.* **taedas:** the torches used in the wedding procession, used by metonymy for marriage; cf. 1.483 *taedas . . . iugales*; Catull. 61.15 (with Fordyce ad loc.), 64.302.

678 pro quo: on lines ending with two monosyllables (far more common than a one-monosyllable ending), see Hellegouarc'h 1964: 52–5 (2% *Met.* 13–14, of which a form of *esse*, as in the following line, is the most common final word); cf. Helzle on *Pont.* 4.2.47. Homoeoteleuton of two monosyllables at the end of the line occurs nowhere else in the *Met.* according to Shackleton Bailey 1994: 75; he cites only *Her.* 17.197 *de te, F.* 3.491 *ne te.*

679 me quoque pignus habes 'and in addition you have my guarantee', *quoque* qualifies the whole sentence. Cf. 3.658–9 (Acoetes) *per tibi nunc ipsum (nec enim praesentior illo | est deus) adiuro*; Prop. 4.2.20 (Vertumnus) *de se narranti tu modo crede deo!* **neque enim sibi notior ille est:** cf. Cipus 15.599–60 *sed nos obstitimus, quamuis coniunctior* *illo* | *nemo mihi est*, *Her.* 20.158 *sed propior certe quam pater ipsa sibi est.* Tissol 1997: 61 comments on Ovid's stylistic play with the disjunctive repetition of pronouns to represent metamorphosis and shape-shifting as a sort of separation from the self.

681 haec loca sola colit: V. stresses his devotion to his and Pomona's native landscape. The two meanings of *colere* as 'inhabit' and 'cultivate' are perhaps here both activated, cf. 624, 687. The majority of MSS have *magna* for *sola* (transmitted in a few late MSS), which is meaningless here. The presence of the demonstrative helps to split up the usual combination of *loca sola* (= 'deserted places') to give the meaning '*these* are the only places in which he dwells', cf. 683 *solique . . . tibi.*

681–2 nec, uti pars magna procorum, | **quam modo uidit amat** 'nor does he fall in love with a girl at first sight, as most suitors do'; cf. Iphis' reaction to Anaxarete in Vertumnus' own tale (698–700n.).

682–3 tu primus et ultimus illi | **ardor eris:** a common amatory claim, but see especially Prop. 1.12.19–20 *mi neque amare aliam neque ab hac desistere fas est:* | *Cynthia prima fuit, Cynthia finis erit.* V. again reveals his familiarity with Propertius' poetry. We are also reminded of the programmatic *primus amor* at *Met.* 1.452, connected with Prop. 1.1.1 *Cynthia prima* (see Nicoll 1980: 177).

683 solique suos tibi deuouet annos: V. follows Ovid's amatory precepts at *AA* 1.42 *elige cui dicas 'tu mihi sola places'*, which quote Prop. 2.7.19 *tu mihi sola places*; cf. *Am.* 1.3.5 *accipe, per longos tibi qui deseruiat annos.* **suos . . . annos** 'his (whole) life' (*OLD* s.v. *annus* 6b).

684 adde quod . . . quod: a rhetorical transition formula which marks V.'s argumentative tone (see McKeown on *Am.* 1.14.13 for the idiom, found predominantly in poetry, esp. Lucretius and Ovid (29 x, *Met.* 4x), but not used by Virgil (*adde* alone at *G.* 2.155), Tib., or Prop.); cf. N–H on Hor. *C.* 2.8.17; K–S II 273.

684–5 naturale decoris | **munus:** cf. Prop. 4.2.21–2 *opportuna mea est cunctis natura figuris;* | *in quamcumque uoles uerte, decorus ero;* [Tib.] 3.8.14 (Vertumnus) *mille habet ornatus, mille decenter habet. naturalis* (also at 9.730, 10.117) is attested in Latin poetry before Ovid only at Lucr. 6.30, 760. McKeown ad loc. compares Dipsas' praise of a prospective male lover at *Am.* 1.8.33–4 *est enim facies, qua se tibi comparet illi:* | *si te non emptam uellet, emendus erat.* **formasque apte fingetur in omnes** ~ Prop. 4.2.47 *formas unus uertebar in omnis* (~Virg. *G.* 4.411 (Proteus) *formas se uertet in omnes*), where Propertius etymologizes Vertumnus' name (cf. 4.2.20–2). Cf. 765, 12.559 (Periclymenus) *formas uariatus in omnes*, *F.* 6.409 (Vertumnus) *conueniens diuersis iste figuris.*

686 iussus, iubeas: polyptoton at the third foot caesura. **iubeas licet** 'though you order' with the subordinate subjunctive in a concessive sense, see 171n. **omnia** 'anything whatever' (*OLD* 7). For the elegiac lover's *obsequium* cf. *AA* 2.198 *fac modo, quas partes illa iubebit, agas*, Tib. 1.4.39–40 *tu puero quodcumque tuo temptare libebit* | *cedas: obsequio plurima uincet amor.*

687–91 V. now tries to convince Pomona of their similar divine vocations and associations. It is possible that these similarities were the motivation for Ovid's invention of their pairing, see Littlefield 1965: 471–2, Barkan 1986: 81–2.

687 quid, quod 'what about the fact that . . . ?'; pointedly rhetorical, deemed 'too prosaic as a rule for the highest poetry' (N–H on Hor. *C.* 2.18.23; McKeown on *Am.* 1.14.5; cf. 2.8.9; K-S II 277 (§192 A 4), 499 (§ 228 A. 1).

688 primus habet: V. evidently received the first-fruits of the seasons, cf. Prop. 4.2.11–13 (Vertumnus) *uertentis fructum praecipimus anni, . . . | prima mihi uariat liuentibus uua racemis;* 41–2 *nam quid ego adiciam, de quo mihi maxima fama est, | hortorum in manibus dona probata meis.* **tua munera** 'your gifts', i. e. the fruits which it is your task to cultivate.

689 sed neque iam 'but as things are now he does not . . . '

690 cum sucis mitibus: ablative of quality or description with *cum.*

691–2 The lover's plea, cf. 9.561 (Byblis) *miserere fatentis amorem,* 13.855 (Polyphemus) *tantum misere precesque | supplicis exaudi,* Virg. *Ecl.* 2.7 *nil nostri miserere?*

692 praesentem 'in person'. Ovid stresses the dramatic irony of V.'s situation here in addressing Pomona on his own behalf, cf. 3.658–9 (Acoetes (Bacchus in disguise?) in another warning tale) *per tibi nunc ipsum (nec enim praesentior illo | est deus) adiuro,* 9.602 (Byblis) *debueram praesensque meos aperire furores.* Johnson 1997: 371–2 suggests that Pomona may by now have seen through his disguise, but this would lessen the drama of his self-revelation at the end of the story (766–7).

693–7 After entreaty, V. now turns to threats, which introduce his narration of the inset tale of Iphis and Anaxarete as a warning to Pomona. The narrative is introduced as a cautionary tale. Cf. other internal narratives in the poem that function as *exempla* (all of which fail as warnings, see 765n.): 2.549–95 (crow to the raven); 6.83–102 (Pallas' tapestry for Arachne), 10.542–707 (Venus to Adonis); see Gieseking 1965: 44–7, 139–40. The elegiac *exclusus amator* often resorts to such threats of retribution: cf. 717–32, Tib. 1.8.28 *persequitur poenis tristia facta Venus,* 77–8 *at te Poena manet, ni desinis esse superba. | quam cupies uotis hunc reuocare diem!*

693 ultoresque deos: cf. *deus ultor* 14.750; both references are deliberately (and threateningly) nonspecific, perhaps including Cupid (*Amor*) and *Anteros* (who avenged unrequited love); for associations with Venus see *TLL* V 1.910.49. The plea for divine vengeance for lovers is frequent in elegy, cf. *Am.* 3.8.65–6 *o si neglecti quisquam deus ultor amantis | tam male quaesitas puluere mutet opes!*, Tib. 1.8.71–2 *hic Marathus quondam miseros ludebat amantes, | nescius ultorem post caput esse deum,* 1.9.4 *sera tamen Poena uenit pedibus,* 11–12 *at deus illa | in cinerem et liquidas munera uertat aquas,* Sen. *Herc. Fur.* 385 *sequitur superbos ultor a tergo deus;* contrast Prop. 3.20.22 *non habet ultores nox uigilanda deos.* **pectora dura:** the conventional hard-hearted mistress, the *puella dura* of elegy, is here evoked (e.g. *Am.* 1.9.19, *AA* 2.527, Tib. 2.6.28, Prop. 1.7.6, 1.17.16, 2.1.78), but in V.'s story the figurative meaning of *dura*, 'hard-hearted', i.e., 'not susceptible to passion' (see McKeown on *Am.* 2.4.23), becomes literal when Anaxarete is transformed into stone, as in the earlier tale of the Propoetides at 10.238–42 (on this kind of wordplay see Tissol 1997: 20–6). It will be the central motif in V.'s story of Anaxarete's petrifaction: *quod fuit in duro iam pridem pectore saxum* (758), cf. 704, 709, 712, 749. Vertumnus himself in Prop. 4.2.23 says that he will become a '*non dura puella*'.

694 Idalien 'Venus', *Aphrodite Idalie* was named after her place of worship in Idalium on Cyprus, cf. e.g. *AA* 3.106, *F.* 1.452, Catull. 61.17 (with Fedeli 1983: 32 'Alexandrian refinement of a rare detail', cf. Theocr. *Id.* 15.100), Virg. *Aen.* 1.681, 5.760, 10.52, 86, Prop. 2.13.54, 4.6.59. The epithet serves to introduce the following inset tale about another cult of Venus on Cyprus. Venus' role here returns emphatically to the erotic realm after her involvement with Aeneas' apotheosis at 581–608. On Venus as vengeful to lovers, cf. Tib. 1.8.28 *persequitur poenis tristia facta Venus*, 1.9.19–20. The anger of Venus has been met with earlier in the tale of Diomedes (477–8). The cycle of erotic tales narrated in *Met.* 10 by Orpheus also takes place on Cyprus and involves Venus (see Knox 1986a: 48–64). On the prominence of Venus in this latter portion of the poem, see Introduction, p. 4, 476–9n. **memorem . . . iram** ~ Virg. *Aen.* 1.4 *saeuae memorem Iunonis ob iram*, cf. *Met.* 14.477–8n., 494 *iratam Venerem*, 4.190 *exigit indicii memorem Cythereia poenam*, 12.583 (Neptune) *memores . . . iras*, *Her.* 21.9 (Diana) *memori . . . ira*. The Virgilian echo gives Vertumnus' introduction a solemn tone, which soon gives way to a stylistic register closer to amatory poetry. It also recalls the similarly Virgilian motivation of the erotic story of Daphne and Apollo at 1.453 *saeua Cupidinis ira*. **Rhamnusidis:** Nemesis, the Greek goddess of retribution, was named from her Temple at Rhamnus in Attica near Marathon (visited by Pausanias 1.33.2). Since the Hellenistic period she was particularly associated with the punishment of over-proud lovers (Herter *RE* XVI.2 2370). She appears elsewhere in Ovid only at 3.406 (Narcissus story) *adsentit precibus Rhamnusia iustis*, *Tr.* 5.8.9 *exigit a dignis ultrix Rhamnusia poenas*; cf. Catullus 50.20 (*Nemesis*); 66.71, 68.77 (*Rhamnusia uirgo*). The Gk form with *-is* is found only here.

695 quoque magis timeas: *quoque = et quo*, introducing a purpose clause including a comparative (K–S II 233, Courtney on Juv. 15.89; cf. e.g. 1.757, 2.44, 3.290). Cf. other warning tales at 10.542–3 (Venus to Adonis) *te quoque, ut hos timeas, siquid prodesse monendo | possit, Adoni, monet*, 6.83–4 (Pallas' tapestry for Arachne) *ut tamen exemplis intellegat aemula laudis | quod pretium speret.* **etenim:** a prosaic word (Axelson 1945: 123 n.15) which occurs only here in the poem, cf. *Pont.* 3.7.13, *Tr.* 1.11.9, 3.3.7. **uetustas:** cf. Athena's appeal to old age for credibility (also in disguise as an old woman) while speaking to Arachne 6.29 *seris uenit usus ab annis*. For the related use of the claim of *uetustas* as the antiquity of a tradition, cf. 1.400 *quis hoc credat nisi sit pro teste uetustas*, *F.* 4.203–4 *pro magno teste uetustas | creditur.* The humour perhaps lies here in the recognition that the tale he is about to narrate traditionally was dated to the fourth century BCE, long after the reign of Proca (see below 698n.).

696 scire dedit: *dare* + infinitive ('permit, enable' *OLD dare* 15 c); the infinitive after concessive or permissive *dare* is frequent in poetry from Lucretius onwards (Austin on Virg. *Aen.* 1.66).

696–7 notissima . . . | facta: typical Ovidian humour, as the story seems to be anything but common (although *tota . . . Cypro* limits this to local knowledge – but how has V. heard the tale?); cf. 2.570 (the crow is speaking) *nota loquor,* 2.591 *res est notissima,* 4.189, *AA* 2.561. V. insists on the veracity of his tale in order to frighten P., a theme which is picked up again at the end of his narration: 759 *neue ea ficta putes*. The contrast between *facta/ficta* and belief and disbelief is made an issue throughout the epic and is especially highlighted in internal narratives because of the presence of an internal audience, on which see esp. Feeney 1991: 224–32.

697 quibus flecti facile et mitescere possis: this looks forward to the lesson of V.'s tale of the fate of the *dura puella* Anaxarete, whose frigidity leads to her petrifaction: 761–2 *quorum memor, o mea, lentos | pone, precor, fastus*. Pomona instead is urged to be pliant and soft (i.e. receptive to his advances): cf. erotic elegy's claim to softening, e.g. *Am.* 2.1.22 *mollierunt duras lenia uerba fores*, Prop. 1.7.19 (with Fedeli), 1.19.24 *flectitur assiduis certa puella minis*, Virg. *Ecl.* 10.61 *deus ille [Amor] malis hominum mitescere discat*. The vocabulary is erotic, but also recalls the language of one of the first transformations in the poem: that of rocks into people (a process which this inset tale will reverse): 1.400–2 *saxa . . . | ponere duritiem coepere suumque rigorem | mollirique mora mollitaque ducere formam*, 409 *quod solidum est flectique nequit, mutatur in ossa*.

698–761 *The tale of Iphis and Anaxarete.* Vertumnus' motive is to frighten Pomona with the story of a hard-hearted and high-born Cypriot woman, Anaxarete, who is punished by Venus with petrifaction for not yielding to the love of the humble Iphis (on the use of mythological exempla for didactic purposes in erotic poetry, cf. *Am.* 3.6.45–82, Prop. 1.20, 3.15, *AA* 3.683–746 (with Gibson 2003: 359)). Ovid hints at Vertumnus' own literary antecedents as a statue in Propertius 4.2 by having him narrate a statue tale which draws heavily on amatory elegiac models of the paraclausithyron. The tale presents a hyperbolically clichéd depiction of the excluded elegiac lover (Galinsky 1975: 218) and parallels Vertumnus' attempts to gain access to Pomona's orchard. The violence and urban setting of the story, however, contrast with the georgic frame narrative and it proves ill-conceived for winning Pomona (765 *nequiquam*), see Segal 1969: 69. Vertumnus' unexpected knowledge of this obscure Cypriot statue tale strikes a humorous note. Ironically the obsessive lover in Vertumnus' tale fares no better than the hard-hearted mistress. The suicide of Iphis has thematic connections with the preceding tragic deaths of Dido and Canens, also for love.

Antoninus Liberalis 39, which is attributed to Hermesianax's *Leontion* book two (fr. 4 Powell, pp. 96–7), preserves a version of this story set within a historical framework. It tells of the love of the humbly born, but wealthy, young man Arkeophon for Arsinoe, the daughter of King Nikokreon, who succeeded to the throne of Salamis in 332/1 BCE. (Diod. Sic. 19.79.5). To fit his narrator's motivation Ovid has changed this story of social inequality (at Ant. Lib. 39.2 the king rejects Arkeophon's suit because of his humble lineage) into an ahistorical tale of spurned love (see Solodow 1988: 179–80). In Ant. Lib. 39 Arsinoe is turned to stone at her window, but the religious *aetion* for the statue (759–61) is missing. Ovid's tale purports to account for a statue on Salamis called *Venus Prospiciens* (14.760–1 *Veneris quoque nomine templum | Prospicientis habet*). Fauth 1966 attempts to reconcile the literary sources on such a cult-representation (only in Ovid, Ant. Lib. 39, and Plut. *Amat.* 20 (*Mor.* 766C–D where a statue called Παρακύπτουσα is mentioned)) with the archaeological evidence. He suggests that in Salamis on Cyprus there was a sanctuary with a cult-representation of Venus called Ἀφροδίτη Παρακύπτουσα, and that the epithet must indicate a unique characteristic of the Salaminian Aphrodite (338–9). He connects this image with the 'woman in the window' Near-Eastern iconographic representation of Astarte. No other sources, however, mention such a cult or temple; see the criticisms of Söderlind 2000, cf. also Borghini 1979. Ovid's source is probably Hellenistic, perhaps the same as that used for Orpheus' Cypriot tale of Pygmalion in *Met.* 10.243f. (possibly Philostephanus' περὶ Νήσων, *On Islands*, *FGH* III 30ff.). The tale also shares a number of similarities with the pseudo-Theocritean *Idyll* 23, in which an unhappy lover commits suicide by hanging at the door of his beloved and is avenged when a statue falls onto his hard-hearted lover. On the episode, see Copley 1956: 134–40, Solodow 1988: 179–80, Jouteur 2001: 107–14, Frings 2005: 171–5.

698–700 The lines are meticulously structured, with anaphora of *uiderat*, dramatic juxtaposition of the names of the two protagonists at the beginning of 699, and chiastic arrangement of their attributes (*generosam–Iphis–Anaxarete–humili de stirpe*), see Bömer ad loc. On the theme of love at first sight, see 349–50n.

698 a ueteris generosam sanguine Teucri: cf. Ant. Lib. 39.2, where Arkeophon is additionally motivated by Arsinoe's impressive lineage. Teucer (Greek *Teukros*), the half-brother of Ajax, banished by his father Telamon, founded a new Salamis on Cyprus (*Il.* 13.170, 177; Soph. *Ajax* 1008ff., Hor. *C.* 1.7.21–32). Briefly mentioned at 13.157, he is to be distinguished from the ancestor of the Trojans with the same name (mentioned at 13.705–6, cf. Virg. *Aen.* 1.235).

699 Iphis Anaxareten: emphatic word-placement by juxtaposition: cf. e.g. 4.55 *Pyramus et Thisbe*, *AA* 1.511 *Hippolytum Phaedra*, 2.353 *Phyllida Demophoon*. Another Iphis appears at 9.666–797 (see Bömer ad loc. on the use of the name in earlier literature and contemporary inscriptions). Anaxarete appears only here; Frings 2005: 172 suggests an allusion to Hermesianax. **humili de stirpe creatus:** a variation of a common epic phrase at line end, cf. 1.760 *caelesti stirpe creatus*, 2.756, 3.543, 13.22 (with Hopkinson ad loc.), Lucr. 1.733, Virg. *Aen.* 10.543 *Volcani stirpe creatus*, Stat. *Theb.* 1.463 *magni de stirpe creatum*. In Ant. Lib. 39 Arkeophon too is of humble birth (39.1 γονέων δὲ οὐκ ἐπιφανῶν), but his wealth has made him socially prominent. The elegiac lover/poet is also conventionally humbly born (and poor), e.g. *Am.* 1.3.7–10 (with McKeown ad loc.), Prop. 2.24c.37–8, 3.2.9–16, Tib. 1.1.

700 totis . . . ossibus: conventional erotic imagery, cf. 351n., 2.410 *accepti caluere sub ossibus ignes*, 7.747–8, *Her.* 4.70 *acer in extremis ossibus haesit amor*, Virg. *G.* 3.258–9 *magnum cui uersat in ossibus ignem* | *durus amor*, *Aen.* 1.660, 4.101, Prop. 3.17.9, *Ciris* 164. **aestum:** cf., of love, 52–3n., 352n.

701–2 luctatusque . . . non potuit 'though he fought against it for a long time, after he could not conquer his passion with reason'; cf. 7.10–11 (Medea) *et luctata diu, postquam ratione furorem* | *uincere non poterat*, *Her.* 16.237 *luctor celare furorem,* | *sed tamen apparet dissimulatus amor.* **furorem:** see 16n. **uincere** introduces the triumph theme, which will be further developed at 718–21.

702–38 The lover's komos at his beloved's locked door was a long established Greek literary theme, especially in epigram and comedy, which was developed fully in Roman erotic elegy, see Copley 1956, Hunter on Theocr. *Id.* 3, McKeown on *Am.* 1.6 (with full bibliography). Ovid 'trips through the commonplaces' of the elegiac paraclausithyron (N-H on Hor. *C.* 1.25, p. 290), as Iphis adopts the conventional behaviour of the *exclusus amator*: he arrives and camps out at his beloved's threshold (717 *ante fores*), suborns her slaves to help him, sends love messages, hangs garlands on her door, and, in desperation, delivers reproaches and threats, cf. *Am.* 1.16, 3.11.9f., Tib. 1.1.55–6, 1.2 (with Maltby), Prop. 1.16 (with Fedeli), Lucr. 4.1177–84. Other episodes in the poem draw on the motif of the paraclausithyron, cf. Narcissus 3.351ff, Pyramus and Thisbe 4.65ff., Polyphemus 13.778ff. At *F.* 4.109–12 Ovid credits the *exclusus amator* with the invention of poetry and also persuasive eloquence (109–11 *primus amans carmen uigilatum nocte negata* | *dicitur ad clausas concinuisse fores,* | *eloquiumque fuit duram exorare puellam*). In Ant. Lib. 39 Arkeophon in the company of friends serenades Arsinoe every evening, bribes her nurse to help him, and finally commits suicide through starvation.

702 supplex: the appropriate attitude for the prospective lover, see *AA* 1.713 *Iuppiter ad ueteres supplex heroidas ibat*, *Am.* 2.5.49, *Her.* 12.185, Tib. 1.2.13–14 *uoce . . . supplice*, 87, Prop. 1.9.3 *ecce iaces supplexque uenis ad iura puellae.* **ad limina** 'the threshold (of the door)', poetic pl., as common; see *TLL* VII 2.1405.5ff. A substantial block of wood (see N–H on Hor. *C.*1.25.4) which provided the traditional location for amatory entreaty, cf. *Am.* 1.6.67–8, Catull. 63.65–6, Tib. 1.2.17, 1.5.71, Prop. 1.16.22.

703 nutrici: the complicit nurse is a conventional figure from Euripides (e.g. *Hippolytus*), New Comedy (Plautus *Asin.* 183ff.), Hellenistic poetry, and elegy (see Kenney on *Her.* 18.97, Lyne on *Ciris* 206–385); cf. 9.707 (Iphis) *conscia nutrix*, 10.382–464 (Myrrha's obliging nurse), *Rem.* 637 *conscia nutrix*. The nurse of Arsinoe plays a larger role in Ant. Lib. 39.3–4, where she is punished for her collusion. **miserum . . . amorem:** the adj. is common of the elegiac lover, cf. e.g. *Am.* 1.1.25, Tib. 1.6.2, Prop. 1.1.1, Catull. 8.1.

704 dura: for the centrality of the theme of *duritia* to this tale, cf. 693n., 709, 712–13, 721, 749, 758; see Pichon 1966: 136. **per spes alumnae** 'by her hopes for her foster-child'; prayers are often introduced by such phrases with *per*, cf. 372, 13.375–6 *per spes nunc socias casuraque moenia Troum | per deos oro* (with Bömer ad loc.), Virg. *Aen.* 6.364 *per genitorem oro, per spes surgentis Iuli*, 10.524. **orauit:** for the komast's prayers, cf. *Am.* 1.6.61–2.

705–6 The primary MSS show widespread confusion on these lines, although an intelligible text is transmitted by later MSS. **de multis . . . cuique ministris** 'each one of her many servants' (*de* is partitive, *OLD* 10); the lover is often encouraged to ingratiate himself with the domestic staff as well as the nurse, cf. *AA* 1.351–2 *sed prius ancillam captandae nosse puellae | cura sit: accessus molliet illa tuos*, 2.251–2 *nec pudor ancillas, ut quaeque erit ordine prima | nec tibi sit seruos demeruisse pudor*, 3.470 *accipiat missas fida ministra notas*, *Rem.* 639–40, *Met.* 6. 461–2 (Tereus) *impetus est illi comitum corrumpere curam | nutricisque fidem.* **blanditus:** for the lover's conventional use of *blanditiae* in winning his love (usually directed towards the mistress, however, not the servants), cf. 18–19, 707, *Am.*1.6.16 *tibi blandior uni* (with McKeown ad loc.), 1.8.103 *lingua iuuet mentemque tegat: blandire noceque*, 2.1.21 *blanditias elegosque leues, mea tela, resumpsi*, 3.1.46 *haec est blanditiis ianua laxa meis*, *AA* 2.527, *Rem.* 35, 507, Prop. 1.16.16. **sollicita . . . uoce** 'with anxious voice' (*OLD sollicitus* 2e), cf. 8.271 *sollicita supplex petiit prece*, 10.639–40 *cum me sollicita proles Neptunia uoce | inuocat Hippomanes;* of lovers, *AA* 3.472 *ex animo sollicitusque roget*, *Am.* 1.15.38 *atque a sollicito multus amante legar* (with McKeown ad loc. for further examples). **propensum . . . fauorem** 'kind favour', cf. *Pont.* 3.4.15 *cunctaque cum mea sint propenso nixa favore.* The adjective (*OLD* 5) draws attention to the meaning of the noun, a figure Kenney suggests we call 'amplificatory pleonasm', see Diggle 2005: 643.

707 ferenda dedit . . . sua uerba 'he gave them messages to bring to her'; *dare* with the gerundive *ferenda* used predicatively (*NLS* § 207 (3)). **blandis . . . tabellis:** the delivery of love-letters (on wooden tablets with a reusable wax surface) by slaves to the beloved is another topos of erotic elegy, cf. *Am.* 1.11.7–8 *accipe et ad dominam peraratas mane tabellas | perfer*, 14 *cetera fert blanda cera notata manu*, 2.19.41, *AA* 1.437–40 (with Hollis ad loc.) *cera uadum temptet rasis infusa tabellis, | cera tuae primum conscia mentis eat; | blanditias ferat illa tuas imitataque amantum | uerba*, 455, Juv. 9.36–7 *blandae adsidue densaeque tabellae | sollicitent.* The topos is also extensively exploited in the story of Byblis at *Met.* 9.518ff.

708–9 madidas lacrimarum rore coronas: the locked-out lover's garlands are conventionally placed on his beloved's door, cf. 733–4, Lucr. 4.1177–8 *lacrimans exclusus amator limina saepe | floribus et sertis operit*, *Am.* 1.6.67–8 (with McKeown), *AA* 2.527–8 *postibus et durae supplex blandire puellae | et capiti demptas in fore pone rosas*, 3.72, *Rem.* 32, Theocr. *Id.* 2.153, Prop. 1.16.7, Tib.1.2.14. These garlands may be wet from perfume (*Am.* 1.6.38 *madidis lapsa corona comis*, *F.* 5.340), but the lover's tears are a common feature of the paraclausithyron, cf. 734, *Am.* 1.6.17–18 *aspice . . . uda sit ut lacrimis ianua facta meis*, 1.4.61 *lacrimis ego maestus obortis*, *Rem.* 36 *exclusus flebile cantet amans*, [Theocr.] *Id.* 23.17, Meleager *AP* 5.191.5f. (*HE* 4382–5), 12.72.5–6, Asclep. *AP* 5.145 (*HE* 860–5), Prop. 3.24.29 *limina iam nostris ualeant lacrimantia uerbis.* For *lacrimarum rore* (*TLL* VII 2.842.42), cf. 9.368–9 *lacrimae . . . inrorant foliis*, 10.360 *tepido suffundit lumina rore.* **postibus intendit** 'stretched from one door-post to the other'.

709–10 posuitque in limine duro | molle latus: the hard threshold (matching the *dura puella*, cf. 693n.) was another conventional complaint of the *exclusus amator*, cf. *Am.* 1.6.68 *dura super tota limina nocte iace*, *Rem.* 508 *nec latus in duro limine pone tuum*, 677, *F.* 5.339, Hor. *Epod.* 11.21–2 *heu | limina dura, quibus lumbos et infregi latus*, Tib. 2.6.47. Lying in front of the door was the most 'abjectly humiliating posture' of the *exclusus amator* (McKeown on *Am.* 2.19.21–2, with numerous further examples, cf. Prop. 1.16.22 *turpis et in tepido limine somnus).* The contrast of *duro/molle* is at the heart of this tale, cf. 697n. **tristisque serae conuicia fecit** 'railed bitterly against the door-bolt'; *tristis* is adverbial, cf. Prop. 1.16.13–14 *haec inter grauibus cogor deflere querelis | supplicis a longis tristior excubiis.* The lover both beseeches and abuses the locked door, cf. *Rem.* 35–6 *et modo blanditias rigido, modo iurgia, posti | dicat*, 507 *nec dic blanditias nec fac conuicia posti*, *Am.* 1.6.61–2 *nec te precibus minisque | mouimus*, *AA* 3.581–2, Prop. 1.16.37–40.

711–13 These are the typical/proverbial reproaches of the frustrated suitor against the unyielding mistress; cf. Polyphemus' long list of negative comparisons concerning Galatea at 13.798ff.

711 saeuior illa freto surgente: *saeuus* is frequently used of love (e.g. *Am.* 1.1.5 *saeue puer*, 2.10.19 *saeuus amor*), the mistress, and her door, cf. 13.798 *saeuior indomitis eadem Galatea iuuencis*, *Her.* 4.166 *eris tauro saeuior ipse truci?*, Tib.1.8.62 *saeua puella*. For the water comparison, cf. 13.799 *fallacior undis*, 801 *uiolentior amne*, Hor. *C.*1.33.14–15 *Myrtale | libertina, fretis acrior Hadriae.* **cadentibus Haedis** 'when the Kids are setting', i.e. when the sea is most dangerous to sail. The *Haedi,* two stars in the constellation *Auriga* 'Charioteer' (on his wrist), were famous weather signs which marked the onset of storms at their setting in late September and rising in the spring, see Arat. *Phaen.* 156–66 (with Kidd on 158), 679–82, cf. Theocr. *Id.* 7.53–4, Call. *Ep.* 18.5–6 Pf. (*HE* 1223–4), *Tr.* 1.11.13, *AA* 1.410, *F.* 5.113, Virg. *Aen.* 9.668 *pluuialibus Haedis*, Hor. *C.* 3.1.27–8. There is contrast in the juxtaposition of *surgente* and *cadentibus*.

Haedis is not in the primary MSS (which have *austris*). Bömer cites Statius, *Theb.* 8.407 with the same phrase at verse end as a convincing parallel.

712–13 durior et ferro . . . | et saxo: stone and iron are proverbial of 'unfeeling' and cruel behaviour since Homer *Od.* 23.103, *Il.* 4.510, 16.33–5, 24.205, Aesch. *Prom.* 242f., Eur. *Med.* 1279–80, cf. 721, 7.32 *ferrum et scopulos gestare in corde fatebor*, 9.614–15, 13.799 *durior annosa quercu*, *Am.* 1.11.9 (with McKeown ad loc. for more examples in Ovid), 3.6.59, Theocr. *Id.* 3.39, [Theocr.] *Id.* 23.20 λάινε παῖ, Tib. 1.1.63–4, 1.10.59–60, Prop. 1.16.29–30 *sit licet et saxo patientior illa Sicano, | sit licet et ferro durior et chalybe*, *Aen.* 4.366–7, Hor. *C.* 1.3.9; see Otto 1890: 134. Zingerle 1869: 44. **Noricus . . . ignis:** Noricum was an eastern Alpine territory (roughly mod. Austria), conquered in 15 BCE, proverbial for the excellence of its iron (Plin. *Nat.* 34.145, Petron. 70.3), cf. Hor. *Ep.* 17.71, *C.* 1.16.9f, (with N-H), Mart. 4.55.11f., and see further Bömer ad loc. **excoquit** 'smelts' (*OLD* 3b).

713 saxo quod adhuc uiuum radice tenetur 'living rock which still is held firm by its root', i.e. is still in its natural state (*OLD uiuus* 4a). The rock is spoken of as a living organism (prefiguring Anaxarete's transformation), cf. 5.317 *factaque de uiuo pressere sedilia saxo* (with Bömer ad loc.), 3.159, 7.204, 13.810–11, *F.* 2.135, *Aen.* 1.167 *uiuo sedilia saxo*, 3.688.

714 spernit et inridet: although *spernere* is common of amatory rejection in the poem (see 35n.), the combination with *inridere* suggests that Anaxarete's behaviour is to be viewed as almost sacrilegious, thus justifying the punishment sure to follow (cf. 736 *impia*, 693–4n.), cf. 3.513–15 *spernit Echionides tamen hunc ex omnibus unus | contemptor superum Pentheus praesagaque ridet | uerba senis*, 5.669 *rident Emathides spernuntque minacia uerba*, 8.612–13 *inridet credentes, utque deorum | spretor erat mentisque ferox, Ixione natus.* **immitibus:** further play with hard/soft contrasts, cf. 697n.

715 uerba superba: the komast typically represents his beloved's refusal of sexual favours as haughtiness, cf. 762, 3.354 (Narcissus) *fuit in tenera tam dura superbia forma*, 13.802, *Am.* 1.6.58 *tecta superba petam* (with McKeown), *F.* 1.419 *sequiturque superbia formam*, *AA* 2.525 *uultu . . . superbo*, 3.509–11, Lucr. 4.1178 *postisque superbos*, Prop. 2.8.15–16 *an usque | in nostrum iacies uerba superba caput?*, Pichon 1966: 271. On the arrogance of lovers as an insult to Venus, see Hor. *C.* 3.10.9 *ingratam Veneri pone superbiam* (with Nisbet and Rudd), [Theocr.] *Id.* 27.15. **ferox:** cf. 377n. **quoque** 'even', qualifying *spe.*

716 non tulit impatiens longi tormenta doloris 'impatient, Iphis could no longer tolerate the torments of his long grief'; cf. 6.134–5 (Arachne tries to hang herself) *non tulit infelix laqueoque animosa ligauit | guttera. tormenta* of love's anguish, cf. *Am.* 3.10.16, Prop. 3.8.17.

717–32 Iphis' final lament. The rejected suitor frequently resorts to abuse and threats, both of future punishment for his beloved (cf. 693–7n.) and of suicide (cf. Theocr. *Id.* 3.9, 25, 53–4, Tib. 2.6.19–20, Prop. 2.17); however, the actual suicide of a male lover is rare. Parallels are found in Ant. Lib. 39 (where Arkeophon starves himself), and in [Theocr.] *Id.* 23, where the unhappy lover, like Iphis, hangs himself. More common in myth is the suicide of unhappy women, often by hanging, see 10.377–81 (Myrrha's attempt), *AA* 1.283–4 (Byblis), *Rem.* 602f. (Phyllis). There are similarities between the introduction of Iphis' final speech and [Theocritus], *Id.* 23.16–17, see Copley 1956: 136–9. At *Rem.* 15–18 Ovid offers help to the suicidal lover: 15–18 *at si quis male fert indignae regna puellae, | ne pereat, nostrae sentiat artis opem. | cur aliquis laqueo collum nodatus amator | a trabe sublimi triste pependit onus?*

717 uerba nouissima 'his last words', cf. 2.363, 11.256, Virg. *Aen.* 4.650 (where Dido also gives a dramatic speech before her suicide) *dixitque nouissima uerba.* Iphis actually stops speaking at 732, arranges the noose, and gets in one more line at 736.

718 uincis: repeated in 721 for pathetic anaphora. *uincere* is frequent in amatory contexts (cf. e.g. 4.356, 6.513, 10.443, *Am.* 1.2.20, 22, 1.7.38, 2.12.2, Prop. 2.8.8 *uinceris*

†*aut uincis,*† *haec in amore rota est*); the verb introduces the triumph imagery of the following lines.

718–19 neque erunt tibi taedia tandem | ulla ferenda mei 'nor need you at last be wearied of me any longer'. The profusion of *t*'s at the end of 718 expresses Iphis' anger. Cf. [Theocr.] *Id.* 23.21–2 'no longer will I vex you with the sight of me'. **laetos molire triumphos** ~ *Am.* 1.7.35 *i nunc, magnificos victor molire triumphos* (see McKeown ad loc.), Sil. 16.630–1. Triumph imagery occurs frequently in erotic contexts in Roman elegy, cf. *Am.* 1.2.19ff., 1.7.35–40, 2.9.15–16, 2.18.18, Prop. 2.8.40, Prop. 3.1.9–12, 4.8.17–18, Galinsky 1969b. This constitutes the second anachronistic mention (cf. 13.251–2) of this exclusively Roman institution, which is first foretold by Apollo at 1.560–1 *tu ducibus Latiis aderis, cum laeta Triumphum | uox canet et uisent longas Capitolia pompas. laetos* is the appropriate epithet for the joyfulness of the triumph, cf. 1.560 (with Bömer), 13.252 *laetos . . . triumphos, Am.* 1.2.39 (with McKeown), *AA* 1.3, 217, *Tr.* 4.2.66, *Pont.* 2.1.57–8.

720 Paeana uoca: instead of the usual Latin ritual cry at the triumph '*io, triumphe*' (see 1.560–1 *laeta triumphum | uox canet, Am.* 1.2.34 *uulgus 'io' magna uoce 'triumphe' canet'*, Hor. *C.* 4.2.49–50, Varro *LL* 6.68) Iphis uses the Greek Paean (παιήων), a song of celebration (e.g. Hom. *Il.* 22.391, Ar. *Av.* 1763), cf. *AA* 2.1–4 *dicite 'io Paean' et 'io' bis dicite 'Paean'*, Virg. *Aen.* 6.657, 10.738 *conclamant socii laetum paeana secuti*, Prop. 3.15.42). Paean is a Greek cult title of Apollo 'the Healer' (Hom. *H. Ap.* 272, 500, 517), cf. 1.566, 15.535 *ope Paeonia, F.* 4.263 (with Bömer ad loc.). **nitidaque . . . lauro:** *nitida* recalls Daphne's metamorphosis into the laurel at 1.552 *remanet nitor unus in illa.* At 1.560–1 Apollo first established the use of laurel for the *triumphator*'s crown in Roman triumphs (see 718–19n.), cf. *Am.* 1.7.36 *cinge comam lauro*, 2.12.1 *triumphales . . . laurus*, Tib. 2.5.5. **incingere** 'bind yourself', a middle-reflexive (passive) imperative, cf. 7.47 *accingere, Am.* 1.1.29 *cingere* (with McKeown ad loc.), see also Bergh 1975: 17–29.

721 ferrea 'iron (hard)-hearted', cf. 712–13n., 13.516, *Am.* 1.6.27 *ferreus orantem nequiquam, ianitor, audis*, 1.7.50, 1.14.28, 2.5.11, 2.19.4, Sen. *Epist.* 56.3 *ferreum aut surdum, TLL* VI 574.31ff.

722–3 'you will at least be forced to praise something about me, and there will be something to commend me to you' (*eritque | quo: OLD sum*[1] A 6a). Many editors adopt the reading *amoris* for *eritque*, but this weakens the following phrase and spoils the parallelism of the three variations on the same idea. For *gratus* in an amatory context, cf. *Am.* 2.19.30 (with McKeown ad loc.), Prop. 1.12.7 *olim gratus eram*, Hor. *C.* 3.9.1 *Donec gratus eram tibi*, Pichon 1966: 160.

724–725 non tamen ante tui curam excessisse memento | quam uitam 'remember, nevertheless, that my devotion to you did not depart until my life did'. For *cura* as 'love' (*OLD* 3), cf. 6.535, *Am.* 1.9.43, *Her.* 8.15, 14.123, *Rem.* 484. *excessisse* with *uitam* as subject is strained (usually *excedo ex uita*) and may be either syllepsis or a textual problem (Heinsius proposed *cessisse* and *fugisse*), see Bömer ad loc., Luck 2005: 221. The imperative *memento* (found only here in the *Met.*, 6x in Ovid's elegies) adds a solemn (didactic) tone to Iphis' injunctions.

725 geminaque . . . luce: Ovid plays on two metaphorical meanings of *lux*, as beloved (*OLD* 6b, cf. e.g., *Am.* 1.4.25 *mea lux*, 1.8.23, 2.17.23, *AA* 3.524, *Tr.* 3.3.52, Prop. 2.14.29) and life (*OLD* 6a, cf. 132, *Tr.* 4.10.116, Virg. *G.* 4.255, 472 *luce carentum*); cf. also Catull. 51.11–12 *gemina teguntur | lumina nocte.*

726–7 'It will be no rumour that comes to you to announce my death; I myself, have no doubt, shall be there and shall be visibly present', cf. 11.666–8 (Ceyx's shade appears to Alcyone) *non haec tibi nuntiat auctor | ambiguus, non ista uagis rumoribus audis; | ipse ego fata tibi praesens mea naufragus edo.* **fama . . . nuntia** is Virgilian (*Aen.* 4.188, 9.474 *nuntia Fama ruit*); cf. 15.3–4, *Her.* 9.143–4 *nuntia uenit fama*, 16.38, *Pont.* 4.4.15–16. On the motif of the announcement of death, cf. Virg. *Aen.* 9.474 (the death of Euryalus), 11.139 (Pallas' death) *Fama uolans, tanti praenuntia luctus*, 6.456–7 (Dido's death) *uerus mihi nuntius ergo | uenerat exstinctam.* See 12.39–63 for Ovid's description of the 'House of Fame'. **adero:** perhaps an echo of Dido's threats to Aeneas at *Aen.* 4.384–6 *sequar atris ignibus absens | et, cum frigida mors anima seduxerit artus, | omnibus umbra locis adero* (Norden 1976 on *Aen.* 6.456–7). **uidebor:** Iphis puns on two possible meanings of the verb, 'I shall be seen as present', and 'I shall seem to be present' (since he will in fact be dead), see Hardie 2002a: 238n.34.

728 corpore . . . exanimi: Lucretian, see *DRN* 3.714 *corpore in exanimo*, 6.705, 1273, cf., *AA* 1.540. **crudelia lumina:** *crudelis* is another frequently used epithet in *sermo amatorius*, cf. 736, *Am.* 1.6.73, *AA* 1.531, 3.581, *Her.* 7.182, Virg. *Aen.* 4.311, 661–2, Prop. 1.8a 16, 16.17, Pichon 1966: 117. **pascas:** cf. 6.280–1 (Niobe to Latona) *pascere, crudelis, nostro, Latona, dolore, | pascere*, 9.176 (Hercules to Juno) '*cladibus*', *exclamat* '*Saturnia, pascere nostris, | pascere et hanc pestem specta, crudelis, ab alto*'.

729 mortalia facta: Ovid's claims for *fama* (cf. 15.871–9) perhaps challenge Hor. *AP* 68 *mortalia facta peribunt.*

730–1 este mei memores . . . | . . . et longo facite ut narremur in aeuo: Iphis' appeal to the gods to be remembered is guaranteed by Vertumnus' narration of his story in Ovid's poem. For Ovid's play with his poetry's commemorative function, see 433–4n., 10.502 *nulloque tacebitur aeuo*, *F.* 5.377 *floreat ut toto carmen Nasonis in aeuo*, Edmunds 2001: 78. **longo . . . aeuo:** cf. 3.445, 15.306; on the claim for literary fame see 15.878 *perque omnia saecula fama*, *Tr.* 5.14.35–6 *aspicis ut longo teneat laudabilis aeuo | nomen inextinctum Penelopea fides?*

732 et quae dempsistis uitae date tempora famae 'and give the time you have taken from my life to my fame', cf. 7.168 (Jason) *deme meis annis et demptos adde parenti*, Hor. *Sat.* 2.5.14–15 *illi quos tibi dempserit | apponet annos.*

733 ornatos saepe coronis: cf. 708–9n., *Rem.* 32 *tegat ornatas multa corona fores.*

734 umentes oculos: cf. 708–9n. **pallida bracchia:** the paleness of lovers (for the colour see Fordyce on Catull. 81.4) is a topos going back to Sappho (fr. 31.14–15 *PLF*), cf. 4.203, *AA* 1.729 *palleat omnis amans: hic est color aptus amanti*, *Am.* 2.7.10, Theocr. *Id.* 2.88–9, Prop. 1.9.17 (*TLL* x 1.129.61f.); here it also signifies Iphis' impending death, cf. 755n., 10.381 (Myrrha attempts suicide) *dixit et aptabat pallenti uincula collo*, *Rem.* 602 (Phyllis' suicide) *spectat zonam pallida facta suam*, Virg. *Aen.* 4.644 (Dido) *pallida morte futura*, *TLL* x 1.130.35f.

735 cum foribus laquei religaret uincula summis 'as he was fastening the bindings of the noose to the top of the doors', cf. the similar preparations in [Theocr.] *Id.* 23.49–52. **foribus . . . summis:** cf. 10.379 *zona summo de poste reuincta.* **laquei . . . uincula:** cf. 10.381 *aptabat pallenti uincula collo*, *Ib.* 614 *uincula per laquei fac tibi guttur eat.* **religaret:** 445n.

736 haec tibi serta placent: the lover in [Theocr.] *Id.* 23.20–1 offers his noose as his final gift. **crudelis et impia:** for *crudelis*, see 728n.; cf. the lover's cry at [Theocr.] *Id.* 23.19 ἄγριε παῖ καὶ στυγνέ. *impia* implies that Anaxarete has somehow broken a lover's faith with Iphis (cf. Prop. 2.9.19–20 *at tu non una potuisti nocte uacare, | impia, non unum sola manere diem*, 2.17.13, Virg. *Aen.* 4.496, Pichon 1966: 171 'inpii dicuntur . . . qui promissam amantibus fidem non seruant'), which represents Iphis' delusional frame of mind and also underlines Vertumnus' arguments that such behaviour is punishable by the gods (750 *deus ultor*, see Bömer on 14.736).

737 inseruitque: verbal play with *serta* in the previous line (Bömer).

738 atque onus infelix elisa fauce pependit 'he hung there by his strangled throat, an unlucky burden', cf. *Her.* 9.98 (Antaeus) *compressa fauce pependit onus*, *Met.* 6.134–5 (Arachne) *non tulit infelix laqueoque animosa ligauit | guttera.*

739 †et multa timentem†: the line is clearly corrupt and a number of editors have deleted this portion of the line and some of the next (*trepidantem . . . sonum* del. Merkel, *et . . . adapertaque* del. Postgate). Shackleton Bailey's 1981: 337 conjecture *aperire iubentem* would make clearer Ovid's macabre point that Iphis' convulsing feet seem to be knocking at the door. Tarrant (in Shackleton Bailey 1981: 337n.2) has suggested that a possible source for corruption may be a memory of 6.522 *trepidamque et cuncta timentem.*

742 (nam pater occiderat): authenticating detail, which adds to the pathos of Iphis' sad fate (Bömer ad loc.). **ad limina matris:** Iphis' body is transferred from Anaxarete's threshold, where he has been camped as *exclusus amator* (702 *supplex ad limina uenit*, 709), to that of his mother.

743–4 complexaque frigida nati | membra sui: *frigidus* is used frequently of the chill of death (*OLD* 7, *TLL* vi 1.1326.26f.) 2.611 [*frigus letale*], 15.153 *gelidae formidine mortis*, Lucr. 3.930, Virg. *Aen.* 4.385 *cum frigida mors anima seduxerit artus*, Stat. *Theb.*

12.29. Clausen on *Ecl.* 5.22 suggests Ovid is thinking of Virgil's lines on the death of Daphnis: *cum complexa sui corpus miserabile nati.*

744–5 miserorum uerba parentum | . . . matrum miserarum facta: the mannered repetition underlines the unspecified, conventional nature of Iphis' (unnamed) mother's expressions of grief, see Rosati 2002: 290, cf. 420–1. The primary MSS read *miserarum* also in 744, but *miserorum* is perhaps preferable for the less-specified *parentum.*

746 funera ducebat: the combination is almost technical for a funeral procession (see Bömer ad loc.), cf. e.g. Cic. *De orat.* 2.283, Virg. *G.* 4.256 *tristia funera ducunt*, Liv. 11.47.11. **lacrimosa** is probably to be taken as fem. nom. sing. (Bömer), rather than modifying *funera*, where there would some repetition with 748–9 *flebilis . . . pompa* and 751 *miserabile funus*, but cf. *Her.* 13.137–18 *Troasin inuideo, quae si lacrimosa suorum | funera conspicient.*

747 luridaque . . . membra: for the paleness associated with death, cf. 734, 11.654, Hor. *C.* 3.4.74–5 *luridum . . . Orcum*, Prop. 4.7.2 *luridaque . . . umbra.* **arsuro . . . feretro:** the funeral bier (Var. *LL* 5.166) was burnt with the corpse, cf. Tib. 1.1.61 *flebis et arsuro positum me, Delia, lecto*, Stat. *Theb.* 6.55–6 *damnatus flammae torus.* A golden line signals the end of the description.

748 domus: Anaxarete's house.

749–50 duraeque . . . Anaxaretes: the declension is Greek (fem. gen. sing.), cf. 10 *Circes. durae* is a final hint of her imminent metamorphosis. **sonus plangoris:** see 421n. **deus ultor:** cf. 693n. *ultoresque deos*, here the singular points more strongly to *Amor.* In Ant. Lib. 39.6 Arsinoe is motivated to look out of her window by pride alone (πρὸς ὕβριν).

751 mota tamen 'moved after all'; contrasting with *durae* (749) and the immobility of her transformed state (755–7).

752 tectum sublime 'the top part of the building', i.e. 'to an upper room'.

753–8 *Anaxarete's metamorphosis into a stone statue.* The are a number of petrifactions in the *Metamorphoses* (see the list in Lafaye 1904: 247–8): cf. in this book, Scylla at 71–4 and the Phaeacians' ship at 563–5. Venus inflicts the same punishment on the Propoetides at 10.238–42 for their neglect of her worship by practising prostitution (cf. 758n), while the following tale of Pygmalion's statue reverses the process to illustrate the power of devotion to Venus and love (10.243f.). The petrifactions of Niobe (6.301–12) and Aglauros (2.814–32) provide a number of verbal parallels (see below). In Ant. Lib. 39.6 Arsinoe's metamorphosis is explicitly said to be a punishment inflicted by Aphrodite: καὶ ἡ μὲν ἐθεᾶτο, μισήσασα δὲ τὸ ἦθος Ἀφροδίτη μετέβαλεν αὐτὴν καὶ ἐποίησεν ἐξ ἀνθρώπου λίθον καὶ τοὺς πόδας ἐρρίζωσεν ἐπὶ τὴν γῆν ('as she cast glances at him, Aphrodite, loathing her character, changed her from her human form into a stone with her feet rooted into the ground' trans. Celoria).

753 uixque bene . . . prospexerat 'she had only just looked out at' (*OLD bene* 13b); the choice of verb anticipates the aetion at 760–1. In all the versions of this tale metamorphosis occurs as the hard-hearted woman looks out of her house at her lover's funeral, cf. Ant. Lib. 39.6 (Arsinoe peeks out of her house to view Arkeophon's body being cremated) ἐκ τῶν οἴκων ἐκκύψασα τὸ σῶμα τὸ Ἀρκεοφῶντος κατακαίομενον ἰδεῖν, Plut. *Amat.* 20 (*Mor.* 766 D) ἀπελιθώθη παρακύψασα τὸν ἐραστὴν ἰδεῖν ἐκκομιζόμενον ('she was turned to stone when she peeked out to watch the funeral procession of her lover').

754 deriguere oculi = Virg. *Aen.*7.447 (Turnus' terrified reaction to Allecto's metamorphosis to her true form), cf. 757n.; the verb appears first in Virgil (also at *Aen.* 3.259–60); cf. Niobe 6.303 *deriguitque malis*, 304–5 *lumina maestis* | *stant immota genis,* 2.348 (Heliades) *deriguisse pedes*; of fear, e.g., 7.115 *deriguere metu Minyae, F.* 3.331–2 *totoque e corpore sanguis* | *fugit et hirsutae deriguere comae.* For hardening in metamorphosis, cf. 503, 564. For the emphasis on Anaxarete's eyes, cf. 728 *crudelia lumina.*

754–5 calidusque e corpore sanguis | inducto pallore fugit 'the warm blood fled from her body as pallor spread'. Anaxarete now shares Iphis' earlier pallor (734 *pallida bracchia*): cf. 2.824 (Aglauros' metamorphosis) *pallent amisso sanguine uenae,* 6.304 (Niobe) *in uultu color est sine sanguine;* more symptoms of fear, cf. 3.39–40, 7.136 *palluit et subito sine sanguine frigida sedit, F.* 331–2 (above). The metaphorical description of Anaxarete's evident horror at viewing the dead Iphis is in the following lines actualized through her metamorphosis.

755–6 conataque . . . conata: underlines Anaxarete's horrified experience of the process of her own metamorphosis. Cf. e.g. 1.233 (Lycaon) *frustraque loqui conatur,* 637, 2.348–9 (Lampetie) *conata uenire,* 820 (Aglauros) *surgere conanti partes,* 829, 5.232, 9.354, 11.81. **haesit:** cf. Ant. Lib. 39.6 τοὺς πόδας ἐρρίζωσεν ἐπὶ τὴν γῆν ('rooted her feet to the ground'), 6.308–9 (Niobe) *nec flecti ceruix nec bracchia reddere motus* | *nec pes ire potest.* **auertere uultus:** *uultus* is poetic pl. Her gaze is fixed on his funeral, as Iphis wished (727–8), and as he fixed his face towards her in death (737 *uersus ad illam*).

757 paulatimque: cf. 432n., 2.827 (Aglauros) *sic letalis hiems paulatim in pectora uenit.* **occupat artus** continues from 754 the allusions to Turnus at *Aen.* 7.446 *tremor occupat artus.*

758 quod fuit in duro iam pridem pectore 'that all along had lurked in her hard heart' (Melville). The well-known metaphor used of Anaxarete's hard-heartedness (693 *pectora dura,* see 704n.) is transformed into physical reality through her metamorphosis, which is presented as almost a natural consequence of her behaviour or character, see Solodow 1988: 179–80, Kenney 1986: 458. *corpore* is the consensus of the major MSS, but the less well attested *pectore* makes clearer the psychological connection between Anaxarete's character and metamorphosis and the spread of her hardness from her heart to the rest of her body (*artus*), see Clausen 1963: 415–16. The Propoetides' petrifaction is similarly tied to their callous natures: 10.241–2 *utque pudor* *cessit sanguisque induruit oris, | in rigidum paruo silicem discrimine uersae*, cf. 2.827 (Aglauros) *sic letalis hiems paulatim in pectora uenit.*

759 neue ea ficta putes: Vertumnus underlines his warning with a 'proof' of its veracity, an aetion for a statue; for similar narrative concerns with belief, cf. 463–4n. **neue** = *et, ne*: cf. 16n.

759–60 dominae sub imagine signum | seruat adhuc Salamis 'Salamis still to this day preserves a statue in the image of the owner of the name', cf. 9.664–5 (Byblis' fountain) *qui nunc quoque uallibus illis | nomen habet dominae nigraque sub ilice manat, AA* 1.288, *F.* 5.128. *adhuc*, like *nunc quoque*, is an aetiological marker of continuation, cf. 2.254–5 *Nilus . . . occuluit caput, quod adhuc latet*, 6.669, 8.719–20 (Baucis and Philemon) *ostendit adhuc Thyneius illic | incola de gemino uicinos corpore truncos, F.* 4.70 *quod adhuc Circes nomina litus habet.*

760–1 Veneris quoque nomine templum | Prospicientis habet: in Ant. Lib. 39 Arsinoe's transformation is effected by Venus (39.6), but there is no mention of a temple of Venus. Plutarch speaks only of a stone statue of the 'peeking' woman (*Amat.* 20, *Mor.* 766c τὴν ἐν Κύπρωι Παρακύπτουσαν ἔτι νῦν προσαγορευομένην). *Venus Prospiciens* (cf. 753 *prospexerat*) seems to translate Παρακύπτουσα (cf. Ant. Lib. 39.6 ἐκκύψασα) and to refer to a specific cult-title or iconographic representation of a woman looking out of a window, see 698–761n. The implication of Venus in Anaxarete's fate is suggested through the identification of the epithet with her temple.

761–4 Vertumnus concludes his long speech in the guise of an old woman (654ff.) with a final plea to Pomona to acquiesce to his desires.

761–2 lentos | . . . fastus 'cold haughtiness', cf. 715 *uerba superba*. For *lentus* of the unresponsiveness of lovers (*OLD* 8), cf. 13.800 *lentior et salicis uirgis et uitibus albis, Am.* 3.6.59–60 *ille habet et silices et uiuum in pectore ferrum, | qui tenero lacrimas lentus in ore uidet,* Prop. 1.6.12, 3.8.20 *hostibus eueniat lenta puella meis*, Tib. 2.6.36, Pichon 1966: 186. *fastus* in elegy also has the specialized meaning of resistance to love: cf. e.g. *Am.* 2.17.9–10 (with McKeown), *AA* 1.715, 2.241 *exue fastus, F.* 1.419 *fastus inest pulchris,* Tib. 1.8.75 *omnes odit fastus* (with Maltby), Prop. 1.1.3 (with Fedeli), Pichon 1966: 142–3. **iungere:** middle-reflexive (passive) imperative 'join yourself'. **nymphe:** the Gk (nom./voc.) form is common (see 333n.), cf. 771.

763–4 Vertumnus concludes with a prayer for the productivity of Pomona's garden, contingent upon her compliance with his desires (*OLD sic* 8d). For such conditional prayers in a komastic context, cf. *Am.* 1.6.25–6 (with McKeown), 3.6.19–20, *Her.* 18.45–6; see also Bömer on 8.857–8, von Albrecht 1964: 67. The natural imagery recalls the erotic theme of youth/spring as the time of beauty and love, e.g.. [Theocr.] *Id.* 23.28–9, Catull. 68.16, *AA* 2.115–16, Tib. 1.8.47. **adurat** 'burn, wither' (*OLD* 6a), of frost damage, cf. *F.* 4.917–18 *nec uenti tantum Cereri nocuere nec imbres, | nec sic marmoreo pallet adusta gelu,* 1.680 *nec noua per gelidas herba sit usta niues, Tr.* 3.2.8, Virg.

G. 1.93 *Boreae penetrabile frigus adurat.* **uenti:** on the harmful effects of wind on plants, cf. 5.483–4, 10.735–9, Virg. *Ecl.* 3.80–1, *G.* 1.316–20.

765 nequiquam: Vertumnus' speech and inset tale in his guise as an old woman do not succeed in persuading Pomona to succumb to his wishes, cf. 641–2 *sed enim superabat amando | hos quoque Vertumnus, neque erat felicior illis.* No lovers in this poem successfully win over the objects of their desire through speech; cf. Circe's attempts at 28–36, 372–6 (382 *frustra*), Apollo at 1.504–24, Byblis at 9.530–63 (564–5 *talia nequiquam perarantem plena reliquit | cera manum*), Polyphemus at 13.789–869 (870 *talia nequiquam questus*), see Tarrant 1995: 70–1. **formas deus aptus in omnes:** the main MS reading recapitulates Vertumnus' versatility immediately before he reverts to his own form, reworking 685 *formasque apte fingetur in omnes* (cf. 12.559 (Periclymenus) *hic ubi nequiquam est formas uariatus in omnes*). Tarrant observes (*per litteras*) that there is no parallel in Ovid for *aptus* constructed with *in*, although Courtney (*per litteras*) points to the reading of the primary MSS at 10.408–9 *et in hoc mea (pone timorem) | sedulitas erit apta tibi,* and an instance at Plin. *Nat.* 16.174 *in delicias cathedrarum aptissimae* (see also Kenney 1999b: 400 on singularity in Ovid as 'not in itself a ground for suspicion'). Tarrant adopts Housman's conjecture *formae deus apta senili*, based on the reading of the first hand in the best MS (*forma* (*formae* Magnus) *deus aptus anili*), but the Cypriot tale does not seem particularly fitting for an old woman and the disguise is also mentioned in the next lines.

766 in iuuenem rediit 'he returned to his form as a young man', cf. 684–5 *adde quod est iuuenis, quod naturale decoris | munus habet,* Prop. 4.2.24 *meque uirum sumpta quis neget esse toga?* Vertumnus has only as yet appeared to Pomona in his rustic disguises; it is unclear how he would now appear so different as to win finally her affection after her earlier resistance. On the scansion of *rediit* (last syllable long), see 101n.

766–7 anilia demit | instrumenta sibi: the *mitra, baculum,* and white hair, which he donned as part of his disguise as an old woman at 654–5; cf. Circe's reversal of her metamorphosis of Odysseus' men at 301–5.

767–9 talisque . . . reluxit 'he appeared to her as when the image of the sun at its brightest has conquered the opposing clouds and has shone out with no cloud to dim it'. The simile contains hints of the dangers divine epiphanies often pose (*euicit*) and is suggestive of the violence Vertumnus is prepared to use against Pomona, cf. 3.308–9 (Jupiter's appearance to Semele) *non tulit aetherios donisque iugalibus arsit*; see Parry 1964: 277, Richlin 1992: 169.

770–1 In a surprisingly abrupt 'happy' ending, Pomona defies expectations and reverses the many paradigms of virginal females in the poem (see 622–697n.) by returning Vertumnus' feelings. Similarities with the ending of an earlier tale where Sol (Apollo) reveals himself to Leucothoe at 4.231–3 (*in ueram rediit speciem solitumque nitorem. | at uirgo, quamuis inopino territa uisu, | uicta nitore dei posita uim passa querella est*) have suggested to some that the hints of violence surrounding Pomona's acquiescence add a note of disquiet, see 770–1n., Myers 1994b: 243–4, Gentilcore 1995: 119–20, Lindheim 1998: 35.

770 uimque parat: on *uis* as sexual violence, see 635n., where *uis* is precisely what Pomona had been fearing. Cf. Neptune's similar exasperation at 2.574–6 and Ovid's cynical advice at *AA* 1.673 *uim licet appelles; grata est uis ista puellis.*

770–1 inque figura | capta dei nymphe est 'the nymph, captivated by the beauty of the god, returned his feelings'. *inque figura | capta . . . est* is constructed on the analogy of expressions such as *aestuare in, ardere in*; this use of *in* with reference to the object of an emotion, especially love, is frequent in Ovid (McKeown on *Am.* 1.9.33–4, see also Bömer on *Met.* 6.116), cf. 4.234–5 *neque enim moderatus in illa | Solis amor fuerat,* 6.490 *in illa aestuat.* 7.21–2 *in hospite regia uirgo | ureris,* 8.50 *deus arsit in illa,* Catull. 64.98 (with Fordyce ad loc.). *capere* is often used of falling in love, cf. 29, *Am.* 1.10.10, 2.17.15–16, Prop. 1.1.1, Hor. *Sat.* 2.7.46, Pichon 1966: 98–9. **mutua uulnera sensit:** for *uulnus* of love, see 23n. For the theme of *amor mutuus*, cf. 7.800 *mutua cura,* 9.720–1 *amor ambarum tetigit rude pectus et aequum | uulnus utrique dedit, Am.* 2.3.2 *mutua . . . gaudia,* Tib. 1.2.65 *amor . . . mutuus* (with Maltby ad loc. for further references), 1.6.76. Hor. *C.* 2.12.15. Elsewhere in Ovid *mutua uulnera* appears only of death-blows, 3.123, 7.141, *Tr.* 2.319.

772–851 Events under Romulus

Ovid's treatment of the Romulus legend is highly selective, focusing on only two events, both also included in the *Fasti*: an episode during the war between the Romans and Sabines, led by Titus Tatius, involving a marvellous water metamorphosis (775–804, *F.* 1.175–7), and Romulus' deification (805–28, *F.* 2.475–512). The following deification of his wife Hersilie (829–51), apparently original to Ovid, functions as a pendant to the Romulus myth. Ovid's depiction of Romulus here is notably brief and colourless, and contrasts with his more complete and complex treatment of Romulus in the *Fasti* (on the latter, see Hinds 1992b, Barchiesi 1997: *passim*, esp. 112–23, 141ff.). On the development of the foundation myth of Romulus and Remus, see Cornell 1975, Bremmer and Horsfall 1987, Wiseman 1995, Carandini and Cappelli 2000.

As founder and law-giver of Rome, and also as the first deified Roman ruler, Romulus was a politically charged mythological figure (cf. 805–28n.), see Evans 1992: 87–108, Weinstock 1971: 175–7. Following Julius Caesar's lead, Augustus made prominent use of Romulean imagery. At one time Octavian thought of assuming the name Romulus (Suet. *Aug.* 7.2, Cassius Dio 53.16.7); on Julius Caesar's use of Romulean imagery, see Weinstock 1971: esp. 180–90, Classen 1962, Burkert 1962; on Augustus, see Scott 1925, Gagé 1930, Zanker 1988: 98, 201–15, von Ungern-Sternberg 1998, Scheid 2003: 132–5. Romulus figured prominently in the Forum of Augustus, both on the pediment of the Mars Ultor Temple and in the central larger niche of the NE portico (facing Aeneas), surrounded by the great men of the Republic

(*F.* 5.565–6 *hinc uidet Iliaden umeris ducis arma ferentem, | claraque dispositis acta subesse uiris*), cf. 609–21n. Romulus and Remus (with the wolf and Mars) also appear in juxtaposition with Aeneas on the reliefs on the front of the Ara Pacis (Zanker 1988: 203–7).

772–5 The Alban king list recommences with *proximus* as if it had not been interrupted, cf. *F.* 4.52–3 *tradita regna Procae; | quem sequitur duri Numitor germanus Amuli.* With extreme compression Ovid refers to the complex legend of the births of Romulus and Remus and the foundation of Rome (cf. similarly *F.* 4.53–6), a myth he treats in numerous widely spread passages in the *Fasti.* Traditional accounts (usually considered to have been established by Fabius Pictor) relate that Amulius seized the throne by force from his older brother Numitor, the rightful king. He then killed Numitor's son and forced his daughter Ilia (see 781), or Rhea Siluia, to become a Vestal Virgin to prevent her having an heir. When later she was impregnated by Mars (*F.* 2.598, 3.11–45, 233, *Am.* 3.6.47–82), Amulius tried to drown her twin infant sons Romulus and Remus, but the twins survived the flooded Tiber and were suckled by a she-wolf (*F.* 2.381–422, 3.11–68). Raised by shepherds, they eventually killed Amulius and, having restored the throne of Alba to their aged grandfather, they set out to found a new city, eventually named Rome (Romulus as eponymous founder of Rome, cf. Var. *LL* 8.18), Remus having died in mysterious circumstances (*F.* 4.807–62). See the extensive accounts of Livy 1.3.10–1.7.3, Dion. Hal. *Ant. Rom.* 1.71.4–87 (1.79.4–83.3 = Fabius Pictor F 5b Peter, fr. 7b Chassignet), Plut. *Rom.* 3.1–8.9 (= Fabius Pictor F 5a Peter, fr. 7a Chassignet).

Amulius belongs to an early version of the Romulus myth and appears in Naevius (*FPL* F 26) and Ennius (*Ann.* 1.xxxix Sk.), who did not recognize the chronological gap between the Trojan War and Rome's foundation (see 609–21n.), as the persecutor of Ilia (the daughter of Aeneas) and of Aeneas' twin grandsons Romulus and Remus (on Amulius' earlier identity, see Skutsch 1985: 212–13). Amulius and Numitor (the latter perhaps a late addition as Ilia's father) would have been added to the end of the Alban king list after its insertion between the two myths of Aeneas and Romulus; see Laroche 1982: 113.

772–3 Ausonias . . . opes 'the Italian state', cf. 7n. *Ausoniae*, 583 *bene fundatis opibus.* **iniusti . . . Amuli:** cf. *F.* 3.49–50 *contemptor Amulius aequi | (nam raptas fratri uictor habebat opes).* **miles** 'the military force' (collective or general sing. (*OLD* 1b)) is a bit odd here (one would expect instead some abstract quality of Amulius himself), but for the emphasis on force in Amulius' rule, cf. *F.* 3.50 *uictor*, Livy 1.3.10 *plus tamen uis potuit quam uoluntas patris.*

773–4 nepotis | munere: Ovid delays mentioning Romulus' name until 799. The singular *nepotis* omits Remus' role in the tradition: cf. *F.* 3.67–8 *Romuleoque cadit traiectus Amulius ense, | regnaque longaeuo restituuntur auo.*

774–5 festisque Palilibus urbis | moenia conduntur: 'Rome is founded in five words, in the passive, with no named agent' (Feeney 1991: 208), cf. *F.* 3.69 *moenia* *conduntur.* In the following book (15.12–59) the foundation of Croton is, by contrast, extensively narrated (see Hardie 2002d: 194). Livy 1.6.3 relates that after the twins handed over Alba Longa to their grandfather Numitor, they conceived a desire to found a city where they were rescued and raised. Ovid's account of Rome's foundation at *F.* 4. 807–62 includes the famous dispute between the brothers and Remus' eventual death at the hands of Celer (not Romulus, as in Livy 1.7.2).

Ovid names (only here in the poem) a specific *Fasti*-type day, April 21, which was celebrated as Rome's birthday (*F.* 4.806 *quod fit natali nunc quoque, Roma, tuo*) and was the date of the *Palilia* (or *Parilia*), a shepherds' purification festival, cf. Prop. 4.4.73–5 *urbi festus erat (dixere Parilia patres), | hic primus coepit moenibus esse dies, | annua pastorum conuiuia*, Varro, *RR* 2.1.9. At *F.* 4.721–862 Ovid gives an account of the festival (723 *pastoria sacra*) and Rome's foundation (807–8 *urbis origo | uenit*), see Fantham on *F.* 4.721–82. For the controversy over the etymology and spelling of *Palilia* (Tib. 2.5.87, Varro *LL* 6.15 *Palilia dicta a Pale*) or *Parilia* (*F.* 4.721, Festus 248L *uel ut alii uolunt dicta Parilia quod pro partu pectoris eidem sacra fiebant*), see *LALE* s.v. *Palilia*, Radke 1979: 242, Bömer on *F.* 4.721. 'Varronian' dating placed the foundation of Rome in 754/3 BCE, cf. Plut. *Rom.* 12. Dion. Hal. *Ant. Rom.* 1.71.4 supports 751/0 BCE and reviews other dates that had been offered, while Ennius had set the date of the foundation of Rome near 1100 BCE (*Ann.* 154–5 Sk), see Feeney 2007: 86–104.

775–804 *Tatius and the Sabines.* Tradition held that the original population of Rome was a union of Romans and Sabines, a story that begins under Romulus with the rape of the Sabine women and the subsequent attack on Rome by the Sabines, led by Titus Tatius, and ends with the unification of the two peoples and the joint rule of Romulus and Tatius, see Livy 1.9–13, Plut. *Rom.* 14–23, Dion. Hal. *Ant. Rom.* 2.2.30–52; on its historicity, see Ogilvie on 1.9–13, Evans 1992: 119–34, Cornell 1995: 75–7. Virgil placed the episode on Aeneas' shield at *Aen.* 8.635–41. Here Ovid omits the reason for the Sabines' attack (776 *bella gerunt*), the rape of the Sabine women, a story he treated at *F.* 3.167–234 and *AA* 1.101–34. His narrative centres instead on an original tale of the Sabines' repulse from the Roman citadel by a flood of hot sulphurous water, providing a quasi-metamorphosis of the spring and an aetion (798n.). The story is found first here and at *Fasti* 1.259–74 (later versions in Macr. 1.9.17–18. Serv. on *Aen.* 1.291, 8.361; Bömer on *F.*1. 263ff. suggests Verrius as the common source). In both poems the story is connected to the myth of Tarpeia. In the *Metamorphoses* Venus calls on local nymphs for assistance in blocking the citadel-gate opened by Juno, while in the *Fasti* the god Janus takes credit for thwarting the Sabines, thus accounting for his famous temple with its 'gates of war'. For comparisons between the two versions (largely concerned with genre), see Heinze 1919: 35–7, Barchiesi 1991: 15–16, 1997: 20–1, Merli 2000: 193–6. 'Epic' features singled out in the *Met.* episode include the battle narrative (in the *Fasti* there is no mention of battle between the Romans and Sabines (273 *pulsis . . . Sabinis*), despite the promise at *F.* 1.260 *Oebalii rettulit arma Tati*), the 'epic' conflict between Juno and Venus, and Tarpeia's punishment.

775 Tatius: king of Cures (778n.), one of the many Sabine towns that attacked Rome after the abduction of the Sabine women. His name explains the existence of the tribe *Titi(ens)es* (Varro, *LL* 5.55) and the priesthood of *sodales Titii* (Ogilvie on Livy 1.10.1). **patresque Sabini:** i.e. fathers of the Sabine women abducted by the Romans; an allusion to the omitted reason for the attack.

776–7 Tarpeia, a Vestal Virgin and daughter of Spurius Tarpeius, commander of the Roman citadel, treacherously admitted Tatius and the Sabines on to the Capitolium (776 *arcisque uia*). In exchange she asked for what the Sabines carried on their arms, meaning their golden armlets, (cf. *F.* 1.261 *armillis capta*); however, once inside, they crushed her to death with their shields (see Livy 1.11.6–9, with Ogilvie ad loc.). The story is attested as early as Antigonus *FGH* 816 F 2, Dion. Hal. *Ant. Rom.* 2.38.2–40.3 (citing Fabius Pictor fr. 8 Peter (fr. 10 Chassignet) and Calp. Piso fr. 11 Forsythe), Plut. *Rom.* 17. According to another version, found in Propertius 4.4, Tarpeia's motive was love for Tatius, not greed (cf. Plut. *Rom.* 17.5, which quotes an elegy of uncertain date by Simylus (*SH* 724) about Tarpeia and her love for the leader of the Gauls, not of the Sabines), see Bremmer and Horsfall 1987: 68–70. At *F.* 1.261–2 Ovid makes no mention of her punishment: *utque leuis custos armillis capta Sabinos | ad summae tacitos duxerit arcis iter.*

Tarpeia was the eponym of the Tarpeian rock, the cliffs of the Capitoline from which traitors were thrown (Livy 6.20.12, Richardson 1992 s.v. *Tarpeia rupes*), and, in addition, *Tarpeius* was also used of the Capitoline itself, e.g. Varro *LL* 5.41 *hic mons ante Tarpeius dictus a uirgine Vestale Tarpeia, quae ibi ab Sabinis necata armis et sepulta: cuius nominis monimentum relictum, quod etiam nunc eius rupes Tarpeium appellatur saxum*, cf. *Met.* 15.866, *F.* 1.79, Prop. 4.4.93, Virg. *Aen.* 8.347, 652, Lucan 1.195–6. The scene of Tarpeia's punishment is the best preserved of the friezes of the *Basilica Paulli/Aemilia* (late first century BCE) in the Roman Forum (panel 3.177, Carettoni 1961: 27–36, fig. 29, 32–8), along with the Rape of the Sabines (panel 3.175) and other scenes from the life of Romulus (see Arya 2000, *LTUR* 1.183–7).

776 arcisque uia: the *arx* was the fortified summit of the Capitoline Hill (Richardson 1992 s. v. *Arx*).

777 'lays down her life worthy of punishment beneath the shields piled on her'; Ovid recalls Prop. 4.4.91 *dixit, et ingestis comitum super obruit armis* and Livy 1.11.7 *obrutam armis necauere*, cf. *Am.* 1.10.49–50 *non fuit armillas tanti pepigisse Sabinas, | ut premerent sacrae uirginis arma caput.* The expression *animam ... exuit* is odd (*TLL* v 2.2114.26f. cites as a parallel only Solinus 30.22); the variant *edidit* is defended by Luck 2005: 221–2 (cf. *Her.* 9.62). Kenney (*per litteras*) proposes *expuit.* The soul was traditionally thought of as leaving through the mouth; and the note of contempt which *expuere* strikes may be suitable for Tarpeia, cf. Sen. *Phoen.* 44 *spiritum inimicum expue, Thy.* 245 *spiritum imimicum expuat*, *TLL* v.2 1909.49–55.

778–99 *The Sabines at Janus' Gate.* The Sabines should have reached the citadel on the Capitoline hill thanks to the assistance of Tarpeia (in Livy 1.12.1 and Dion. Hal.

Ant. Rom. 2.41.1 they occupy the citadel), but are now found approaching another gate that has been opened for them by Juno (diagram in Carafa 2000: 334–5). This gate (possibly the Romulean *porta Ianualis*, Var. *LL* 5.165) is associated with the temple (or shrine) of Janus Geminus/Quirinus, located at the base of the Capitoline close to where the Argiletum entered the forum, until it was moved by Domitian to the Forum Transitorium (796 *gemini . . . postes*, cf. *F.* 1.258 *hic ubi iuncta foris templa duobus habes*, Livy 1.19.2), see Granobs 1997: 26–7, Porte 1985a: 170–1, Richardson 1992 s.v. *Ianus Geminus*, *LTUR* 3.92–3). At *F.* 1.263–4 Janus describes the Sabines as reaching the Capitoline and then descending down the slope to the forum '*inde, uelut nunc est, per quem descenditis', inquit* | *'arduus in ualles per fora cliuus erat'*. Janus' narrative in the *Fasti* purports to explain the dedication to him, as a monument to his intervention on this occasion against the Sabines (*F.* 1.275 *ara mihi posita est paruo coniuncta sacello*), of a shrine and altar which seem to be associated with the temple of Janus Geminus (*F.* 1.257–8, 277, Macrob. Sat. 1.9.17–18, Serv. on *Aen.* 1.291); Livy 1.19.2 attributes the foundation of Janus' temple to Numa. There was also a story that Tarpeia let in the Sabines through a *Porta Saturnia* (Festus 246L, 496L, see Richardson s.v. *Porta Pandana*).

778 sati Curibus : Cures was a Sabine town on the left bank of the Tiber, 30 miles up the Tiber valley (NW of mod. Corese Terra). It was also the birthplace of Numa; see Ogilvie on Livy 1.13.5, Horsfall on *Aen.* 7.710. For the elevated *satus*, see 10n. (unusually here with a place name, see Bömer). **tacitorum more luporum:** cf. *F.* 1.261–2 *Sabinos* | . . . *tacitos*; wolf similes occur in Homer (e.g. *Il.* 10.334) and Virgil (e.g. *Aen.* 2.355–9 *inde, lupi ceu* | *raptores . . . uadimus*).

779 ore premunt uoces 'suppressed their voices', an epic phrase, cf. 9.692 *premit uocem*, Virg. *Aen.* 9.324 *sic memorat uocemque premit.*

779–80 corpora uicta sopore | **inuadunt:** according to Prop. 4.4 the Romans had been celebrating the Parilia festival on the night of Tatius' attack (4.4.85 *omnia praebebant somnos*). *sopor* is suggestive of a deep sleep, often alcohol-induced (*OLD* 1d), cf. *F.* 1.422 *corpora . . . uicta sopore*, *Her.* 16.102, Tib. 1.2.2. Bömer points to a model at Virg. *Aen.* 2.265 (the Greeks attack from the Trojan horse) *inuadunt urbem somno uinoque sepultam.*

781 Iliades 'Romulus, son of Ilia', a unique and lofty hybrid matronymic (with a patronymic ending) from Ilia, daughter of Numitor, descendant (or daughter, see 772–4n.) of Trojan Aeneas (the alternative name Ilia reflects the influence of the Aeneas legend), first found in Ovid; cf. (of Romulus and Remus) 824, *Am.* 3.4.40, *F.* 3.62, 4.23, 5.565, *Tr.* 4.3.8; also *Met.* 10.160 (of Ganymede, descendant of Ilus; see Hardie 2002c: 349 on the connection between Ganymede and Romulus). The matronymic provides epic elevation and evokes Romulus' Trojan background.

781–2 Juno reveals her continuing enmity towards the Romans (see 581–2n.) by removing a bolt from the gate to admit the Sabines, cf. *F.* 1.265–6 *et iam contigerat* *portam, Saturnia cuius | dempserat oppositas inuidiosa seras.* Ovid has in mind Juno's opening of the doors of Janus' temple at Virg. *Aen.* 7.621–2 *cardine uerso | Belli ferratos rumpit Saturnia postis.*

782 Saturnia: an Ennian patronymic: see *Ann.* 53 Sk. *Iuno Saturnia*, with Skutsch ad loc.: 'Hera is called daughter of Kronos in Homer, *Il.* 5.721, *al.* Ennius may have coined Saturnia as a metrically convenient tag, or he may have meant to hint that after her original hostility she would eventually become the *dea sospes* of the *Saturnia terra*'. Cf. Enn. *Ann.* 445 Sk., *F.* 1.265, *Met.* 3.271, Virg. *Aen.* 1.23, 3.380, 4.92, 9.2, *al.* Cf. 320n. *Saturnia proles.* Serv. *auct.* on *Aen.* 4.92 suggests the epithet is characterizing: *ubi nocituram Iunonem poeta uult ostendere Saturniam dicit* (cf. on *Aen.* 1.23); see Anderson 1958: 523–5, Feeney 1991: 201 on Virgilian wordplay on *Saturnia* and *satiare.* Bömer observes that *Saturnia* is used of Juno more often in the Greek myths earlier in the poem (11x in books 1–5) than in the later books (only here and at 9.176), although the epithet associates her with Italy, cf. Barchiesi on 3.271.

783 sola Venus: in the *Fasti*, the god of the month, Janus, instead takes credit for the deed: *F.* 1.268 *ipse meae moui callidus artis opus, | oraque, qua pollens ope sum, fontana reclusi.* For the prominence of Venus in *Met.* 14–15, see 476–9n.

784–5 clausura fuit 'would have shut it', cf. 72n. **nisi quod rescindere numquam | dis licet acta deum:** cf. *F.* 1.267 (Janus' rationale) *cum tanto ueritus committere numine pugnam.* For the sentiment, see 2.677–8, 3.336–7 (*neque enim licet inrita cuiquam | facta dei fecisse deo*), Eur. *Hipp.* 1328ff. *rescindere . . . acta* is legal terminology (*OLD rescindo* 3). **nisi quod** 'but for the fact that . . .' **Iano loca iuncta:** The shrine of Janus Geminus was often referred to simply as *Ianus* (Livy 1.19.2, Hor. *Epist.* 2.1.255).

786 Naides Ausoniae: for Italian nymphs, see 326–62 (catalogue of Italian river nymphs), on the form *Naides* see 328n. **gelido . . . fonte** is anticipatory; the cold of the fountain is stressed before its transformation to a hot spring, cf. 794–5.

787–8 nec . . . sustinuere 'nor did they refuse' (*OLD* 4c). **iusta petentem:** the Roman perspective, solemnizing Venus' position, cf. 13.466 *ite procul, si iusta peto.* **uenasque et flumina:** hendiadys 'streaming veins' (Miller-Goold). *uena* is a common term for underground channels of water (*OLD* 5), cf. 792, 9.657, *F.* 3.298, 271 (cit. 791–3). On *uenae aquarum*, see Vitruv. 8.3.26, Plin. *Nat.* 2.166, Sen. *NQ* 3.20.1–2.

789–90 nondum . . . erant 'not yet, however, were the entrances of Janus' open gate impassable'. On anticipatory *nondum*, cf. 158n.

791–3 The description of the heating of the waters takes on some of the scientific colouring of Pythagoras' description of the fires of Aetna at 15. 350–1 *siue bitumineae rapiunt incendia uires | luteaue exiguis ardescunt sulphura fumis.* cf. 15.340–1, *F.* 1.271–2 (Janus' claim to the same phenomenon) *madidis subieci sulpura uenis, | clauderet ut Tatio feruidus umor iter.* Similarly, at 9.657–8 Naiads create under Byblis' tears an underground water-source, *Naiadas his uenam, quae numquam arescere posset,* | *supposuisse ferunt.* Cf. the cold/hot stream of Ammon, one of the water marvels listed by Pythagoras (15.309–10), and Vitruv. 12.3.1 on sulphurous waters.

791 lurida . . . sulphura 'yellow sulphur'.

792 cauas . . . uenas: *caua* here suggests perhaps the scientific theory of underground cavities through which air, as well as water, passed. Lucretius (6.680–702) explains volcanoes as a result of underground hot-air activity (6.682 *totius subcaua montis* | *est natura*, cf. *Aetna* 94–101, *passim*). **bitumine** 'tar' was used to kindle fires, cf. Virg. *Ecl.* 8.82, Hor. *Epod.* 5.82.

793 uiribus his aliisque 'by means of these and other powers'; *aliisque* is strangely vague after the specification of the previous line.

793–4 ad ima | fontis = *imum fontem; ima* is an adj. used as a neut. pl. subst., with a gen. noun (a metrically useful Grecism, see Skutsch 1985 on Enn. *Ann.* 84, Bömer on *Met.* 8.335 *ima lacunae*, K–S I 230, 433), cf. 814, 5.41 *in gurgitis ima.* **Alpino . . . rigori:** of extreme cold, cf. Virg. *Ecl.* 10.47 *Alpinas . . . niues.*

795 audebatis . . . ceditis: apostrophe to the water personifies it and makes the scene more emotionally charged: cf. 1.728 (Nile), 2.406–7 (personification of rivers).

796 A golden line rounds off the metamorphosis: see 184n. **flammifera:** the adj. appears earlier only in Ennius, *Alcmeo* 25 J (see Kenney 2002: 63); cf. 2.155, 5.442, 15.849, *Her.* 16.46. **gemini . . . postes:** cf. *Aen.* 7.607 *sunt geminae Belli portae* (*sic nomine dicunt*), Plut. *Numa* 20.1. Numismatic representations of the Janus Geminus Temple show the twin doors (see *RIC* 1^2 177 N. 439, 169 N.323, *LTUR* 3.92–3, Fig. 56–7). Varro *LL* 5.156 reports the existence of hot springs near the temple of Janus Geminus: *Lautolae a lauando, quod ibi ad Ianum Geminum aquae caldae fuerunt.* Richardson 1992 (s.v. *Lautolae*) suggests that the spring (not hot) might have been located at the NE base of the Capitoline.

797 portaque . . . promissa: promised, presumably, by Tarpeia. **rigidis . . . Sabinis** 'rugged' or 'uncouth', a common epithet for the proverbial austerity and hardiness of the early Sabines, cf. *Am.* 2.4.15 *rigidas . . . Sabinas*, 3.8.61 *tetricas . . . Sabinas*, Hor. *Epist.* 2.1.25 *rigidis . . . Sabinis*, Prop. 2.32.47 *durosque Sabinos*, Virg. *Aen.* 8.638 *Curibusque seueris*, Livy 1.18.4; see Dench 1995: 85–94. H–E–A ad loc. observe the wordplay with *rigori* in 794.

798 fonte . . . nouo 'by a new spring', aetiological, implying a sort of metamorphosis, cf. 390. At *Fasti* 1.274 Janus says that he removed the hot flood after repulsing the Sabines, '*quae fuerat, tuto reddita forma loco est*'.

798–9 dum . . . | indueret 'until [such a time as] the Roman army could put on their weapons' (*NLS* §224 a type of final clause). *Martius . . . miles* (collective singular, 772n.) is so-called from Romulus' father: cf. *F.* 3.59 (of Romulus and Remus) *Martia . . . proles*, *Pont.* 1.8.24 *Martia . . . Roma*, 4.9.65–6, *Tr.* 3.7.52.

799–804 A bridging passage (three of six lines enjambed), which speeds the transition to the next episode of Romulus' deification by quickly summarizing the war between Romulus and the Sabines and its resolution.

799–800 quae postquam Romulus ultro | obtulit 'which Romulus brought out on his own initiative', *quae* is a connective relative (referring to *arma*). *ultro* stresses Romulus' initiative and agression (H–E–A ad loc.), cf. Virg. *Aen.* 9.127 [Turnus] *ultro animos tollit dictis atque increpat ultro.*

800–1 et strata est tellus Romana Sabinis | corporibus strata estque suis: an artfully composed phrase, with pointed juxtaposition of *Romana* and *Sabinis*, repetition (*strata est*), with *tellus Romana* and *corporibus* to be understood with the second clause as well. **strata estque:** the delayed placement of *–que* is metrically convenient., cf. e.g. 11.264, 15.694.

801–2 generique . . . soceri: the relationships were established through the abduction of the Sabine women. Ovid takes his cue from Livy 1.13.2 *hinc patres, hinc uiros orantes, ne se sanguine nefando soceri generique respergerent, ne parricidio macularent partus suos, nepotum illi, hi liberum progeniem.* Cf. *F.* 3.201–2 *intumuere Cures et quos dolor attigit idem: | tum primum generis intulit arma socer,* 225–6 *gladiisque remotis | dant soceri generis accipiuntque manus*, 6.95, *Am.* 2.12.23–4, Lucan 1.118. The relationship of Julius Caesar and Pompey was also thus characterized: cf. Catull. 29.24 *socer generque, perdidistis omnia,* Virg. *Aen.* 6.830–1, Lucan 1.289–90, Martial, *Ep.* 9.70.3–4. **impius ensis:** cf. 1.145–9 (on the Iron Age) *non socer a genero [tutus]. . . uicta iacet pietas,* 7.396 (Medea's sword).

803–4 'yet they resolved that the war be ended in peace and not to fight with the sword to the finish and that Tatius join in rule'. In most literary versions peace is established between the Romans and Sabines through the intervention of the Sabine women (including Romulus' wife Hersilia, cf. 829f.n. below): see *F.* 3.203–28, Livy 1.13.1–5, Dion. Hal. *Ant. Rom.* 2.45–6, Plut. *Rom.* 19. On Aeneas' shield in Virgil's *Aeneid* Tatius and Romulus are shown ratifying the treaty between the two peoples with a sacrifice: *Aen.* 8.639–41 *post idem inter se posito certamine reges | armati Iouis ante aram paterasque tenentes | stabant et caesa iungebant foedera porca.* **in ultima:** neut. pl. as substantive (cf. 483); an unusual expression (*TLL* VII 1.763.8ff. offers no exact parallel), cf. *OLD ultimus* 6d (*Aen.* 2.446 *his se, quando ultima cernunt | extrema iam in morte parant defendere telis*). **accedere regno** 'share the reign' (*OLD accedo* 16), cf. 390, 15.818, *Am.* 2.9.53. The reading of the main MSS *excedere* does not align with the prevailing tradition that Tatius was made co-ruler/regent with Romulus: cf. *F.* 6.93–5 (Concordia gives the etymology of June) *haec ubi narrauit Tatium fortemque Quirinum | binaque cum populis regna coisse suis, | et lare communi soceros generosque receptos, | 'his nomen iunctis Iunius' inquit 'habet'*, Livy 1.13.4 *nec pacem modo sed ciuitatem unam ex duabus faciunt. regnum consociant: imperium omne conferunt Romam,* Dion. Hal. *Ant. Rom.* 2.46.2, Cic. *Rep.* 2.13.

805–28 *The deification of Romulus.* Romulus vanished on the Nones of July (7th) in the year 716 BCE; Plutarch tells us he was said to be 54 years old and in the 38th year of his reign (Plut. *Rom.* 29.7). The sources give two widely divergent accounts of Romulus' end, one supernatural or poetic and the other 'historical' or 'rationalizing'. His disappearance was explained either as deification by his father, Mars, or as murder and dismemberment by senators or the populace in anger at his increasing despotism; all sources agree that there is no accepted tradition about his fate (see Bremmer and Horsfall 1987: 45–7). Dionysius of Halicarnassus finds Romulus' political murder 'more plausible' (*Ant. Rom.* 2.56.3), while accepting the possibility that illustrious persons might be elevated to heaven (56.6). Livy is cautious both about the story of murder (1.16.4 *sed perobscura fama*) and Julius Proculus' testimony to Romulus' deification (1.16.5 *et consilio etiam unius hominis addita rei dicitur fides*, cf. 1.16.8). In the *Met.* the supernatural version alone appears, while in Ovid's parallel account of the apotheosis at *F.* 2.475–512 the charge of murder is mentioned only to be rejected (497 *falsaeque patres in crimine caedis*) and Romulus appears and announces his new divinity to Julius Proculus (499–509), as in Livy, cf. Plut. *Rom.* 28, *Numa* 2.1–3, Dion. Hal. *Ant. Rom.* 63.3.

Ennius is our earliest literary source for Romulus' deification, which may be his invention (*Ann.* 54–5 Sk., Skutsch 1985: 205, cf. *Ann.* 110–11 *Romulus in caelo cum dis genitalibus aeuom | degit*). In both of his versions Ovid has Mars quote the same line from Ennius' poem concerning Romulus' ascension (see 814n.). Romulus' apotheosis seems to have been the final episode in *Annales* 1 and Ovid acknowledges his source through its similar placement at the end of the book as a closural device (Hardie 2002d: 193; Cole 2004: 365 observes that Romulus' apotheosis is also the latest event referred to in surviving fragments of Varro's *De gente pop. Rom.* fr. 18 Peter).

In the *Met.* Romulus' divinity is achieved through divine action, the intervention of his father Mars (cf. Venus' involvement in Aeneas' and Caesar's divinizations), with no enumeration of Romulus' exploits, which traditionally won him immortality and probably formed the basis of Ennius' euhemeristic account of his apotheosis (Skutsch 1985: 260–1), cf. Livy 1.15.6 *haec ferme Romulo regnante domi militiaeque gesta, quorum nihil absonum fidei diuinae originis diuinitatisque post mortem creditae fuit.* Cicero uses Romulus in his *Rep.* (and elsewhere) as an example to support euhemeristic belief that those now worshipped as gods were originally men of great achievement (*Rep.* 2.4 *bene meriti de rebus communibus ut genere etiam putarentur, non solum ingenio esse diuino*, 2.17 *Romulus . . . deorum in numero collocatus putaretur; quam opinionem nemo umquam mortalis assequi potuit sine eximia uirtutis gloria*, 6.13.1, *Cat.* 3.2, *Sest.* 143; see *Rep.* 2.18 (with Zetzel ad loc.), Cole 2006). Hercules was an important paradigm for his apotheosis: see 581– 608n., 818–24n, Hor. *C.* 3.3.9–12, Livy 1.7.15, Anderson 1928: 29–31. Romulus figures in traditional literary canons of deified human benefactors as the first Roman, e.g. Cic. *Leg.* 2.19 *diuos qui caelestes semper habiti sunt colunto et ollos quos endo caelo merita locauerint, Herculem, Liberum, Aesculapium, Castorem, Pollucem, Quirinum*, *Tusc.* 1.28, Hor. *C.* 3.3.15–16, *Epist.* 2.1.5–6, Ovid, *Am.* 3.8.51–2 (see further 581–608n.). In the *Fasti* there is brief mention of Romulus' achievements before his apotheosis at 2.481–2 *postquam noua moenia uidit | multaque Romulea bella peracta manu*; for comparative readings of the two narratives in the *Fasti* and *Met.*, see Gosling 2002, Heinze 1919: 39–41.

At some point the deified Romulus was identified with Quirinus, an ancient war-god claimed as Sabine who was worshipped in a temple on the Quirinal hill, which may have been decorated in imperial times with representations of Romulus' *augurium*, see 837, *F.* 2. 475–50. Quirinus had a *flamen Quirinalis*, and a festival, the *Quirinalia* (17 Feb.), discussed at *F.* 2. 475–512; on Quirinus see Plut. *Rom.* 29, Porte 1981, Radke 1987: 138–56, 1981, Bömer on *F.* 2.475, Ogilvie on Livy 1.16. The identification was debated and subjected to political pressures, especially during the development of the imperial ruler-cult, see Barchiesi 1997a: 112ff., 144, Classen 1962, Jocelyn 1989, Granobs 1997: 54–61. The association was probably not in Ennius (the prayer to Quirinus at Enn. *Ann.* 99–100 Sk. is placed before Romulus' deification, see Skutsch 1968: 130–7, 1985 ad loc., Jocelyn 1989: 46–7), nor is it in Livy, and it seems to betray its novelty at Cicero *Off.* 3.41 *pace uel Quirini uel Romuli dixerim* and *Nat. deor.* 2.62 *Romulum, quem quidam eundem ac Quirinum putant* (cf. *Rep.* 2.20 (with Zetzel ad loc.), *Leg.* 1.3). The impetus for the synthesis may have come from the Julian *gens*, and was promoted by Caesar and Augustus, see Classen 1962: 192–9, Burkert 1962. A statue of Julius Caesar was set up by the Senate in the temple of Quirinus in 45 BCE (Dio Cass. 43.45.3, Weinstock 1971: 186–8) and Augustus restored the temple, whose construction Caesar had begun, in 16 BCE (Aug. *RG* 19, *LTUR* 5.183–5). The statue of Romulus in Augustus' forum (see 772–851n.) bore the inscription *receptusque in deor[um] numerum Quirinu[s] appellatu[s est]* (*CIL* 1.1^2 p. 189 = *ILS* 64). Augustan literature contains a number of references to the association of Romulus and Quirinus, e.g. Virg. *Aen.* 1.292 *Remo cum fratre Quirinus*, 6.859, *G.* 3.27, Prop. 4.10.11, Hor. *Epod.* 16.13, *C.* 1.2.46. Ovid identifies the two here and at *F.* 2.475–6 *Quirino, | qui tenet hoc nomen (Romulus ante fuit)*, cf. *Met.* 15.572, 756.

805–17 Both the *Met.* and *Fasti* episodes open with a divine scene between Mars and Jupiter, in which a speech by Mars wins Jupiter's assent to Romulus' deification. As in the deifications of Hercules (Jupiter and the gods 9.239–61), Aeneas (Venus and Jupiter 585–608), and later Caesar (Venus and Jupiter 15.760–842), Romulus' apotheosis is brought about through divine intervention and preceded by a divine exchange. Romulus' father Mars reminds Jupiter of his promise of Romulus' divinity, which he claims was given earlier at a council of the gods (812). The meeting here referred to is evidently the council of the gods held before the twins are exposed in Ennius' *Annales* 1 (see Skutsch 1985: 202–6). Horace *C.* 3.3.35f. perhaps also recalls this same council, at which Juno consented to Romulus' apotheosis: 33–6 *illum ego lucidas | inire sedes, discere nectaris | sucos, et adscribi quietis | ordinibus patiar deorum;* see 581–2n., Feeney 1984: 185–91, Nisbet and Rudd 2004: 36. The language is stylistically elevated throughout the scene and marked by strong Ennian colour.

805 Occiderat Tatius: a quick end to Tatius' co-regency; after ruling jointly with Romulus for some years Tatius was killed in Lavinium, following a dispute over his failure to punish some of his clansmen who had attacked people of Lavinium, see Livy 1.14.1–3, Dion. Hal. *Ant. Rom.* 2.51–2, Plut. *Rom.* 23, Enn. *Ann.* 104 Sk. The pluperfect tense and the imperfect *dabas* prepare for the inverted *cum* clause of 806.

805–6 populisque . . . duobus: the Romans and Sabines. **aequata . . . iura dabas** ~ *Aen.* 1.292–3 *Remo cum fratre Quirinus | iura dabunt*; cf. 823 *non regia iura, F.* 2.492 *forte tuis illic, Romule, iura dabas, F.* 3.61 *Iliadae fratres iura petita dabant,* Livy 1.8.1 *vocataque ad concilium multitudine quae coalescere in populi unius corpus nulla re praeterquam legibus poterat, iura dedit. aequata* 'equal' seems to mean equal treatment for Romans and Sabines, but may also refute the negative tradition which saw Romulus killed for being a tyrant (Dion. Hal. *Ant. Rom.* 2.56.3, Barchiesi 1997a: 167). Cf. 15.832–3 (of Augustus) *pace data terris animum ad ciuilia uertet | iura suum legesque feret iustissimus auctor.*

806–7 posita . . . parentum: the sentence strikes a lofty tone with its numerous archaisms (see Coleman 1999: 58–9). *posita . . . casside* provides a humorous detail and conciliatory gesture; for the disarming of Mars in a context of peace, cf. *F.* 3.1–2 *depositis clipeo paulisper et hasta, | Mars, ades et nitidas casside solve comas,* 171 *sic posita dixit mihi casside Mauors.* The archaic *cassis* is used in place of the usual classical *galea.* **cum:** for the inverted *cum* clause, see 532–8n. **Mauors:** archaic and poetic form for Mars (cf. Enn. *Ann.* 99 Sk.). **adfatur** is archaic and elevated; Cicero (*Cat.* 1.1) uses the word in an Ennian context (see Horsfall on *Aen.* 7.544). **diuumque hominumque parentem:** renders the Homeric πατὴρ ἀνδρῶν τε θεῶν τε, e.g *Il.* 1.544, 15.47, see 91n.; cf. Enn. *Ann.* 203–4 Sk. *tum cum corde suo diuom pater atque hominum rex | effatur,* 591 *diuomque hominumque pater,* 592, Virg. *Aen.* 1.254, 10.2, 743. *diuum* for *deorum* is also an archaism. For double *-que*, see 78n.

808 tempus adest is to be taken with the infinitives *soluere* and *imponere* at 811. See 584n. for similar expressions of the timing of deification. **genitor:** see 84, 91nn. Ennius *Ann.* 444 *o genitor noster, Saturnie, maxime diuom* may belong to the assembly in *Annales* 1 concerning Romulus' apotheosis (see Skutsch ad loc.). Romulus is the son of Mars and Ilia (772) and Mars is the son of Zeus and Hera (Hes. *Th.* 921–3, Hom. *Il.* 5.892–8). In an alternative version at *F.* 5.229–58 the goddess Flora claims that Juno secretly conceived Mars from a flower.

808–9 quoniam fundamine magno | res Romana ualet nec praeside pendet ab uno 'since the Roman state stands firm on its great foundation and does not depend on the protection/strength of one leader alone'. See 583n. on the deification of Aeneas, and cf. Mars' similar argument at *F.* 2.483–4 *habet Romana potentia uires; | sanguinis officio non eget illa mei.* The phrase as a whole may recall (and form a contrast with?) Ennius *Ann.* 156 Sk. *moribus antiquis res stat Romana uirisque.* **fundamine:** cf. 583 *bene fundatis opibus crescentis Iuli,* 15.433 (of Rome's foundation) *rerum fundamina ponit. fundamen* is better suited to dactylic verse than the more usual *fundamentum*, cf. *F.* 4.835, Virg. *G.* 4.161, and see Kenney 2002: 68. **res Romana:** see 610n. **nec** was restored by Heinsius from later MSS, the primary MSS read *et* (Tarrant '*fort. recte*'). *nec* is supported by the parallel passage from *Fasti* 2.483–4 (cited above). Adopting *et* would require lengthening the quantity of the short final syllable of *ualet* (which is allowed, cf. 250n., 491), but, more importantly, it would significantly change the import of the line. *uno* may simply signify Romulus' sole rule, as opposed to sharing with Tatius (805–6), but the suggestion that the stability of the state depended on Romulus alone does not support Mars's argument for his translation to heaven. Earlier at 583 Venus argues for Aeneas' deification on the basis of the guarantee of his successor Iulus (*bene fundatis opibus crescentis Iuli*). The dependence of the state on one extraordinary individual is an idea which recurs in Augustan and imperial panegyric, as at 15.819–20 *qui* [Augustus] *nominis heres | impositum feret unus onus* (cf. Tac. *Ann.* 1.9.4 *non aliud discordantis patriae remedium fuisse quam ut ab uno regeretur*), and 758–9 *quo praeside rerum | humano generi, superi, fauistis abunde;* see Hardie 1993: 5–6. Reading *nec* thus may imply a contrast between an earlier and stronger Rome, and her later dependence on a sole leader, or represent, perhaps, a stronger challenge to imperial rule, see Bömer ad loc. On the theme of the appropriation of the corporate by the individual in Ovid's imperial apotheoses, see Feeney 1991: 213–16. On the important (Augustan) issue of political succession cf. 15.1–2 (Numa's accession) *Quaeritur interea quis tantae pondera molis | sustineat tantoque queat succedere regi*, and see Feeney 1999: 28.

810 praemia iam promissa: promised in Ennius' *Annales*, that is. Cf. 818. At *Aen.* 9.107 Cybele likewise calls in Jove's promise of the deification of her fleet: *ergo aderat promissa dies*. Jupiter offered Venus Aeneas' deification as a *munus* (594 *caelesti munere*). **dignoque nepoti:** cf. Venus' arguments for Aeneas at 588–9n. (*auum*) and Jupiter's response to her at 594–5 *'estis' ait 'caelesti munere digni, | quaeque petis pro quoque petis'*, 833 (of Hersilie) *dignissima*.

811 ablatum terris imponere caelo: *imponere caelo* is used elsewhere mostly of catasterism: 2.507 (Callisto and Arcas) *imposuit caelo*, 4.614 (Bacchus), *Phaen.* fr. 2 *FLP* p. 308, Manil. 1.337. Cf. 9.254–5 (Hercules' apotheosis) *idque ego defunctum terra caelestibus oris | accipiam*, 15.818 (Caesar) *ut deus accedat caelo*, 846 *caelestibus intulit astris*, 15.839 (Augustus) *aetherias sedes cognataque sidera tanget*, 869–70 *orbe relicto | accedat caelo*, *F.* 3.703 (Caesar) *ille quidem caelo positus Iouis atria uidit.*

812–15 Mars recalls the promise Jupiter made to him at the council of the gods which was held in Ennius' *Annales* 1.xxx–xliv (51–6 Sk., see Skutsch 1985: 202–6) and he quotes verbatim a line spoken by Jupiter on this occasion in the earlier poem (814 = *Ann.* fr. 54–5 Sk), as he does at *F.* 2.487. At this council, which has been placed either before the twins were exposed (Skutsch 1985: 202) or just before the actual foundation of Rome (Feeney 1984: 90), Mars seems to have remonstrated with Jupiter and received the guarantee of Romulus' ascension. In Horace, *C.* 3.3.15ff. Juno makes a speech to a council of the gods in which she consents to the deification of Romulus; this may refer to the same model, see 581–2n. The passage constitutes a famous example of the Ovidian self-conscious character-narrator aware of his own literary past, cf. 165–6n., and see Conte 1986: 57–9, Skutsch 1985: 205, Tissol 2002: 330–2. Mars's quotation serves to authenticate both his and Ovid's statements from outside the text of the poem by the appeal to the authority of Ennius, see Hinds 1998:

14–16. For the framing words *tu mihi . . . dixisti*, cf. Mars' opening at *F.* 2.488 *tu mihi dixisti.*

812 concilio quondam praesente deorum 'once in the presence of the council of the gods' On *quondam* as an allusive temporal marker, see 160–1n.

813 'for I recollect, since I recorded your faithful words in my retentive mind' (*-que* epexegetic (*OLD* 6a 'explains and enlarges')); cf. 15.814–15 (Jupiter on Augustus' deification) *legi ipse animoque notaui | et referam, ne sis etiamnum ignara futuri*, 9.778 *memorique animo tua iussa notaui.* Mars' words signal the Ennian allusion as 'a memory' (Hinds 1998: 15), cf. 465–6n. *pia uerba* urges Jupiter to fulfil his (familial) vow (*OLD pius* 3) and also perhaps compliments Mars's literary source, Ennius. On divine *pietas*, cf. Virg. *Aen.* 2.536 *si qua est caelo pietas quae talia curet*, 4.382, 5.687.

814 = Enn. *Ann.* 54 Sk. Ennius' words continue further to the next line, *Ann.* 54–5 *unus erit quem tu tolles in caerula caeli | templa.* **unus:** refers to the fact that of the twins only Romulus will survive and be deified, cf. *F.* 2.485–6 *redde patri natum: quamuis intercidit alter, | pro se proque Remo qui mihi restat erit.* **caerula caeli** 'the blue of the sky', cf. Lucr. 1.1090 *per caeli caerula*, 5.772 *per caerula mundi*; on the construction, see 793–4n.

815 uerborum summa tuorum 'the full import of your words'.

816–17 Jupiter's assent is accompanied by the traditional weather signs of his authority (cf. 542n., *F.* 2.489–90 (the same scene of Romulus' deification) *Iuppiter adnuerat. nutu tremefactus uterque | est polus, et caeli pondera mouit Atlas*, Virg. *Aen.* 9.106), but also recalled is the tradition that Romulus' disappearance and deification occurred during a storm (*F.* 2.493–5, Livy 1.16.1, Plut. *Rom.* 27.6) and, according to some sources, was even accompanied by an eclipse (Cic. *Rep.* 1.25, 2.17, Plut. *Cam.* 33.7). **omnipotens:** another word with an Ennian pedigree, *Ann.* 447 Sk., cf. *FLP* pp. 67–8, Lucr. 5.399, Catull. 64.171, Virg. *Aen.* 10x, Ovid *Met.* (only) 7x. **tonitru:** cf. 542 *intonuit . . . tonitrum*, *F.* 2.495 (the storm at Romulus' ascension) *hinc tonat, hinc missis abrumpitur ignibus aether*, *F.* 4.833–4. **terruit urbem** localizes the action, cf. Hor. *C.* 1.2.2–4 *Pater et rubente | dextera sacras iaculatus arces | terruit urbem*, Virg. *Aen.* 4.187 *magnas territat urbes. orbem* is the reading of the main MSS (Tarrant '*fort. recte*'), which would nicely extend the imperial implications of Jupiter's approval, cf. *Tr.* 2.35 [Jupiter] *detonuit strepituque exterruit orbem*, Sil. 3.230.

818–24 Mars carries Romulus up to heaven in his chariot, a scene found probably first in Ennius (*Ann.* 1.54–5 Sk.), see Skutsch 1985: 260; cf. *F.* 2.496 *rex patriis astra petebat equis*, Hor. *C.* 3.3.15–16 *Quirinus | Martis equis Acheronta fugit.* Cf. also Hercules at 9.271–2 *quem pater omnipotens inter caua nubilia raptum | quadriiugo curru radiantibus intulit astris;* probably on the model of Romulus, see Feeney 1991: 208.

818 rapinae: similarly of apotheosis at 15.840 (Caesar) *hanc animam interea caeso de corpore raptam*, 845–6, 2.506 (Callisto), 9.271 (Hercules), *F.* 2.188 (Callisto), 3.701

(Caesar), Livy 1.16.2 (of Romulus) *sublimem raptum procella*, Lucan 1.197 *rapti secreta Quirini. rapina* elsewhere in the *Met.* is used of rape, 5.492, 10.28 (both Pluto and Proserpina), cf. *F.* 5.203, *AA* 1.675.

820 conscendit equos 'climbed up behind his horses' (Hill), i.e. he mounted his chariot (synecdoche), cf. Virg. *Aen.* 12.735–6 *prima in proelia iunctos | conscendebat equos, Rem.* 6 *in liquidum rediit aethera Martis equis.* **Gradiuus** is a title of Mars derived by the ancients from *gradior* (Serv. on *Aen.* 3.35, *LALE* s.v., cf. *F.* 169–74 *Gradiue . . . gressus*), but of obscure origin and significance (cf. 6.427, 15.863, *F.* 2.861, 3.169, 5.556, Virg. *Aen.* 3.35, 10.542, Serv. on *Aen.* 1.292 (*Mars enim cum saeuit Gradiuus dicitur, cum tranquillus est Quirinus),* Val. Fl. 4.602, Sil. It. 15.15 (see Horsfall on *Aen.* 3.35, Ogilvie on Livy 1.20.4). The prosody of the *a* (here long, as at 15.863) varies; at 6.427 it is short.

822 constitit in summo nemorosi colle Palati: Mars stands where Romulus had received the omens for founding Rome, cf. *F.* 4.815 *nemorosi . . . Palati, AA* 1.105 *nemorosa Palatia.* In the *Fasti,* as well as in Livy 1.16.1, Romulus disappears on the Campus Martius, near the marsh of Capra (*F.* 2.491–2 *est locus, antiqui Caprae dixere paludem: | forte tuis illic, Romule, iura dabas*), where he was holding an assembly of the people (cf. Plut. *Rom.* 27.6) or addressing and reviewing his troops (Dion. Hal. *Ant. Rom.* 2.56.2, Livy 1.16.1).

823 reddentemque . . . non regia iura 'giving judgements that were not despotical', *OLD reddo* 14a; cf. 805–6n. **suo . . . Quiriti:** collective singular. Singular forms of *Quirites* occur elsewhere in Augustan poetry only at *Am.* 1.7.29, 3.14.19, *Tr.* 2.569, Hor. *C.* 2.7.3, *Epist.* 1.6.7 (see McKeown on *Am.* 1.7.29) and only in the oblique cases. Quirites was a name for the Roman people in their peacetime/civic function and the standard form for addressing the popular assembly, and so appropriate here. It also pointedly refers to the new Sabine element in the populace (cf. *F.* 4.855 *tum iuuenem* (sc. *Remum*) *nondum facti fleuere Quirites,* 2.505). A popular etymology derived the name *Quirites* from *Cures* (Varro, *LL* 6.68 *Quirites a Curensibus; ab his cum Tatio rege in societatem uenerunt ciuitatis*, Livy 1.13.5 *Quirites a Curibus appellati*).

824 Iliaden: see 781n.

824–6 Ovid's remarkable use of a slingshot bullet simile to describe the physical process of Romulus' apotheosis strikes an incongruous scientific note at a highly supernatural moment. The simile (and language) is Lucretian, employed to illustrate the production of lightning through swift air friction at *DRN* 6.177–9 *ut omnia motu | percalefacta uides ardescere, plumbea uero | glans etiam longo cursu uoluenda liquescit,* and 306–8 *non alia longe ratione ac plumbea saepe | feruida fit glans in cursu, cum multa rigoris | corpora dimittens ignem concepit in auris.* For the widely held ancient belief in the melting of leaden pellets in their passage through the air, cf. Arist. *De cael.* 2.7, Virg. *Aen.* 9.588–9, Sen. *NQ* 2.57.2, Lucan 7.513, Stat. *Theb.* 10.533. Ovid uses the same simile quite differently at 2.726–9, where it is applied to Mercury's heated passion for Herse. For his use of other Lucretian similes of meterological phenomena to describe metamorphosis, cf. 3.487–90, 4.121–4, 9.219–25, 13.600–7; see Due 1974: 32–3, Myers 1994a: 47–9.

824–5 corpus mortale per auras | dilapsum tenues 'his mortal body dispersed (melted) through the thin air'. Romulus' body disappears as his immortal soul reaches heaven (for purification by fire, cf. Hercules' deification 9.262–70). On the mortality of the body, see 598–608n.; cf. Plutarch on the separation of body and soul in his discussion of Romulus' apotheosis at *Rom.* 28.6–8 (28.7 ψυχὴ . . . ὥσπερ ἀστραπὴ νέφους διαπταμένη τοῦ σώματος 'the soul flies from the body as lightning from a cloud').

825–6 ceu lata plumbea funda | missa solet medio glans intabescere caelo 'just as a lead pellet shot from a broad sling will melt in the middle of the sky'. The sling was part of the armoury of the Roman legion (Watson 1969: 60–1), but is also in Homer and Virgil (*Il.* 13.599–600, 716, *Aen.* 7.686–7 (with Horsfall), 9.586–9 (with Hardie), 11.579–80. *ceu* (attested in only one MS, but preferred as *lectio difficilior*) is an epic poetic archaism (Enn. *Ann.* 361 Sk., Lucr. 4x, Virgil 24x, Ovid, *Met.* 9x). *intabescere* (or *tabescere*) is more often used of the 'wasting' or even rotting of the body, cf. Canens at 432n., 2.780, 15.363, but also of the melting of wax at 3.487–8 *ut intabescere flauae | igne leui cerae solent.* For *lata* Hardie proposes *torta* (cf. Prop. 4.3.65 *plumbea cum tortae sparguntur pondera fundae*, Val. Fl. 3.96 *tortae pondera fundae*, Stat. *Theb.* 7.338), see also Ramírez de Verger 2006: 329.

827 pulchra subit facies 'a beautiful countenance appears in replacement' (*OLD subeo* 9b, c); cf. *F.* 2.503–4. *pulcher et humano maior trabeaque decorus | Romulus*, 6.375 *lituo pulcher trabeaque Quirinus*, Plut. *Rom.* 28.1. The adj. *pulcher* is used of Romulus in Enn. *Ann.* 75 Sk. (cf. of Mars at *Ann.* 38 Sk. (with Skutsch)). Cf. 4.541 (the deification of Ino and Melicertes) *faciemque nouauit.* **puluinaribus altis:** a *puluinar* was a special couch on which images of the gods were placed and offered a sacrificial feast at the *lectisternium* of Roman cult; see Bömer ad loc., Latte 1960: 242–4, Ogilvie on Livy 5.13.6, Feeney 1991: 208. Upon deification Romulus will participate in the gods' banquets in heaven (*altis*); cf. Hom. *Od.* 11.602f. (Hercules), Theocr. *Id.* 17.22ff. (Ptolemy Soter), Hor. *C.* 3.3.11–12 (the deified Augustus).

828 qualis trabeati forma Quirini 'the form which Quirinus has in his ceremonial cloak'. The *trabea*, a short toga with a reddish-purple border, was a ceremonial garment worn by the early kings (Livy 1.41.6 (Servius Tullius), Virg. *Aen.* 7.187 (Picus), 11.334), and later Roman magistrates and *equites* (see Bömer on *F.* 6.375, Bonfante 1975: 592, 613–14). It was frequently associated with Romulus/Quirinus, cf. *F.* 1.37 *trabeati cura Quirini*, 2.503, 6.375 *lituo pulcher trabeaque Quirinus* (with Bömer), 796, Virg. *Aen.* 7.612 *Quirinali trabea* (see Horsfall ad loc.), Juv. 8.259. The adj. *trabeatus* appears here first (cf. *F.* 1.37). On Romulus' identification with Quirinus, see 805–28n. Since we have been given a detailed account of the divine mechanisms of Romulus' apotheosis, the usual pendant to the myth, in which Julius Proculus informs the Roman people that the deified Romulus appeared to him and announced that he had been taken up into heaven (see *F.* 2.499–513, Livy 1.16), is not necessary, although in the following lines Iris performs a similar function in announcing Romulus' divinity to his wife Hersilie and repeatedly confirming his identification with Quirinus (see 834, 836–7, 851).

829–51 *The deification of Hersilie.* Romulus' deification is followed by that of his wife, Hersilie, into *Hora Quirini,* which seems to be an Ovidian invention. Ennius mentioned a *Hora* (with a long *o*) *Quirini* at *Ann.* 100 Sk. *Quirine pater ueneror Horamque Quirini,* where Skutsch comments: 'feminine abstract nouns denoting functions or manifestations of major gods and regularly linked with their names were early misunderstood as names of their attendants or wives' and concludes that 'it is a little difficult to credit Ennius with the Ovidian metamorphosis which turns Hersilie into Hora'; cf. *id.* 1968: 132–7, Latte 1960: 55–6, Ogilvie on Livy 1.11.1–4. Feeney 1984: 189 has suggested that 'Juno's reconciliation in *Annales* 1 might have involved her playing some part in the marriage of the newly enrolled god'. *Hora Quirini* was given offerings on 23 Aug. (Degrassi XIII.2 pp. 500–2), see Plut. *Quaest. Rom.* 46, Gell. 13.23.2, Bömer on *Met.* 14.829–51, Radke 1979: 145. On the episode, see Granobs 1997: 61–70, Domenicucci 1991, Tissol 2002: 332–5.

Hersilie was a Sabine (832), but accounts vary both as to how she was taken during the abduction of the Sabine women by the Romans and to whom she was married (see Plut. *Rom.* 14.6–7, Dion. Hal. *Ant. Rom.* 2.45, Wiseman 1987: 288–9). She appears as the wife of Romulus also in Livy 1.11.2 and Sil. Ital. 13.812, but elsewhere she is married to a certain Hostus Hostilius and becomes grandmother of Tullus Hostilius (Macrob. 1.6.16, Dion. Hal. *Ant. Rom.* 3.1.2–3). She is mostly commemorated for her role in mediating between the Roman and Sabine armies (e.g. *F.* 3.205–12 and Livy 1.11.1–4, Enn. *Ann.* 101 Sk.). Her catasterism prefigures that of Caesar in the following book, where the manoeuvre of adding an original metamorphosis (Ovid's own, 15.871–9) after an imperial one (Augustus) is repeated. The closural strategy is used here to end a book, as there to end the poem. Considering the importance of Romulus as a prototype for the first imperial deifications (see 805–28n.), it is possible that Hersilie may be meant to suggest Augustus' wife Livia (see Flory 1995: 129–30, Domenicucci 1991: 227–8), cf. 833–4n. Augustus is said to have referred to Hersilie as the woman who introduced marriage customs to Rome (Cassius Dio 56.5.5), which would fit with the ideology of Livia as a model *matrona* (*Tr.* 1.6.25–6 *femina seu princeps omnes tibi culta per annos | te docet exemplum coniugis esse bonae,* Barrett 2002: 115ff.) and hints at her future divinization (*F.* 1.536 *sic Augusta nouum Iulia numen erit*). Alternatively, Romulus' parallelism with Hercules may suggest that Hersilie is deified to provide him with a divine consort to correspond with the goddess Hebe, see Granobs 1997: 67–70.

829 Flebat . . . coniunx: on a wife's grief see also Canens 14.416–34 and Egeria 15.485–551; cf. *F.* 3.873–4 (Phrixus) *flebat, ut amissa gemini consorte pericli, | caeruleo iunctam nescius esse deo.* **cum:** inverted *cum*-clause, see 535–8n. **regia Iuno** is a Virgilian formula (*Aen.* 1.443, 4.114, 7.438, 10.62, always in the same metrical *sedes*), which may render the Homeric πότνια Ἥρη and recalls the Roman cult of *Iuno Regina* (Tarrant on Sen. *Ag.* 350), cf. 6.94, 9.21, *Pont.* 1.4.39. Juno, as goddess of marriage, takes full authority for Hersilie's deification, while Jupiter had requested her assent for those of Hercules and Aeneas. It is from Juno's temple that Hersilie exhorts the Sabine women at *F.* 3.205; on Juno Regina and Roman matrons, see Hänninen 1999.

830–1 Irin: cf. 85n. **Hersilien:** Ovid uses throughout the passage a Grecizing form of her name instead of the usual Hersilia (she is -ία in Dionysius and Plutarch). Tarrant (p. 488) shows that the Latin form *–iam* has strong authority in the primary MSS in 830 and 839; if they are right, 848 may have to be considered corrupt (see below). **limite curuo:** the rainbow, Iris' usual route to earth, cf. 838, 11.590 *arcuato . . . curuamine*, 6.63–5. The connection between Iris and the rainbow is common in Virgil (*Aen.* 4.694–702, 5.657–8, 9.14–15 (with Hardie)), cf. Stat. *Silu.* 5.1.103–4, *Theb.* 10.82–3. **imperat:** with acc. and inf., see *OLD* 4c. **uacuae** 'solitary' (*OLD* 8c); Liberman 2004: 87 cites the variant *uiduae* (not in Tarrant).

832–3 'o et de Latia, o et de gente Sabina | praecipuum, matrona, decus': a passage remarkable for multiple anaphora, hiatus, and monosyllables (see Hellegouarc'h 1964: 257), as well as accentual variation (*ó et . . . o ét*). For the highly artificial word order (*praecipuum, matrona, decus*) see 472n. **de Latia . . . de gente Sabina** stresses Hersilie's dual heritage. *gente* is to be taken *apo koinou* with *Latia*. The address recalls Virgil's praise of Maecenas at *G.* 2.40 *o decus, o famae merito pars maxima nostrae*, and Horace's at *C.* 1.1.2 *o et praesidium et dulce decus meum.*

833–4 dignissima tanti . . . uiri, coniunx: recalls conventional praise of women in Roman epitaphs (e.g. *CIL* VI 2.9334, p. 1229) and Ovid's praise of Livia elsewhere (Bömer ad loc.), cf. *F.* 1.650 *sola toro magni digna reperta Iouis*, *Tr.* 2.161–2 *Liuia . . . quae, nisi te, nullo coniuge digna fuit*, *Pont.* 1.4.55 *turaque Caesaribus cum coniuge Caesare digna*, 3.1.118 *sola est caelesti digna reperta toro.* Juno, who had earlier betrayed the Romans by opening a gate for the Sabines (781–2), now has words of praise for Romulus. **uiri** 'mortal husband'.

836–7 lucum . . . colle Quirini | . . . templum Romani regis: the Quirinal hill: for the etymology see *F.* 2.511 *templa deo fiunt: collis quoque dictus ab illo est*, Varro, *LL* 5.51. The large and ancient temple of Quirinus was traditionally founded in immediate response to the deified Romulus' appearance to Iulius Proculus (*F.* 2.499–512, Cic. *Rep.* 2.20.3). There is evidence of an early temple (436/5 BCE = Livy 4.21.9, Plin. *Nat.* 15.120; 293 BCE = Livy 10.46.2, Plin. *Nat.* 7.213), which was ultimately completely rebuilt and rededicated in 16 BCE by Augustus (*RG* 19, Cass. Dio 54.19.4, Richardson 1992 s. v. *Quirinus, Aedes*). Evidence of an actual grove is found only here (two sacred myrtles are mentioned at Plin. *Nat.* 15.120); but such sites are frequent in Ovid's metamorphic landscape, cf. e.g. 3.175–6 (Actaeon), 5.391 (Proserpina). **Romani regis:** the styling of Romulus/Quirinus as *rex* is unexpected after 823 *non regia iura*, cf. 805–6n.

838 pictos . . . per arcus 'along her coloured arches', i.e. rainbow, cf. 830n.

840 uerecundo . . . uultu: Hersilie shows appropriate matronly modesty (see Kaster 2005: 13–25 on *uerecundia*). Ovid uses *uerecundus* 8x (only once elsewhere in this poem, cf. 1.484 (Daphne) *pulchra uerecundo suffunditur ora rubore*; Horace 4x, not in Virgil, Tibullus, Propertius), see McKeown on *Am.* 1.5.7–8.

841–2 'o dea (namque mihi nec quae sis dicere promptum est | et liquet esse deam) 'O goddess! (for though I cannot tell who you are, you are clearly a goddess)'. *namque* introduces the reason for addressing Iris simply as *dea*, cf. 12n.; Hersilie is suitably cautious about misidentifying a goddess. *nec . . . et* 'while not . . . (yet) at the same time' (otherwise apparently prosaic), cf. 2.42 (with Bömer), *F.* 4.485, *Her.* 20.177–8, and see *OLD neque* 8a, K–S II 48. Ovid evokes Aeneas' address to the disguised Venus at *Aen.* 1.328 '*o, dea certe | (an Phoebi soror? an Nympharum sanguinis una?), | sis felix nostrumque leues, quaecumque, laborem'*, cf. *Aen.* 8.351–2 *'hoc nemus, hunc' inquit 'frondoso uertice collem | (quis deus incertum est) habitat deus'* (Wills 1996: 340). For the expression *dicere promptum est*, cf. 13.10–11 (Ajax) *nec mihi dicere promptum | nec facere est isti*, 3.96, *F.* 4.717. **duc, o duc:** cf. 4.583 *accede, o coniunx, accede*, Virg. *Aen.* 2.644 *sic, o sic*, 6.258 *procul, o procul*, *G.* 4.358 *duc, age, duc* (see Wills 1996: 89–95, on the (rare) gemination and separation of imperatives in Latin poetry).

843 ora: poetic pl.; perhaps a pun on Hersilie's new name *Hora* (Wiseman 1987: 289n.38).

844 caelum accepisse fatebor 'I shall confess that I have gained heaven', cf. 6.356–7 (Latona asks for a drink) *haustus aquae mihi nectar erit, uitamque fatebor | accepisse simul; uitam dederitis in unda*, 7.60–1 (Medea) *quo coniuge felix | et dis cara ferar et uertice sidera tangam*. Hersilie uses *caelum* metaphorically in a proverbial expression connoting the pinnacle of happiness (see Otto 1890: 62, no. 9; Bömer ad loc. cites Cic. *Att.* 2.19.1 *in caelo sum*). For Hersilie, the greatest happiness will be in being reunited with her husband, which will, of course, occur when she too is literally transported to heaven, i.e. divinized (see Tissol 2002: 335 on this type of Ovidian wordplay). Cf. Bacchus to Ariadne in *AA* 1.557 *munus habe caelum*.

845–6 Romuleos . . . colles: poetic pl. (to avoid hiatus in 846), in this case the Quirinal, cf. 836–7. Romulus was more usually associated with the Palatine (cf. 822–3n.; for the *casa Romuli* preserved on the Palatine, see Dion. Hal *Ant. Rom.* 1.79.11, Prop. 4.1.9–10). The poetic adjectival form *Romuleus* (see 1n.) balances the weighty Gk adj. at the end of the line. **cum uirgine Thaumantea** 'with the virgin daughter of Thaumas', cf. 4.480 *Thaumantias Iris*, 11.647 *Thaumantidos*. Thaumas (son of Pontos and Gaia) is first named as the father of Iris in Hes. *Th.* 780, cf. Call. *H. Del.* 67, Cic. *ND* 3.51, Virg. *Aen.* 9.5. The Greek quadrisyllabic patronymic adj. (only here) creates a spondaic fifth foot (*spondeiazon*), a Grecizing metrical effect often associated with neoteric technique (rarer in Ovid than Virgil), cf. 1.14 *Amphitrite*, 690 *Nonacrinas*, 2.226 *Appenninus*, 5.607 *Cyllenenque*; see Fordyce on Virg. *Aen.* 7.631, Soubiran 1969.

The ancients connected Thaumas' name with θαυμάζω 'I wonder' in reference to the marvel of the rainbow (see Hardie on *Aen.* 9.5, Pease on Cic. *ND* 3.51).

846–8 Hersilie's apotheosis combines the portent of her burning hair and her translation to heaven by a star (suggesting catasterism). For the form of the divine omen, cf. Virg. *Aen.* 7.72–7 *Lauinia uirgo* | *uisa (nefas) longis comprendere crinibus ignem* | *atque omnem ornatum flamma crepitante cremari* | *regalisque accensa comas, accensa coronam* | *insignem gemmis; tum fumida lumine fuluo* | *inuolui*, 2.681f. (Iulus), 8.680–1 (Augustus), Livy 1.39.1f. (Servius Tullius). A similar phenomenon accompanies Caesar's catasterism, which Hersilie's prefigures, at 15.847 *dumque tulit, lumen capere atque ignescere sensit* and 849 *flammiferumque . . . crinem.* Caesar's comet (the *sidus Iulium,* 15.749 *in sidus uertere nouum stellamque comantem,* 841) shone on seven nights at Octavian's games in his honour in July 44 BCE and was regarded as a sign of his deification (Plin. *Nat.* 2.93–4), see Weinstock 1971: 370–84, Suet. *Iul.* 88, Virg. *Ecl.* 9.47–9, *Aen.* 8.681, Hor. *C.* 1.12.47.

847–8 a cuius lumine . . . in auras 'Hersilie, her hair burning from its light, departed with the star into the air'. **crines** is an acc. of limitation with *flagrans,* a poetic Grecism (*NLS* § 19 (i)). The stress on Hersilie's hair in her catasterism recalls Catullus 66, the translation of Callimachus' *Coma Berenices*, a poem about the catasterism of a lock of the Ptolemaic Queen's hair (cf. Knox 1986a: 76, on Caesar's comet and hair in *Met.* 15 (cf. 15.749, 849, quoted above) and its associations with the *Coma*). **cessit:** perhaps echoes Catull. 66.40 *inuita, o regina, tuo de uertice cessi*, cf. Prop. 3.18.34 *Caesar, ab humana cessit in astra uia.* **in auras:** cf. 432n.

849 Romanae conditor urbis: an honorific title for Romulus after the ellipsis of the founding of the city at 774–5, cf. *F.* 3.24, 1.27, *Am.* 2.14.15–16, *Aen.* 8.313 *rex Euandrus, Romanae conditor arcis.* Ovid's depiction of Romulus' reception of his wife takes on an oddly formal tone (cf. *manibus . . . notis*).

850–1 priscum . . . nomen | **mutat Horamque uocat:** on the change of name after apotheosis, cf. 607–8 Aeneas–Aeneas Indigetes, 828 Romulus–Quirinus, 4.451 Ino and Melicertes–Leucothoe and Palaemon (*imposuit nomenque simul faciemque nouauit*, cf. *F.* 6.550 *nomina mutarunt: hic deus, illa dea est*). The short *o* in *Hora* (vs. Ennius' long) is 'undoubtedly correct' (Skutsch on *Ann.* 99 Sk.); cf. Plut. *Quaest. Rom.* 46. Etymologies derived her name from *orare* and *hortari* (Plut. *Mor.* 275F–276A). *corpore* and *mutat* recall Ovid's prooemium at 1.1–2 *In noua fert animus mutatas dicere formas* | *corpora.* **nunc dea iuncta Quirino est** 'now as a goddess she is joined to Quirinus'; this also refers to the fact that her new name was *Hora Quirini. nomen* and *nunc* are etymological markers, see 90n., 73n. The book ends with unusual finality. Continuity with the following book is provided by the chronological continuation of the king list 15.1–2 *Quaeritur interea quis tantae pondera molis* | *sustineat tantoque queat succedere regi.*

BIBLIOGRAPHY

1. ABBREVIATIONS

Axelson	B. Axelson, *Unpoetische Wörter* (Skrifter utgivna av Vetenskaps-societeten i Lund 29). Lund 1945.
CIL	*Corpus inscriptionum Latinarum*. Berlin 1863–.
Degrassi	A. Degrassi, *Inscriptiones Italiae* XIII. *Fasti et elogia*. Rome 1963.
D–S	C. Daremberg and E. Saglio, eds. *Dictionnaire des antiquités grecques et romaines*. Paris 1875–1912.
EGF	M. Davies, ed. *Epicorum Graecorum fragmenta*. Göttingen 1988.
EV	*Enciclopedia virgiliana*. Rome 1984–91.
FGH	F. Jacoby *et al.*, eds. *Die Fragmente der griechischen Historiker*. Leiden 1923–.
FLP	E. Courtney, ed. *The fragmentary Latin poets*. Oxford 1993.
FPL	W. Morel, ed. *Fragmenta poetarum Latinorum epicorum et lyricorum*. Leipzig 1927, repr. Stuttgart 1963.
G–L	B. W. Gildersleeve and G. Lodge, *Gildersleeve's Latin Grammar*. London 1960.
HE	A. S. F. Gow and D. L. Page, *Hellenistic Epigrams* I–II. Cambridge 1965.
H–E–A	M. Haupt and R. Ehwald, eds. *P. Ovidius Naso: Metamorphosen*. Vol. I 9th edn, II 4th edn, rev. by M. von Albrecht. Zurich and Dublin 1966.
H–S	J. B. Hofmann and A. Szantyr, *Lateinische Syntax und Stilistik*. Munich 1965.
ILS	H. Dessau, *Inscriptiones latinae selectae*. Berlin 1892–1916.
K–S	R. Kühner and C. Stegmann, *Ausführliche Grammatik der lateinischen Sprache*. 3rd edn, ed. A. Thierfelder, 2 vols. Leverkusen 1955.
LALE	R. Maltby, *A lexicon of ancient Latin etymologies*. Leeds 1991.
Latte	K. Latte, *Römische Religionsgeschichte*. Munich 1960.
Leumann	M. Leumann, *Lateinische Laut- und Formenlehre*. Munich, 1977.
LIMC	*Lexicon iconographicum mythologiae classicae*. Zurich and Munich 1981–97.
LSJ	H. G. Liddell and R. Scott, *A Greek-English Lexicon*. New edn H. S. Jones. 2 vols. Oxford 1940 and repr.
LTUR	M. Steinby, ed. *Lexicon topographicum urbis Romae*. Rome 1993–.
N–H	R. Nisbet and M. Hubbard, *A commentary on Horace: Odes Book I* 1970; *Book II* 1978. Oxford.
NLS	E. C. Woodcock, *A new Latin syntax*. London 1959, repr. Bristol 1987.

N–W	F. Neue and C. Wagener, *Formenlehre der lateinischen Sprache*, 3rd edn, 4 vols. Leipzig and Berlin 1892–1905.
OLD	P. G. W. Glare, ed. *Oxford Latin dictionary*. Oxford, 1982.
Peter	H. Peter, ed. *Historicorum Romanorum reliquiae*. 2 vols. repr. Stuttgart 1967.
RAC	T. Klauser, *Reallexicon für Antike and Christentum*. Stuttgart 1950–.
RE	A. Pauly, G. Wissowa and W. Kroll, eds. *Real-Encyclopädie der classischen Altertumswissenschaft*. Stuttgart 1893–.
Roscher	W. H. Roscher, ed. *Ausführliches Lexicon der griechischen und römischen Mythologie*. Leipzig 1884–1937.
RRC	M. H. Crawford, *Roman Republican coinage*. Cambridge 1975.
SH	H. Lloyd-Jones and P. Parsons, eds. *Supplementum Hellenisticum*. Berlin and New York 1983.
Talbert	R. J. A. Talbert, *Barrington atlas of the Greek and Roman world*. Princeton 2000.
TLL	*Thesaurus linguae Latinae*. Munich 1900–.
Walde–Hofmann	A. Walde, *Lateinisches etymologisches Wörterbuch*, 3rd edn. rev. J. B. Hofmann. Heidelberg 1930–55.

2. EDITIONS, TRANSLATIONS, AND COMMENTARIES

Barchiesi	A. Barchiesi, *Ovidio Metamorfosi*, vol. I. Milan 2005.
Barchiesi and Rosati	A. Barchiesi and G. Rosati, *Ovidio Metamorfosi*, vol. II. Milan 2007.
Bömer	F. Bömer, *P. Ovidius Nasonis Metamorphosen*, 7 vols. Heidelberg 1969–86.
Hill	D. E. Hill, *Ovid Metamorphoses XIII–XV.* Warminster 2000.
Hollis	A. S. Hollis, *Ovid Metamorphoses Book VIII*. Oxford 1970.
Hopkinson	N. Hopkinson, *Ovid Metamorphoses Book XIII*. Cambridge 2000.
Melville	A. D. Melville, *Ovid Metamorphoses*. Translation. Oxford 1986.
Miller–Goold	F. J. Miller, *Ovid Metamorphoses*. Loeb Classical Library, vol. I, 3rd edn, vol. II, 2nd edn; rev. by G. P. Goold. Cambridge MA and London, 1977.
Moore-Blunt	J. J. Moore-Blunt, *A commentary on Ovid Metamorphoses II*. Uithorn, 1977.
Simmons	C. Simmons, *P. Ovidii Nasonis Metamorphoseon XIII—XIV*. London 1899.
Tarrant	R. J. Tarrant, *P. Ovidii Nasonis Metamorphoses*. Oxford 2004.

3. OTHER WORKS

Adams, J. N. (1982) *The Latin sexual vocabulary*. London.

Adams, J. N. and R. G. Mayer, eds. (1999) *Aspects of the language of Latin poetry*. Oxford.

Ahl, F. (1982) 'Amber Avallon, and Apollo's singing swan', *AJP* 103: 373–411.
(1985) *Metaformations. Soundplay and wordplay in Ovid and other Classical poets*. Ithaca.
Albrecht, M. von (1964) *Die Parenthese in Ovids Metamorphosen und ihre dichterische Funktion*. Hildesheim.
(1968) 'Ovids Humor', in M. von Albrecht and E. Zinn, eds. *Ovid* (Darmstadt) 405–37.
(1982) 'Venus in Ovids *Metamorphosen*', *Vichiana* 11: 319–31.
Alföldi, A. (1965) *Early Rome and the Latins*. Ann Arbor.
Alton, E. H., D. E. W. Wormell, and E. Courtney (1985) *P. Ovidius Nasonis Fastorum libri sex*. 2nd edn. Leipzig.
Anderson, A. R. (1928) 'Heracles and his successors: A study of a heroic ideal and the recurrence of a heroic type', *HSCP* 39: 7–58.
Anderson, W. S. (1958) 'Juno and Saturn in the *Aeneid*', *SPhNC* 55: 519–32.
(1963) 'Multiple changes in the *Metamorphoses*', *TAPA* 94: 1–27.
Andrae, J. (2003) *Von Kosmos zum Chaos: Ovids Metamorphosen und Vergils Aeneis*. Trier.
André, J. (1967) *Les noms d'oiseaux en Latin*. Paris.
Andreae, B. (1984) *Odysseus: Archäologie des europäischen Menschenbildes*. Frankfurt am Main.
D'Anna, G. (1996) 'Alba Longa in Nevio, Ennio e nei primi annalisti', in A. Pasqualini, ed. *Alba Longa: mito storia archeologia* (Rome) 101–25.
Arnott, W. G. (1977) 'Swan songs', *G&R* 24: 149–53.
Arya, D. (2000) 'Il fregio della Basilica Paulli (Aemilia)', in Carandini and Cappelli 2000: 303–19.
Austin, C. and G. Bastianini, eds. (2002) *Posidippi Pellaei quae supersunt omnia*. Milan.
Austin, R. G. (1955) *P. Vergili Maronis Aeneidos liber quartus*. Oxford.
(1964) *P. Vergili Maronis Aeneidos liber secundus*. Oxford.
(1971) *P. Vergili Maronis Aeneidos liber primus*. Oxford.
(1977) *P. Vergili Maronis Aeneidos liber sextus*. Oxford.
Baier, T. (1997) *Werk und Wirkung Varros im Spiegel seiner Zeitgenossen*. Stuttgart.
Baldini Moscadi, L. (1976) '*Murmur* nella terminologia magica', *SIFC* 48: 254–62.
Baldo, G. (1986) 'Il codice epico nelle Metamorfosi di Ovidio', *MD* 16: 109–31.
(1995) *Dall' Eneide alle Metamorfosi: il codice epico di Ovidio*. Padua.
Bandiera, E. (1986) 'La mitologia arcaica di Ascanio-Iulo', *Studi di Filologia e Letteratura* 1: 13–61.
Barchiesi, A. (1979) 'Palinuro e Caieta: Due "epigrammi" virgiliani (*Aen.* 5.870 e 7.1–4)', *Maia* 31: 3–11.
(1991) 'Discordant Muses', *PCPS* 37: 1–21.
(1992) *P. Ovidii Nasonis Epistulae Heroidum 1–3*. Florence.
(1993) 'Future reflexive: two modes of allusion and Ovid's *Heroides*', *HSCP* 95: 333–65.
(1997a) *The poet and the prince: Ovid and Augustan discourse*. Berkeley.
(1997b) 'Endgames: Ovid's *Metamorphoses* 15 and *Fasti* 6', in D. Roberts, F. Dunn, and D. Fowler, eds. *Classical closure* (Princeton) 181–208.

(1999) 'Venus' masterplot: Ovid and the Homeric Hymns', in Hardie, Barchiesi, and Hinds 1999: 112–26.
(2001) *Speaking volumes: narrative and intertext in Ovid and other Latin poets*. London.
(2002a) 'Martial arts. Mars Ultor in the Forum Augustum: a verbal monument with a vengeance', in G. Herbert-Brown, ed. *Ovid's Fasti: historical readings at its Bimillennium* (Oxford) 1–22.
(2002b) 'Narrative technique and narratology in the *Metamorphoses*', in Hardie 2002b: 180–99.
(2005) *Ovidio Metamorfosi*, vol. I. Milan.
Barkan, L. (1986) *The gods made flesh: metamorphosis and the pursuit of paganism*. New Haven.
Barrett, A. (2002) *Livia: first lady of Imperial Rome*.New Haven.
Bassett, S. (1919) '*Versus tetracolos*', *CP* 144: 216–33.
Bergh, B. (1975) *On passive imperatives in Latin*. Stockholm.
Bernbeck, E. J. (1967) *Beobachtungen zur Darstellungsart in Ovids Metamorphosen*. Munich.
Boldrer, F. (1999) *L'Elegia di Vertumno (Properzio 4.2)*. Amsterdam.
Bömer, F. (1957) 'Interpretationen zu den Fasti des Ovid', *Gymnasium* 64: 112–35.
(1959) 'Ovid und die Sprache Vergils', *Gymnasium* 66: 268–87.
(1986) 'Aeneas landet bei Cumae: zu Verg. *Aen.* VI.2 und Ov. *Met.* XIV.102ff.', *Gymnasium* 93: 97–101.
Bonfante, L. (1975) *Etruscan dress*. Baltimore.
Borghini, A. (1979) 'Riflessioni antropologiche sopra un mito di proibizione: la ragazza alla finestra (Ovidio *Metamorphoses* 14.795–861 e Antonio Liberale *Metamorphoses* 39)', *MD* 2: 137–61.
Boyd, B. W., ed. (2002) *Brill's Companion to Ovid*. Leiden, Boston, Köln.
Bramble, J. C. (1970) 'Structure and ambiguity in Catullus LXIV', *PCPS* 16: 22–41.
Bremmer, J. N. and N. M. Horsfall, eds. (1987) *Roman myth and mythography*. London.
Brugnoli, G. (1983) '*Reges Albanorum*', in *Atti del convegno Virgiliano di Brindisi nel bimillenario della morte* (Perugia) 157–90.
(1996) 'I *Reges Albani* di Ovidio', in A. Pasqualini, ed. *Alba Longa: mito storia archeologia* (Rome) 127–34.
Buffière, F. (1962) *Allégories d'Homère*. Paris.
Burkert, W. (1962) 'Caesar und Romulus-Quirinus', *Historia* 11: 356–76.
Cairns, F. (1989) *Virgil's Augustan epic*. Cambridge.
(1996) 'Ancient "etymology" and Tibullus: on the classification of "etymologies" and on "etymological markers"', *PCPS* 42: 24–59.
(2002) 'The nomenclature of the Tiber in Virgil's *Aeneid*', in J. Booth and R. Maltby, eds. *What's in a name?* (Swansea) 65–82.
Cameron, A. (2004) *Greek mythography in the Roman world*. Oxford.
Capanna, E. (2000) 'Pico, Fauno e Latino', in Carandini and Cappelli 2000: 225.
Carafa, P. (2000) 'La battaglia tra Romani e Sabini', in Carandini and Cappelli 2000: 334–5.
Carandini, A. and R. Cappelli, eds. (2000) *Roma, Romolo, Remo e la fondazione della città*. Rome and Milan.

Carettoni, G. (1961) 'Il fregio figurato della Basilica Emilia', *RIA* 10: 5–78.
Casali, S. (1995a) 'Altre voci nell' *Eneide* di Ovidio', *MD* 35: 59–76.
(1995b) *P. Ovidii Nasonis: Heroidum Epistula IX*. Florence.
(2006) 'Other voices in Ovid's *Aeneid*', in P. E. Knox, ed. *Oxford readings in Ovid* (Oxford) 144–65.
(2007) 'Correcting Aeneas's voyage: Ovid's commentary on *Aeneid* 3', *TAPA* 137: 181–210.
Casson, L. (1994) *Ships and seafaring in ancient times*. Texas.
Castagnoli, F. (1982) 'La leggenda di Enea nel Lazio', *Studi Romani*: 30: 1–15.
(1983) 'Commentaires topographiques à l'Énéide', *CRAI*: 202–15.
Celoria, F. (1992) *The Metamorphoses of Antoninus Liberalis. A translation with commentary*. London and New York.
Chiarucci, P. (2000) 'Ascanio fonda Alba', in Carandini and Cappelli 2000: 219–21.
Clarke, W. M. (1972) 'Intentional rhyme in Vergil and Ovid', *TAPA* 103: 49–77.
Classen, C. J. (1962) 'Romulus in der römischen Republik', *Philologus* 106: 174–204.
Clausen, W. (1963) 'Two conjectures', *AJP* 84: 415–17.
(1979) 'Ovid, *Met.* 15.90', *AJP* 100: 247–9.
(1986) 'Cicero and the New Poetry', *HSCP* 90: 159–70.
Clay, J. (1972) 'The *planktai* and *moly:* divine naming and knowing in Homer', *Hermes* 100: 127–31.
Coarelli, F. (1987) *I santuari del Lazio in età repubblicana*. Rome.
Cole, S. (2006) 'Cicero, Ennius, and the concept of apotheosis at Rome', *Arethusa* 39: 531–48.
Cole, T. (2004) 'Ovid, Varro, and Castor of Rhodes: the chronological architecture of the *Metamorphoses*', *HSCP* 102: 355–422.
(2008) *Ovidius mythistoricus: legendary time in the Metamorphoses*. Frankfurt am Main.
Coleman, R. (1971) 'Structure and intention in the *Metamorphoses*', *CQ* 21: 461–77.
(1999) 'Poetic diction, poetic discourse and the poetic register', in Adams and Mayer 1999: 21–96.
Connors, C. (2004) 'Monkey business: imitation, authenticity, and identity from Pithekoussai to Plautus', *ClAnt* 23: 179–207.
Conte, G. B. (1986) *The rhetoric of imitation. Genre and poetic memory in Virgil and other Latin poets*. Translated by C. P. Segal. Ithaca.
Copley, F. O. (1940) 'The suicide-paraclausithyron: a study of Ps.-Theocritus, *Idyll* XXIII', *TAPA* 71: 52–61.
(1956) *Exclusus amator. A study in Latin love poetry*. APA Monographs no. 17. Madison.
Cornell, T. J. (1975) 'Aeneas and the twins: the development of the Roman foundation legend', *PCPS* 21: 1–31.
(1977) 'Aeneas' arrival in Italy', *LCM* 2: 77–83.
(1995) *The beginnings of Rome*. London and New York.
Courtney, E. (1965) 'Ovidian and non-Ovidian *Heroides*', *BICS* 12: 63–9.
(1985) 'Three poems of Catullus', *BICS* 22: 85–100.
(2001) *A companion to Petronius*. Oxford.

(2004) 'The "Greek" accusative', *CJ* 99: 425–31.
(2005) 'Three conjectures on Ovid', *Maia* 57: 39–40.
Cova, P. V. (1994) *Il libro terzo dell'Eneide*. Milan.
Crane, G. (1986) 'Tithonus and the prologue to Callimachus' *Aetia'*, *ZPE* 66: 269–78.
Crump, M. (1931) *The epyllion from Theocritus to Ovid*. Oxford.
Curran, L. (1972) 'Transformation and anti-Augustanism in Ovid's *Metamorphoses'*, *Arethusa* 5: 71–91.
Currie, H. MacL. (1981) 'Ovid and the Roman stage', *ANRW* 31.4: 2701–42.
Davies, M. (1989) *The epic cycle*. Bristol.
Davis, G. (1980) 'The problem of closure in a *Carmen Perpetuum*: aspects of thematic recapitulation in Ovid's *Metamorphoses* 15', *Grazer Beiträge* 9: 123–32.
(1983) *The death of Procris: 'amor' and the hunt in Ovid's Metamorphoses*. Rome.
Deichgräber, K. (1971) 'Überlegungen zu den Gedichten und Gedichtbüchern der Neoteriker', *Hermes* 99: 46–70.
Dench, E. (1995) *From barbarians to new men*. Oxford.
Desmond. M. (1993) 'When Dido reads Vergil: gender and intertextuality in Ovid's *Heroides* 7', *Helios* 20: 56–68.
Dewar, M. (1991) *Statius Thebaid IX*. Oxford.
Diggle, J. (2005) 'Tibullus 2.1.45–6 and "amplificatory pleonasm"', *CQ* 55: 642–643.
Dippel, M. (1990) *Die Darstellung des trojanischen Krieges in Ovids Metamorphosen*. Frankfurt am Main.
Doblhofer, E. (1959–60) '*Ovidius Urbanus:* eine Studie zum Humor in Ovids *Metamorphosen*', *Philologus* 103–4: 63–91, 223–35.
Domenicucci, P. (1991) 'La caratterizzazione astrale delle apoteosi di Romulo ed Ersilia nelle Metamorfosi di Ovidio', in I. Gallo and L. Nicastri, eds. *Cultura poesia ideologia nell'opera di Ovidio* (Naples) 221–8.
Döpp, S. (1968) *Vergilischer Einfluss im Werk Ovids*. Diss. Munich.
(1991) 'Vergilrezeption in der Ovidischen *Aeneis*', *RhM* 134: 327–46.
Duckworth, G. E. (1969) *Vergil and classical hexameter poetry*. Ann Arbor.
Due, O. S. (1974) *Changing forms: studies in the Metamorphoses of Ovid*. Copenhagen.
Dury-Moyaers, G. (1981) *Énée et Lavinium*. Brussels.
Edmunds, L. (2001) *Intertextuality and the reading of Roman poetry*. Baltimore and London.
Eller, H. M. (1938) 'Studies in *apo koinou* in Ovid'. Diss. Chicago.
Ellsworth, J. D. (1986) 'Ovid's "Aeneid" reconsidered (*Met.* 13.623–14.608)', *Vergilius* 32: 27–32.
(1988a) 'The episode of the Sibyl in Ovid's *Metamorphoses.*', in R. Hadlich and J. D. Ellsworth, eds. *East meets West* (Honolulu) 47–55.
(1988b) 'Ovid's "Odyssey": *Met.* 13.623–14.608', *Mnem.* 41: 333–40.
Ernout, A. (1957) *Philologica*, vol. II. Paris.
Esposito, P. (1994) *La narrazione inverosimile: aspetti dell'epica ovidiana*. Naples.
Evans, J. (1992) *The art of persuasion*. Ann Arbor.
Fabre-Serris, J. (1986) 'La narration illustrée: étude de quelques digressions dans l'Énéide ovidienne', *REL* 64: 172–84.

Fantazzi, C. (1976) 'The revindication of Roman myth in the Pomona-Vertumnus tale', in N. Barbu, E. Dobroiu and M. Nasta, eds. *Ovidianum. Acta conuentus omnium gentium Ouidianis studiis fouendis* (Bucharest) 283–93.

Fantham, E. (1990) '*Nymphas . . . e navibus esse*: Decorum and poetic fiction in *Aen.* 9.77–122 and 10.215–59', *CP* 85: 102–19.

(1993) '*Sunt quibus in pluris ius est transire figuras*: Ovid's self-transformers in the *Metamorphoses*', *CW* 87: 21–36.

(1998) *Ovid Fasti Book IV*. Cambridge Greek and Latin Classics. Cambridge.

Faraone, C. (1999) *Ancient Greek love magic*. Cambridge, MA.

Farrell, J. (1992) 'Dialogue of genres in Ovid's lovesong of Polyphemus (*Met.* 13.719–897)' *AJP* 113: 235–68.

Fauth, W. (1966) *Aphrodite Parakyptusa: Untersuchungen zum Erscheinungsbild der vorderasiatischen Dea Prospiciens*. Abhandlungen der Geistes und Sozial wissenschaftlichen Klasse 6. Mainz, Wiesbaden.

(1980) '*Venena amoris*: die Motive des Liebezaubers und der erotischen Verzauberung in der augusteischen Dichtung', *Maia* 32: 265–82.

(1999) *Carmen magicum: das Thema der Magie in der Dichtung der römischen Kaiserzeit*. Frankfurt am Main.

Fedeli, P. (1965) *Properzio Elegie Libro IV, Testo critico e Commento*. Bari.

(1980) *Sesto Properzio. Il primo libro delle elegie*. Florence.

(1983) *Catullus' Carmen 61*. Amsterdam.

(1985) *Properzio. Il libro terzo delle Elegie*. Bari.

Feeney, D. (1984) 'The reconciliations of Juno', *CQ* 34: 179–94.

(1991) *The gods in epic*. Oxford.

(1992) '*Si licet et fas est:* Ovid's *Fasti* and the problem of free speech under the Principate', in A. Powell, ed. *Roman Poetry and Propaganda* (Bristol) 1–25.

(1998) *Literature and religion at Rome: cultures, contexts, and beliefs*. Cambridge.

(1999) '*Mea tempora*: patterning of time in the *Metamorphoses*', in Hardie, Barchiesi, and Hinds 1999: 13–30.

(2007) *Caesar's calendar: ancient time and the beginning of history*. Berkeley and London.

Flory, M. (1995) 'The deification of Roman women', *AHB* 9: 127–34.

Forbes Irving, P. M. C. (1990) *Metamorphosis in Greek myths*. Oxford.

Fordyce, C. J. (1977) *Virgil Aeneid VII–VIII*. Bristol.

Forsythe, G. (1994) *The historian L. Calpurnius Piso Frugi and the Roman annalistic tradition*. Lanham, New York, London.

Fowler, W. W. (1908) *The Roman festivals of the period of the Republic*. London.

Fraccaro, P. (1907) *Studi Varroniani*. Padua. Reprinted Rome, 1966.

Frécaut, J.-M. (1972) *L'esprit et l'humeur chez Ovide*. Grenoble.

Frederiksen, M. (1984) *Campania*. Ed. N. Purcell (British School at Rome). London.

Frier, B. W. (1979) *Libri annales pontificum maximorum: the origins of the annalistic tradition*. Rome.

Frings, I. (2005) *Das Spiel mit eigenen Texten. Wiederholung und Selbstzitat bei Ovid*. Munich.

Fulminante, F. (2000) '*Tumulo/heroon* di *Indiges*/Enea a Lavinio (Pratica di Mare)', in Carandini and Cappelli 2000: 213–15.
Fusco, U. (2000) 'Ricostruzione dell'esedra occidentale del Foro di Augusto', in Carandini and Cappelli 2000: 223–4.
Gagé, J. (1930) 'Romulus–Augustus', *Mélanges d'archéologie et d'histoire: école francaise de Rome* 47: 138–81.
Galasso, L. (2006) 'L'edizione di Richard Tarrant delle Metamorfosi di Ovidio: una discussione', *MD* 56: 105–36.
Gale, M. (1997) 'The shield of Turnus (*Aeneid* 7.783–92)', *G&R*: 44: 176–196.
Galinsky, G. K. (1969a) *Aeneas, Sicily, and Rome*. Princeton.
(1969b) 'The triumph theme in the Augustan elegy', *WS* n.s. 3: 75–107.
(1972) *The Herakles theme*. Oxford.
(1975) *Ovid's Metamorphoses: an introduction to the basic aspects*. Berkeley and Los Angeles.
(1976) 'L'eneide di Ovidio (met. XIII 623-XIV 608) ed il carattere delle Metamorfosi', *Maia* 28: 3–18.
(1983) 'Aeneas in Latium: Archäologie, Mythos und Geschichte', in V. Pöschl, ed. *2000 Jahre Vergil: ein Symposion* (Wiesbaden) 37–62.
(1996) *Augustan culture*. Princeton.
(1999) 'Ovid's *Metamorphoses* and Augustan cultural thematics', in Hardie, Barchiesi, and Hinds 1999: 103–111.
Gassner, J. (1972) *Kataloge in römischen Epos: Vergil, Ovid, Lucan*. Augsberg.
Gee, E. (2000) *Ovid, Aratus and Augustus. Astronomy in Ovid's Fasti*. Cambridge.
Gentilcore, R. (1995) 'The landscape of desire: the tale of Pomona and Vertumnus in Ovid's *Metamorphoses*', *Phoenix* 49:110–20.
Gibson, R. (2003) *Ovid: Ars Amatoria Book 3*. Cambridge.
Gieseking, K. (1965) *Die Rahmenerzählung in Ovids Metamorphosen*. Tübingen.
Glenn, J. (1972) 'Virgil's Polyphemus', *G&R* 19: 47–59.
Goldhill, S. (1991) *The poet's voice*. Cambridge.
Goold, G. P. (1965) '*Amatoria critica*', *HSCP* 69: 1–107.
(1966) '*Noctes Propertianae*', *HSCP* 71: 59–106.
(1967) Review article. *AJP* 88: 120–22.
Gosling, A. (2002) 'Sending up the founder; Ovid and the apotheosis of Romulus', *AClass* 45: 51–69.
Gow, A. S. F. and D. Page (1965) *The Greek anthology: Hellenistic epigrams*. Cambridge.
Gow, A. S. F. and A. F. Scholfield (1953) *Nicander: the poems and poetical fragments*. Repr. New Hampshire 1988.
Gradel, I. (2002) *Emperor worship and Roman religion*. Oxford.
Graf, F. (1988) 'Ovide, les Métamorphoses et la véracité du mythe', in C. Calame, ed. *Métamorphoses du mythe en Grèce ancienne* (Geneva) 57–70.
(1997) *Magic in the ancient world*. Cambridge, MA.
(2002) 'Myth in Ovid', in Hardie 2002b: 108–121.
Grandazzi, A. (1986) 'La localization d'Albe', *MEFRA* 98: 47–90.

Granobs, R. (1997) *Studien zur Darstellung römischer Geschichte in Ovids Metamorphosen.* Frankfurt am Main.
Gratwick, A. S. (1979) '*Quam lepide lexeis compostae. . .*: Catullus 64.174', *CQ* 29:112–16.
Green, C. (2007) *Roman religion and the cult of Diana at Aricia.* Cambridge.
Green, S. (2004) *Ovid, Fasti 1: a commentary*. Leiden and Boston.
Grimal, P. (1969) *Les jardins Romains*. Paris.
Gross, N. P. (1985) *Amatory persuasion in antiquity*. Newark, London, and Toronto.
Gruen, E. (1990) *Studies in Greek culture and Roamn policy.* Leiden and New York.
(1992) *Culture and national identity in Republican Rome.* Ithaca.
Guthmüller, H.-B. (1964) *Beobachtungen zum Aufbau der Met. Ovids*. Diss. Marburg.
Guttmann, K. (1890) *Sogenanntes instrumentales ab bei Ovid.* Dortmund.
Hänninen, M.-L. (1999) 'Juno Regina and the Roman matrons', in P. Setälä and L. Savunen, eds. *Female networks and the public sphere in Roman society* (Rome) 29–38.
Hardie, A. (forthcoming) '"Canens" (Ovid *Metamorphoses* 14.320–434)', *SIFC.*
Hardie, P. R. (1986) *Virgil's Aeneid: cosmos and imperium.* Oxford.
(1987a) 'Aeneas and the omen of the swans (Verg. *Aen.* 1. 393–400)', *CP* 82: 145–50.
(1987b) 'Ships and ship-names in the Aeneid', in Michael Whitby, P. Hardie, and Mary Whitby, eds. *Homo viator: classical essays for John Bramble* (Bristol) 163–71.
(1990) 'Ovid's Theban history: the first Anti-*Aeneid*?' *CQ* 40: 224–35.
(1991) 'The Janus episode in Ovid's *Fasti*', *MD* 26: 47–64.
(1992) 'Augustan poets and the mutability of Rome', in A. Powell, ed. *Roman poetry and propaganda in the age of Augustus* (London) 59–82.
(1993) *The epic successors of Virgil: a study in the dynamics of a tradition.* Cambridge.
(1994) *Virgil Aeneid Book IX.* Cambridge Greek and Latin Classics. Cambridge.
(1997a) 'Closure in Latin epic', in D. Roberts, F. Dunn, and D. Fowler, eds. *Classical closure* (Princeton) 139–62.
(1997b) 'Questions of authority: the invention of tradition in Ovid *Metamorphoses* 15', in T. Habinek and A. Schiesaro, eds. *The Roman cultural revolution*, (Cambridge) 182–98.
(2002a) *Ovid's poetics of illusion.* Cambridge.
(2002b) *The Cambridge Companion to Ovid.* Cambridge.
(2002c) 'Another look at Virgil's Ganymede', in T. P. Wiseman, ed. *Classics in Progress* (Oxford) 333–61.
(2002d) 'The historian in Ovid. The Roman history of *Metamorphoses* 14–15', in D. S. Levene and D. P. Nelis, eds. *Clio and the Poets* (Leiden) 191–209.
(2004) 'Ovidian middles' in S. Kyriakidis and F. de Martino, eds. *Middles in Latin Poetry* (Bari) 151–82.
(forthcoming) *Commentary on Ovid Metamorphoses* 13–15. Fondazione Lorenzo Valla.
Hardie, P. R., A. Barchiesi, and S. Hinds, eds. (1999) *Ovidian transformations.* Cambridge.
Harmon, D. P. (1986) 'Religion in the Latin Elegists', *ANRW* II.16.3: 1909–73.
Harrison, E. L. (1986) 'Achaemenides' unfinished account: Vergil, *Aen.* 3.588–691', *CP* 81: 146–7.

Harrison, S. J. (1991) *Vergil Aeneid 10*. Oxford.
Haupt, M. (1967) *Opuscula*, vol. II. Hildesheim.
Heinze, R. (1919) *Ovids elegische Erzählung*. Leipzig.
Hellegouarc'h, J. (1964) *Le monosyllabe dans l'hexamètre latin*. Paris.
Helzle, M. (1989) *Publii Ovidii Nasonis Epistularum ex Ponto liber IV. A commentary on poems 1 to 7 and 16*. Hildesheim, Zürich, and New York.
Herescu, N. I., ed. (1958) *Ovidiana: recherches sur Ovide publiées à l'occasion du bimillénaire de la naissance du poète*. Paris.
Heubeck, A. and A. Hoekstra (1989) *A commentary on Homer's Odyssey*, vol. II. Oxford.
Herbert-Brown, G. (1944) *Ovid and the Fasti*. Oxford.
Heyworth, S. J. (1994) 'Some allusions to Callimachus in Latin poetry', *MD* 33: 51–79.
Hill, D. E. (1973) 'The Thessalian trick', *RhM* 116: 221–38.
Hinds, S. E. (1987a) *The metamorphosis of Persephone: Ovid and the self-conscious Muse*. Cambridge.
(1987b) 'Generalizing about Ovid', in A. J. Boyle, ed. *The Imperial Muse. Ramus essays on Roman literature of the Empire* (= *Ramus* 16) (Victoria) 4–31.
(1992a) '*Arma* in Ovid's *Fasti* part 1: genre and mannerism', *Arethusa* 25: 81–112.
(1992b) '*Arma* in Ovid's *Fasti* part 2: genre, Romulean Rome and Augustan ideology', *Arethusa* 25: 113–53.
(1993) 'Medea in Ovid: scenes from the life of an intertextual heroine', *MD* 30: 9–47.
(1998) *Allusion and intertext: dynamics of appropriation in Roman poetry*. Cambridge.
(1999) 'After exile: time and teleology from *Metamorphose* to *Ibis*' in Hardie, Barchiesi, Hinds 1999: 48–67.
(2003) 'Ovid', in S. Hornbower and A. Spawforth, eds. *The Oxford Classical Dictionary*. Revised 3rd edn (Oxford) 1084–7.
Hofmann, J. B. (1951) *Lateinische Umgangssprache*. 3rd edn. Heidelberg.
Holland, L. (1935) 'Place names and heroes in the *Aeneid*', *AJP* 56:202–15.
Hollenburger-Rusch, C. (2001) *Liquitur in lacrimas : zur Verwendung des Tränenmotivs in den Metamorphosen Ovids*. Hildesheim and New York.
Holzberg, N. (1998) '*Ter quinque uolumina* as *carmen perpetuum*: the division into books in Ovid's *Metamorphoses*', *MD* 40: 77–98.
(1999) 'Apollos erste Liebe und die Folgen. Ovids Daphne-Erzählung als Programm für Werk und Wirkung', *Gymnasium* 106: 317–34.
Hopkinson, N. (1982) 'Juxtaposed prosodic variants in Greek and Latin Poetry', *Glotta* 60: 162–78.
Horsfall, N. (1974) 'Virgil's Roman chronography: a reconsideration', *CQ* 24: 111–15.
(1985) 'Illusion and reality in Latin topographical writing', *G&R* 22: 197–208.
(1986) 'The Aeneas-legend and the *Aeneid*', *Vergilius* 32: 8–17.
(1987) 'The Aeneas-legend from Homer to Virgil', in J. N. Bremmer and N. M. Horsfall, eds. *Roman myth and mythography* (London) 12–24.

(1991) '*Externi duces*', *RFIC* 119: 188–92.
ed. (1995) *A companion to the study of Virgil.* New York.
(2000) *Virgil, Aeneid 7: a commentary.* Leiden, Boston, and Köln.
(2003) *Virgil, Aeneid 11: a commentary.* Leiden, and Boston, and Köln.
(2006) *Virgil, Aeneid 3: a commentary.* Leiden, and Boston, and Köln.
Housman, A. E. (1972a) 'Greek nouns in Latin poetry from Lucretius to Juvenal', in J. Diggle and F. R. D. Goodyear, eds. *The classical papers of A. E. Housman* II (Cambridge) 817–37.
(1972b) '*Ovidiana*', in J. Diggle and F. R. D. Goodyear, eds, *The classical papers of A. E. Housman* III (Cambridge) 917–39.
Hunter, R. (1989) *Apollonius of Rhodes: Argonautica Book III.* Cambridge Greek and Latin Classics. Cambridge.
Hutchinson, G. O. (2002) 'The new Posidippus and Latin poetry', *ZPE* 138: 1–10.
(2006) 'The metamorphosis of metamorphosis: P. Oxy. 4711 and Ovid', *ZPE* 155: 71–84.
(2007) 'The monster and the monologue: Polyphemus from Homer to Ovid', in P. J. Finglass, C. Collard, and N. J. Richardson, eds. *Hesperos* (Oxford) 22–39.
Jameson, M. H. and I. Malkin (1998) 'Latinos and the Greeks', *Athenaeum* 86: 477–85.
Jocelyn, H. D. (1989) 'Romulus and the *di genitales*', in J. Diggle, J. B. Hall, and H. D. Jocelyn, eds. *Studies in Latin literature and its tradition in honor of C. O. Brink* (Cambridge) 39–65.
Johnson, P. J. (1996) 'Constructions of Venus in Ovid's *Metamorphoses* V', *Arethusa* 29: 125–49.
Johnson, W. R. (1997) 'Vertumnus in love', *CP* 92: 367–75.
Jones, P. (2001) 'Aversion reversed: Ovid's Pomona and her Roman models" *CW* 94: 361–76.
(2005) *Reading rivers in Roman literature and culture.* Lanham.
Jouteur, I. (2001) *Jeux de genre dans les Métamorphoses d'Ovide.* Louvain.
Junod, H. (1991) '*Barbarus ensis* (*Met.* 14.574) ou les ambiguités de l'*Enéide* ovidienne', *Études de Lettres*: 43–75.
Kaiser, E. (1964) 'Odyssee-Szenen als Topoi', *MH* 21: 197–224.
Kambylis, A. (1965) *Die Dichterweihe und ihre Symbolik.* Heidelberg.
Kaster, R. (2005) *Emotion, restraint, and community in ancient Rome.* Oxford.
Keith, A. (1992) *The play of fictions: studies in Ovid's Metamorphoses Book 2.* Ann Arbor.
(2002) 'Sources and genres in Ovid *Metamorphoses* 1–5', in Boyd 2002: 235–70.
Kennedy, D. (1982) 'Gallus and the *Culex*', *CQ* n.s. 32: 377–82.
Kenney, E. J. (1958) '*Nequitiae poeta*', in Herescu 1958: 201–9.
(1959) 'Notes on Ovid: II ', *CQ* 9: 240–60.
(1970) 'Notes on Ovid: III ', *HSCP* 74: 169–85.
(1971) *Lucretius De Rerum Natura Book III.* Cambridge Greek and Latin Classics. Cambridge.
(1972) Review of Bömer's commentary on *Met.* 1–3. *CR* 22: 38–42.
(1973) 'The style of the *Metamorphoses*', in J. W. Binns, ed. *Ovid* (London) 116–53.

(1976) '*Ovidius prooemians*', *PCPS* 22: 46–53.
(1982) 'Ovid', in E. J. Kenney and W. V. Clausen, eds. *The Cambridge History of Classical Literature.* II *Latin literature* (Cambridge) 420–57.
(1986) Introduction and commentary, *Ovid's Metamorphoses*. Translated by A. D. Melville. Oxford.
(1988) Review of Bömer's commentary on *Met.* 14–15. *CR* 38: 247–9.
(1993) '*Ovidiana*', *CQ* 43: 458–67.
(1996) *Ovid Heroides XVI–XXI* (C.G.L.C.), Cambridge.
(1999a) 'Greek feminines in *-ias*: an Ovidian predilection', *CQ* 49: 330–32.
(1999b) '*Vt erat nouator*: anomaly, innovation and genre in Ovid', in Adams and Mayer 1999: 399–414.
(2001a) '"*Est deus in nobis . . .*": Medea meets her maker', in T. D. Papanghelis and A. Rengakos, eds. *A Companion to Apollonius Rhodius* (Leiden, Boston, Köln) 261–83.
(2001b) 'Textual notes on Ovid, *Metamorphoses* 7–9', *CQ* 51: 545–50.
(2002) 'Ovid's language and style', in Boyd 2002: 27–89.
(2003) 'Vain repetitions? Notes on the text of Ovid, *Ars Amatoria* 2.593 and *Metamorphoses* 14.240', *CQ* 53: 619–20.
(forthcoming). '*Metamorphoses*', in P. E. Knox, ed. *A Companion to Ovid.*
Kidd, D. (1997) *Aratus Phaenomena*. Cambridge.
King, H. (1986) 'Tithonos and the tettix', *Arethusa* 19: 15–35.
Kinsey, T. E. (1979) 'The Achaemenides episode in Virgil's *Aeneid* III', *Latomus* 38: 110–24.
Knauer, G. N. (1964) *Die Aeneis und Homer*. Göttingen.
Knox, P. E. (1986a) *Ovid's Metamorphoses and the traditions of Augustan poetry*. Cambridge.
(1986b) 'Adjectives in *-osus* and Latin poetic diction', *Glotta* 64: 90–101.
(1995) *Ovid Heroides. Select Epistles* (C.G.L.C.), Cambridge.
(2002) 'Representing the Great Mother to Augustus', in G. Herbert-Brown, ed. *Ovid's Fasti: historical readings at its Bimillenium* (Oxford) 155–74.
Kroll, W. (1988) 'La lingua poetica romana', in A. Lunelli, ed. *La lingua poetica Latina.* 3rd edn (Bologna) 1–66.
Kyriakidis, S. (2002) 'The Alban kings in the *Metamorphoses:* an Ovidian catalogue and its historiographical models', in D. S. Levene and D. P. Nelis, eds. *Clio and the Poets* (Leiden) 211–29.
Lafaye, G. (1904) *Les Métamorphoses d'Ovide et leurs modèles grecs*. Paris.
Lamacchia, R. (1960) 'Ovidio interprete di Virgilio', *Maia* 12: 310–20.
(1969) 'Precisazioni su alcuni aspetti dell'epica Ovidiana', *Atene e Roma* 14: 1–20.
Landolfi, L. (2003) '*Posse loqui eripitur* (Ov. *Met.* 2.483). Perdita di parola, perdita d'identità nelle *Metamorfosi*', in L. Landolfi and P. Monella, eds. *Ars adeo latet arte sua: riflessioni sull' intertestualità ovidiana* (Palermo) 29–58.
Laroche, R. A. (1982) 'The Alban king-list in Dionysios I 70–7', *Historia*: 133–55.
Latte, K. (1960) *Römische Religionsgeschichte*. Munich.
Lattimore, R. (1965) *The Odyssey of Homer*. Translation. New York.
Lausberg, M. (1982) *Das Einzeldistichon: Studien zum antiken Epigramm*. Munich.

Leumann, M. (1945) 'Der lateinische Genetiv Achilli', *MH* 2: 237–58.
(1959) *Kleine Schriften*. Zürich.
Liberman, G. (2004) 'Observations sur le texte des Métamorphoses d'Ovide', *RPh* 78: 57–90.
Lieberg, G. (1970) 'Apotheose und Unsterblichkeit in Ovids Metamorphosen', in *Silvae: Festschrift für E. Zinn* (Tübingen) 125–35.
Lindheim, S. (1998) 'I am dressed, therefore I am? Vertumnus in Propertius 4.2 and in *Metamorphoses* 14.622–771', *Ramus* 27: 27–38.
Liou-Gille, B. (1980) *Cultes 'héroiques' romains*. Paris.
Lissarrague F. (1990) 'The sexual life of satyrs', in D. Halperin, J. Winkler, and F. Zeitlin, eds. *Before sexuality: the construction of erotic experience in the ancient Greek world* (Princeton) 53–81.
Littlefield, D. (1965) 'Pomona and Vertumnus: a fruition of history in Ovid's *Metamorphoses*', *Arion* 4: 465–73.
Littlewood, A. R. (1968) 'The symbolism of the apple in Greek and Roman literature', *HSCP* 72: 147–81.
Lloyd, R. B. (1957) '*Aeneid* III and the Aeneas legend', *AJP* 78: 382–400.
Loehr, J. (1996) *Ovids Mehrfacherklärungen in der Tradition aitiologischen Dichtens*. Stuttgart and Leipzig.
Löfstedt, E. 1942, 1956. *Syntactica. Studien und Beiträge zur historischen Syntax des Lateins*. I *Über einige Grundfragen der lateinischen Nominalsyntax*. 2nd edn. Lund, Leipzig, and London. II *Syntaktische-stilistische Gesichtspunkte und Probleme*. Lund.
Luck, G. (1982) 'Notes on the text of Ovid's *Metamorphoses*', *AJP* 103: 47–61.
(2005) 'Naugerius' notes on Ovid's *Metamorphoses*', *ExClass* 9: 155-224.
(2006) 'Missing letters in Ovid's *Metamorphoses*?' *Myrtia* 21: 113–21.
Ludwig, W. (1965) *Struktur und Einheit der Metamorphosen Ovids*. Berlin.
Lundström, S. (1980) *Ovids Metamorphosen und die Politik des Kaisers*. Uppsala.
Lunelli, A. (1988) *La lingua poetica Latina*. 3rd edn. Bologna.
Lyne, R. O. A. M. (1978) *Ciris : a poem attributed to Vergil*. Cambridge.
McCartney, E. S. (1960) 'Vivid ways of indicating uncountable numbers', *CP* 55: 79–89.
Mckay, A. G. (1970) *Vergil's Italy*. Greenwich, CN.
Mackay, T. S. (1975) 'Three poets observe Picus', *AJP* 96: 272–5.
Maltby, R. (1993) 'The limits of etymologizing', *Aeuum Antiquum* 6: 257–75.
(1999) 'Technical language in Tibullus', *Emerita* 67: 231–49.
McKeown, J. C. (1979) 'Augustan elegy and mime', *PCPS* 25: 71–84.
(ed.) (1987) *Ovid: Amores* Vol. I. *Text and Prolegomena*. Liverpool.
(1989) *Ovid: Amores* Vol. II. *A commentary on Book One*. Leeds.
(1998) *Ovid: Amores* Vol. III. *A commentary on Book Two*. Leeds.
Malkin, I. (1998) *The returns of Odysseus. Colonization and ethnicity*. Berkeley, Los Angeles, and London.
Maltby, R. (2002) *Tibullus Elegies*. Francis Cairns, Cambridge.
Marouzeau, J. (1958) 'Un procédé Ovidien', in Herescu 1958: 101–5.

Marquis, E. C. (1974) 'Vertumnus in Propertius 4.2', *Hermes* 102: 491–500.
Maurach, G. (1995) *Lateinische Dichtersprache*. Darmstadt.
Mayer, R. (1981) *Lucan Civil War VIII*. Warminster.
Meister, K. (1916) *Lateinisch-Griechische Eigennamen*. Leipzig and Berlin.
Merli, E. (2000) *Arma canant alii: materia epica e narrazione elegiaca nei Fasti di Ovidio*. Florence.
Michalopoulos, A. (2001) *Ancient etymologies in Ovid's Metamorphoses: a commented lexicon*. Leeds.
Miller, J. (1982) 'Callimachus and the Augustan aetiological elegy', *ANRW* II.30.1: 371–417.
(1993) 'Ovidian allusion and the vocabulary of memory', *MD* 30: 153–64.
Monteleone, C. (1979) 'Cornelio Gallo tra Ila e le Driadi (Virgilio, Properzio e una controversia letteraria)', *Latomus* 38: 28–53.
Monti, R. (1994) 'The identification of Vergil's cave of the Cumaean Sibyl in *Aeneid* 6', *Vergilius* 40: 19–34.
Moorton, R. (1988) 'The genealogy of Latinus in Vergil's *Aeneid*', *TAPA* 118: 253–9.
Morison, B. (1995) 'Two notes on Ovid, *Met.* XIV, 196 and 211', *Latomus* 54:106–9.
Myerowitz, M. (1985) *Ovid's games of love*. Detroit.
Myers, K. S. (1994a) *Ovid's causes: cosmogony and aetiology in the Metamorphoses*. Ann Arbor.
(1994b) '*Ultimus ardor:* Pomona and Vertumnus in Ovid's *Met.* 14.623–771', *CJ* 89: 225–50.
(1999) 'The metamorphosis of a poet: recent work on Ovid', *JRS* 89: 190–204.
(2004–5) 'Italian myth in *Metamorphoses* 14', *Hermathena* 177–8: 91–112.
Nagle, B. R. (1988a) 'Erotic pursuit and narrative seduction in Ovid's *Metamorphoses*', *Ramus* 17: 32–51.
(1988b) 'Ovid's "reticent" heroes', *Helios* 15: 23–39.
(1988c) 'A trio of love-triangles in Ovid's *Metamorphoses*', *Arethusa* 21: 75–98
Navarro Antolín, F. (1996) *Lygdamus*. Leiden, New York, and Köln.
Nelis, D. (2001) *Vergil's Aeneid and the Argonautica of Apollonius Rhodius*. Leeds.
Newlands, C. (2005) 'Ovid', in J. M. Foley, ed. *A companion to ancient epic* (Oxford) 476–91.
Nicoll, W. S. M. (1980) 'Cupid, Apollo, and Daphne (Ovid, *Metamorphoses* 1.452ff.)', *CQ* 30: 174–82.
Nisbet, R. G. M. and N. Rudd (2004) *A commentary on Horace: Odes Book III*. Oxford.
Nock, A. D. (1972) *Essays on religion and the ancient world* I . Cambridge, MA.
Norden, E. (1913) *Agnostos Theos*. Leipzig.
(1926) *P. Vergilius Maro Aeneis Buch VI* ^{6}. Leipzig and Berlin.
O'Connor, E. M. (1989) *Symbolum salacitatis: a study of the god Priapus as a literary character*. Frankfurt am Main, Bern, New York, Paris.
Ogilvie, R. M. (1970) *A commentary on Livy Books I–V*. Repr. with addenda. Oxford.
O'Hara, J. J. (1990) *Death and the optimistic prophecy in Vergil's Aeneid*. Princeton.
(1996a) *True names. Vergil and the Alexandrian tradition of etymological wordplay*. Ann Arbor.

(1996b) 'Vergil's best reader? Ovidian commentary on Vergilian etymological wordplay', *CJ* 91: 255–76.

(2001) 'Callimachean influence on Vergilian etymological wordplay', *CJ* 96: 369–400.

Oliensis, E. (1991) 'Canidia, Canicula, and the decorum of Horace's *Epodes*', *Arethusa* 24: 107–138.

Otis, B. (1970) *Ovid as an epic poet*. Cambridge.

Otto, A. (1890) *Die Sprichwörter und sprichwörtlichen Redensarten der Römer*. Leipzig.

Owen, S. G. (1924) *P. Ovidi Nasonis Tristium liber secundus*. Oxford.

Papaioannou, S. (2000) 'Virgilian Diomedes revisited: the re-interpretation of the *Iliad*', *Mnem.* 53: 193–217.

(2005) *Epic succession and dissension*. Berlin.

(2007) *Redesigning Achilles: 'recycling' the epic cycle in the 'Little Iliad' (Ovid, Metamorphoses 12.1–13.622)*. Berlin and New York.

Papathomopoulos, M. (1968) *Antoninus Liberalis: Les Métamorphoses*. Paris.

Parke, H. W. (1988) *Sibyls and Sibylline prophecy in classical antiquity*. London.

Parker, H. (1997) *Greek gods in Italy in Ovid's Fasti*. Lampeter.

Parry, H. (1964) 'Ovid's *Metamorphoses*: violence in a pastoral landscape', *TAPA* 95: 268–82.

Paschalis, M. (1997) *Virgil's Aeneid: semantic relations and proper names*. Oxford.

Pearce, T. E. V. (1966) 'The enclosing word order in the Latin hexameter. I, II', *CQ* 16: 140–71, 298–320.

Pease, A. S. M. (1920) *M. Tulli Ciceronis De divinatione: liber primus*. Illinois studies in languages and literature, v. 6.

(1935) *Publi Vergili Maronis Aeneidos, liber quartus*. Repr. Darmstadt 1967.

(1955–8) *Tulli Ciceronis De natura deorum*. Repr. New York 1979.

Petersmann, M. (1976) *Die Apotheosen in den Metamorphosen Ovids*. Diss. Graz.

Philips, C. R. (1992) 'Roman religion and literary studies of Ovid's *Fasti*', *Arethusa* 25: 55–80.

Pianezzola, E. (1991) *Ovidio. L'arte di amare*, with commentary by G. Baldo, L. Cristante, E. Pianezzola. Milan.

Pichon, R. (1966) *Index verborum amatoriorum*. Hildesheim (=*De sermone amatorio apud Latinos elegiarum scriptores*, Diss. Paris [1902]) 75–303.

Platnauer, M. (1951) *Latin elegiac verse*. Cambridge.

Porte, D. (1981) 'Romulus-Quirinus, prince et dieu, dieu des princes. Étude sur le personage de Quirinus et sur son évolution, des origins à Auguste', *ANRW* 2.17.1: 300–42.

(1985a) *L'étiologie religieuse dans les Fastes d'Ovide*. Paris.

(1985b) 'L'idée romaine et la métamorphose', in J. M. Frécault and D. Porte, eds. *Journées Ovidiennes de Parméne. Actes du Colloque sur Ovide* (Brussels) 175–98.

Possanza, M. (2002) 'Penelope in Ovid's *Metamorphoses* 14.671', *AJP* 123: 89–94.

Potter, D. S. (1990) *Prophecy and history in the crisis of the Roman Empire: a historical commentary on the Thirteenth Sibylline Oracle*. Oxford.

(1994) *Prophets and emperors*. Cambridge, MA.

Poucet, J. (1983) 'Un culte d'Énée dans la region Lavinate', in H. Zehnacker and G. Hentz, eds. *Hommages à Robert Schilling* (Paris) 187–201.

Price, S. (1987) 'From noble funeral to divine cult: the consecration of Roman emperors', in D. Cannadine and S. Price, eds. *Rituals of royalty* (Cambridge) 56–105.

Putnam, M. C. J. (1967) 'The shrine of Vortumnus', *AJA* 71: 177–9.

(1995) *Virgil's Aeneid.* Chapel Hill and London.

Quint, D. (1993) *Epic and empire: politics and generic form from Virgil to Milton.* Princeton.

Radke, G. (1977) '*Nerio.* Beobachtungen zu einem Götternamen', *MH* 34: 191–8.

(1979) *Die Götter Altitaliens.* Fontes et Commentationes, Universität Münster, Heft 3. Münster.

(1981) 'Quirinus. Eine kritische Überprüfung der Überlieferung und ein Versuch', *ANRW* 2.17.1: 276–99.

(1987) *Zur Entwicklung der Gottesvorstellung und der Gottesverehrung in Rom.* Darmstadt.

Ramírez de Verger, A. (2006) 'A new edition of Ovid's *Metamorphoses*', in C. Deroux, ed. *Studies in Latin literature and Roman history* 13 (Brussels) 315–34.

Ramminger, J. (1991) 'Imitation and allusion in the Achaemenides scene (Vergil, *Aen.* 3.588–691)', *AJP* 112: 53–72.

Ramsby, T. (2005) 'Striving for permanence: Ovid's funerary inscriptions', *CJ* 100: 365–92.

Reitz, C. (1999) 'Zur Funktion der Kataloge in Ovids Metamorphosen', in W. Schubert, ed. *Ovid Werk und Wirkung* 1 (Studien zur klassischen Philologie 100. Frankfurt am Main) 359–72.

Renehan, R. (1977) 'Compound-simplex verbal iteration in Plautus', *CP* 72: 243–8.

Richardson, L., Jr. (1992) *A new topographical dictionary of ancient Rome.* Baltimore.

Richlin, A. (1992) 'Reading Ovid's rapes', in A. Richlin, ed., *Pornography and representation in Greece and Rome* (Oxford) 158–79.

Ridgway, D. (1992) *The first western Greeks.* Cambridge.

Rieks, R. (1980) 'Zum Aufbau von Ovids Metamorphosen', *WJA* 6: 85–103.

Roller, L. (1999) *In search of god the mother: the cult of Anatolian Cybele.* Berkeley.

Rosati, G. P. (1983) *Narciso e Pigmalione. Illusione e spettacolo nelle Metamorfosi di Ovidio.* Florence.

(1996) *P. Ovidii Nasonis Heroidum epistulae XVIII–XIX : Leander Heroni, Hero Leandro.* Florence.

(1999) 'Form in motion: weaving the text in the *Metamorphoses*' in Hardie, Barchiesi, Hinds 1999: 240–53. Repr. in P. E. Knox, ed. *Oxford readings in Ovid* (Oxford 2006) 334–50.

(2002) 'Narrative techniques and narrative structures in the *Metamorphoses*', in Boyd 2002: 271–304.

Rosenmeyer, P. A. (1999) 'Tracing *medulla* as a *locus eroticus*', *Arethusa* 32: 19–47.

Rosivach, V. (1980) 'The genealogy of Latinus and the palace of Picus', *CQ* 30: 140–52.

Ross, D. O. (1975) *Backgrounds to Augustan poetry: Gallus, elegy, and Rome*. Cambridge.

Salzman, M. R. (1998) 'Deification in the *Fasti* and the *Metamorphoses*', in C. Deroux, ed. *Studies in Latin literature and Roman history* 9 (Brussels) 314–46.

Scheid, J. (2003) 'Cults, myths, and politics at the beginning of the Empire', in C. Ando, ed. *Roman religion* (Edinburgh) 117–40.

Schiesaro, A. (2002) 'Ovid and the professional discourses of scholarship, religion, rhetoric', in Hardie 2002b: 62–78.

Schilling, R. (1979) 'Le culte de l'*Indiges* a Lavinium', *REL* 57: 49–68.

Schmidt, E. A. (1991) *Ovids poetische Menschenwelt*. Heidelberg.

Scott, K. (1925) 'The identification of Augustus with Romulus-Quirinus', *TAPA* 56: 82–105.

Scullard, H. H. (1981) *Festivals and ceremonies of the Roman Republic*. New York.

Seaford, R. (1984) *Euripides Cyclops*. Oxford.

Segal, C. P. (1968) 'Circean temptations: Homer, Vergil, Ovid', *TAPhA* 99: 419–42.

(1969) *Landscape in Ovid's Metamorphoses*. Wiesbaden

(1997–8) 'Ovid's metamorphic bodies: art, gender, and violence in the *Metamorphoses*', *Arion* 3rd ser. 5(3): 9–41.

(2000) '*Tantum medicamina possunt*: la magie dans les *Métamorphoses* d'Ovide', in A. Moreau and J.-C. Turpin, eds. *La magie du monde latin au monde contemporain* (Montpelier) 45–70.

(2003) 'Black and white magic in Ovid's *Metamorphoses*', *Arion* 9: 1–34.

Shackleton Bailey, D. R. (1956) *Propertiana*. Cambridge.

(1981) 'Notes on Ovid's *Metamorphoses*', *Phoenix* 35: 332–7.

(1994) *Homoeoteleuton in Latin dactylic verse*. Stuttgart and Leipzig.

Sharrock, A. (1994) *Seduction and repetition in Ovid's Ars Amatoria 2*. Oxford.

Simmons, C. (1899) *P. Ouidii Nasonis Metamorphoseon XIII–IV*. London.

Simon, E. (1990) *Die Götter der Römer*. Munich.

Skutsch, O. (1968) *Studia Enniana*. London.

(1985) *The Annals of Q. Ennius*. Oxford.

Smith, R. A. (1997) *Poetic allusion and poetic embrace in Ovid and Virgil*. Ann Arbor.

Söderlind, M. (2000) 'The woman in the window: a motif in Ovid's *Metamorphoses*', in A. Jönsson and A. Piltz, eds. *Språkets speglingar. Festkrift till Birger Bergh* (Lund) 627–35.

Solodow, J. B. (1986) '*Raucae, tua cura, palumbes*: study of a poetic word order', *HSCP* 90: 129–53.

(1988) *The world of Ovid's Metamorphoses*. Chapel Hill.

Soubiran, J. (1966) *L'élision dans la poésie latine*. Paris.

(1969) Les hexamètres spondaiques à quadrisyllabe final', *GIF* 21: 329–49.

Stanford, W. B. (1963) *The Ulysses theme*. Oxford.

Stitz, M. (1962) *Ovid und Vergils Aeneis: Interpretation Met.* 13.623–14.608. Freiburg.

Suits, T. A. (1969) 'The Vertumnus elegy of Propertius', *TAPA* 100: 475–86.

Summers, K. (1996) 'Lucretius' Roman Cybele', in E. Lane, ed. *Cybele, Attis and related cults: essays in memory of M. J. Vermaseren* (Leiden) 337–66.

Tarrant, R. J. (1976) *Seneca Agamemnon*. Cambridge.

(1982) 'Editing Ovid's *Metamorphoses:* problems and possibilities', *CP* 77: 342–60.

(1989a) 'The reader as author: collaborative interpolation in Latin poetry', in J. N. Grant, ed. *Editing Greek and Latin texts* (New York) 121–62.

(1989b) 'Silver threads among the gold: a problem in the text of Ovid's *Metamorphoses*', *ICS* 14: 103–17.

(1995) 'Ovid and the failure of rhetoric', in D. Innes, H. Hine, and C. Pelling, eds. *Ethics and rhetoric* (Oxford) 63–74.

(2000) 'The soldier in the garden and other intruders in Ovid's *Metamorphoses*', *HSCP* 100: 425–38.

(2002) 'Ovid and ancient literary history', in Hardie 2002b: 13–33.

(2005) 'Roads not taken: untold stories in Ovid's *Metamorphoses*', *MD* 54: 65–90.

Tavenner, E. (1916) 'Three as a magic number in Latin literature', *TAPA* 47: 117–43.

Theodorakopoulos, E. (1999) 'Closure and transformation in Ovid's *Metamorphoses*', in P. Hardie, A. Barchiesi, and S. Hinds 1999: 142–61.

Thilo, G. and H. Hagen (1878–1902) *Servius. Commentary*, 3 vols. Leipzig.

Thomas, R. F. (1986) 'From *recusatio* to commitment: the evolution of the Vergilian programme', *PLLS* 5: 61–73.

(1988) *Virgil's Georgics*, 2 vols. Cambridge Greek and Latin Classics. Cambridge.

(1998) 'Melodious tears: sepulchral epigram and generic mobility', in M. Harder, R. Regtuit, and G. Wakker, eds. *Genre in Hellenistic poetry* (Groningen) 205–23.

(2001) *Virgil and the Augustan reception*. Cambridge.

Thompson, D' A. W. (1918) 'The birds of Diomede', *CR* 32: 92–6.

(1936) *A glossary of Greek birds*. 2nd edn. Oxford.

Tilly, B. (1959) 'Vergil's *periplus* of Latium', *G&R* 6 1959: 194–203.

Tissol, G. (1992) 'An allusion to Callimachus' *Aetia* 3 in Virgil's *Aeneid* 11', *HSCP* 94: 263–8.

(1997) *The face of nature. Wit, narrative, and cosmic origins in Ovid's* Metamorphoses. Princeton.

(2002) 'The house of fame: Roman history and Augustan politics in *Metamorphoses* 11–15', in Boyd 2002: 305–35.

Tränkle, H. (1960) *Die Sprachkunst des Properz und die Tradition der lateinischen Dichtersprache*. Hermes Einzelschriften 15. Wiesbaden.

Van Tress, H. (2004) *Poetic memory: allusion in the poetry of Callimachus and the* Metamorphoses *of Ovid*. Leiden and Boston.

Trieber, C. (1894) 'Zur Kritik des Eusebios', *Hermes* 29: 124–42.

Tupet, A.-M. (1976) *La Magie dans la poésie latine*. Paris.

Ungern-Sternberg, J. von (1998) 'Die Romulusnachfolge des Augustus', in W. Schuller, ed. *Politische Theorie und Praxis im Altertum* (Darmstadt) 166–82.

Vallet, G. (1958) *Rhégion et Zancle*. Paris.

Van Dam, H.-J. (1984) *P. Papinius Statius Siluae Book II*. Leiden.

Wackernagel, J. (1953–79) *Kleine Schriften*. 3 vols. Göttingen.

Waser, O. (1894) *Skylla und Charybdis in der Literatur und Kunst der Griecher und Römer.* Zurich.
Watson, G. R. (1969) *The Roman soldier.* London.
Watt, W. S. (1995) 'Ovidiana', *MH* 52: 90–107.
Weinstock, S. (1971) *Diuus Julius.* Oxford.
Wheeler, S. M. (1999) *A discourse of wonders.* Philadelphia.
(2000) *Narrative dynamics in Ovid's Metamorphoses.* Classica Monacensia 20. Tübingen.
White, K. D. (1967) *Agricultural implements of the Roman world.* Cambridge.
(1975) *Farm equipment of the ancient world.* Cambridge.
Wilkinson, L. P. (1955) *Ovid recalled.* Cambridge.
(1963) *Golden Latin artistry.* Cambridge.
Williams, G. (1994) *Banished voices: readings in Ovid's exile poetry.* Cambridge.
Williams, R. D. (1960) *Aeneidos Liber Quintus.* Oxford.
(1962) *Aeneidos Liber Tertius.* Oxford.
Wills, J. (1996) *Repetition in Latin poetry: figures of allusion.* Oxford.
(1997) 'Homeric and Virgilian doublets: the case of *Aeneid* 6.901', *MD* 38: 185–202.
Wiltshire, S. F. and A. Krickel (1982) 'Diomedes and Aeneas: a Vergilian paradox', *CB* 58: 73–6.
Wimmel, W. (1960) *Kallimachos in Rom.* Wiesbaden.
Winbolt, S. E. (1903) *Latin hexameter verse.* London. Reprinted 1978. New York.
Wiseman, T. P. (1984) 'Cybele, Virgil and Augustus' in A. Woodman and D. West, eds., *Poetry and politics in the age of Augustus* (Cambridge) 117–28.
(1987) 'The wife and children of Romulus', in *Roman Studies* (Liverpool) 285–92.
(1995) *Remus: a Roman myth.* Cambridge.
(2002) *Classics in progress: essays on ancient Greece and Rome.* Oxford and New York.
Wlosok, A. (1967) *Die Göttin Venus in Vergils Aeneis.* Heidelberg.
Yarnall, J. (1994) *Transformations of Circe.* Urbana.
Zanker, P. (1968) *Forum Augustum: das Bildprogram.* Tübingen.
(1988) *The power of images in the age of Augustus.* Ann Arbor.
Zingerle, A. (1869) *Ovidius und sein Verhältniss zu den Vorgängern und gleichzeitigen römischen Dichtern* I. Innsbruck.
Zissos, A. and I. Gildenhard (1999) 'Problems of time in *Metamorphoses* 2', in Hardie, Barchiesi, and Hinds 1999: 31–47.

INDEXES

1 Subjects

Italic numbers refer to pages, non-italic numbers to lemmata in the Commentary
This index is selective; not all incidental personal names are listed, nor major characters in the text of Metamorphoses 14

2 Latin words

3 Passages discussed